ECONOMICS FOR THE COMMON GOOD

This volume provides an introduction to economics in terms of human rather than material welfare. In the face of increasing marketization, declining community and growing inequality, the author argues the case for a broader, more sensitive economic science. Building on a venerable social economics tradition, this volume proposes a more rational economic order and develops new principles of economic policy. The issues covered include:

- the inadequacy of individualistic economics in guiding policy formation
- a logical critique of economic rationality
- rethinking the modern business corporation
- a critique of modern trade theory and unregulated international competition
- how standard economic theory encourages major ecological problems

Economics for the Common Good introduces social economics concepts and demonstrates their continuing relevance to the ills of an increasingly global society. In approaching problems generally conceived to be purely *economic*, from a social and ecological perspective centered on basic material needs, human dignity, and the laws of thermodynamics, the author explores the vital interface between economics, ethics and politics. The reader is challenged to look beyond the confines of mainstream economic thinking to find new solutions to some of the fundamental issues facing us today. As such it will be of interest to students of economics, philosophy, sociology and politics.

Mark A. Lutz is Professor of Economics at the University of Maine.

ADVANCES IN SOCIAL ECONOMICS
Edited by John B. Davis
Marquette University

This series presents new advances and developments in social economics thinking on a variety of subjects that concern the link between social values and economics. Need, justice and equity, gender, cooperation, work poverty, the environment, class, institutions, public policy, and methodology are some of the most important themes. Among the orientations of the authors are social economist, institutionalist, humanist, solidarist, cooperatist, radical and Marxist, feminist, post-Keynesian, behaviouralist, and environmentalist. The series offers new contributions from today's most foremost thinkers on the social character of the economy.

Published in conjunction with the Association of Social Economics.

Books published in the series include:

SOCIAL ECONOMICS
Premises, findings and policies
Edited by *Edward J. O'Boyle*

THE ENVIRONMENTAL CONSEQUENCES OF GROWTH
Steady state economics as an alternative to ecological decline
Douglas Booth

ECONOMICS FOR THE COMMON GOOD
Two centuries of social economic thought in the humanistic tradition
Mark A. Lutz

THE HUMAN FIRM
A socio-economic analysis of its behavior and potential in a
new economic age
J. Tomer

ECONOMICS FOR THE COMMON GOOD

Two centuries of social economic thought
in the humanistic tradition

Mark A. Lutz

London and New York

First published 1999
by Routledge
11 New Fetter Lane, London EC4P 4EE

Simultaneously published in the USA and Canada
by Routledge
29 West 35th Street, New York, NY 10001

© 1999 Mark A. Lutz

Typeset in Garamond by
BC Typesetting, Bristol
Printed and bound in Great Britain by
MPG Books Ltd, Bodmin

British Library Cataloguing in Publication Data
A catalogue record for this book is available from the British Library

Library of Congress Cataloging in Publication Data
A catalog record for this book has been requested

ISBN 0–415–14312–8 (hbk)
ISBN 0–415–14313–6 (pbk)

To three eminent contemporary social economists –
John Culbertson, Herman Daly and David Ellerman –
for their efforts in proposing new avenues for a more humane
and socially just world in the third Millennium.

CONTENTS

PREFACE

Little did I know that the preferred vacation spot of my boyhood would contain a thread that would link me to my future. The old Swiss castle, Schloss Brunegg, located about one hour from Zurich, served as the summer residence of my favorite playmate. His father, Professor Jean Rudolf von Salis, was the widely known biographer of the nineteenth-century Swiss historian and economist J. C. L. Simonde de Sismondi. When visiting in those early years I was more interested in the outdoors than social philosophy. Still, the kind professor, with his stacks of papers, piles of books and the intellectual ambiance of the place, must have left an impression at some deeper level, a subtle influence that manifested itself two decades later.

After completing a Ph.D. in economics at the University of California, Berkeley, and having taught the subject for some years at the University of Maine, I was to make the fateful acquaintance of Ken Lux, a psychologist with a consuming interest in economic matters. Ken, deeply suspicious of the prevailing way economists approach their subject matter, and after prolonged discussions, managed to overpower all my learned defenses. As a result of this slow and arduous process of "deprogramming," of questioning and shedding more and more the conventional way of looking at things, we co-authored *The Challenge of Humanistic Economics* (1979). In the process of writing that book and tracing the history of this type of economics, I soon discovered Sismondi's work, much of it translated into many languages but scarcely, at least until very recently, into English. And ever since, I have found it stimulating to indulge in his new brand of economic thought, so utterly different from modern standard economics and so much more humane. In particular, it is striking how much the problems and issues he discussed almost 200 years ago are still relevant today: a teaching of how to study economic activity and institutions without losing sight of the human, social dimension and (more recently also of the) ecological dimensions of things.

Modern economics is the science of self-interest, of how to best accommodate individual behavior by means of markets and the commodification of human relations. Much of it still reflects the particular philosophic tradition of British culture inaugurated by Hume and his followers. In this economic world view, the traditional human faculty of reason gets short-changed and degraded to act as the servant of sensory desires. There is no room for a logic of human values and rationally founded ethics. Human aspirations are watered down to skillful shopping behavior and channeled into a stale consumerism. One would think that there must be an alternative way to conceptualize the economy.

Decades ago, many disenchanted students were lured into the Marxist camp where they were soon forged into materialists of an even more brazen kind. Today, opposing souls full of compassion for the have-nots and underdogs are attracted to thinkers who reject reason altogether, or else subject it to cultural considerations: a new but strange home drifting in the relativistic and nihilistic waters of postmodern thought with its deconstructive undertones. Economy and society, meanwhile, are confronted with mounting problems, some of which are pushing us dangerously close to the abyss of an environmental disaster on a global scale.

The faith in a better alternative, both more human and more rational, led me to look for wisdom and inspiration in the economic philosophy of Sismondi and a time-honored tradition of *social economics* as further developed by some of its outstanding contributors. It's an economics of human equality and well-being based on a recognition of human self-awareness, genuine rationality and objective social values rooted in the basic needs and intrinsic dignity common to all. Its line of inquiry opens up a complete criticism of contemporary economic thought and the foundation of public policy analysis in industrial society. Its bottom line is a normative, social-values-directed economics that downplays and replaces much of the conventional emphasis on economic rationality and economic efficiency.

The plan of the book

I like to think of this book as having an introduction, three parts and a conclusion. The first chapter, which serves as the introduction, familiarizes the reader with the essential elements of an economics that emphasizes the pitfalls of individualism: the fallacy of composition, as well as the social and moral dimension impinging on economic theory and activity. The book's first part, beginning with Chapter 2, recounts a distinct history that goes back to the year 1815 when Sismondi had finished outlining a new set of economics principles that would soon evolve into the French *économie sociale*. This new "social school" in economics, as shown in Chapters 3 and 4, was further developed by some outspoken representatives in England, culminating in the work of John Hobson. During its 185-year history, this humanistic perspective has mounted various challenges against the orthodox *laissez-faire* doctrine. On the macro side, it developed a full-blown underconsumption theory rooted in an unequal distribution of income and wealth. With respect to microeconomics, they objected to reasoning from overly abstract and counterfactual premises, like the deducing of public policy objectives on the basis of selfish and one-dimensional "Economic Man." They preferred to recalibrate their compass for a true social good to combat economic maldistribution, unemployment and a degrading workplace. In short, all these pioneers called for an *ethical* component to economics.

The book's second part highlights some of the basic issues raised by Sismondi and Hobson within contemporary economic thought. Chapter 5 offers a critical assessment of the standard belief that economics must be a positive science uncontaminated by ethical judgments, yet still capable of providing meaningful guidance to the public policy maker. The demonstrated inadequacy of the New Welfare Economics cries out for a more reasonable reconstruction, something that is attempted in Chapter 6. Finally, in Chapter 7, the concept of economic rationality, at the very heart of the contemporary economics establishment, is shown to be both logically over-ambitious and humanly impoverished. A non-algorithmic rationality is proposed, a rationality rooted in a "dual self" conception of the person, which seems the only way to accommodate qualitative human *judgments* in the choice of alternatives.

The third part of the book introduces the reader to three basic applications of modern social economics. They were selected from a much larger set that also includes such problematic issues as degrading work, poverty and hunger, unwarranted inequality, discrimination by race and gender, the sale of body parts and organs, markets for adoptions, the limitations of cost–benefit analysis and current economic development strategies. Chapter 8 discusses property theory and seeks to make a case for democratizing the modern investor-owned corporation. Chapter 9 examines both modern trade theory and globalization in the critical light of national well-being and suggests the possibility of a Sismondi–Hobson-type crisis scenario. The interface between the natural environment and the economy is presented in Chapter 10 as the "ultimate challenge" facing humanity. In all three policy-oriented chapters, the standard criterion of economic efficiency is subordinated to the social values calling for material sufficiency and respect for human dignity of all members of the economy.

The conclusion, Chapter 11, argues for the timely relevance of this type of economic thinking in recovering the vanishing social fabric and the impaired natural environment.

During the last ten years a number of highly valuable books have been published in the field, including B. Buergenmeier's slender but informative *Social Economics* (1992); the well-known masterpiece *For the Common Good* (1994) by H. Daly and J. Cobb; as well as the more sociological text by A. Etzioni, *The Moral Dimension: Toward a New Economics* (1988). There are also two new anthologies, one edited by J. Davis and E. O'Boyle, *The Social Economics of Human Material Need* (1994), the other by myself: *Social Economics: Retrospect and Prospect* (1990). What makes the present book unique is that it builds on the classic branch in social economics in order to honor and develop the new offshoots it has produced in the last few decades. In the process, it not only questions some of the fundamental elements of modern economic science, but it is also driven beyond the present-day microeconomic confines to encompass the issue of macroeconomic instability arising from global markets.

It is my hope that the reader will agree that the present *tour de force* of a more extensive and more humanistic social economics goes a long way toward casting a new light on the state of economic science and the contemporary social order. As such, the present book is well suited as a supplementary text in college classes that address the linking of basic economic theory to social institutions and policy. Although it has been written with the aspiring economics student in mind, it should be a reader-friendly and accessible introduction for anybody interested in the state of academic economics and the usefulness of the discipline in its present form to help keep humanity out of troubled waters.

Acknowledgments

I am deeply grateful to my colleagues who have been kind enough to read certain chapters and have provided highly valuable suggestions for improvement: Professor John Davis, Marquette University; Professor Robert Heibronner, The New School; Professor Daniel Hausman, University of Wisconsin; Professor Mike Montgomery, University of Maine; Dr David Ellerman, economist at the World Bank; and Professor Herman Daly, University of Maryland. My friend and intellectual collaborator, psychologist Dr Kenneth Lux, deserves special thanks for having read the entire manuscript as it developed and who helped shape and improve it considerably.

My debt and gratitude also go to my graduate students who tested a preliminary version in a class on the history of economic policy and who gave me much valuable feedback on the book's suitability as a teaching tool. They made innumerable suggestions and corrections. Among this group, my special thanks go to Ke "Art" Hao and the enthusiastic encouragement and the constructive criticism he so generously provided as the manuscript developed. I am also grateful to the many undergraduate students in my course on the History of Economic Thought for their input on the chapters on Sismondi and Hobson, particularly Catherine Blount-Helmke who was always cheerfully ready to help with translating Sismondi's French into English.

This book could have never materialized without the crucial assistance of three persons: my father, Robert H. Lutz, who helped generously with the finance, Robert Lawson, who brooded sentence by sentence over the entire manuscript and helped mold it into more acceptable English, and Gail Fernald, who took charge of all word-processing and necessary administrative details involved in cleaning up and formatting the manuscript. Just as Sir Edmund Hillary could not have reached the peak of Mount Everest without the partnership of Sherpa Tenzing, so would this book have never made it to the publisher without Gail's tireless, skillful and always dependable assistance. My whole-hearted thanks to you!

Finally, my wife Carol B. Arone deserves my particular gratitude for all the love, tolerance, understanding and forbearance she demonstrated during the long, two-year gestation process of this work.

SOURCE ACKNOWLEDGMENTS

We would like to thank all those who have granted permission to reproduce copyright material in this volume:

Cambridge University Press, Cambridge (Shackle, G. L. S., *Decision, Order and Time in Human Affairs*, 1961); Harcourt Brace & Company, New York (Friedman, M. and Friedman, R., *Free to Choose: A Personal Statement*, 1990); Harvard University Press, Cambridge, MA (Hirsch, F., *Social Limits to Growth*, 1976); McGraw-Hill, New York (Samuelson. P. *Economics*, 1992); Macmillan Press Ltd. (Pearce, D. (ed.), *The MIT Dictionary of Economics*, 1992); Oxford University Press, Oxford (Berlin, I., *Four Essays on Liberty*, 1969); Random House Inc. , New York. (Samenow, S. E. *Inside the Criminal Mind*. New York Times Books, 1984); Regnery Publishing Inc., Washington, DC (Mirandola, G. P. della, *Oration on the Dignity of Man*, 1956); Routledge, London. (Roy, S., *The Philosophy of Economics: On the Scope of Reason in Economic Inquiry*, 1989); Rowman and Littlefield Publishing, Lanham, MD (Ellerman, D., *Intellectual Trespassing as a Way of Life*, 1995); Transaction Publishers, New Jersey (Sismondi, J. C. L., *The New Principles of Economy* [1827] 1991); Worldwatch Institute, Washington DC ("Promoting Sustainable Fisheries" in *State of the World*, 1998).

1

INTRODUCING SOCIAL ECONOMICS

With the unexpectedly rapid demise of Marxist economic ideology, the 1990s have witnessed the triumph – as yet unchallenged – of orthodox mainstream economic theory, whose textbooks are required reading for students all over the world. A new generation is taught to think along market economic lines, approaching the subject scientifically, and to keep clear of any contact with social values. What counts are carefully conceived models constructed with analytical and mathematical rigor. How else can one make sense of the otherwise stunning answer some 200 aspiring economics doctoral students in leading American universities gave to the question, "Which characteristic will most likely place students on the fast track," that is, make them successful members of the discipline? The two most common responses were "being good at problem solving" and "excellence in mathematics." The two least-marked answers were "having a broad knowledge of the economic literature" and "having a thorough knowledge of the economy." Only three respondents considered the latter characteristic "very important" for success.[1] Imagine an equivalent set of answers from medical students on track to becoming surgeons and discounting the importance of a thorough knowledge of human anatomy. True, modern economics is not modern medicine, but it is also true that the foremost standard taught in either discipline ought to be the promotion of health, be it the human or the socioeconomic organism.

One could, with little risk of exaggeration, see the present age as dominated by a *religion of economic efficiency*. Everything is to be interpreted in its light. Efficiency is the catalyst for maximum possible economic growth, which will then provide the arsenal of resources conducive to redistribution of income, to the combating of mass unemployment, even to assuring a more ecological approach to a battered environment. Increasingly, institutions must justify their existence in the name of efficiency, the state itself being no exception. The maxim of "efficiency first" inculcates a new generation of policy makers with a predisposition to a *laissez-faire* approach to domestic and international matters. And quite often, when the invoked forces of competition do not deliver the expected results, the blame is put elsewhere: not on the theory, but on a deficient reality. Meanwhile, the fabric of society wears thin as people increasingly find themselves in a world of widespread and mounting unemployment, harsh corporate down-sizing (sometimes called "right-sizing"), growing income and wealth disparity, and alarming environmental deterioration. The mainstream economist, confronted with these challenges, counsels patience and confidently prescribes a greater faith in the eventual good of market outcomes.

How much longer can the social fabric tolerate the doctrines and medicines of an economic orthodoxy that appears inept at coming to grips with the socioeconomic problems people contend with every day? What are the credible alternatives? Certainly, the sudden breakdown of Marxist economics has further diminished the number of possibilities, but at the same time, its collapse, like the sudden crash of a forest giant, has brought to light an older critique of economics, *social economics*, a noble tree which was overshadowed by the Marxist approach. This economic perspective with social values has co-existed with mainstream analysis for almost two centuries and is offered as a possible alternative. This book promotes a social economics in the *humanistic tradition*, arguably the oldest and perhaps least-articulated tradition within the social economy school.

1. The nature of social economics

Over the last hundred years, social economics has had several different definitions. Stripped of all extras and subtleties, the following catches its essence: it's an economics exploring the principles on which production of goods and services can be undertaken such that human welfare in its broadest sense is maximized.[2] An abbreviated description of social economics should include two related ingredients: first, it recognizes a *common good* that gives direction to social science in general and to economics in particular. Second, it makes room for a *social dimension* in economic analysis and thought. These two elements, visibly absent from the orthodox individualistic creed, suggest a critical re-examination of the way mainstream economics treats matters of methodology, rationality and efficiency.

Acknowledging the common good

The very notion of *the* common good is not easily grasped in an intellectual community with a prevailing individualist liberalism. In fact, since the eighteenth century, classical liberalism has denied that there is a common good. Outside neo-liberal economics, the common good is the same as the common interest of members of society, and this common interest goes beyond the traditionally narrow economic domain to include interest in the quality of *social* relations.[3] In other words, appeals to the common good

2

should be understood as arguments of how to organize the social economy so as to allow its members to realize a common interest in the provision of certain basic goods to all members of the community.

The philosophy of a sound common good is based on the old republican tradition as practiced by ancient Greeks and Romans and revived by Thomas Aquinas in the Middle Ages. This venerable tradition lasted in England until the eighteenth century when it was replaced by a new liberal creed, which has dominated political philosophy and economics ever since. In England, classical liberalism first took the form of a demand for religious liberties and toleration, and soon thereafter also a demand for a constitutional guarantee of political rights. Subsequently, the additional demand for economic liberty with its underlying creed of a self-regulated market unrestrained by political intervention was added to the liberal agenda. This last step, aimed at the free-wheeling power of kings and mercantilist statesmen, sought to rein in government as the following statement by the nineteenth-century essayist Thomas Macaulay nicely illustrates:

> Our rulers will best promote the improvement of the nation by confining themselves strictly to their legitimate duties, by leaving capital to find its most lucrative course, commodities their fair price, industry and intelligence their natural reward, idleness and folly their natural punishment, by maintaining peace, by defending property, by diminishing the price of law and by observing strict economy in every department of the state. Let the Government do this, the people will assuredly do the rest.[4]

The central idea of republicanism was the notion of *citizenship*, a term implying the mutual sharing of burdens and benefits of certain aspects of social life. As part of this system, some assets relevant to the provision of the public good were equalized under the direction of the community. Morally responsible to uphold this goal, citizens viewed excessive social and economic inequality and dependence as detrimental to the common good. Jean Jacques Rousseau appealed to the state to promote equality: "It is one of the most important functions of government to prevent extreme inequality of fortunes; not by taking wealth from its possessors, but by depriving all the means to accumulate it; not by building hospitals for the poor, but by securing the citizens from becoming poor."[5] Thomas Jefferson, who opposed the development of large-scale domestic manufacturing on the grounds that a decentralized agrarian economy would diminish the number of small landholders, noted that "dependence begets subservience and venality and suffocates the germ of virtue."[6] A century later, uncontrolled and concentrated corporate power was seen as inimical to liberty. In England, around the turn of the century, and as a prelude to the subsequent ascent of social democracy, Thomas H. Greene, Leonard T. Hobhouse, John A.

Hobson and others led a movement to reorient classical liberalism in a more communitarian direction.[7]

Much like the Gestalt idea that the whole is more than the sum of its parts, the common good philosophy goes beyond the pale of English philosopher Jeremy Bentham's stance that the interest of the community is nothing more "than the sum of the interests of the several members who compose it."[8] However, any composition implies a *harmonious relation* of its parts. And such relation cannot be found adhering to the individuals, but has an existence of its own. A prosperous society, for example, will have a unity of purpose, whereas a fragmented society can be characterized by antagonistic social relations. The nurturing and maintenance of a well-ordered society reinforces both personal and *social* values. Such wholism, being the counterpoint of individualism, not only recognizes but also emphasizes the quality of social relations, as demonstrated by conviviality, fairness, social justice and mutual respect.

At this point it might be helpful to anticipate and respond to a typical objection to the concept of a general good – that a basic social goal common to all will lead society to the horrors of *absolutism* and *totalitarianism*. It is true that the humanistic perspective assumes a shared natural inclination for the common good precedes any particular group identification with institutions, class, ethnicity and gender, despite the tempering of a person's particular life history and social environment. This does not preclude that the perceptions cannot evolve over time.[9] Another and related objection concerns the alleged assumption that the common good is ironclad and incontestable, to be the expression of the "general will" of a collective citizenry posturing as a single "body politic" possessing and "defending" *the* truth against dissenters. Here there is indeed little or no space between persons, no room for argument or legitimate opposition. It certainly is not what American history was about and it is not what is wanted now. In terms of a political vision, Michael Sandel effectively states the case: "[This vision] does not despise differentiation. Instead of collapsing the space between persons, it fills the space with public institutions that gather people together in various capacities, that both separate and relate them. These institutions include the townships, schools, religions, and virtue-sustaining occupations that form the 'character of mind' and 'habits of the heart' a democratic republic requires."[10]

Individualistic classical liberalism views the concept of a "common good" as incompatible with an interpretation of liberty that centers on the need for individuals to choose their own ends as they see fit. This inability to acknowledge the organic structure of society sees the common good as a mere aggregate of individuals in constant interaction, each being propelled by assertive self-interest. This perspective allows no room for a social and moral dimension to individualist economics; any claim of being motivated by the social good is immediately suspect and seen as a mere *pretension*. Decades before Adam Smith's famous dictum: "I have never known much good done by those who affected to trade for the public good. It is an affectation, indeed, not very common among merchants, and very few words need be employed in dissuading them from it," Joshua Tucker had stated the case in his *Elements of Commerce* (1755). There he criticized the "pretense of the public good" when in fact private advantage is the only point aimed at.[11] In contrast, a more communitarian view recognizes a person's ability to set aside the narrower self in favor of a wider self which grows and manifests its own reality as he identifies his good with that of others. Similarly, for the classical liberalism inherited and enshrined by mainline economists, the concept of citizenship is now almost completely drained of its traditional republican meaning, standing, as it does, for a particular bundle of private and property rights bestowed by positive law on individual members of society.

What does an alternative economics, an economics that recognizes a common good or a common goal that stands in direct contrast to an economics based on individualist liberalism, look like? Because it is seen as a *moral* rather than a natural science, it embodies ethics and considerations of social justice. Even Leon Walras, who did pioneering work in abstract and mathematical economics, saw this moral orientation as the very essence of social economics. He wrote: "If [there is] any science [which] espouses justice as its guiding principle, surely it must be the science of the distribution of social wealth, or as we shall designate it, *social economics*."[12] To Walras, this school of thought asks the following questions: "What mode of appropriation [or distribution of profits] is compatible with justice? Which mode of appropriation subordinates the destiny of some to the destiny of others? What mode of appropriation does reason recommend as compatible with the requirements of moral personality?"[13] In short, the key words are justice, distribution of wealth and income, and the "mode of appropriation" or the way productive services of land, labor and capital are appropriated.

It seems strange that economics and ethics have been kept apart for so long. Both disciplines deal with what is valuable, and both refer to the same social life. One social economist blames Kantian ethics in part for this separation.[14] Kant's approach to ethics posits a duality between happiness on the one hand, and moral obligation on the other. This viewpoint plays into the hands of the economic philosophy espoused by Smith and his followers, which regards the pursuit of happiness as an essentially private quest of agents who know what is best for themselves. Ever since Kant and Smith, society has come to accept these as two separate domains: happiness, guided by the principle of economic rationality, and ethics, based on the principle of moral personality. Any integration of happiness and moral obligation would have to rest on a demonstration that there is indeed social mediation in the formation of individual preference; in other words, that the pursuit of happiness is more than a merely private affair. In this context, keep in mind two cases in which the social category enters in individual preference formation: first, people are not born with a fully developed set of preferences but acquire wants in large part according to their social surroundings of parents, schools and work. Second, people periodically reflect about their inclinations and their behavior. Due to the influence of social standards of propriety and moral responsibility during these moments of critical self-awareness, people often modify their tastes and preferences.

One meaning of the "social" in *social* economics is best understood in contrast to its opposite, an *asocial* or individualistic approach to economics. It includes decision makers who function neither as mechanical atoms nor as subordinated cells nourished and controlled by social processes. Instead, persons as *social individuals* are embedded in a web of constitutive social relations: they value persons and evaluate institutions as to their responsiveness to people. Human beings have a special consciousness or sense of what is common to all. One socially sensitive economist defined the *social point of view* quite accurately nearly a century ago as "the point of view of an individual who, being conscious of a mass of feelings, beliefs, and purposes, which he shares with those with whom he comes into contact, acts in such a way as to preserve society."[15] Broadly speaking, social persons refrain from antisocial behavior, particularly activities that violate the moral codes of society or otherwise inflict damage on others. In addition, such persons will protect the social fabric by their ability to care for others and to be compassionate and affectionate.

An economic philosophy that accommodates the common good leads to an economics that does not shy away from ethical considerations and distinguishes itself by focusing on persons as citizens who stand in relation to each other, instead of treating people as acquisitive consumers. This alternative perspective of the good of society also affects the perception of the good of the person, the nature of the self, as well as the varied sources of motivation that this perspective entails.

Recognizing a social dimension

One could say that orthodox economists approach the economy with a false compass, working toward something other than maximum possible human welfare. Social economists, on the other hand, tend to equate human welfare with a just society in which a person's well-being is measured by the standard of individual material well-being, as well as by distributional and moral factors. Thus, it is vitally important that a *social dimension* to well-being be taken into account when looking at the social economics equation.

Being a philosophical concept, the social dimension is a qualitative category that does not easily lend itself to being treated mathematically, or ex post grafted on in the form of an afterthought. Instead, it adds a new qualitative dimension whose incorporation will lead to novel conclusions. To continue the compass analogy, classical individualism not only sets it incorrectly, but also fails to operate it properly. It is a question of false methodology, which prevents complete understanding of how the economy really functions and diagnosis of its malfunctioning. In other words, the neglect of a social perspective seriously impedes the vision of conventional economics, leading to a whole set of questionable assertions and findings.

In its simplest form, refusing to acknowledge the social dimension manifests itself in the lack of recognition of the aggregate effect of human interaction. People can recognize the absurdity of everybody standing up to see better at a ball game. What initially looks worthwhile for each fan produces through social interaction a result that makes everyone worse off. Similarly, seeking personal benefits at the expense of others may make sense to the individual, but from a social perspective such leapfrogging is at best a zero-sum game. In such cases, individual actions rarely add up to meaningful and purposeful social choice. Examples in economics abound. For instance, a state or a municipality may be willing to make what appear to be considerable sacrifices to attract new firms, yet when its rivals do the same, all are worse off. Such myopic vision of subsidized piecemeal and fragmented choices does not take all the relevant factors into account. Consider, for instance, the sum effect of *individually* rational choices on an independently owned, local bookstore:[16] when discount books are purchased at the supermarket rather than the local bookstore, people are choosing the same for less. But such purchases will eventually drive the specialty store out of business, thereby narrowing future shopping possibilities. The English economist Alfred Kahn referred to this type of problem as the "tyranny of small choices" adding up to an undesirable aggregate outcome.[17]

What is common to all these illustrations is the simple fact that adding up all the parts does not produce a whole. Or what may be true for each part is not necessarily true for the whole. Logicians identify this essential limitation of atomistic individualism as the *fallacy of composition*. A leading economics textbook describes it as a "fallacy in which what is true of a part is, on that account alone, alleged to be also necessarily true of the whole."[18] Although earlier introductory economics textbooks explained and illustrated this fallacy, today, as in the Samuelson text, the fallacy is only briefly elucidated: "What is prudent behavior for an *individual* may at times be folly for a *nation*."[19] Samuelson is clearly alluding to Adam Smith's debatable dictum: "What is prudent in the conduct of every private family, can scarce be folly in that of a good Kingdom."[20] The gradual de-emphasis of the fallacy of composition in textbooks may be due to recent changes in macroeconomics, the effect of analyzing private and public spending in the aggregate. Analytically, the fallacy of composition can be conceptualized in two ways. On the one hand, spatial wholes should not and cannot be reduced to their atomistic parts if the common good is more than the aggregation of individual goods. As previously discussed, a wholistic approach must account for the social relations between the individual parts, including the application to such distinct concepts as social selves, social rationality and social standards.

7

Besides imagining spatial wholes and the repercussions they imply, one can also imagine the whole–part relationship in a temporal dimension. It would thereby follow that the long run is not merely the additions arrived at by the logic of short-term maximizations. Yet this is precisely what atomistic reasoning seeks to accomplish by unwarranted mathematical reduction, with the result that for all practical purposes the long run gets de-emphasized.

The fallacy of composition in its spatial and temporal dimensions manifests itself both in macroeconomic and microeconomic analysis. In the macro sphere, as demonstrated by the "paradox of thrift," if everybody tries to save more, everybody may end up saving less. As John Maynard Keynes demonstrated, uninvested savings reduce national income and thereby the very source of savings. In other words, there may be an incompatibility between some kinds of individual behavior and the desired collective results. Another macroeconomic manifestation of this fallacy runs like this: an individual firm may benefit by reducing workers' wages or benefits, but if all other companies follow the same strategy, the result is likely to be detrimental to the community since lower wages decrease not only production costs, but also employee incomes and consumption power. For these reasons, it was quite natural that the birth of social economics, the topic of Chapter 2, coincided with the birth of macroeconomic analysis. Similarly, Keynes, a towering figure in the field, subscribed to a more wholistic conception of society and was careful to avoid the fallacy. He stressed the importance of (psychological, institutional and historical) context in establishing facts and scientific regularities, which led him to question a method that relies too much on induction and empirical correlations.[21] It is only more recently that macroeconomists have been backsliding: in aspiring to be good (albeit atomistic) scientists, they have been seeking to reduce macroeconomics to its micro counterpart by trying to squeeze it onto a micro foundation. This approach is blatantly oblivious to a qualitatively distinct (and irreducible) social dimension.[22] In contrast, applications in the temporal sphere are less striking, but one could argue that ultimately what will benefit a particular generation in terms of national output and its use of natural resources will not necessarily be good for the life span of humanity.

When turning to microeconomics, the fallacy of composition causes trouble in many situations. Most obviously, it happens when individuals seek private gain at the expense of others, thereby driving a wedge between the sum of individual interests and the common good. Such socially dysfunctional behavior manifests itself in the *free rider problem* of "public goods," whose services can be simultaneously shared, and whose benefits cannot be withheld from any individual. The classic example of this has been the lighthouse protecting ships at sea; another is public radio and television. The Germans have coined the phrase *Trittbrett Fahrer* for somebody who rides the city tramways without paying the fare. In all these cases, it pays for the users of these services to try to get "something for nothing" and let the others pay. Yet, opportunistic behavior of this kind will backfire because if everybody shirks from paying his or her fair share, then the good won't be provided at all. Other examples showing the fallacy are cases of reaping private gain by exploiting or cheating others, or more generally, where there is "cost shifting" from the factory owner to the public at large, as happens with polluters of the environment. In short, there are only too many instances where individual gain-seeking undermines the common good.

In the temporal domain the fallacy of composition shows itself clearly in the orthodox business practice of focusing only on short-run profit maximization. Yet, as most business managers know, it is more often than not a good strategy to sacrifice some short-run profits in order to maximize returns over time. In many ways, the modern Japanese economy has long been seen as a model of a more wholistic economic approach, whereas American firms under competitive pressure have been compelled to focus too much on short-run profits. Another problem caused by shortsightedness is illustrated by competitive price wars initiated by a firm with surplus production capacity that cuts prices to draw customers away from its rivals, but, as other competitors match the price cuts, all find themselves in a worse position. In all these cases individual or short-run decision making by the parts is not likely to enhance the long-run interest of industry.

More recently, the social dimension has been profiled in game theory. The prisoners' dilemma game shows that cooperation cannot be explained in terms of self-interest, thereby voiding Bertrand Russell's claim, long promulgated by individualistic liberalism: "If men were actuated by self-interest . . . the whole human race would cooperate."[23] In other words, analysis in terms of strategic interaction demonstrates that although we may know that in a certain situation it would be in our self-interest to cooperate, this realization alone does not make for cooperation; instead we must rely on altruism and moral commitment. Game theory shows that there are limits to self-interest, and the only way to overcome them is to make room for a qualitatively different type of motivation.

Reassessing rationality, welfare, efficiency and competition*

Recognizing a social dimension opens the way to reconceptualize such elemental economic concepts as the self, rationality, welfare, efficiency, competition and market economy. Social philosophy ultimately hinges on the conception of the self. From the standard economic point of view, the self is atomistic, concerned only with self-advancement and aggrandizement. If an "other" exists, it only has instrumental significance and it is treated as a mere object of use and experience. One could even say that there is no self

---

*The reader with little background in economic theory may want to skip this section and continue on page 15.

in standard economics: an individual is pictured as nothing but a bundle of well-behaved preferences. Everybody is believed to be equipped with a preference ordering in choosing commodity bundles. In contrast, from a social point of view, a self with both egoistic and altruistic dimensions does exist. In the latter case a person identifies with the interests of other or of society in general.

Any identification beyond one's own good, any identification with the good of another, means there are correspondingly *multiple* criteria for making choices, and therefore also *multiple* preference orderings. In seeing the person as multidimensional, human agents are portrayed as persons with qualitatively different identifications and attachments. The self becomes structured: on one level individuals operate with a narrow self, on another they operate with a more "expanded," inclusive or "whole" self that manages over time. This psychological process is often referred to as self-realization.

Intimately connected with the view of the self is the *rationality postulate*. In standard economics, to be rational is to have a preference ordering that is transitive and complete (meaning essentially that one's preferences are not contradictory and that one can always rank any possible bundle among the alternatives offered) and to act in a manner to best satisfy such "well-behaved" preferences. Known as "utility maximization" or *instrumental rationality*, the rationality postulate is a purely *formal* concept so that one does not know what the agent is maximizing; it could be self-regarding preferences (egoism) or other-regarding preferences (altruism or morality). Whatever the end, rationality only pertains to the proper selection of the available means (bundles of goods and services) to attain that end. To say that people are and do whatever they are and do may be true, but it does not help much in predicting and explaining human behavior. So, to go about their business, economists are compelled to assume that an agent's preferences are based on self-interest. But clearly not all actions undertaken for the sake of expediency and personal gain, for instance, robbing a bank or cheating a customer, do conform to the dictates of reason. In other words, what is economically rational is often socially and morally unreasonable. Besides, isn't economic rationality itself irrational whenever it entails the fallacy of composition? Isn't it after all a *logical* fallacy, a fallacy of reason? Furthermore, a careful analytical investigation of instrumental rationality shows that it is an incomplete explanation of human action, being unable to explain the institutional and informational structures necessary for instrumentally rational action.[24]

When moving from instrumental rationality to social economics, the concept of rationality changes drastically. Besides recognizing tastes and preferences, social values and a commitment to those values must also be factored in. Individual choices can be seen to be guided and motivated by such social norms as truthfulness, fairness and justice. To obey or break such a norm can produce either self-esteem and self-respect or shame and guilt, alternative motives which cannot be easily reduced to the rational calculus professed by economists.[25] Because self-imposed norms containing ethical elements do often play an important role in the economic process,[26] a rationality consistent with the common good will have to recognize that there is more than just self-interest guiding the decision maker. There is a potential conflict between a conduct that is selfishly motivated and one following a social or moral norm. Also, the fact that social norms can be backed up by impersonal reasons implies that a person, after due reflection and deliberation, can accept those reasons as his or her own and act accordingly. Often the choice of ends is not just a private affair because such choices often necessitate communication and dialogue. As one scholar put it: "Until I debate and negotiate with others and coordinate my choices with theirs, I will not be able to [truly] follow my interest and act rationally."[27] But regardless of whether social rationality is internal or external to the person, it does not alter the basic fact that individuals remain at all times free *not* to follow the norms or the dictates of reason, instead surrendering to the sweet temptations of individual gain. Accordingly, whether in economic life or elsewhere, we tend to face a distinctly human choice between different *ends* of action. And it is precisely this human experience that is denied by the individualistic concept of instrumental (or economic) rationality in which reason only dictates the means of best satisfying self-interest. The broader concept of rationality applying to both ends and means is sometimes called *expressive rationality*[28] or *extended rationality*.[29]

When discussing normative economics, students learn that economic outcomes and events are to be evaluated in terms of the consequences to individual welfare, which is to be measured by how well personal preferences are satisfied. In order for such inferences about personal well-being to be possible, preferences are assumed to be both self interested and *well informed*. Although economists are adamant that people know what is best for themselves, in a recent study, two leading philosopher-economists point out a number of serious problems when identifying individual welfare with preference satisfaction.[30] Imagine somebody who experiences a change in preferences (perhaps someone who has overcome a phobia about computers and decides to enter the market to buy one); it is not at all clear whether to privilege the old set of preferences or the new in evaluating the consequences for this consumer's satisfaction. One cannot assume that the newer preferences are the relevant ones because "if one says that satisfying past desires does not count, because giving people what they no longer want brings them no 'satisfaction,' then one has shifted from a preference-satisfaction to a mental-state theory of welfare."[31] Other problems involve the satisfying of preferences that are based on false beliefs, that are idiosyncratic, obnoxious, unfair and so on. Why base an evaluation of social policy or social institutions on such preferences? If there are no shared or social values, by what standard can individual tastes and preferences be assessed?

Social economics measures welfare in a very different manner than ordinary economics. Rather than focusing on preference satisfaction, the preferred criterion is the satisfaction of basic material *human needs*, such as the need for food, shelter and a minimum standard of living. Since some needs are more urgent than others, a comparison can be made of different levels of need satisfaction between individuals and social groups. Unmet needs, in contrast to subjective preferences, are to be understood as an objective, empirical and measurable criterion of social well-being.

The preceding considerations of the limitations of the standard conception of rationality and welfare help explain the social economist's skepticism of efficiency: a core orthodox concept. In standard theory efficiency is defined by the Pareto Criterion, a social state in which nobody can be made better off without hurting somebody else. The layman will be surprised to know that economic efficiency is a highly abstract notion that has little to do with beating down costs of production. Using it as a yardstick for socio-economic policy won't get you very far since any change in the status quo is bound to have both winners and losers, and therefore it encourages leaving things unchanged. Amartya Sen, one of today's foremost scholars, illustrates his growing frustration with the Pareto Criterion in a vivid manner: "a state in which some people are starving and suffering from acute deprivation while others are tasting the good life can still be Pareto optimal if the poor cannot be made better off without cutting into the pleasures of the rich – no matter by how small an amount." And he adds, "Pareto optimality is faint praise indeed."[32] Not surprisingly, standard economics largely confines its use of the Pareto Criterion to the mathematical exercise of demonstrating the superiority of perfectly competitive markets, a "proof" that involves a host of highly unrealistic assumptions including the absence of (social) interdependencies in consumption and production, and also the presence of future markets for *all* goods and services.[33]

A distorted view of economic reality lies in the standard economist's insistence that social situations and institutions are *only* to be evaluated and compared by the extent of preference satisfaction or welfare to the exclusion of other factors such as distributional justice, fairness and respect for personal rights. In contrast, the conservation of key natural resources and a life-sustaining ecology that would allow future generations to meet their needs must be seen in itself as an important criterion for insisting on sustainable economic processes whether or not the current generation can muster preferences in this regard.

An efficiency-based economics presents other problems. First, it is predicated on the notion that society can be evaluated by means of individual preferences that are *exogenously given* (preferences determined outside economics), meaning that any questions about how preferences are determined and shaped are suppressed and relegated to other disciplines.

Although it is true that people are born with certain distastes or preferences that remain fairly stable, it is important to note that personal values are not at all like tastes. They are more often something about which we argue, something that is amenable to rational persuasion and very much affected by our own experience in the social economic universe. Therefore it makes little sense to talk about our values as "exogenously given" preferences. Instead, they need to be understood as largely *endogenous* to the prevailing social order and codetermined by a person's upbringing, socioeconomic circumstances and social institutions. For example, a strong case can be made that one of the most significant factors in character formation, or the growth of the self, is a person's work experience, a factor that can hardly be treated as *independent* of the prevailing industrial order. The late E. F. Schumacher defined alienation in the workplace as a kind of negative education that encourages the formation of inferior preferences, such as a taste for alcoholism, or an inclination toward domestic violence.[34] Because a worker's preferences are not fixed for all time, but are subject to change and improvement, the social economist does not seek to build social institutions and the social order on the basis of a "given" set of preferences, but sees both preferences and social institutions in mutual interplay. Thus, he believes that the improved environment of a more just social order will serve as a catalyst for the formation of better values and preferences.

A second issue relates to the weighing of individual preferences in determining social outcomes. The standard economist measures the relative importance of a preference by a person's willingness to pay. Because this process favors the rich over the poor, most social economists would reject efficiency as a yardstick in public policy. Why in the name of *real* efficiency should grain ever be used to feed the pleasure horses of the rich rather than to feed the unemployed and their families? Willingness to pay too often reflects an ability to pay, which is determined by the distribution of wealth and income. In other words, the "given preferences" on which the economist constructs the exotic house of efficiency are to some extent merely a reflection of a "given" socioeconomic inequality. Readily granting that some income differentials are legitimate, one must nevertheless examine the very roots of unwarranted inequality exhibited in society. As an example, an argument (to be presented in Chapter 8) can be made that the absentee ownership of productive capital assets does not necessarily entitle the owner to a claim on profits. Neither is it always clear that discrepancies in pay are productivity related. Similarly, unemployment and the underemployed are to a large extent problems of social origin and not of individual making.

The social economics alternative to economic efficiency as defined by Leon Walras "espouses justice as its guiding principle."[35] It is concerned with the distribution of benefits and burdens throughout society in a market economy. The overriding importance of just institutions was also emphasized by philosopher John Rawls when he wrote:

> Justice is the first virtue of social institutions, as truth is of thought. A theory however elegant and economical must be rejected or revised if it is untrue; likewise laws and institutions no matter how efficient and well-arranged must be reformed or abolished if they are unjust.[36]

Obviously, the actual measuring of social justice is not an easy matter, but one must try. The challenge for the social economist, therefore, is to articulate rational normative principles that are also in tune with people's intuitive understanding of the concept of justice and – in a second step – to systematically bring those principles to bear on the evaluation of the socioeconomic order.

The downplaying of individual preferences and a de-emphasis of economic efficiency goes hand-in-hand with a more guarded assessment of competition. Although competition can be, and very often is, a very dynamically beneficial and socially constructive force, such concession does not imply that the more of it a society has, the better. In fact, competition can also be socially *destructive* when its aims are achieved at the cost of downgrading social goals, conventions and standards. It is for this very reason, of course, that all competitive sports have rules assuring an outcome that is in the social interest. Without such rules, whether in sports or in the economy, competition becomes dysfunctional. Even a relatively innocent-looking price war between competitors may be an instance of destructive competition: it may hurt socially responsible and efficient firms while benefiting the ruthless firms with "deeper pockets" that either ignore social standards or seek to overpower and monopolize rivals. More generally, competition as a social coordinating device can also exhibit highly dysfunctional aspects in a world of mounting social scarcity because certain goods like coastal property, a top position in the job hierarchy and so forth, cannot be reproduced. In situations such as these, the acquisition of socially scarce goods implies denying them to others. At best it is a zero-sum game. The fiercer the competition, the more resources consumed, and the more divisive and socially wasteful the competitive solution is likely to be. One example of competing for a finite resource is the costly lengthening of the obstacle course of requirements when applying for a leadership job. First it was a high school diploma, then it was a bachelor's degree, now it is often necessary to have a master's degree and, if the past is a guide for the future, a doctorate will soon be a must. Or the American phenomenon of moving to the country: as more and more people move to the suburbs in order to be closer to nature, that wholesome quality becomes increasingly scarce and, at the same time, leads to more congested roads and longer commutes. The late Fred Hirsch deplored these tendencies of what he labeled *positional competition*.[37]

As is to be expected, an acute awareness of the limits of standard rationality and efficiency also has the effect of looking at market processes in a much more critical light. To point out the social consequences of market behavior has long been a distinguishing characteristic of social economics. The market outcomes of poverty amidst plenty, for example, have from the very beginning been at the top of the social economics agenda. There is nothing sacred about the free market. It is not an institution dictated by some (higher) natural law, but is, like private property, a social institution, socially created and subject to being reined in if it does not perform adequately.

In summary, being mindful of a common good and a social dimension in matters of rationality, welfare, efficiency and the social order is the heart of social economics. Among other things, it deals with such issues as the protection of a person's rights, including property rights, the redistribution of income and wealth, the regulation of wages, land use and the social consequences of free-flowing capital; in short, with the social control of business. Ultimately, one must ask, what is the basic purpose of both the economy and economics as a discipline? What are they about? An ever-growing average real income, or an adequate provisioning of all persons so as to increase the quality of life?

2. Toward a humanistic social economics

This chapter has surveyed individualistic economic liberalism, the pseudo-religion of economic efficiency and competition, as well as identifying elements of the criterial stance common to social economists, and a common good that is characterized by a shared vision of a better social order and a better social economy. At the same time, it should be stressed that social economics, especially today, is a highly heterogeneous and pluralistic affair; it bristles with diversity and includes adherents with ties to American neo-institutionalism, solidarism, cooperativism, post-Keynesianism, humanism, feminism, neo-Marxism and environmentalism.

Social economics, now 170 years old, can be metaphorically understood as a tree trunk constituting the initial work of the Swiss economist Sismondi, the founder of a human-centered social economics. The trunk leads to three main stems, the largest of which represents the Catholic solidaristic school, the next continues the humanistic tradition, and the third marks the development of a direction that flourished early and then became intertwined with what is now known as the Austrian School of Economics. After a century of vigorous growth, nurtured by organizational homogeneity and the strength of Catholic social thought, the solidarist branch overshadowed the other growth to such an extent that by 1970 it was quite natural to regard it as the whole tree. But, since then, new offshoots, most strongly a branch denoting American economic institutionalism, as well as others representing versions of humanism and Marxism, have been growing rapidly. This proliferation has increased in the last decade with new shoots articulating postmodern thinking, or professing feminism and environmentalism. These various branches and twigs have been growing in different directions, each emphasizing a certain

15

epistemological and methodological position, each embracing some sort of ethics and each preoccupied with issues that are of special interest to its constituents.

This study will familiarize the reader with the original human-centered approach as it developed in Europe and America during the last two centuries, providing a genealogy of humanistic social economic thought and following its development to contemporary times.

What is distinctive about the humanistic perspective expressed here is its focus on the human being, on what is *common* to all persons regardless of gender, race or cultural background. The image of a shared humanity, the emphasis on the distinctly human, gives this tradition an all-encompassing scope and ability to make certain claims that transcend space and time, a rather ambitious undertaking which is defensible only if it operates with some minimal assumptions concerning human nature and an ethics that will command the widest possible assent: every person has an inalienable right to life and a right to be treated in a manner that respects his or her personal dignity. Such a minimalist social ethic and morality serves as a yard-stick in the evaluation of economic phenomena in all cultures and societies. Contrary to the pragmatic American-institutionalist wing of social eco-nomics, the ideas of right and wrong and the reactions of admiration and moral condemnation that they evoke are more than a matter of culture or social agreement; they are grounded in a universal structure of reason and conscience. It does make a big difference. For example, the gruesome story of the late King Bokassa of the Central African empire, as recounted in *The Economist*, epitomizes what can happen when there is a disregard for this ethic.

> It was said that [the King] discovered his lion-keeper feeding the lions' dinner to his own family. Mr. Bokassa had him thrown to the lions but they, recognizing their keeper, did not touch him. So Mr. Bokassa fed the keeper to his crocodiles which showed less discriminating taste.[38]

A more drastic violation of the humanistic ethic is hard to imagine. Even if King Bokassa's subjects, being from a very different culture, all agreed that the lion-keeper got what he deserved, social agreement does not make it right. For the humanistic social economist, right and wrong are not matters to be resolved by counting noses.

The social value of human dignity holds a central place in this book. Even though virtually all social economists would readily grant that human dignity is an important social value, there is some disagreement as to its ontological status, that is, the nature of its existence. A pragmatist, for example, would hold that human dignity is something that society confers and that society can also abrogate, deny and deprive somebody of. In contrast, a humanistic view would hold that personal dignity inheres in human nature, and is there-

16

fore inalienable. Of course, the *claims* of personal dignity deriving from the inalienable may be disrespected or violated, but no social convention or institution can decree who has human dignity and who has not.[39] Similarly with legal justice and laws; in the humanistic tradition statutory or positive law, constitutional law and acts of legislation, regardless of how much popular assent they may command, are never above critical reasoning and evaluation. In other words, positive justice may be considered unjust by some "higher law" or some standard that transcends a particular society. Again, not all social economists can be expected to endorse without hesitation such metaphysical propositions.

On a more basic level, the humanistic version of social economics, in its affirmation of the principle of human equality, does so on *a priori* grounds; that is, on validity independent of observation. In contrast, many other social economists, especially the pragmatists, would very much prefer to ground the ideal of human equality in social agreement. But, logically, it cannot be done. Any agreement necessitates a prior consensus about who ought to be participating in making the agreement and who excluded. Look, for instance, at questions of suffrage. Questions such as the following arise: should women or senior citizens or non-whites be given the right to vote? In order to answer the question, a procedural question must be solved first: that is, who is to participate in deciding who decides about the vote? Do women, senior citizens, or non-whites have a vote on that prior question? And if it is assumed that they do, on what basis other than a *metaphysical* (pre-agreement) principle that all human beings are "born equal" and are therefore equally entitled to participate? This manifests the need for metaphysics and also demonstrates the limits of a purely scientific approach. The calling for additional reliance on philosophy is a methodological stance that has from the beginning been fully acknowledged by the humanistic social economist and is an integral part of his or her economic equation.

On this fundamental point regarding the inalienable nature of human dignity, human equality and the nature of positive law, there is a close affinity between the humanistic tradition and Catholic solidarism, historically a relationship that has been quite friendly. Both orientations appeal to a value standard that is to some extent *external* to a particular society. But at the same time, that affinity was never close enough to suggest a virtual union of the two. Whereas this external standard is grounded in human nature for one tradition, it is based on the social doctrine of the Church and its pope in the other. Not surprisingly, from the very start members of the humanistic tradition have been voicing concern about the parochial nature of a Church-centered economics. Sismondi, in commenting on a new book giving birth to the Catholic version of social economics, expressed displeasure not so much about the "mixing of charity with political economy" as about the "confounding [of] religion with Catholicism" and the potential of a hidden agenda "to put all public charity into the hands of the priesthood, and [which] at the same time would give them all political power."[40]

One final characteristic of the human-centered approach is the distinction made between *humanistic* as opposed to *naturalistic*, the latter expressing a monistic metaphysical doctrine that there is but *one* system or level of reality and that the behavior of this system is reducible to a set of causal laws.[41] As a result, naturalism as a creed has long sought to reduce the human mind to nothing but physics and brain chemistry. In this context, psychologist Abraham Maslow popularized the designation "humanistic" through an approach to psychology that rejected this type of naturalism. To him, little was to be learned from animal research simply because human beings had a "higher nature," a personality, and were subject to a much richer variety of motivations. In humanistic economics, the rejection of naturalistic leveling manifests, for example, in the belief, grounded in introspection, that agents have not only preferences, but also higher-level "meta" preferences.[42] Such preferences about our preferences (such as "I prefer not to prefer to smoke") are intimately connected to the human capacity for self-reflection, freedom of the will and moral personality; they are not subject to causal analysis and empirical observation, but nevertheless are very real. Like the hierarchical part–whole relation discussed earlier, these meta-preferences imply a *vertical* dimension. They translate into a "dual self" view of the person, a philosophical anthropology which is central to an understanding of what is distinctly *human* and an economics that goes with it.

Having mentioned the basic elements of the humanistic approach, the following chapters will be a quick tour of the evolving nature of this tradition over the last two centuries. In addition, several distinct issues fundamental to humanistic social economics have been singled out for special attention in separate chapters. They include discussions of the self, well-being and rationality; economic democracy; the theory *and* reality of global competition; as well as the environmental challenge. All these topics center on the notion of human equality and personal dignity, thereby allowing us to bring to bear a humanistic ethics that clings to the common good in evaluating real world institutions and policies.

Notes

1 A. Klamer and D. Colander, *The Making of an Economist*, Boulder, CO, Westview Press, 1990, p. 18.

2 This description paraphrases the characterization by W. H. Richmond, in "John A. Hobson: Economic Heretic," *American Journal of Economics and Sociology*, July 1978, vol. 37:3, p. 291.

3 B. Jordan, *The Common Good: Citizenship, Morality, and Self-Interest*, New York, Basil Blackwell, 1989, p. 73.

4 T. B. Macaulay, "Southey's Colloquies on Society" (January 1830), in *The Complete Works of Lord Macaulay*, vol. VII, London, Longmans Green and Co., 1898, p. 502.

5 Quoted in Jordan, *The Common Good*, p. 72.
6 ibid.
7 See, for example, J. Allett, *New Liberalism: The Political Economy of J. A. Hobson*, Toronto, University of Toronto Press, 1981; P. Clarke, *Liberals and Social Democrats*, Cambridge, Cambridge University Press, 1978.
8 J. Bentham, *An Introduction to the Principles of Morals and Legislation*, London, T. Payne and Sons, 1789, pp. 1.4–5.
9 See, for example, M. Raskin, *The Common Good: Its Politics, Policies, and Philosophy*, New York, Routledge and Kegan Paul, 1986, p. 31.
10 M. Sandel, "America's Search for a New Public Philosophy," *The Atlantic Monthly*, March 1996, p. 70.
11 J. Tucker, *The Elements of Commerce and the Theory of Taxes*, Yorkshire, S. R. Publishers, 1755, p. 7; A. Smith, *An Inquiry into the Nature and Causes of the Wealth of Nations* [1776], Chicago, IL, University of Chicago Press, 1976, vol. I, p. 478.
12 L. Walras, *Elements of Pure Economics* [1926], reprinted by Augustus Kelley, New York, 1977, p. 79.
13 ibid., pp. 77–78.
14 J. B. Davis, "The Science of Happiness and the Marginalization of Ethics," *Review of Social Economy*, December 1987, vol. 45:3, pp. 298–311.
15 L. Haney, "The Social Point of View in Economics," *Quarterly Journal of Economics*, November 1913, vol. 27, p. 134.
16 F. Hirsch, *Social Limits to Growth*, Cambridge, MA, Harvard University Press, 1976, p. 40.
17 A. Kahn, "The Tyranny of Small Decisions: Market Failures, Imperfections, and the Limits of Economics," *Kyklos*, 1966, vol. 19:1, pp. 23–47.
18 P. Samuelson, *The Principles of Economics*, 9th edn, New York, McGraw-Hill, 1973, p. 14.
19 ibid.
20 Smith, *An Inquiry into the Nature and Causes of the Wealth of Nations* [1776], Chicago, IL, University of Chicago Press, 1976, vol. I, p. 478.
21 E. K. Brown-Collier, "Keynes' View of an Organic Universe," *Review of Social Economy*, 1985, vol. 93:2, pp. 14–23.
22 E. K. Brown-Collier, "The Fundamental Difficulty in Basing Macroeconomic Policy on Microeconomic Theory," *Forum of Social Economics*, Fall 1996, vol. 26:1, pp. 47–56.
23 B. Russell, quoted in Hirsch, *Social Limits to Growth*, p. 135.
24 S. Hargreaves Heap, *Rationality in Economics*, New York, Basil Blackwell, 1989.
25 K. Koford and J. Miller (eds), *Social Norms and Economic Institutions*, Ann Arbor, MI, University of Michigan Press, 1991.
26 D. M. Hausman and M. S. McPherson, *Economic Analysis and Moral Philosophy*, Cambridge, Cambridge University Press, 1996, ch. 5; A. Sen, *On Ethics and Economics*, Oxford, Basil Blackwell, 1987a.
27 E. Phelps, *Political Economy: An Introductory Text*, New York, W. W. Norton, 1985, p. 114.
28 Hargreaves Heap, *Rationality in Economics*, ch. 8.
29 A. P. Hamlin, *Ethics, Economics and the State*, New York, St. Martin's Press, 1986.
30 Hausman and McPherson, *Economic Analysis and Moral Philosophy*.
31 ibid., p. 76.
32 A. Sen, "The Profit Motive," *Lloyds Bank Review*, January 1983, no. 147, p. 6.
33 For a good critique of Paretian welfare economics supporting competitive capitalism, see J. Stiglitz, *Whither Socialism?*, Cambridge, MA, MIT Press, 1994, chs. 3–4.

34 E. F. Schumacher, "Philosophy of Work," *The Catholic Worker*, February 1977a, p. 1.
35 Walras, *Elements of Pure Economics*, p. 79.
36 J. Rawls, *The Theory of Justice*, Cambridge, MA, Harvard University Press, 1971, p. 3.
37 See Hirsch, *Social Limits to Growth*, for a comprehensive cataloguing of such perverse effects.
38 November 9, 1996, p. 105.
39 For a good essay on human dignity, see H. Spiegelberg, "Human Dignity: A Challenge to Contemporary Philosophy," in R. Gotesky and E. Laszlo (eds), *Human Dignity*, New York, Gordon and Breach, 1970, pp. 39–64.
40 J. C. L. Simonde de Sismondi, *Political Economy and the Philosophy of Government* [1847], New York, Augustus M. Kelley, 1966b, p. 452.
41 I. Jenkins, "Naturalism," in D. Runes, *Dictionary of Philosophy*, Totowa, NJ, Littlefield, Adams and Co., 1962.
42 H. G. Frankfurt, "Freedom of the Will and the Concept of a Person," *Journal of Philosophy*, January 1971, vol. 68:1, pp. 5–20.

2

THE GRANDFATHER OF
SOCIAL ECONOMICS:
J. C. L. SIMONDE DE SISMONDI

Jean Charles Léonard Simonde de Sismondi, or, as he preferred, Sismondi, entered and left this world amid revolutionary turmoil and armed conflict. His sixty-nine years (1773–1842) spanned the American Revolution, the French Revolution, the Napoleonic wars and the European social tension leading to the turmoil of 1848. Due to the stormy events in the aftermath of the French Revolution, young Sismondi was forced to break off his apprenticeship to a silk dealer in Lyons and to seek asylum in England, a circumstance that taught the French-speaking man from Geneva not only English, but also much about the British socioeconomic landscape. Upon his return to Geneva, the family assets were sequestered and the 21-year-old was to taste prison life for the first time. A close friend who was sheltered in the family estate was dragged from the home and shot nearby by revolutionary guards. Sismondi's refuge in Tuscany blessed him with three more stints in prison, incarcerated by both parties in the ongoing revolutionary turmoil.

But, just as significantly, Sismondi's life coincided with that agitated period, now called the Industrial Revolution, which ushered in a new type of economy bearing little resemblance to the one Adam Smith had described. It was his determined and passionate response to the social injustices that surfaced in the wake of such industrial innovations as the spinning and weaving of textiles in a factory complex, the concentration of laborers in factory compounds, and the massing of capital in the hands of industrial barons, that reverberated through nearly two centuries of economic schools of thought.

During the Industrial Revolution, factory work replaced agricultural labor and artisans, new industries created whole new cities: Manchester and Birmingham in England; Lille, Rouen and Mulhouse in France. The decades following the Napoleonic wars witnessed the rise of a new working class leading a generally impoverished life toiling long hours at low wages under conditions of precariously low job security. Part of the problem was caused by the general demobilization following Waterloo. According to one estimate, some 300,000 British soldiers returned to civilian life and the job market in 1815, joined by another 100,000 who had lost their jobs in war-related industries.[1]

Aggravating this period of widespread unemployment, the new industrial society experienced for the first time recurrent economic crises or "slumps," the most serious occurring in 1816–1822, 1825–1831 and 1839–1842, forcing the shutdown of many shops and causing periodic sharp increases in unemployment and poverty. Meanwhile, the ceaseless introduction of new machinery was seen by many as threatening their job security, and – by cutting prices and pushing cheap goods – depreciating their skills. Because labor unions were non-existent and forbidden by law, workers responded with Luddite riots (the sabotage of machinery, originally by means of the French workers throwing their wooden shoes or sabots into the jacquard spinning looms) and political unrest. On one occasion, the infamous Peterloo Massacre of August 1819, troops opened fire on some 50,000–80,000 men marching as a protest demonstration in Manchester, killing 8 and wounding 400.

The leading spokesmen of Sismondi's day, David Ricardo, Thomas Malthus and James Mill, offered little by way of helpful insights or policies to ameliorate the evils of industrialization. These classical economists opposed humanitarian relief of poverty because of their apprehension that such policies would be a stimulus to population growth. During the debate concerning the Poor Laws, it was therefore claimed that to provide more liberal provisions to the unemployed poor was not only a violation of liberty, but of the principles of political economy as well.[2] The road to social improvement, according to classical economists, consisted in promoting capital accumulation and economic growth through minimal taxation and maximum profits and savings. Not surprisingly, in the eyes of these experts, the alleged problems of recurring slumps and technological unemployment were best left to the self-adjusting market mechanism under the guise of a *laissez-faire* policy orientation. It was in such a socioeconomic climate that Sismondi entered the economic fray and proposed an alternative theoretical approach.

Interestingly enough, Sismondi was not the flaming revolutionary type one would expect, considering the ambitious task he set himself up to pursue. In contrast to his rather awkward appearance, he had a reputation of being extremely mild-mannered and very kind. He was a sought-after guest at the Château of Coppet near Geneva where Madame de Staël entertained a small circle of prominent intellectuals. Yet he was a man of integrity and great courage, as the following anecdote told by one of his contemporaries suggests:

> Though he was apparently pacific by nature, he on more than one occasion confronted formidable aggressions rather than compromise a friend. He was connected with a celebrated Review in which was inserted an article that wounded the feelings of a man who was too vain of his nobility. He accused Sismondi of its authorship and required him to acknowledge the charge or name the real author. Sismondi refused him any answer. A challenge was sent. Sismondi

accepted it, received the fire of his adversary, and fired his own pistol in the air, declaring for the first time that he was not the writer of the article. He retired from this ridiculous conflict with all the honours of war.[3]

An accomplished historian, having just completed a sixteen-volume *History of the Italian Republic* (1815), Sismondi had always felt the potential importance and relevance of economic science in guiding the thinking of statesmen. Passionately yearning for social progress and justice, he could not remain on the sidelines as an ever-growing segment of citizens was denied an adequate share of social output and relegated to some newly constituted underclass. Sismondi, upholding the ultimate value of human well-being and human dignity for every citizen, responded to the prevailing view that equated economics with the quest for material wealth. The following section, after briefly discussing his first book, *De La Richesse Commerciale* (1803), surveys his creation of a new social economics through the concepts and theories put forth in his *New Principles* (1819).

1. Sismondi's *De la Richesse Commerciale* (1803)

This first work tackling the basic issue of commercial wealth predates in so many ways the real Sismondi who was to rewrite economics. Still, it is not an insignificant book and sets the stage for much that he had to say later on. Its modest purpose, according to the author, was to present the doctrines of Adam Smith in a briefer and tidier manner to the people of France, as well as to apply their lessons to their own situation. Possibly for this reason, it has been ignored by so many students of the history of economics. But there were also exceptions: Joseph Schumpeter, for example, remarked: it really is "not quite the Smithian brew that it has been made out to be."[4] There are, for instance, several novelties, one pertaining to the meaning and aim of political economy. Sismondi was already defining this as a branch of "science of government" in charge of securing "le bien des peuples" (the common good) rather than merely the accumulation of abstract wealth. Another novelty was the author's focus on the nation's capital, how it circulates through the economy, how it affects income distribution among the classes, and under what conditions it can reproduce itself. Sismondi does all this in the first part of the book in which he presents a distinct model of the circular flow, and in the process articulates one of the very first formal macroeconomic models of equilibrium national income and expenditures expressed in rudimentary fashion, as shown in Box 2.1.

In order to take a closer look at this novel approach, and to understand and appreciate its significance, one must first do some bushwhacking through the thicket of classical economics. Sismondi follows Adam Smith in distinguishing two types of capital: first, there is *fixed capital* consisting in the main of

---

Box 2.1

Sismondi's Mathematical Macro Model*

Appelons P la production du travail national pendant l'année; N le salaire nécessaire antérieur auquel ce travail est dû. P–N sera le revenu. Que D soit la dépense, X la différence entre le salaire nécessaire antérieur, et celui avancé dans l'année courante, différence qui peut être ou nulle ou positive ou négative, en sorte que $\overline{N+X}$ sera ce dernier salaire. Enfin C représente les dettes ou créances sur l'etranger.

Lors qu'une nation n'a point de commerce extérieur, sa consommation est égale à sa production: or cette consommation c'est $D+\overline{N+X}$. Or $D+\overline{N+X}=P$. Ou $D=P-\overline{N+X}$. Lorsqu'elle en a un, si elle emprunte des étrangers, sa consommation non-seulement égale sa production, mais elle comprend de plus l'emprunt qu'elle fait aux étrangers, ensorte que $D+\overline{N+X}=P+C$; soit $D=P+C-\overline{N+X}$. Lorsqu'enfin la nation préte chaque année aux étranger, il s'en faut de toute la valeur de ce prêt que sa consommation égale sa production; alors $D+\overline{N+X}=P-C$, soit $D=P-C-\overline{N+X}$. D'où il résulte que l'état progressif ou rétrograde de la nation dépend toujours de l'évaluation de X ou de la différence entre le salaire nécessaire d'une année et celui de la suivante.

---

*Here is how Sismondi apologetically introduced his model:

Those who are not familiar with the language of mathematics won't pay any attention to calculations that are presented to them in that form. Those, on the other hand, who have acquired the habit of thinking in abstract numbers and ideas are repelled by numerical suppositions that appear to them implausible or inexact. In order to satisfy both groups I will generalize in this note what is put forth in the text, and I shall adopt this time only the language of exact sciences; but only this one time because to apply the mathematical language to a science which is not exact is to continuously expose oneself to error. Political economy is not founded solely on numbers, it is rather an assemblage of moral observations which cannot be submitted to calculation and which continuously change the facts. The mathematician who wants to constantly make abstractions is bound to suppress haphazardly essential variables in each of his equations. (J. C. L. Simonde de Sismondi, *De La Richesse Commerciale*, Geneva, Paschoud, 1803, pp. 104–106, translated by the author.)

land (ready for cultivation), buildings (factories, grain mills and so forth), agricultural and industrial machinery and equipment (for example, water-wheels), as well as the available means of transportation (roads, canals, carriages, boats and so on). In being put to productive use, this fixed capital will generate an income which Sismondi chose to call "rent." Second, there is also *circulating capital* made up of the value of the necessary wage goods, which the capital owner or capitalist has to finance or "advance" in order for his work force to produce the next harvest or the next period's commercial output. The forthcoming output minus its costs, namely the "necessary wages," is appro-priated by the owners of capital as *profits*. Together with the rents, this return to investment income stands for a society's total annual *revenue*. It can be spent on consumption, that is *dépense*, or reinvested in the form of another outlay of necessary wages to produce the next harvest or period's output.

Since Sismondi, like the other economists of his time, was primarily inter-ested in understanding the growth of a nation's wealth, he centered his atten-tion on capital and the causes for its enlargement. In particular, he wanted to demonstrate, against the mercantilist doctrines, that nations can grow wealthy even in the absence of a foreign trade surplus. Instead – and here comes his new idea – he was to analyze the effect of a national (macro) balance between a society's revenue and its total expenditures. For that purpose, he starts out with the novel notion that in a national economy overall consump-tion and production need to balance, since "if it produced more than it could consume, absent exports, a part of the fruit of their labor would be useless, thereby lowering prices and halting production for the following year."[5] In other words, national income is in balance when overall consumption (both productive, that is, in today's language, "investment," and unproductive, today simply "consumption") is equal to national output. Given this require-ment, he now postulates an equilibrium between society's *dépense*, which is consumption minus what is saved for necessary wages, and its *revenue*, the national income minus the necessary wages. Since "necessary wages" can be canceled out on both sides of the equation (assuming that workers produce what they consume), macro equilibrium is determined by the mutual relation of capitalists' consumption and income. But now Sismondi goes one step further by introducing intertemporal relations and so allowing for unequal values in "necessary wages" between two periods, implying net investment or disinvestment taking place in the second period, resulting in economic growth or decline. His equation of dynamic national balance now looks like this:

capitalist revenue = capitalist consumption + in(de)crease in necessary wages.

In Sismondi's own symbolic terms: $R = D + X$. Clearly, the gap between revenue and consumption, Sismondi's "increase in necessary wages" or "X," constitutes in this model both savings and investment. If capital owners every year were to accumulate by spending their revenue more on wages of productive workers than on luxury goods, national wealth would increase. This process can go on without reliance on the growth of exports, the key point Sismondi wanted to make. To demonstrate this further, Sismondi then modifies the domestic national balance by adding a factor representing net imports. In his model it can be readily shown that as long as net investment is larger than net imports, the economy will still grow.[6]

It is only at some scattered points in his analytic description of the economic process that one can see the humanistic Sismondi who would some dozen years later challenge his contemporaries with a new political economy. So, for example, after analyzing and denying the possibility of higher than subsistence wages as a way to boost national product, he laments: "no man of sensibility can without sorrow see the most significant class in the nation, that which supports the whole society by the fruits of its labors, deprived of its enjoyments in order to share them with people of leisure or with those who burden him with taxes."[7] The real Sismondi shines through his discussion when he questions the right of landowners to appropriate the rent, or of capital owners to siphon off the entire surplus in the form of profits. While firmly believing in private property of both land and capital, such property rights were to him not absolute and based on natural law, but instead on social utility. He felt that it would be from a social point of view senseless to have a system in which the entire fruits of economic growth go to one side, while leaving the bulk of society at a continuing subsistence level.[8] In brief, the early Sismondi's support of the system was contingent on it functioning in the social interest.

The second half of *De la Richesse Commerciale*, which deals with the determination of price and discusses commercial policy, is, unlike the first half, very "Smithian." This is also apparent in how he chooses to define the common good: while not all people are artisans or landowners or folks engaged in commerce, they all are *consumers*, thereby enabling the evaluation of an economy's institutions and policies by the yardstick of *consumer satisfaction*. Clearly, the young Sismondi was a classical liberal with a strong faith in market freedoms, free competition and a government that does best by governing least.

Whether or not the *Richesse Commerciale* was in fact "a perfectly traditional exposition of the doctrine of Adam Smith," as one leading scholar[9] maintains, it certainly was not a great academic, let alone commercial, success. It went through only one edition, it was never translated into any language, and there are only very few copies left in libraries today. Perhaps its lack of success can be partially explained by an unhappy coincidence: another Frenchman, Jean Baptiste Say, published in the same year his *Treatise on Political Economy*, a work that was written with a quite similar purpose and that proved much more popular. Before long, Say's book established itself as *the* authoritative text in France, going through five editions. Meanwhile, Sismondi turned his back on political economy and instead devoted the next dozen years to the study of the history of the Italian Republic.

2. The *New Principles of Political Economy*

Sismondi a decade later, in 1815, was to contribute an article on *political economy* for the prestigious *Brewster's Edinburgh Encyclopedia*. It was an invitation he gladly accepted, thinking that all he had to do was write a short and clear exposition on a doctrine "on which all theorists . . . were in universal agreement."[10] He explained that since the requirements of brevity and clarity generally demand that an author follow his own ideas rather than someone else's, he had refrained from reading any recent book on the subject and decided to "walk alone" and rely on both his memory and his own observations of economic life. "In this way," he recalled, "I remained unconstrained by any settled authority." But it quickly became apparent to him that some of these observed real world facts – particularly the ongoing European business crisis and the cruel suffering of factory workers – seemed to contradict the principles he had held so dearly. As a result, Sismondi experienced some sort of Gestalt switch:

> Suddenly, [the stubborn facts] seemed to fall into place, to clarify each other, because of the new development I gave to my theory. The more I progressed, the more I became convinced of the importance and the truth of the modifications I brought to the system of Adam Smith. When considered from this new viewpoint all that had heretofore remained obscure in this science, became clear, and my assumptions gave me solutions to difficulties I had never dreamed of before.[11]

It was this piece for the *Encyclopedia*, some 120 pages long, written in 1815 and eventually published in 1824, that marked the birth of his social economics.[12] As Sismondi recalled, twenty-five years later: "In this [article] I laid down my first sketch of my system of Political Economy, on the abuse of labour, of competition, on the excess of production."[13] Although the essay was only a sketch, it provided a perfect outline for what was to come: each of its six chapters was developed and expanded to become the six "books" making up his *New Principles of Political Economy*, the first edition of which was published as early as the spring of 1819. A slightly revised second edition that was published in 1827, and only very recently translated into English,[14] serves as the primary reference in what follows. The various aspects that as an ensemble make it the first basic text of social economics include: a concern with the economy's tendency to macroeconomic instability, thus aggravating the sorry lot of the work force; a reconceptualization of economic thought in terms of its methodology and scope; together with a critical assessment of the basic institutional framework leading to a rejection of the prevailing *laissez-faire* policy prescriptions.

The problem of overproduction and business cycles

Sismondi had used his concise macroeconomic model in *Richesse Commerciale* to demonstrate that the value of national production logically also entails an equivalent national income, thereby precluding any possibility that capital will remain idle. Now in U-turn fashion he embraces the opposite point of view, allowing for the possibility that income may not be able to buy all that is produced, at least not at profitable prices. This allows for a temporary period of generally glutted markets, or an economic crisis. There are two interconnected aspects of his crisis theory, one explaining recurrent business slumps in terms of overproduction, the other blaming a lopsided income distribution for generating a growing tendency toward underconsumption.

In Sismondi's intricate explanation of business cycles, he paints a picture of growth as a rather fragile balance between consumption and production, a balance which can easily be disturbed by too great a boost in the saving and investment rate causing an unsustainable spurt in economic activity. Using a dynamic method of period analysis, similar to the one in his earlier book, a new problem is encountered: income of one year (similar to the harvest in an agricultural economy) must be balanced with production and consumption of the following year. Since income is a historical or "predetermined quantity," limiting current aggregate spending, it may not be able to fully absorb an increased level of production, not necessarily yielding the expected profits on the invested capital. For example, a capital owner after having marketed his previous product with great ease, may decide to invest a much larger proportion of his revenue this time around. In the process, production increases sharply while the (predetermined) income remains the same. As a consequence, demand falls short and output cannot be sold at a price that covers costs, inventories rise and markets are glutted, leading to subsequent cutbacks and recession. Obviously, the logic of such a restrictive assumption does make continuous growth problematic, and it is true that explicit consideration of depreciation of fixed capital would render any gap between available income and the supply of available goods less pronounced.

Generally, Sismondi felt that the process of accumulation if "executed with prudence and moderation can perpetuate itself."[15] More specifically, if the increase in output is sufficiently moderate, the inevitable losses will be small and widely dispersed with the result that "everyone bears it without complaining about his income" and will be willing to continue to invest, and so it is "the chain of these small sacrifices [that] adds to capital and public prosperity." Only if there exists "a great disproportion between the new and the previous production," will accumulation cease and bring about a situation in which there will be great suffering, "and the nation regresses instead of advancing."[16]

At that time, he put most of the blame on government policies (war-related expenditures, export subsidies and so forth), but in his later works he accused bankers of being too eager to furnish (fictitious) capital to profit-hungry speculators wanting to set up new factories. "Capital so easily obtained," he declared, "incites too hazardous enterprises, which the authors would have hesitated to undertake," if they had been "commanding of a vast capital which [did] not belong to themselves," for investing recklessly.[17]

Now the question arises, why is it that an excessive amount of production cannot always be sold at prices and profits that would guarantee continued reproduction of output? The answer for Sismondi is quite simple. Consumption power is relatively limited and grows only slowly with population and the incomes of agricultural and industrial workers, both groups increasingly constituting the bulk of society. In addition, human needs are limited: people can only consume so much food, clothing and shelter. Even to the extent that they might want more "exquisite aliments" or more extravagant clothes, the problem is only alleviated or postponed, but not solved. Moreover, many of these potential luxuries are incompatible with the life of the working man sweating twelve to fourteen hours a day. Why would he want to labor in velvets and gold brocades? he asks. Additional consumption necessitates some leisure, which, for the most part, was reserved for the wealthy few. More generally, no additional consumer goods would be worth the effort.[18]

Overproduction, according to Sismondi, was less of a problem in earlier times when producers could estimate the extent of their market and gear their overall output to demand. But with the onset of mass production, farmers and entrepreneurs now face an impersonal market with little reliable knowledge of the forthcoming consumption. Blinded by this uncertainty, and hoping for the best, there is an inclination to optimistically "shoot for the moon" by expanding output as much as possible. This was a new problem caused by the Industrial Revolution.

The underlying idea of an equilibrium rate of growth in output and income has been recognized by economic historians as a worthwhile contribution. As Joseph Schumpeter, who otherwise had little sympathy for Sismondi, put it: "[his] great merit is that he used, systematically and explicitly, a schema of periods, that is, that he was the first to practice the particular method of dynamics that is called period analysis."[19] In such a model, future output is a function of current profits and *expectations*. Another economic historian, Thomas Sowell, notes this process can be described in what is known as the cobweb theorem.[20] He demonstrates, and in graphical terms rigorously "proves," that we need not play the game in terms of a harvest model and still get Sismondi's results. All that is needed is a situation in which capitalists overestimate the prospective profits on their planned investment for the resulting aggregate output to fall short of its cost of reproduction.[21] In other words, due to imperfect foresight and false expectations, output can only be sold at substandard profits or losses which implies, at least for some time, glutted markets.

Sismondi's claim of the possibility of general gluts flew in the face of the prevailing conventional wisdom, which was cemented some ten years before the publication of his *New Principles.* Earlier, responding to a pamphlet written by a certain William Spence, who had voiced concern that enriched landlords may hurt the economy by not spending all their proceeds, James Mill countered:

> If a nation's power of purchasing is exactly measured by its annual produce, the more you increase the annual produce . . . the more by the very act you extend the national market, the power of purchasing and the actual purchases of the nation. Whatever be the additional quantity of goods therefore which is at any time created in any country, an additional power of purchasing, exactly equivalent, is at the same instant created; so that a nation can never be naturally overstocked either with capital or with commodities; as the very operation of capital makes a vent for its produce.[22]

Later on, in France, J. B. Say used similar language to express the same faith: "The mere circumstance of the *creation of one product* immediately *opens a vent* for other products," says Say. "*Demand* is only limited by *production*," repeats David Ricardo. Mill's proposition (paraphrased today as "supply creates its own demand") came to be known as an early articulation of what we now call "Say's Law." According to its logic it was foolish to say that the volume of production could in any way exceed the general level of demand. In other words, this reasoning implied, contra Sismondi, that any size accumulation, regardless of how large, would automatically produce a national purchasing power to absorb the new production. Of course, there could be *partial* gluts disturbing certain parts of the economy, but logic dictated that if too little was spent in one place, too much had to be spent in another, thus driving up profits and employment in those industries. It should be noted that to Mill, Ricardo and Say, "equilibrium" or "balance" meant something quite different from what Sismondi intended, namely that all branches of the economy were producing output in proportion to consumer demand.

It was not long before Sismondi was attacked, first by J. R. McCulloch, the leading follower of the reigning economics pope, David Ricardo, and then by J. B. Say himself. The issue was Say's Law. It was a messy debate, one side defending it by arguing in terms of the method of comparative statics, while Sismondi argued the case in terms of his short-term intertemporal model of national income determination. In hindsight, Sismondi can be seen to have managed to hold his own,[23] persuading his countryman, Say, to acknowledge in his revised text Sismondi's point of there being indeed consumption-induced limits to successful accumulation and production.[24] Perhaps because Say's new and corrected fifth edition was never translated into English, the British held to the prevailing static interpretation of Say's Law. Nevertheless, it was Sismondi who, implicitly in 1815 and explicitly in 1819, first seriously challenged the prevailing orthodoxy of Say's Law, a distinction that makes him a pioneer of macroeconomic thought.[25]

The tendency toward underconsumption

Sismondi was not only the father of business cycle theory, but also the very first economist to attempt a macro theory of underconsumption based on the distribution of income between the owners of capital and workers.[26] "It is not unimportant for the well-being of citizens," Sismondi declares, "whether everyone's share of ease and enjoyment approximates equality, or whether a small number has luxuries while a great number is reduced to subsistence"; the two distributions of income have different effects on the progress of commercial wealth. "Equality of benefits," he says, "must result in steady expansion of manufacturers' markets; inequality, always, furthers contraction." The problem has two basic dimensions. Sismondi explains:

> The same income is used by the rich as well as the poor, but it is not used in the same way. The former use much more capital and much less labor than the latter; they benefit the population much less and, as a consequence, contribute less to the reproduction of wealth.[27]

It is the poor who spend their incomes more on consumer goods instead of saving, and thereby contribute to the economy growing at a slower but steadier pace.

Moreover, a further contraction comes about through the rapid growth of large-scale factories replacing small workshops, thereby also affecting the power of consumption. He compares the spending of a manufacturer employing 1,000 workmen and paying subsistence wages with that of 100 manufacturers each employing 10 workers far less poor. In one case, there is one rich family demanding fancier articles of better quality, better workmanship, made from more refined materials and often imported, such as silks, fancy ribbon, spices, Greek liquors, cashmere shawls and Persian rugs. Domestically, it will "remunerate magnificently the efforts, the elegance, and the taste" of artisans. At the same time, the remaining ninety-nine families will have to live in wretched poverty on a diet of potatoes and milk, and clothe themselves in cheap textiles. In the case of small-scale production, on the other hand, there would be 100 families being able to afford better bread, meat, wine, enough spare linen and several suits of clothes, in other words, a demand that would give much greater encouragement to farmers and domestic manufacturers. In short, the ongoing transformation in production, replacing many small firms with a few large ones, in and of itself exerts a force restricting consumption. Add to this the fact that "the effect of great opulence is almost entirely to exclude the [very] produce of those large manufactures from the consumption of the opulent man," since the rich prefer the objects crafted by skilled artisans to the qualitatively more inferior machine-made ones.[28] In other words, the growing concentration of industry in a few hands undermines the demand for the very goods it grinds out. This in turn forces industry to look abroad, especially among the "barbarous nations," for new markets in an effort to unload their unsold merchandise. Yet it will not take long to discover that the extent of the world market too is circumscribed, "that the general optimism of all producers who sold abroad has everywhere raised production above demand." The result is that the international rivals attempt to undersell each other, even at a loss if necessary, and in the process tend to provoke defensive measures among the importing countries in the form of tariff barriers. As this safety valve has been closing, "Europe at present knows not how to dispose [of its superabundant labor] and to terminate [the] distress into which the poor are plunged."[29]

Sismondi's underconsumption forces are to a major part driven by competition, not only in the world market but also at home. And competition meant for Sismondi primarily "underselling" in the product market where it manifests in ruthless cost (read wage) cutting among rivals trying to snatch each other's customers. Underselling also makes for self-inflicted pain among desperate laborers for whom any pay is better than none at all. Workers have no choice but to consent to work longer hours in order to maintain their incomes. As a result, production increases more than the combined incomes of workers, owners, and bankers loaning the capital. Sismondi tries to prove the point with a numerical example of a cloth manufacturer who manages with the same staff to double production while combined incomes increase only by a little more than half, thereby precipitating a glut.[30] Unfortunately, it was not a successful demonstration since he neglected to consider the additional purchasing power among consumers of the cloth that would be generated by the logically necessary drop in its price from the initial £4.50 per ell to £2.20 per ell. This error was to be an easy target for economists eager to discredit him, yet the miscarriage of Sismondi's attempted proof may be exaggerated within the overall context of his analysis of the "struggle to produce cheaper." Another objection to this type of competition was the fact that it leads to the squeezing and eventual elimination of the independent small farmers and artisans in the process. The result is a new social order composed of two classes: rich capitalists employing a multitude of day laborers together with a growing mass of dependent industrial "proletarians," a word Sismondi coined. In the process, bargaining power between

The two classes becomes extremely lopsided. They need each other in the production process, "but the necessity weighs daily on the workman; [who] must work that they may live, [while the capitalist] may wait and live for a time without employing workmen."[31] The result of this unequal power play is "constantly a sacrifice of the class which is poorer, [and] more numerous," wages fall relative to profits and the whole economy becomes more and more vulnerable to aggregate demand failure.

Demographically, the new economic dependency creates a problem of its own. Both the agricultural day laborer and the industrial worker have lost control over their lives and destinies, living on a day-by-day basis never knowing when capital will dispose of them as redundant. Drifting as they do, they have lost any reason to exercise foresight and have acquired an inclination to reproduce themselves without restraint. Those "wretched souls," through no fault of their own, cannot be expected to have any aspirations for their children. In fact, the more rapidly the employee produces offspring, thereby adding a surplus of new workers to the world, the sooner can he count on a new source of family income. So the laid-off worker, interested in finding bread at whatever price, is driven to self-destructive behavior: "he will [be willing to] work 14 hours a day, will bring his children to a factory at the age of six, and will endanger with his health and life the existence of his whole class, to escape the pinch of dire need."[32] The growing surplus of labor seeking employment further depresses wages and the purchasing power of the mass of consumers. The root of the problem begetting Sismondi's gloomy perspective is the growing divorce of ownership from labor, which acts to curb the growth of consumption while production soars.

The influence of machinery

The new phenomenon of machine production, spreading from England to the Continent, further aggravated underconsumption. Since the invention of the steam engine, British economists had given machines their unqualified blessing. It was only in 1817 that the worldly philosophers were challenged by a humanitarian country gentleman, John Barton, from Stoughton in Sussex. In a widely read pamphlet he offered the following hypothetical case:

> A manufacturer possesses a capital of £1,000 which he employs in maintaining twenty weavers, paying them £50 per annum. His capital is suddenly increased to £2,000. With double means he does however hire not double the number of workmen, but lays out £1,500 in erecting machinery, by the help of which five men are enabled to perform the same quantity of work as twenty did before. Are there not then fifteen men discharged in consequence of the manufacturer having increased his capital?[33]

33

In anticipating economists' objections, Barton goes on to demonstrate that even if we take the work for the construction and repair of the machine into account, this could never account for more than three machine-makers in addition to the five weavers still employed. More than that, the increased profits of the manufacturer enable him to maintain two additional domestic servants, making now a total of ten persons in all. In short, the doubling of capital went hand-in-hand with a slicing of the employed labor force in half. From which Barton concluded: "The demand for labor depends then on the increase of circulating (or human), and not fixed capital [embodied in machines]."[34] That negative assessment, brought to the attention of David Ricardo via Thomas Malthus, may have been instrumental in the latter's change of mind and his belated admission that the idea long popular with the working class, of machinery being detrimental to their interests, is not ill-founded on prejudice and error. Rather, it "is conformable to the correct principles of political economy."[35]

Sismondi, when he met Ricardo in July of 1822, must have been made aware of Barton's work, which he promptly and very favorably reviewed in a French journal.[36] After quoting in full Barton's numerical example, he commented: "By this process, the prodigious augmentation of industrial capital has merely meant more and more machines which, far from leading to an increase in the demand for labor and a rise in wages, have only brought about the dismissal of numerous workmen and the lowering of the wages for the rest of them."[37] Ricardo's lending credibility and respectability to Barton's attempted proof may have emboldened Sismondi to go one step further to blame the improper use of mechanization for a macroeconomic instability. By the time he revised his *New Principles* (1827), Sismondi had already gained the reputation of being against progress. In order to combat this impression, he added the following note comparing the effects of machinery under different social organizations:

> It is not the improvement of machines which is the true calamity, it is the improper distribution we make of their products. The more we can produce with a given quantity of labor, the more we must increase either our enjoyments, or our leisure; the worker who is his own master, when he would have produced in two hours with the help of a machine, what he had before in twelve, would have stopped after two hours, if he had no need, and could not use a larger product. It is our actual social organization, it is the dependency of the worker that brings him to work, not less but more hours per day, for the same wages, while the machine enhances his powers of production.[38]

Applying this enhanced power everywhere is especially socially questionable when there is already excess capacity and unemployed labor. "When consumption is limited and cannot grow, when workers are already in excess in factories, when by the use of all their capacities they obtain only an insufficient wage," Sismondi warns, "the invention of a machine which replaces a number of hands by inanimate force is a calamity, because the inventor, instead of using it to assist his own workers, employs it to kill the workers of his rival."[39] And he adds that: "surely no one will maintain that it can be advantageous to substitute a machine for a man, if this man cannot find work elsewhere; or that it is not better to have the population composed of citizens than of steam engines, even though the cotton cloth of the first should be a little dearer than that of the second."[40]

But what about the claim that new technology lowers not only costs but also prices? Would not lower prices benefit the consumer and allow for additional expenditure on other goods, thereby counteracting the direct effect of lower incomes? Sismondi, anticipating this objection, replied that "there will never be any proportion[al relationship] between this new demand and the labor suspended on account of it." He offers two basic reasons. First, prices need not decline at all; consumers "make use of goods a little finer, a little prettier, at the same price," and second, labor costs are only a fraction of total costs. As an illustration he points to the invention of the stocking frame, which boosted labor productivity a hundredfold, but reduced prices of stockings by a mere 10 percent. Examples such as this and others would suggest that improved manufactures "have never diminished the price of their product except in arithmetical progression, while they have suspended workmanship in geometrical progression."[41] Once again the Sismondian world is one in which wages fall and profits soar, with both affecting income distribution in a manner where the "turning [of] workers into steam engines" contributes to the making of underconsumption together with overinvestment, resulting in more excess capacity and generally glutted markets.

The problematic process of market adjustments

Right or wrong, today few economists would take seriously any macroeconomics that incorporates consideration of income distribution. But Sismondi made another basic point. He did not question that the free market process would eventually find a new and satisfactory equilibrium, but it was the nature of this slow and painful adjustment process that was a real problem to Sismondi. Market adjustments take time, and that fact alone causes "long and cruel sufferings." The new factory system greatly aggravated the situation, something that he was never tired of emphasizing. Supply reacts slowly to changes in demand. This lethargic response is due to the immobility of both labor and capital. Workers having invested in long years of apprenticeship are reluctant to change their occupation. As a result, even if there were a constant demand for his services in another trade, Sismondi noticed that a worker will generally be inclined to prefer wage cuts combined with longer hours and stay put rather than switch occupations. "He will remain at work for fourteen hours, and will not rest on holidays; he will deny himself the time devoted previously to pleasure and dissipation, and the same number of workers will turn out more goods."[42] With respect to capital, there are similar obstacles to mobility: a cotton producer is operating with a very specialized set of equipment as his capital, "one-half, three-quarters of his fortune are irrevocably destined to produce cotton cloth." Sismondi asks us to imagine that the price of cotton declines to a level below costs and poses the question: will the entrepreneur because of this shut down his factory? He answers in the negative, and explains: "in agreeing to lose one half of the income of his fixed capital, he continues to produce, and he will realize the other half, but, if he closes his factory, he will lose all his income." Therefore production continues unabated in the face of vanishing demand, until eventually a number of factory owners are abruptly forced into bankruptcy. Tragically, by that time, "a part of the work force will have died from misery."[43]

Sismondi concludes that it was David Ricardo's basic error to extrapolate from switches in product demand *within* an industry (for example, changing one's cotton assortment from striped velour to single color) to the more general situation of changes in demand *between* industries, as, for example, from cotton to steel manufacture. It is particularly in the latter situation in which the turnover of investment capital operates with "extreme slowness." The real world circumstance of sluggish market adjustments has macro-economic significance, something that Sismondi tried to impress on Ricardo when they met in Geneva in 1822. He argued his case in an 1824 article, "On the Balance of Consumption with Production," which he later appended to the second edition of his *New Principles*. It shows a more mature Sismondi, and is a good illustration of the level of analytic proficiency with which he attempted to persuade his fellow economists to change course.

According to Sismondi, their talk focused on the "fundamental question" that divided Say and Ricardo from Malthus and himself: whether or not an increased production, in this case due to technological change, would also generate the necessary consumption to absorb it? Ricardo confidently argued that it would:

> Suppose a hundred cultivators produce a thousand bags of corn, and a hundred wool manufacturers produce a thousand ells of cloth; viewing only them in the world, abstracting from all other goods useful to men, of all middlemen, they exchange their thousand ells against their thousand bags; let us then assume that with successive progress of industry the productive powers of labor increase by one-tenth; the same men exchange eleven hundred ells against eleven hundred bags,

and everyone of them will find himself better clad and fed; a new advance will exchange twelve hundred ells against twelve hundred bags, and so forth; the increase in product will always increase the pleasures of those who produce them.[44]

Sismondi answers that the abstraction we are asked to make is much too extreme and, therefore, misleading, "hiding from our view all the successive operations by which we can distinguish truth from error."[45] The main problem is that it lacks institutional detail, the way society is actually organized: workers without property whose wages are fixed by competition and who may be dismissed any time the master no longer needs them. Sismondi offers a thoughtful and sophisticated numerical counterexample, one that takes full account of those frictional details, giving way to a more pessimistic conclusion. It talks about a hypothetical situation in which technological change (for example, a new type of plow) allows annual production in agriculture to increase 50 percent. But, due to lack of additional arable land available, the representative cultivator increases output by only 5 percent, and produced now with 30 percent fewer farm hands. Sismondi then demonstrates, in quantitative terms, how the laid-off workers further impact employment in the other industries that had been supplying them with other basic manufactures: in his example, consumption is cut by one-third, and through these secondary effects, one-third of the community's work force is now unemployed and "will not have yet received their bread." At the same time, profits are up, creating a strong demand for luxury goods, a new demand which takes time to be met: "new coach builders, glass makers and watch makers have to be born, or at least learn their newly demanded trades." Similarly, new machines must be built or ordered from abroad. Till that time, the redundant farm hands shifting toward the new occupations making luxury goods "are still very far from eating the corn of our cultivators, [or] from wearing the clothes of our basic manufactures."[46] Everything depends on the swift build-up of the luxury trades. Only after they are established will the obstacle be finally removed and a new equilibrium with full employment regained.

> We come to find, like Mr. Ricardo, that at the end of the cycle, if it is in no way impeded, production will have created a consumption; but this is done by abstracting from time and space, as the German metaphysicians would do; this is by abstracting from all the obstacles which can halt this circulation; and the more we look at them more closely, the more we see that these obstacles are multiplied.[47]

This example demonstrates that Sismondi, despite some glitches in earlier years, can prove his points even against the most formidable and respected opponents, and can do so in a fairly rigorous manner. He showed how easily Say's Law can fail due to frictions caused by the relative immobility of capital and labor: production does not automatically generate more demand, except in the long run, after many have died of starvation and deprivation.

In conclusion, Sismondi's pioneering thought in macroeconomics constructs a rich and complex fabric of interwoven strands that work through both overproduction and underconsumption. Whether the initial problematic impetus turns out to be lack of information to realistically and adequately forecast business demands and profits, or whether it is the rapid introduction of machinery and other cost and wage reduction measures, or whether it is simply the slow way markets respond to major shifts in industrial demand, in all these cases the subsequent chain of further events and adjustments can all too easily upset the fragile balance between sufficient purchasing power and the supply of products. Moreover, these processes generally weaken the bargaining power of workers and via subsequent shifts in income distribution from wages to profits, reinforce macroeconomic failure with its dire collateral effects for large numbers of citizens.

All this raises the question, why did it take a *socially oriented economist* to point out these problems? The answer undoubtedly is to be found in concern for the new suffering among the impecunious masses caused by the new phenomenon of recurring business slumps. The conventional economist, preoccupied with the accumulation of material wealth rather than the well-being of the people producing it, gave little attention to such temporary blips in the growth-producing economic engine. What mattered to them was that in the *long run* the self-adjusting market mechanism would always re-establish equilibrium and enable national wealth to resume its expansion. Yet, it was precisely these intervals, the periods while the gluts lasted, that were responsible for hunger and general immiseration, if not death, of multitudes of innocent human beings. It was this very alarming new situation which, in the name of the tragedies "that afflict today such a large number of brethren, and which the old science neither teaches us to understand, nor to prevent," provoked Sismondi to carry economics "forward to new ground." He believed that political economy, unlike the natural sciences, had to be approached by appealing both to reason *and to the heart*. "The observer is called upon to recognize unjust suffering that comes from man, and of which man is the victim," Sismondi insists, and adds, "We cannot consider them coldly and pass them over, without seeking some remedy."[48] Elsewhere, after discussing the misery caused by glutted markets, he emphatically points out that "this great European calamity cannot be viewed without turning, with all our hearts, our minds, to search for cures that will put an end to so much suffering."[49] In short, social economics reckons with the *human* costs of unmet needs and, in those days especially, this was bound to lead to giving primary attention to macroeconomic instability and crisis.

Political economy and the abstract method

Sismondi's career as an economist started, it will be remembered, with his earlier book introducing the French to Adam Smith's teachings. Part of his mission was to emulate and spread his master's method as he understood it, a method which emphasized the observation of facts over abstract theorizing. Already in his *Richesse Commerciale* he made it clear that economics is "not founded on dry calculations, nor on a mathematical chain of theorems, deduced from some obscure axioms, given as incontestable truth"; instead, he says, "[it] is founded on the study of man and of men; human nature must be known, as well as the condition and life of societies in different times and different places."[50] In the following two decades he continued to regard Adam Smith as an exemplar of good economics, since in his search for truth, Smith never neglected "to examine each fact in the social context to which it belonged." But now Sismondi upholds Smith's approach to economics against Smith's self-avowed followers in England, men who had "thrown themselves into abstractions which make us lose from view entirely the human being to whom the wealth belongs, and who ought to enjoy it." Under their reign the science became increasingly speculative and divorced from all practical applications so essential to good government. To this Sismondi added:

> One would believe at first sight that in freeing the theory from all surrounding circumstances, one would make it clearer and easier to comprehend; the opposite has happened; the new English economists are extremely obscure and can only be understood with much effort, while our mind is loath to accept the abstractions they require of us. But this very aversion is a warning that we move away from the truth, because, in the social sciences where everything is connected, we have to make great efforts to isolate a principle and see nothing but it alone.[51]

He singled out David Ricardo, in particular, whose *Principles of Political Economy and Taxation* (1817) had already proved immensely influential. Ricardo was portraying economics as a highly abstract undertaking in which the economy moved from one equilibrium state to another in the manner of comparative statics in physics. On the other hand, for Sismondi the historian, the real issue was the *process* of establishing equilibrium. We have already seen how he likened Ricardo to a German metaphysician abstracting from time and real world institutional content. Elsewhere he warns the reader: "Let us beware of this dangerous equilibrium theory that reestablishes itself by its own accord. Let us beware of believing that it does not matter on which side of a scale one puts or takes a weight, because the other will quickly adjust itself," and he even makes the claim that "every abstraction is always a deception." At the same time, Sismondi granted that it is human to simplify everything, to generalize everything, and he further concedes that this trait "is the very cause of all basic advances in science." But, to the extent that people must make abstractions, people should not "surrender to [this practice] in a thoughtless manner." He further cautions, that political economy is not a mathematical science, but a moral science, meaning that "it misleads if one wants to be guided by numbers; it only leads to a goal if the feeling, the needs, and the passions of mankind are taken into account."[52]

Sismondi preferred to study economic phenomena by means of the concrete historical method within a particular institutional context. An excellent illustration of this approach is his measured assessment of the two sides in the debate of opening up British agriculture to foreign competition and imports. Taking place in the first three decades of the nineteenth century, this was the first big controversy on free trade in economic history. Sismondi's careful analysis of the various pros and cons concludes in asking the reader to consider the following three basic questions:

(1) If the wheat produced by serf cultivation [in Poland and Southern Russia] costing nothing to its seller, comes to England without duties, will it be possible for one single English farmer to continue sowing a single wheat field?

(2) If the English nation, finding it cheaper to buy foreign wheat, gives up wheat farming, what will be the decrease in the number of hands employed in agriculture? What will be the expense to the manufacturing classes to maintain, in workhouses, all the families of dismissed farm hands? What will manufacturers lose from the suspension of consumption by a whole class of English workers who make up close to one-half of the nation?

(3) On what security can a nation count whose subsistence depends totally on foreigners? . . . What will become of English honor if the Russian czar, every time he should want some concession from England, can starve her by closing the Baltic ports?[53]

To Sismondi, at least, it was not at all clear that choosing the approach that leads to the lowest wheat price is the only position that is harmonious with the principles of sound political economy. The whole matter was considerably more complicated than that.

On the scope and aim of political economy

As in method so also in the scope or range of economics, Sismondi considered himself the true follower of Smith, developing his thought by means of the same principles, but taking into account the experience of the half century since the publication of his *Wealth of Nations*, thereby arriving at new conclusions. In this respect, the novel problem of macro imbalance and crisis has already been discussed. But in one important aspect he did depart from his master. The focus now changed from wealth and its accumulation to the *enjoyment* of wealth and its *diffusion* among the people at large. For Sismondi, everything centered on how the economy affects human well-being, creating a "new economics of men" to replace the old economics of wealth. He explained: "we lose ourselves whenever we attempt to consider wealth abstractly. Wealth is a modification of the state of Man: it is only by referring it to man that we can form a clear idea of it."[54] Here his social economics takes on a distinctly humanistic flavor. What did Sismondi intend by his new "economics of man"?

For one, he maintained that a truly prosperous economy would have to spread the advantages of national fortune to every citizen, including the poor. Specifically:

> The enjoyments of the poor are composed of the abundance, of the variety, and of the wholesomeness of their nourishment, of the sufficiency of clothes relative to climate, and of their cleanliness; of the convenience and of the salubrity of their lodging, also as regards the climate and the quantity of fuel which it requires; lastly, of the certainty that the future will not be inferior to the present, and that a poor man can by the same labour obtain at least the same enjoyment.[55]

In other words, economics should be about fulfilling the basic material needs of all. More than that, Sismondi claimed that such subsistence "is the common *right* of man" and must be secured to all those "who do what they can to forward common labour."[56] As a result, Sismondi redefined economics as "the management of the national fortune for the happiness of all." This radically new perspective implies reliance on government as the protector of the poor, something that goes far beyond the *laissez-faire* doctrine championed by Smith. Sismondi, being fully aware of the implications of this new way of thinking, comments that "it is not true that the contest of individual interests suffices to produce the greatest good of all," but that "in the administration of the fortune of the public, it is necessary that sovereign authority should watch over and restrain particular interests to make them subservient to the general interest, that this authority should never lose sight of the formation and distribution of income, for it is income which spreads ease and prosperity throughout all classes." Government, as seen by Sismondi, now assumes a positive role as the "representative of the long-term, if quiet, interest of all, against the temporary, if vociferous interest of each."[57]

This then is an economics that aims at the common good. Here it is no longer sufficient to merely focus on the interest of the consumer, to aim at producing everything as cheaply as possible. In stark contrast to his earlier finding, he now maintains that whoever says "that each one being a consumer, the interest of the consumer is the interest of all, deceives us by an abstraction." This is especially true when one deals with luxury goods in which expenses are usually "calculated to afford relative rather than absolute enjoyment." This is an anticipation on Sismondi's part of the keeping-up-with-the-Jones's syndrome. But the economist must go beyond consumption and come to the realization that "the producer [meaning the worker] ought to be considered first of all." In conclusion, pursuit of the social interest of society demands that "perfect certainty of subsistence is more important than low prices to the consumer himself."[58]

A new economics of human well-being and the common good therefore goes beyond treating work as a mere input to greater wealth and consumption. Instead, work becomes a primary determinant of the quality of life, serving as a catalyst in human development, by cultivating and strengthening the intellect and character. First and foremost, this means that the worker needs to have job security. It is one thing for the savage hunter who dies for want of game, but quite another for an artisan to be dismissed from his workshop: in the latter case "he is still surrounded with riches; he still sees beside him, at every step, the food which he requires; and if society refuses him the labour by which he offers, till the last moment, to purchase bread, it is men, not nature, that he blames." Unemployment is a social disease and deserves the foremost attention of the social economist in terms of both macroeconomic analysis and remedial policies. Similarly, low-paying and degrading work must also be seen as a problem within the scope of economics. Primarily due to unequal bargaining power, a laborer's remuneration is so miserable as to scarcely maintain life. In addition to hunger and suffering dominating their lives, such deprivation also "stifles in them all moral affections." Sismondi explains the latter as follows:

> When every hour is a struggle for life, all passions are concentrated in selfishness; each forgets the pain of others in what he himself suffers; the sentiments of nature are blunted; a constant, obstinate, uniform labour, debases all the faculties. One blushes for the human species, to see how low on a scale of degradation it can descend; how much beneath the condition of animals it can voluntarily submit to maintain life.[59]

Sismondi also blamed the false gospel of universal competition, preached by the economists, for social immiseration and disintegration because, as he saw it, the paying of lowest possible wages and exploitative conditions are two of its "irresistible fatalities." The manufacturer's capital is all invested in the factory and the work force; "to pay their workmen, they must sell; to sell they must lower their prices; to lower their prices they *must* offer their workmen insufficient wages, whatever may be their humanity, their generosity." Competition and the "seduction of cheapness" will work to undermine human well-being of the largest class of citizens, and do so even in a world of moral employers. The social organization has reduced the worker to a state of deprivation and dependency, to a *proletarian*, who is a stranger to property, who has been "habituated to know no future further removed than next Saturday, when his weekly wages are paid." Much of the income will be spent on drink, and in matters of intimacy, with the moral sensitivities deadened: they "will conceive for the objects of their affection only the desires they have for themselves," mindlessly breeding offspring, regardless of an ability to provide for their sustenance.[60]

Bringing the nature of work into economics also entails the importation of a moral dimension. In Sismondi's time workers, artisans and peasants were not treated well in France, which had just entered the Industrial Revolution on the heels of the British. The country was suddenly face-to-face with the "Social Question," and Sismondi's new economics was a sensitive response to it. Naturally, the conditions and quality of work are a primary element of the common good. Certainly, more work adds to national enjoyment, but Sismondi was adamant that "as soon as those who perform it are *not* taken into account, it can easily transform itself into a frightful disaster." Factory work in those days was especially cruel and monotonous. Workers became appendages of machines and similarly dispensable, engendering a degradation of the human species for which no increase of wealth could compensate.[61] Clearly, the quality of work is the hub around which a human economy revolves. Good work builds character and ennobles preferences. Demeaning and degrading work has its effect on economic behavior.

Critical analysis of socioeconomic institutions

The treating of economics as a moral science with a social dimension, rather than as a natural science in quest of discovering natural laws, involves an explicit focus on socioeconomic institutions. These are now seen as socially created, with a social purpose and for a social use, and must be evaluated as to their current usefulness in promoting the public interest. On this question, too, Sismondi has much to say.

Being a historian at heart, Sismondi was all too well aware of how property had been forcefully appropriated through the ages, and how different cultures and societies had different property arrangements to underwrite the private ownership of agricultural land as a "natural right" guaranteeing possession and exclusive use. To him, the reality was quite different: "the division of rights to property is born from special circumstances, from chance schemes, often from passion or vanity." Therefore, ownership needed to be based on a principle of public utility. Ultimately, for any structure of basic property rights the *sine qua non* is that no one should die of hunger, and only on such condition should property be acknowledged and guaranteed.[62]

More particularly, it is because land ownership is "for society's advantage, for the poor as well as the rich, that it has taken the landlords under its protection." But the state can attach conditions to a concession that it grants: "it must submit property in land to legislation which will indeed bring about the general good, because it is the general good that alone justifies such ownership." Sismondi recommended that economists should promote those property rights structures that allow for the largest number of users, rather than aiming for profitability only. Accordingly, he considered the small family-owned farm vastly superior to large-scale cultivation by absentee landowners. Sismondi was no socialist advocating public ownership of land or factories. Instead of abolition, he fought for a diffusion of private property, thereby allowing everybody to participate in ownership and have a stake in property, "giving habits of order and economy" to the owners. Large-scale farms operated by hired labor are likely to be less efficient than family farms: "The [farm] hand has no participation in property, nothing to hope for from the fertility of the soil, or the propitiousness of the season; he plants not for his children; he entrusts not to the ground the labour of his young years, to reap the fruit of it, with interest, in his old age."[63]

The situation is no different with industry, where Sismondi championed proprietorships and independent small owner-operated business. For Sismondi, the root of all the social problems of his time, ranging from underpaid workers and degrading working conditions to periodic overproduction and excessive population growth, could be found in the separation of property from labor. He illustrated this general insight with the example of technological innovation:

> It is not in any way against machines, against inventions, against civilization that I raise my objections, it is against the new organization of society which, by taking away from the working man all property except his arms, gives him no guarantee against competition, a mad auction conducted to his disadvantage, and one of which he must necessarily be the victim. Let us assume that all men share equally the product of their labour in which they have cooperated; then every invention in the trades will in all instances, be a blessing for all of them; because, after every advancement in industry, they will always be able to choose, either to have more leisure with less labour, or to have with the same labour more pleasures. Today, it is not the invention that is the evil; *it is the unjust division man makes of its results.*[64]

An unjust division of the fruits of progress comes about from the new state of society where we "incline to separate completely any property from all types of labour, to break all ties between the worker and his employer, [and] to exclude the former from all types of participation in the profits of the latter." The result is a two-class society, with an increasingly prosperous group of powerful owners of capital confronted by a growing mass of dispossessed, dependent and wretched laborers. Here again Sismondi makes history, in painting a picture of increasingly antagonistic class struggle (another expression coined by him) long before Marx. Yet, he aspired to reform capitalism by reuniting capital and labor rather than by abolishing it. In his eyes the evil of the separation of ownership rights from labor was ushered in by a new social order where labor was a commodity to be bought and sold in the marketplace. Sismondi's voice here, not surprisingly, was not much appreciated by his fellow economists and statesmen, who saw nothing wrong with the social order progressing in this new direction. Sismondi pointed out that even slavery and serfdom were more successful in their earlier stages, before they became more and more dysfunctional and began to impose "frightful calamities on humanity." Similarly, Sismondi believed that its modern counterpart, the new wage system, was not to be seen as the final truth; that, on the contrary, history would reveal this new social order, too, to have been a "fundamental mistake." And he went on to make the prophetic prediction that "the time will undoubtedly come when our descendants will judge us not any less barbarous for having left the working class without security, as they will judge, and as we judge ourselves as barbarous, those nations who have reduced the same classes to slavery."[65]

As should be clear by now, Sismondi was the first economist rejecting *laissez-faire* and calling for an active government. What is the role of government in his opinion? Like most economists of his time, Sismondi believed that it ought to serve commerce by "rendering all communication easy, preparing roads, canals and bridges, protecting property, securing a fair administration of justice," and to finance these services through taxation. Beyond these and other conventional measures (such as control of monopoly, coinage and so forth), government, in his view, was also to be the protector of the poor and the weak in society. It was to make sure that wealth proceeded in a stable and socially just manner. Ironically, the existing social order in Sismondi's time was supported by legislation which favored the strong over the weak: laws that opposed the division of inheritances, that favored the formation and conservation of great fortunes (thereby discouraging the distribution of land in small parcels to those who worked it), and finally, laws that protected coalitions of masters against workmen and which also deprived workers of "their natural means of resistance," meaning their right to organize trade unions and to strike. What was necessary was to "level the playing field," to stop favoritism and to "intervene to abolish the evil it has produced."[66] But ultimately, the task of "protecting the poor" meant considerably more than the measures so far alluded to. At this point one is led into the brand new territory of radical institutional reform proposals. Still,

Sismondi was too much of a liberal to propose heavy-handed government decrees in furthering his agenda. Instead, he suggests that government action, when necessary, be indirect through the establishment of incentives and disincentives that encourage behavior congruent with the social interest.

Reforming the system

Scattered throughout *New Principles* are policy proposals including such measures as prohibition of Sunday work, limitations on child labor and regulation of hours of labor, all of which earned him the reputation of being one of the first to propose factory legislation in France. Included among his policy recommendations are suggestions for circumscribing or eliminating patent rights to slow down technological change.[67] In his subsequent works, Sismondi offers additional proposals such as the need for government to collect labor statistics and to act as employer of last resort by means of offering public works programs that would also provide new skills to the unemployed.

But keep in mind that for Sismondi the key to solving social problems is the realization that they are caused by the new system of production for profit with a work force that no longer has access to capital. Therefore it is the challenging task of the legislator "to bring together anew the interests of those who cooperate in the same production instead of setting them in opposition." It is this question that is addressed in the last two chapters of the book, "How Government Must Defend the Population against the Effects of Competition" and "The Worker Has the Right to Receive Job Security from His Employer." The problem in terms of the first is the self-destruction aspect of competition. It happens when conditions make for self-exploitation. Government is to protect against self-destructive, sacrificial behavior that by itself might appear to make sense to the individual, such as "to prevent that a man, after having worked ten hours daily would agree to work twelve, fourteen, sixteen, and eighteen hours, [and] that in always outbidding his neighbor, he lowers himself to the most frightful misery." In agriculture, these considerations lead to two basic conclusions. First, it means protecting the day-laborers living under the risk of being dismissed at a day's notice by allowing those who work the land a share in the property (for example, sharecropping). Second, the adoption of measures that would encourage the division of large estates and thereby allow for more family farming.[68]

Another example of the citizen having to be guarded against the effects of competition relates to the idea of wanting to raise a family without adequate means. In particular, the poor "are the people who marry soonest, produce most children, and consequently lose most; but they do not lose their children, till after being themselves exposed to a competition which deprives them successfully of all the sweets of life." The remedy lies in legislating a minimum wage that allows the employee to maintain a family as well as providing laborers with the additional security of sharing in the property of their work place. The legislator ought to encourage a situation where the worker "after a probationary period would come to possess a right of ownership in the business to which he gives his sweat." What Sismondi had in mind was a 50/50 profit sharing between capital and labor, convinced that by such arrangement workers with aspirations would tend to postpone marriage till they were made partners.[69]

Going beyond these indictments against competition, Sismondi wanted to find a general rule that would protect the entire working population "against the competitive folly to which the actual organization of society exposes them." What he came up with was a formidable new principle of institutional reorganization that would, through economic and political incentives, work toward a reunification of capital and labor. Furthermore, it would also provide an effective antidote to the various diseases that had been inflicted on the social body by the competitive wage system. This new idea is proposed in the final chapter of his book, which may be seen as a high point of his contribution to social economics. He starts out by reminding the reader that the activity of production is a natural partnership of contributors cooperating in a spirit of solidarity and commonality. All through the ages, even in slavery, it was a recognized obligation of the masters to take care of their subjects when afflicted with misfortune, old age or sickness. It was only during Sismondi's time that the employers abandoned "'sacred obligation' and [threw] it on the backs of compatriots." Under the prevailing system, when a large landowner hires farm hands:

> he seeks to reduce their wages to the lowest possible rate, to receive for that wage the most work possible. If such labor exhausts them and they fall sick, the parish will provide for them; if the fields do not give suitable work to the women, children, and old people, the parish will care for them. By means of competition, the large farmer obtains the greatest possible amount of labor from the strongest men, in the best season, and for the least price, while he shares with the small farmer, and the freeholders, the obligation to provide income to the families of the workers, for all the labor he does not put to work.[70]

In other words, the small farmers subsidize, under the name of poor rates, the subsistence wages of those workers who cultivate the fields of the rich. Not surprisingly, Sismondi bolts at such an unjust policy and offers this perverse policy as a reason why the small farmer cannot compete and why large farms have been taking over.

The same problem occurs in industry. Workers no longer needed (because they are sick, old or otherwise redundant) are laid off, "so that public welfare, the hospitals, in England the parish, attend to their wretched existence."[71]

47

According to Sismondi, the manufacturer has every interest to get the profits denied him by consumers from his diligent workers instead. Beyond that, the manufacturer fights to reduce his wage bills further by shifting his costs, letting society make up for the niggardly pay. Again, the small independent businessman and the artisan end up subsidizing their large-scale competitors, a practice that sooner or later will seal their fate.

To get to the root of this type of competitive cost-shifting, Sismondi offers his ingenious new idea: make the employer, whether agriculturist or capitalist, legally responsible to maintain the laborer during a period of dead season, illness or old age. It's like a social insurance scheme where the employer pays all the premiums in proportion to the costs that the conduct of his own business inflicts on society. The state, family farmers and small businesses are no longer called upon to underwrite private costs disguised as public charity. Large-scale landlords, knowing that they are ultimately responsible to pay for the sick and the old, will soon learn that the cheapest way consists in giving their workforce "the most enduring interest in life, that will tie them in the best way to their own tillage, that will sustain their spirits, their health, their physical strength the most, and therefore comes closest to ownership."[72]

Similarly with the large-scale manufacturer who believes that he can profit either by selling at a high price, or by paying a lower wage: under this new proposal "he would learn that he can make no profit except by selling; and that all he takes away from the worker, will no longer be provided by society, but by himself as support for the worker." Similarly, the large capitalist would no longer have an interest in beating down wages and would think twice about introducing new machinery. Instead, he would have every incentive to "bind his worker ever closer to himself, to hire them for longer periods and to have them share in his profits." In Sismondi's words:

> Today the manufacturer, after having hired many families, leaves them all of a sudden without work, because he has discovered that a steam engine can do all their work; then he would discover that the steam engine would not produce any savings, if all people who worked find no other means of working again, and he were bound to support them at the hospital while he stoked his boilers. This cost, which would fall on his shoulders alone, would be in strictest justice; because he makes a profit today from the life of these hands, and all the injuries this causes he puts back on the shoulders of society. If the wages he pays are adequate, if they provide not only for the productive age of his workers, but for their childhood, their old age, their sickness; if the work he tells them to do is not unhealthy, if the machines he invents provide only, as he asserts, an occasion to produce a larger output, then the responsibility that will be placed on his shoulders alone will not be a cost at all; he

will have no occasion to complain. If it is onerous then his industry is a declining industry; it would be better that he gave it up, rather than make society support its losses.[73]

Through this pioneering scheme, which based economic policy on incentive, ideally manufacturers would rack their brains for ideas and measures to lift their workers to their level, to interest them in ownership and economy, and "to make them finally men and citizens, whereas today [the manufacturers] labor incessantly to turn them into machines."[74]

Sismondi, with his usual honesty and integrity, wastes no time in pointing out that there are likely to be formidable obstacles to implementation. For one, it would necessitate identifying and keeping occupational records for all unemployed, injured, sick or old workers. Then one would have to expect political obstacles from the ruling elite, the rich landowners and large capitalists, "with whom such proposal will likely arouse indignation," not being in the position to benefit by the implementation of this kind of legislation.[75] Still, the idea is in theory simple and it is fair; it is non-coercive, democratic, couched in terms of the common good, and fully integrated with the theoretical body and distinctive themes of his *New Principles*. Quite conceivably, there was another reason for the lack of response: it was simply too much ahead of its time.

In conclusion, Sismondi's proposals were original, far-reaching and sound; probably he had quite a lot more to say than any other economist in the first four decades of the nineteenth century. As already noted, in France his work more than that of any other economist inspired the early development of social legislation. It seems curious that countless historians of economics have been especially critical about this dimension of Sismondi's work. His entreaties to the legislators are frequently described as "extraordinarily timid," "full of self-doubt," "helpless," "bewildered," "impotent," "incompetent," and paralyzed by the contradiction of what appealed to his passions and what to his reason.[76] To back up these unflattering ascriptions, his detractors typically cite the following passage in which Sismondi confesses:

> After having shown what, in my opinion, the principle is, where justice lies, I confess that I feel powerless to sketch the means of its implementation. The distribution of the fruits of labor, between those who cooperate to produce them, appears to me viscous; but it seems to me to be almost beyond human capability to imagine an arrangement of ownership entirely different from the one we know from experience.[77]

But that declaration needs to be read in the context in which it was written; to distance himself from the highly specific social architecture of the Utopian socialists. Compare this paragraph with the following passage, written on a different occasion:

> We do not have confidence enough in ourselves to show [the econo-mists] what would be the truth; it is one of the greatest efforts to which we can force our minds to visualize the actual structure of society. Who would then be the man enlightened enough to imagine a structure that does not yet exist, to see the future when we have already so much trouble to see the present? Still, if all the enlightened minds finally agree to seek the security society owes to the classes charged with feeding it, perhaps what a single mind cannot accomplish, the joining of the knowledge of all will be able to accomplish.[78]

It appears to be more of a statement indicating modesty and wisdom, attributes not always found among economists, even today. Beyond that, it is a plea for others to develop this new policy, stated as a new *principle*, by exploring how it could be *applied* and implemented in an existing socio-economic and political context. Genuinely, new ideas of an almost visionary quality rarely come "out of box" complete with detailed, operational direc-tives. Usually it takes quite some time to work out the flaws. Much of the humanistic tradition in social economics can be seen as trying to accomplish this undertaking.

Conclusion

After devoting himself to history for another two decades, Sismondi, suffering from stomach cancer, passed away on 25 June 1842. He did not die a happy man. In spite of his writings the gospel of greed and opulence prevailed, and industrialization and immiseration of the working class continued unabated. One of his last diary entries conveys the immense suffering that this painful realization provoked:

> I cry, take care, you are bruising, you are crushing miserable persons who do not even see from whence comes the evil which they experi-ence, but who remain languishing and mutilated on the road which you have passed over. I cry out, and no one hears me: I cry out and the car of the Juggernaut continues to roll on, making new victims.[79]

Already in 1836, voicing disappointment that no one in France or England had shown much interest in his work, he comforted himself with the realiza-tion that economics is a subject "on which each one has his opinion settled, and finds it more easy to let his adversary's book fall unnoticed than to answer it." Many others following in his footsteps must at times have had

50

similar thoughts. They, too, have had to learn that writing makes little impression when it attacks a dominant system, but may take comfort in Sismondi's teaching that "facts are more obstinate and more rebellious," that "they do not manifest themselves less from its being supposed that they can be refuted without being heard" and that "they often increase from having been neglected, and that they fall with their whole weight on the most skillfully constructed theory, crushing and overthrowing it at the very moment when its author was congratulating himself on having victoriously refuted all his adversaries."[80]

Today, Sismondi is more recognized as being a great economist. A recent and authoritative text features his *New Principles* as one of the nine most important economics publications in the first half of the nineteenth century.[81] He was the first to attack the orthodox doctrine of harmony of interests, to show the limitations of *laissez-faire* and individual self-interest parading as the common good. He was the first to practice social economics, the first to show that economics could be done differently, and that people are more important than things. And even though he had no direct disciples, his humanitarian work inspired many more to confront orthodoxy in a similarly wholehearted way. This work and particularly the following chapters honor him by introducing the reader to a representative sample of the work done by social economists in the same spirit.

Notes

1 G. Sotiroff, *Ricardo und Sismondi: Eine aktuelle Auseinandersetzung über Nachkriegs-wirtschaft vor 120 Jahren*, Zurich and New York, Europa, 1945.
2 For a good discussion of economists' attitude toward Poor Law reform, see R. K. Kanth, *Political Economy and Laissez-Faire: Economics and Ideology in the Ricardian Era*, Totowa, NJ, Rowman and Littlefield, 1986, ch. 3.
3 From: A. Stevens, *Madame de Staël, a Study of Her Life and Times: The First Revolution and the First Empire*, vol. II, London, John Murray, 1880, p. 19.
4 J. Schumpeter, *History of Economic Analysis*, New York, Oxford University Press, 1954, p. 493.
5 J. C. L. Simonde de Sismondi, *De la Richesse Commerciale*, Geneva, J. J. Paschoud, 1803, p. 96. As Thomas Sowell (*Say's Law: An Historical Analysis*, Princeton, NJ, Princeton University Press, 1972) adds, the "useless" production was, as Sismondi's subsequent footnote (pp. 111–112) suggests, to be understood as unwanted additions to inventories which in turn would trigger price reductions and curtailment of the production process.
6 Sismondi's algebra using his own symbols is as follows:

Let production $= P$; $N =$ necessary wages of previous period; $X =$ growth of necessary wages between this year and last; $D = dépense$ (capitalists' consumption); and $C =$ net imports. Now, since macro equilibrium requires total production to be equal to total consumption, we have the following equation:

$$(1) \qquad\qquad P = D + N + X.$$

By subtracting N from both sides, we obtain:

(1b) $$P - N = D + X$$

where $P - N$ is what constitutes national revenue which in Sismondian manner we might designate by R:

(2) $$R = D + X.$$

By introducing foreign trade in the form of Sismondi's net imports C, we get the more general equilibrium condition:

(2b) $$R + C = D + X$$

which demonstrates that as long as C is more than offset by X there will be growth even in an economy where capitalists indulge in buying foreign luxury goods.

7 Sismondi, *De la Richesse Commerciale*, p. 109.
8 A. Amonn, *Simonde de Sismondi als Nationaloekonom: Darstellung seiner Lehren mit einer Einführung und Erläuterungen*, Bern, Francke, 1945–1949, vol. I, pp. 50–52.
9 M. Blaug, *Great Economists Before Keynes*, Atlantic Highlands, NJ, Humanities Press International, Inc., 1986, p. 228.
10 J. C. L. Simonde de Sismondi, *New Principles of Political Economy* [1827], trans. R. Hyse, New Brunswick, NJ, and London, Transaction Publishers, 1991, p. 1.
11 ibid., p. 2.
12 J. C. L. Simonde de Sismondi, *Political Economy* [1815], New York, Augustus M. Kelley, 1966a.
13 J. C. L. Simonde de Sismondi, *Political Economy and the Philosophy of Government* [1847], New York, Augustus M. Kelley, 1966b, p. 458.
14 Sismondi, *New Principles of Political Economy*.
15 ibid., p. 104.
16 ibid., pp. 104, 105.
17 Sismondi, *Political Economy and the Philosophy of Government*, p. 212.
18 Sismondi, *New Principles of Political Economy*, p. 75.
19 ibid., p. 496.
20 Sowell, *Say's Law*, p. 56.
21 ibid., p. 60.
22 Quoted in M. F. Bleany, *Underconsumption Theories: A History and Critical Analysis*, New York, International Publishers, 1976, p. 38.
23 The reader may want to form his/her own opinion by consulting the appended chapters of the second 1827 edition of the *New Principles of Political Economy* (Sismondi, pp. 593–648).
24 For a summary account of Say's recantation, see T. Sowell, *Classical Economics Reconsidered*, Princeton, NJ, Princeton University Press, 1974, pp. 47–48.
25 Malthus published his own (similar) views early in 1820, after he had been made familiar with Sismondi's new thinking.
26 The essentials of the theory are described in Sismondi, *New Principles of Political Economy*, pp. 273–280.
27 ibid., p. 274.
28 Sismondi seems to neglect here the possibility that the highly paid craftsmen catering to the rich may very well fill in some of the demand for these manufactured goods.
29 Sismondi, *New Principles of Political Economy*, pp. 276, 277.
30 ibid., pp. 303–304.
31 ibid., p. 285.
32 ibid., p. 164.

33 The full title of the pamphlet is rather long: *Observations on the Circumstances which Influence the Conditions of the Labouring Classes of Society*. Among other places it has been reprinted by G. Sotiroff as part of J. Barton's *Economic Writings*, Regina, Sask., Lynn Publishing Co., 1962, p. 15.

34 ibid., p. 16.

35 P. Sraffa (ed.), *The Works and Correspondence of David Ricardo*, Cambridge, Cambridge University Press, 1951, p. 392.

36 J. C. L. Simonde de Sismondi, "Review of John Barton's Observations and Inquiry," *Annales de Législation et d'Economie Politique*, November 1822, pp. 82–119.

37 ibid., p. 96.

38 Sismondi, *New Principles of Political Economy*, pp. 558–559.

39 ibid., p. 266.

40 ibid., p. 299.

41 ibid., pp. 559–560.

42 ibid., p. 256.

43 ibid.

44 ibid., pp. 620–621.

45 ibid.

46 ibid., pp. 621, 625.

47 ibid., p. 624. Sismondi then works his example in a different way, assuming that after the new innovation all 10 workers remain employed, allowing the annual output to increase to 180 bags. This scenario now works via competitively depressed wages to underconsumption, crisis, and eventually to a new equilibrium with a greatly enhanced population. He concludes the example by generalizing it to a situation where labor productivity increases by 33 percent everywhere, finding that "every invention decreases the demand for already existing factories, and creates one, as an offset, that is directed to factories that do not yet exist" (ibid., pp. 625–627).

48 ibid., p. 13.

49 ibid., p. 613.

50 Sismondi, *De la Richesse Commerciale*, vol. I, p. xv.

51 Sismondi, *New Principles of Political Economy*, pp. 54, 55.

52 ibid., pp. 487, 232, 459, 232.

53 ibid., pp. 204–205.

54 Sismondi, *Political Economy and the Philosophy of Government*, p. 127.

55 ibid., p. 127.

56 ibid.

57 Sismondi, *New Principles of Political Economy*, pp. 27, 53; *Political Economy and the Philosophy of Government*, pp. 243–244.

58 Sismondi, *New Principles of Political Economy*, p. 162; *Political Economy and the Philosophy of Government*, pp. 161, 162, 163.

59 Sismondi, *New Principles of Political Economy*, pp. 556, 555.

60 Sismondi, *Political Economy and the Philosophy of Government*, p. 212; ibid., p. 521.

61 Sismondi, *New Principles of Political Economy*, p. 289; *Political Economy and the Philosophy of Government*, p. 166.

62 Sismondi, *New Principles of Political Economy*, p. 132; *Political Economy and the Philosophy of Government*, p. 222.

63 Sismondi, *New Principles of Political Economy*, pp. 139, 181.

64 ibid., p. 628, emphasis added.

65 ibid., pp. 628, 629.

66 ibid., pp. 342, 647.

67 ibid., p. 265.
68 ibid., pp. 635, 570.
69 ibid., pp. 572, 573.
70 ibid., pp. 572, 580.
71 ibid., p. 583.
72 ibid., pp. 579–580.
73 ibid., pp. 583, 585, 584.
74 ibid., p. 585.
75 ibid., p. 581.
76 The latter-type contention seems to be implying that his heart must have been driving him to embrace socialism, while his intelligence admonished him to hang on to capitalism; hence the contradiction and indecision.
77 Sismondi, *New Principles of Political Economy*, p. 584.
78 ibid., p. 634.
79 Sismondi, *Political Economy and the Philosophy of Government*, p. 455.
80 ibid., pp. 454, 150.
81 H. Landreth and D. C. Colander, *History of Economic Thought*, 3rd edn, Boston, MA, Houghton Mifflin Co., 1994. Similarly, Sismondi made the list of the 100 greatest economists before John M. Keynes (see Blaug, *Great Economists before Keynes*).

3

THE GERMINATION OF SOCIAL
ECONOMICS ON BRITISH SOIL

Tracking the humanistic spirit of Sismondi in Great Britain might appear daunting in light of Thomas Sowell's opinion. Sowell – one of the most knowledgeable contemporary defenders of Sismondi's challenge to Say's Law – claimed that "he [Sismondi] left no disciples and his eclecticism provided no dogma around which a school could crystallize."[1] Certainly such a bleak assessment is not without truth, but it overlooks too much. Charles Rist's classic assessment of Sismondi is probably closer to the mark when he points out that his sympathy for the working classes, his critique of an industrial regime driven by competition, his refusal to recognize personal interest as the only economic motive and his plea for corrective state intervention was to give rise to several powerful currents of thought.[2] That Sismondi had considerable influence both in France and Germany, even in Russian intellectual history, nobody will dispute.

The French economist Eugene Buret early declared himself a wholehearted disciple of Sismondi. His work echoes all the great themes of his master: blaming classical economists for making far too many abstractions divorced of social content; for their preoccupation with wealth rather than welfare and the study of poverty; for a blind faith in free competition; and an unwarranted (macroeconomic) faith "that an active and assured consumption should always follow production."[3] Unfortunately, Buret died prematurely at the age of thirty-two, having just completed his only work, *De la Misère des Classes Laborieuses.*[4]

Sismondi's lasting imprints

In his book on the *History of Political Economy* (1837/1842), Jerome A. Blanqui, a noted French economist and a contemporary of Buret, praised Sismondi's *Nouveaux Principes* as "the best critical work in existence in political economy" and credited him with having been a founder of the "new economic school." Blanqui also called it the "social school,"[5] an English translation for the French *économie sociale*. A number of economists, besides Buret, made up this school: Charles de Coux, Joseph Droz, M. Dunoyer, Frederic LePlay and

55

Alban Villeneuve-Bargemont. Typically, they sold their books under the new label of *social* economy, rather than political economy.[6] Although they all generally approached economics in a fashion akin to Sismondi: that is, motivated by a deep concern with poverty, distribution, human dignity, social welfare and a lack of belief in Say's Law, there was some disagreement among them about such matters as property, tariffs and population theory. They also showed a tendency to shift emphasis for social improvement from government to family, and to stress moral education and individual responsibility. Most promoted the idea of special banks to encourage more thrift among the working class, as well as corporations of workmen which would favor the spirit of association and mutual help. Perhaps their chief distinguishing characteristic was to be found in a shared purpose: "to unite closely, by an indissoluble link the science of material wealth with the science of moral wealth; in a word, to take as a foundation the great civilizing power of Christianity."[7] In short, they sought to unite science and the Catholic faith, something Sismondi had very much opposed. This branch of economic thought had an enormous importance within the Catholic social economics movement. It not only formed the historical root of Pope Leo XIII's famous encyclical *Rerum Novarum*, issued in 1891, aiming to solve the conflict between labor and capital on Christian principles, but also continued to develop and inspire other Papal Encyclicals to this day. Above all, more than half a century ago it was instrumental in forming the Association of Catholic Economics, later renamed the Association for Social Economics.

Besides France, Sismondi also had a rather profound influence in Germany, serving as one of the earliest precursors of both the Historical School and Marxist economic thought. In fact, the influence on Marx is likely to have been enormous. Marx must have studied Sismondi in his early years in Paris, evidenced by praise for his work as having

> dissected with great acuteness the contradictions in the conditions of modern production. It laid bare the hypocritical apologies of economists. It proved, incontrovertibly, the disastrous effects of machinery and division of labour; the concentration of capital and land in a few hands; over-production and crises; it pointed out the inevitable ruin of the petty bourgeois and peasant, the misery of the proletariat, the anarchy in production, the crying inequalities in the distribution of wealth, the industrial war of extermination between nations, the dissolution of old moral bonds, of the old family relations, of the old nationalities.[8]

Marx not only learned much of his general economics from Sismondi, but it is also said that even the very heart of Marxian economics, the concept of surplus value, was inspired by him. Sismondi, employing the French term *mieux valeur*, used it to explain the difference between what the worker gets and what the employer gets out of the worker:

> the capital which pays the wages of labor and makes work possible, never remains in the hands of those who work. It is a consequence of a more or less unequal division between the capitalist and the worker, a division in which the capitalist is determined not to leave the worker more than what is just necessary to maintain life, and keeps for himself all that the worker has produced over and above the value of that life.[9]

The fact that Marx often cites Sismondi in *Das Kapital*, but omits to discuss Sismondi's conceptual ideas in his *Theories of Surplus Values*, can be seen to support the presumption that Marx did not want to expose what may have been the main source of his own critique.[10]

Sismondi's macroeconomic doctrines also left an imprint on Robertus and Rosa Luxemburg and were at the center of the Russian debate between Lenin and the Russian Narodniks in the 1890s. All in all, it's a legacy that commands some admiration and respect.

The British scene

Turning from the Continent to Great Britain, the home ground of the developing science of orthodox classical economics, Sismondi's influence at first appears close to nil. His *New Principles* was not translated into English, and he was much better known as a historian than an economist. In part this may be explained by the cool reception awaiting any doctrine that challenged Say's Law, something that had also haunted Malthus' thoughts on the subject. Moreover, Sismondi's attempt at reorienting political economy from a science of wealth to an art of socioeconomic welfare met with strong opposition. In 1836, Nassau Senior, a leading political economist, made it very clear that a real economist must abstain from wanting to gain "a knowledge of all the facts which affect the social condition of every community whose conduct the Economist proposes to influence," because they are bound to exceed the powers of a single mind.[11] To him, it was imperative to overcome the temptations of wandering "into the more interesting and more important, but far less definite fields by which the comparatively narrow path of political economy is surrounded." And he added, "the business of a political economist is neither to recommend nor to dissuade, but to state general principles which it is fatal to neglect."[12] In short, economics, as a *science*, dealt with wealth only, while the discussion of happiness, virtue and institutional reform was to be kept *outside* the discipline and left to the statesmen. Part of the reason for this scientism was that the followers of Ricardo saw their new industrial order as a product of nature, a datum that needed to be understood in the light of natural science. Thus, wanting to reform the status quo was like trying to condemn and banish the force of gravity.

Socially, the British intellectual scene after David Ricardo's death was characterized by the meteoric rise of the Philosophical Radicals clustered around the social doctrines of Jeremy Bentham, a confirmed Voltairian. Forming their own political party in 1824, the Philosophical Radicals published the *Westminster Review* to propagate their views, and followers of the school soon established and occupied university chairs in leading institutions, including Oxford where Nassau Senior taught political economy. The Benthamites professed to be against the aristocracy, the Church and metaphysics, and were anti-communitarian, highly individualistic, materialistic, scientistic and rationalistic. They fought for individual liberty, political equality and parliamentary reform, including universal suffrage. All existing social institutions were to be questioned and scrutinized according to whether or not they produced the "greatest good for the greatest number." In matters of psychology, Bentham's new school promulgated a scientific approach that sought to reduce all motives to a calculus of pleasure and pain, thereby leaving no specific room for emotions, conscience or morality.

The Benthamite program initially resonated with the working class who, in those years of high food prices and taxes, increasingly resented the privileged aristocracy and readily blamed them and their Corn Laws for their misery. With the ascent of the Philosophical Radicals came a triumph of political economy under the leadership of James Mill (an early articulator of Say's Law), J. R. McCulloch (with whom Sismondi had crossed swords in the early 1820s) and Nassau Senior. Under their reign, political economy further developed along Ricardian lines: a highly abstract discipline arguing deductively from first principles by assuming free competition between selfish individuals in the quest for wealth and fortune with little regard for the social consequences of their behavior. Politically, they were free traders agitating for the repeal of the Corn Laws and ardent defenders of *laissez-faire*, a predisposition that led them to actively oppose poor relief, factory legislation to limit hours of work and child labor, and the toleration of trade unions.

The opposition to combinations of labor was defended, once again, on supposedly scientific grounds rooted in the abstract economics upholding the doctrine of the *wages fund*. Rudimentary traces of that theory were first contained in the writings of Smith and Malthus, but it was only explicitly formulated by McCulloch in 1828 and carried into politics by Senior in his *Lectures on the Rates of Wages* (1830). In McCulloch's words:

> It is on the amount of capital, applicable to the payment of wages in its possession, that the power of a country to support and employ labourers must depend. . . . It is a necessary consequence of this principle, that the amount of subsistence falling to each labourer, or the rate of wages, must depend on the proportion which the

whole capital bears to the whole labouring population . . . and it is
further evident, that this rate of wages could not be increased unless
the amount of capital were increased in a greater proportion than the
number of labourers, or the number of labourers diminished more
than the quantity of Capital.[13]

In other words, according to Wages Fund doctrine, workers' pay is advanced
out of a capital fund having a certain fixed size. The more workers seeking
employment, the less everybody can be paid; with the implication that any
attempt through unionization or otherwise to raise wages of a particular
group of workers simply reduces wages elsewhere, or comes at the expense
of investment and growth. This is one of the basic principles of political economy that, according to Senior, it would be *fatal* to neglect: allowing workers
to raise wages through granting the right to strike hurts rich and poor alike
by reducing profits and future accumulation. In short, from a social point of
view, unionism is a negative sum proposition. The Wages Fund doctrine
rapidly gained popularity both in academic circles and among the public
where it was readily used as a potent weapon in the struggle against the
workers' movement. Only in the 1860s was it to be questioned from several
sides and unmasked as wrong and discarded.

As a result of classical political economy's new authority concerning the
conduct of social affairs in the 1830s and 1840s, it also came more and more
to be identified as the voice of the propertied industrial class to the detriment
of the poor. Increasingly alienated from the Benthamites, the working class,
therefore, formed their own political associations. At the same time, the
Conservatives, representing the landed interests, began to attack the inhumane
conditions prevailing in the factories and the ever-growing commercialization
of society. During the 1830s and 1840s, in an unusual new alliance with the
working classes, the Conservatives legislated such reform measures as the prohibition of child labor and the introduction of a 10-hour day, over the opposition
of the Liberal party and some of the most noted economists. This disillusionment
with radical individualism and *laissez-faire* led to a new humanistic spirit in
Victorian England, and also prepared the soil for the eventual birth of a British
social economics tradition.

From Sismondi to Carlyle

The cold shoulder given to Sismondi by his British contemporaries would
have under normal circumstances been enough to effectively insulate the
developing science of wealth from his unwelcome ideas, but thanks to some
peculiar historical circumstances and the more favorable intellectual climate
of the mid-nineteenth century, the French tradition of a more humanistic
economics was able to take root, albeit in a roundabout fashion. It initially
sprouted on Scottish soil in Edinburgh and wound through social philosophy

and sociology. Born there of Calvinist parents, by the age of twenty-three Thomas Carlyle was an impecunious young man who had struggled to prepare for the ministry at the local university, only to change his mind in the midst of his studies. Having tested the waters of school teaching, and then having spent a semester studying law under David Hume, a nephew of the famous skeptic philosopher, he decided to devote himself to literature. In order to make ends meet, in 1818 he accepted employment working for the *Edinburgh Encyclopedia* under the editorship of Dr. Brewster. One of his assignments was to translate Sismondi's submitted 200-page contribution on political economy.[14] It was this acquisition of economic knowledge, in combination with a continuing struggle for existence, that made him sympathetic to the miserable lot of the laboring classes. The 1819 bloody Peterloo Massacre and an on-going militant suppression of worker discontent and desperation led Carlyle to seriously question his faith in a just universe and a Christian God. His spiritual crisis was alleviated by the Transcendental philosophy he found in the German literature of Schiller, Goethe, Kant and Fichte. Carlyle eventually rejected the prevailing intellectual materialism and entrusted himself to the ultimate reality of a benevolent and just Universal Spirit who rules humanity through the heart and the dictates of the conscience.

He published his first attack on materialism and the heartless new science of political economy in "The Signs of the Times," in the *Edinburgh Review* (1829). In this essay he condemned *laissez-faire*, industrialism and the poverty of the masses in no uncertain terms and urged readers to redeem themselves in seeking a more just and humane path in matters of political economy. The essay was soon reprinted in French and aroused the interest of the followers of the Utopian social reformer Saint-Simon, an eclectic group that at this time included the great sociologist and philosopher Auguste Comte.

At this juncture Carlyle's imprint on humanizing economics can be traced along two very different trails. On the one hand, he soon started a prolonged friendship with his contemporary, John Stuart Mill, who had just become acquainted with the doctrines of Comte. On the other hand, and more significantly, Carlyle's subsequent writings, particularly *Past and Present* (1843), attracted the maverick philosopher of art, John Ruskin, who cast his idealistic social ideas into a new moral political economy.

Carlyle and John Stuart Mill

The rather dramatic intellectual life of John Stuart Mill is a story in itself, perhaps best told in Mill's autobiography, but several of its salient features should be alluded to here. Under the strict regime of his father, James Mill, John was raised on the educational philosophy of his father's close friend and mentor Jeremy Bentham. It was an education that stressed the importance of logical thinking over the cultivation of feelings. Poor John learned a lot, just about everything there was to know, but the one thing he did not learn was how to be happy. At the age of twenty, he fell into a deep depression that lasted a couple of years and from which he was only able to escape by reading the work of the Romantic poet Wordsworth. Mill credited the healing power of poetry with enabling him to feel empathy for others and to be more at peace with the world. He became interested in the philosophy of history as propounded by Samuel Coleridge as well as Comte, entertaining the possibility that social philosophy evolves through stages, and that there may very well be something beyond the radical Benthamism of his father.

In the summer of 1830, he visited Paris and was persuaded by two leaders of the St. Simonian school, with whom Comte was associated, to read Sismondi, whose new way of economic thinking, it is said, did much to convince Mill of the inequities of the factory system.[15] He began to realize the "very limited and temporary value of the old political economy, which assumes private property and inheritance as indefeasible facts, and freedom of production and exchange as the 'dernier mot' of social improvement."[16] It was at this time that Mill wrote *The Spirit of the Age* (1831), an essay expressing his faith in the reconstruction of social order on the basis of intrinsic merit. Carlyle, having read the piece, immediately suspected a kindred soul and left for London to meet Mill, kindling a friendship that lasted two decades. In spite of their mutual differences, both agreed that political reform held little promise without addressing the underlying economic ills. As one scholar put it: "They [both] knew that the system of irresponsible private property and free competition, which enslaved the many and materialized the few, was impoverishing the nation physically, morally and intellectually, and sowing the seeds of class war."[17]

In his famous *Principles of Political Economy with Some of Their Applications to Social Philosophy* (1848), Mill's new attitude, as suggested by the second half of the title, was now manifest. Although the first part of the treatise is essentially a more readable restatement of classical economics in the Smith–Ricardo tradition with all its assumptions of a class-divided society, self-interested economic agents and unlimited competition, the second part of the book discusses distribution and contains the revolutionary statement:

> [The Distribution of Wealth] . . . is a matter of human institution solely. The things once there, mankind, individually or collectively, can do with them as they like. They can place them at the disposal of whomsoever they please, and on whatever terms. Further, in the social state, in every state except total solitude, any disposal whatever of them can only take place by the consent of society, or rather of those who dispose of its active force. Even what a person has produced by his individual toil, unaided by any one, he cannot keep, unless by the permission of society. Not only can society take it from him, but individuals could and would take it from him, if society only

remained passive; if it did not either interfere *en masse*, or employ and pay people for the purpose of preventing him from being disturbed in the possession. The distribution of wealth, therefore, depends on the laws and customs of society. The rules by which it is determined are what the opinions and feelings of the ruling portion of the community make them, and are very different in different ages and countries; and might be still more different, if mankind so chose.

Society can subject the distribution of wealth to whatever rules it thinks best; but what practical results will flow from the operation of those rules, must be discovered, like any other physical or mental truths, by observation and reasoning.[18]

The treatise was an inquiry into the justice and utility of the existing system of distribution. Like Sismondi, he accepted private property but had harsh words for the dehumanizing effects of a system leaving distribution to ruthless competition. To Mill, "the best state for human nature is that in which, while no one is poor, no one desires to be richer, nor has any reason to fear being thrust back by the efforts of others to push themselves forward." Similarly, he was one of the first orthodox economists to question *laissez-faire*, a policy that he felt might have outlived its usefulness and would soon expire. "Peace be with its ashes when it does expire, for I doubt much if it will reach the resurrection."[19] In a chapter titled "On the Probable Futurity of the Labouring Classes," he outlined his vision of a cooperative society in which workers would render capitalist employers obsolete by the setting-up of self-governing cooperative enterprises.

Mill also removed one of the biggest obstacles hindering the labor movement. In 1869 he emasculated the Wages Fund doctrine in agreeing with a lesser-known economist, whose book he reviewed, that "there is no law of nature making it inherently impossible for wages to rise to the point of absorbing not only the funds which he had intended to devote to carrying on his business, but the whole of what he allows for his private expenses, beyond the necessaries of life." He concluded that this doctrine, lacking any scientific foundation, "must be thrown aside."[20]

All in all, Sismondi would have no doubt cheered the humanistic turn in the vision of Great Britain's leading mid-nineteenth-century economist, but just how much he helped through Carlyle in bringing about such a breakthrough is a matter of conjecture.[21] It should also be added that Mill, particularly in his early writings, strongly opposed any ideas about underconsumption or overproduction. Partly due to his own earlier work, Say's Law as articulated by his father and Ricardo had by now solidified into an unquestionable, almost dogmatic creed and was to remain that way for another century.

Carlyle and John Ruskin

Carlyle's more direct influence was, as previously noted, on another literary giant of the nineteenth century: John Ruskin. In the late 1840s, Ruskin, a famous art critic, wondered why medieval Venice had produced masterpieces of architectural beauty in contrast to the drab structures of his contemporary England. The answer, he believed, was that Venice had been constructed by professional guilds of workmen who took pride in what they did, rather than by construction companies working for profit, employing hirelings with little interest in their work. Such was the message of Ruskin's famous *Stones of Venice*, which was published in the early 1850s. Carlyle, who in an earlier publication *Past and Present* (1843) had railed against what he called the "dismal science" of political economy as a gospel of despair and had heaped praise on the feudal past when commerce was still governed by a hefty dose of chivalry, immediately recognized in Ruskin a kindred spirit. Soon, after some initial reluctance, the eloquent art critic was persuaded by his new mentor to try his critical pen on political economy and in the service of social reform. He did so in a series of articles entitled *Unto This Last*, written for the *Cornhill Magazine* in 1860, only to receive the following oratorical letter of congratulation from Carlyle:[22]

Chelsea, 29 October, 1860

Dear Ruskin,

You go down thro' those unfortunate Dismal-Science people, like a Treble-x of Senna, Glauber and Aloes; like a fit of British Cholera, — threatening to be fatal! I have read your paper with exhilaration, exultation, often with laughter, with "Bravissimo!" — Such a thing flung suddenly into half a million dull British heads on the same day, will do a great deal of good.

I marvel, in parts, at the Lynx-eyed sharpness of your logic, at the <u>*pincer-grip*</u> *(red hot pincers) you take of certain bloated cheeks and blown-up bellies: — more power to your elbow (tho' it is cruel in the extreme)! If you chose to stand to that kind of work for the next 7 years, and work out there a result like what you have done in painting: yes, there were a "something to do," — not easily measurable in importance to these sunk ages. Meantime my joy is great to find myself henceforth in a minority of* <u>*two*</u> *at any rate! —*

The Dismal-Science people will object that their Science expressly <u>*abstracts*</u> *itself from moralities, from etc etc: but what you say, and show, is incontrovertibly true, that no "Science" worthy of men (and not worthier of dogs or of devils) has a right to call itself "Political Economy," or can exist at all except mainly as a fetid nuisance and public poison, on* <u>*other*</u> *terms than those you now shadow out to it for the first time.*

On your last page, and never till then, I pause slightly, not too sorrowfully, and appeal to a time coming. Noble is the spirit then too, my friend; but alas it is not Philanthropisms that will do then, — it is Rhadamanthisms (I sorrowfully see) which are yet at a very great distance! Go on and prosper. I am yours always (sleeping a little better, and hoping an evening soon)

T. Carlyle

Ruskin's critique of political economy was not so well received in other circles. In fact, the editor of the *Cornhill Magazine* felt compelled to cut short Ruskin's series after four installments due to numerous protests among offended subscribers and readers. Clearly, Ruskin was not the first to use scornful language in labeling his target: Carlyle had for some time been using terms like "pig philosophy" and "dismal science," and others talked about "plutonomy," "foul philosophy," "pseudo-science" and so forth. However, Ruskin's vocabulary became more acrimonious: political economy further deteriorated to the "bastard science" and was described as "the most cretinous, speechless, paralyzing plague that has yet touched the brains of mankind" and much more. Yet, hidden behind such uncompromising language and occasional vitriolic outbursts, one finds a rather profound critique of the method and scope of political economy.

Economics and the soul

Ruskin's primary target was the creature invented by Nassau Senior and John Stuart Mill some twenty-five years earlier: *Homo Oekonomicus*, a new species whose activities were understood *solely* as a being who desires to possess wealth. In J. S. Mill's words, "it makes abstraction of every other human passion or motive," constituting "an arbitrary definition of man," deliberately hypothetical. To the extent that other motives (altruism, moral obligation and custom) and other "disturbing forces" are involved, the deductions based on the premises of self-interest and greed would only be true in the abstract, and would have to be modified before applying them in practice. To Mill, this modification was a matter of "adding" and "subtracting," an essentially mechanical process of working with multiple congruent causes and determining their composite force. Ruskin paraphrases this methodology before severely criticizing it:

> The social affections are accidental and disturbing elements in human nature; but avarice and desire for progress are constant elements. Let us eliminate the inconstants, and considering the human being as a covetous machine, examine by what laws of labour, purchase and sale, the greatest accumulative result in wealth is obtainable. Those laws once determined, it will be for each individual afterwards to introduce as much of the disturbing affectionate element as he chooses, and to determine for himself the results on the new conditions supposed.[23]

Ruskin opposed this approach on a fundamental principle that says much about the difference between a mechanistic, atomistic economics and an organic, communitarian approach. To him social affections and moral sentiments were qualitatively not of the same kind as the initial premise of greed and self-interest. "They alter the essence of the creature under examination the moment they are added; [and] operate, not mathematically, but chemically, introducing conditions which render all previous knowledge unavailable." Human beings, he maintained, are not rats or steam engines, but have a *soul*, and it is the force of this particular agent which "enters into all political economists' equations, without his knowledge, and falsifies every one of their results."[24] This insight is illustrated by the employment relationship in which the greatest effort and quantity of work is only achievable when the worker's will is "brought to its greatest strength by its own proper fuel: namely, by the affections." If one observes in modern industry a lack of moral animation, according to Ruskin, it must be due to the prevailing practice of engaging "a workman at a rate of wages variable according to the demand for labor, and with the risk of being at any time thrown out of his situation by chance of trade."[25] To Ruskin, it was clear that workers assured of a living wage would be more eager to exert themselves on behalf of their employer.

Armed with the realization that the effect of combining different forces will yield something more than their sum, Ruskin warned that economic laws assuming a perfectly competitive and atomistic society cannot be easily applied to a society as an organic whole. The idea that the social whole is more than the sum of its parts implies a non-mechanical, non-additive relation between original premise and the "disturbing forces," something that was bound to be ignored by the "dismal science" folks who consistently talked about society and psychology in mechanical metaphors: witness Senior's "machinery" of civilized society worked by many "antagonistic springs," Mill's appeal to centripetal and tangential forces of astronomy for learning about the conduct of man in society, and McCulloch's manner of dealing with "disturbing forces" akin to "the engineer [who] must allow for the friction and resistance of matter."

Ruskin's methodological criticism explains why social economists of the humanistic tradition have always remained skeptical about the relevance of orthodox economic analysis based on interacting Economic Men for purposes of public policy. Lacking *the* faith, they felt free to go ahead with their own theories of what makes for greater *human* welfare. This skepticism is also intrinsically related to another of Ruskin's criticisms relating to the *scope* of socioeconomic analysis: the injection of ethics into economics. As he puts it: "The idea that directions can be given for the gaining of wealth, irrespective of the considerations of its moral sources . . . is perhaps the most insolently futile of all that ever beguiled men through vices."[26] To him, the perspective of the person as a *social* being necessitates attention to morality, dictates of conscience and ethical values. For most members of the German Historical School, the latter were mere cultural or historically variable facts to be studied and grafted to economic values, but here they are seen as universal and absolute, and thereby able to direct economic analysis in a normative manner.

Life, not wealth

Besides his strong criticism of the narrow-minded scope and method of economists, Ruskin's most important contribution to social economics was his recentering of economic theory and social policies on a human standard. Instead of measuring the value of production and consumption in mercantile fashion by money, income and wealth, he proposed to assess a product in terms of how much it "avails towards life," that is, has properties that not only enable material need satisfaction but also engage intellectual, spiritual and aesthetic dimensions "animating the senses *and* the heart." In the process he expressed his famous maxim: "there is no wealth but life," the latter including "all its powers of love, joy and admiration." And he proclaimed:

> That country is the richest which nourishes the greatest number of noble and happy human beings; that man is the richest, who having perfected the functions of his own life to the utmost, has also the widest influence, both personal and by means of his possessions, over the lives of others.[27]

Ruskin used his "vital value" criterion to gauge the benefits and costs of production and consumption in order to demonstrate the discrepancies between monetary and human value. In short, he ambitiously sketched a vision of an economics of the quality of life in which work can be meaningful and creative rather than merely painful or even degrading. Unfortunately, his constructive insights of social reform were too scattered and unsystematic to impress his intellectual contemporaries. His teachings, put forth in excessively ornamental language, were perceived by the Victorian upper class as much too radical. So, for example, he held in Marxian fashion that labor was exploited by their employer whose greater bargaining power appropriated all the "surplus" as profits. Similarly, interest on capital was condemned as usury, which he defined broadly as "the taking of money for the loan or use of anything (over and above what it pays for wear and tear), such use involving no care or labour on the part of the lender; it includes all investments of capital whatsoever, returning 'dividends', as distinguished from labour wages or profits."[28] In short, the British socioeconomic system of his day was a "Devil's Economy," a "system of inequity" in which the rich trampled the poor, at the same time making the economy prone to cyclical instability. In one of his "Letters to the Workmen and Labourers of Great Britain," published in 1876, Ruskin intimated that abolishing, or at least restricting, interest and rent would redirect income from those who hoard it toward those who spend it, would tend to encourage consumption and thereby rein in periodic overproduction, or what he preferred to call "over-destruction."[29]

In one area, Ruskin was way ahead of his times. His concern with vital value and the quality of life made him an early environmentalist condemning the "diabolic work" of air and water pollution. He complained about industrialism turning every river of England into a common sewer and making "that great foul city of London . . . a ghastly heap of fermenting brickwork, pouring out poison at every pore." He warns of a time when the soil will be so poisoned as to be made uninhabitable.[30]

Ruskin: success or failure?

Radical social economy? Yes, and a vision perhaps not unappealing, but Ruskin did not make it convincingly clear or attractive. His amorphous arguments, couched in vituperative language and thrown at the "Dismal Science People," did not persuade political economists, who, not surprisingly, simply pretended he did not exist. *Unto This Last* sold fewer than 900 copies in its first ten years. However, following Ruskin's death in 1900 the papers in England and the United States were filled with eulogies. The American correspondent of *The Times* reported:

> He was, perhaps, the one writer on art who reached the mind and sympathies of the American people generally. He did not like us, but that passed as caprice unresented. He was the most stimulating personality we knew in art literature, and, *while Americans rightly neglected his teachings on political economy and other matters not within his range,* they were and are profoundly grateful to him as one who opened the eyes of multitudes who before him had not had revealed to them the true meaning of art and its true place in national and individual life.[31]

It's not a flattering verdict for Ruskin the would-be economist, yet only ten years later, *Unto This Last* had become a widely read book with sales exceeding 100,000 copies.[32] Apparently, early twentieth-century events, to be discussed in Chapter 4, contributed to Ruskin's popularity as a social critic.

Conclusion

Sismondi's French legacy of an *économie sociale* had not visibly borne much fruit among Anglo-Saxon economists, except perhaps as a softening agent on John Stuart Mill. Very likely, part of the problem was that both Carlyle and Ruskin, for all their sympathy for the poor, were not progressive thinkers. Their reaction to the social troubles of the modern economy was to look backward, seeking comfort and salvation in some version of medieval feudalism. Both were suspicious of liberty and democracy, and took a stand against universal suffrage, even showing a complacent attitude toward slavery.

Both exhibited a type of paternalism which preferred benign mastership and obedience to profit sharing and worker cooperatives. Neither did their elitism make room for the basic notion of human equality. As one scholar put it so well with respect to Ruskin: "The organic unity of society [is to him] like that of a painting of a cathedral. It depends on the 'helpful' cooperation of unequal parts in a hierarchy, not the mechanical addition of equal parts in a democracy."[33]

In spite of all these shortcomings, their voluminous and eloquent writings did at times soften the hearts of the well-to-do, a most welcome counterforce to the works of the followers of Ricardian economics in the 1830s and 1840s, which had enabled the propertied classes to feel absolved of responsibility toward the unlucky poor. In this sense, the writings of Carlyle, Mill and Ruskin, in spite of their differences, can be seen as an effective antidote to the anodyne of abstract Ricardian classical economics, which professed that poverty and misery were the result of iron natural laws and that higher wages would only act to reduce accumulation and speed up the growth of the indigent population. More importantly, Ruskin's vision directly inspired John Hobson, another great exponent of social economics in the humanistic tradition and the subject of the next chapter. Hobson concluded in his rendering of Ruskin's "Indictment of Political Economy":

> By insisting upon the reduction of all economic terms, such as value, cost, utility, etc., to terms of "vitality," by insisting upon the organic integrity and unity of all human activities, and the organic nature of the co-operation of the social units, and finally by furnishing a social ideal of reasonable humanity, Mr. Ruskin has amply justified his claim as a pioneer in the theory of Social Economics.[34]

And it was Hobson who celebrated this pioneering spirit by cleansing it of some of its excesses.

Notes

1 T. Sowell, "J. C. L. Simonde de Sismondi," in J. Eatwell *et al.* (eds), *The New Palgrave Dictionary: Social Economics*, New York, W. W. Norton, 1989, p. 18.
2 C. Gide and C. Rist, *A History of Economic Doctrines*, 2nd English edn, London, George G. Harrap and Co., 1948, p. 210.
3 Quoted in M. Tuan, *Simonde de Sismondi as an Economist*, New York, Columbia University Press, 1927, p. 163.
4 E. Buret, *De la Misère des Classes Laborieuses*, 2 vols, Paris, Paulin, 1840.
5 J. Blanqui, *History of Political Economy in Europe* [1837/1842], translated from the 4th French edn, New York, G. P. Putnam's Sons, 1880, pp. 473, 475, 479.
6 For a genealogy and sketch of their work see T. Nitsch, "Social Economics: The First 200 Years," in M. Lutz (ed.), *Social Economics: Retrospect and Prospect*, Boston, MA, Kluwer Academic Publishers, 1990, pp. 5–90.

7 Villeneuve, quoted in Tuan, *Simonde de Sismondi as an Economist*, p. 139.
8 Quoted in J. C. L. Simonde de Sismondi, *New Principles of Political Economy* [1827], trans. R. Hyse, New Brunswick, NJ, and London, Transaction Publishers, 1991, p. 92.
9 ibid.
10 This is at least how Richard Hyse sees it (ibid., p. 97, note 7). Marx, *Theories of Surplus Value* was published posthumously by Karl Kantsky in three volumes, 1905–1910.
11 N. W. Senior, *An Outline of the Science of Political Economy* [1836], New York, Augustus M. Kelley, 1965, p. 2.
12 ibid., p. 3.
13 J. McCulloch, *The Principles of Political Economy*, London, Ward Lock and Co., 1825, pp. 379–380.
14 Only recently has it been established that Sismondi had not submitted his manuscript in English and that it was Carlyle who translated it. We can read in the *Collected Letters of Thomas and Jane Welsh Carlyle*, Ch. Sanders and K. Fields (eds), Durham, NC, Duke University Press, 1970, vol. I, p. 259: "Although Carlyle appears to have kept the fact quiet in the main it can now be definitely stated that he translated the long article 'Political Economy' which Sismondi wrote for *Brewster's Edinburgh Encyclopedia*." This volume came off the press in December of 1824. The editors also speculate that "Carlyle's familiarity with Sismondi's ideas about economics at this early date is significant and undoubtedly influenced his own later thinking on the subject" (p. 260).
15 E. Neff, *Carlyle and Mill*, New York, Columbia University Press, 1926, p. 257.
16 J. S. Mill, quoted in Neff (ibid.).
17 ibid., p. 390. Nevertheless, Mill was unwilling to "charge upon competition the economical evils which at present exist," J. S. Mill, *Principles of Political Economy with Some of Their Applications to Social Philosophy*, vol. II, New York, D. Appleton and Co., 1891, p. 378.
18 Mill, *Principles of Political Economy*, pp. 258–259.
19 Quoted in J. C. Sherburne, *John Ruskin or the Ambiguities of Abundance*, Cambridge, MA, Harvard University Press, 1972, p. 117.
20 J. S. Mill, "Thornton on Labour and Its Claims," *Fortnightly Review*, May–June 1869, pp. 505–518.
21 The French historian of economic thought, Hector Denis, was one of the earliest scholars to suggest the possibility of a link between Sismondi and Mill's new treatment of the laws of distribution in his *Histoire des Systèmes Economiques et Socialistes*, Paris, V. Giard and E. Briere, 1904 edn, vol. II, p. 275.
22 G. A. Cate (ed.), *The Correspondence of Thomas Carlyle and John Ruskin*, Stanford, CA, Stanford University Press, 1982, p. 89.
23 J. Ruskin, *Unto This Last* [1861], Lincoln, NE, University of Nebraska Press, 1967.
24 ibid., pp. 12, 15.
25 ibid., pp. 15, 18.
26 ibid., p. 58.
27 ibid., p. 156.
28 J. Ruskin, *Fors Clavigera: Letters to the Workmen and Labourers of Great Britain* [1876], vol. III, Boston, MA, Colonial Press Co., 1880, p. 264.
29 See Ruskin's relevant passages cited by Sherburne, *John Ruskin or the Ambiguities of Abundance*, p. 180.
30 ibid., p. 175.

31 Quoted in J. Abse, *John Ruskin: The Passionate Moralist*, New York, Alfred A. Knopf, 1981, p. 330, emphasis added.
32 ibid., p. 178.
33 Sherburne, *John Ruskin or the Ambiguities of Abundance*, p. 217.
34 J. A. Hobson, *John Ruskin: Social Reformer*, Boston, MA, Dana Estes and Co., 1898, p. 102.

4

IN SISMONDI'S SPIRIT:
JOHN A. HOBSON

In 1859, about the time Ruskin took the plunge into economics, John Hobson was born. In his own words, he was bred "in the middle stratum of the middle class of a middle-sized industrial town of the Midlands" during the self-confident years of the "mid-Victorian era." His father, editor and co-owner of a local newspaper, and his mother, Josephine, had four children, one of whom (Ernest W. Hobson) became a famous mathematician at Cambridge University. The younger John, in contrast, decided to study classics at Oxford where he was to "imbibe" the atmosphere created by the presence of such greats as T. H. Green and John Ruskin. After graduating, Hobson returned home to help his father with the newspaper. During this period he met and married Florence Edgar, an American woman with feminist aspirations. The turning point in Hobson's life came in 1887 when he moved to London to work as a University Extension Lecturer in Literature and Economics.

In London, Hobson was brought face to face with the problems of unemployment and poverty in the midst of plenty. To a large extent the social problem that confronted him was aggravated by a stubborn economic depression that characterized most of the years between 1883 and 1894. In fact, matters were so bad that a twenty-three-member Royal Commission, which included two economists, sought explanations for its causes. Their 1886 report blamed overproduction aided by unfair tariff policies by Britain's economic rivals as the major culprit for the glutted markets at home.[1] The general concern and public discussions surrounding the slump soon led Hobson to team up with A. F. Mummery, a London businessman and famous mountain climber, to co-author *The Physiology of Industry* (1889). In his autobiography Hobson recounts that his collaborator "entangled [him] in a controversy about excessive saving which he [Mummery] regarded as responsible for the unemployment of capital and labour in periods of bad trade." Hobson continues, "for a long time I sought to counter his arguments by the use of the orthodox weapons," and concedes that the businessman finally "convinced me and I went with him to elaborate the over-saving argument."[2] The 1889 study marks the beginning of Hobson's fifty-year endeavor to approach social problems from a non-individualist perspective and rearticulate a macroeconomic approach that was very similar to Sismondi's attempt sixty years earlier.

1. *The Physiology of Industry* and Hobson's macroeconomics

The Physiology of Industry starts with a bang: the Preface targets the old creed restated by John S. Mill that saving, unlike spending, enriches the community along with the individual, raising wages, giving work to the unemployed and thereby scattering blessings on every side. In the authors' interpretation, the blessing was an "assertion that the effective love of money is the root of all economic good." In spite of the fact that the underlying Wages Fund doctrine had by then long been exploded, this creed managed to survive mainly due to "the commanding height of the great men who asserted it." Against the prevailing opinion, they sought to establish the probability that an undue exercise of the habit of saving "impoverishes the Community, throws labourers out of work, drives down wages, spreads that gloom . . . known as Depression," thereby establishing that "the effective love of money is the root of all economic evil."[3]

Two early chapters, "The Scope of Production" and "The Balance between Production and Consumption," paint a picture of products moving from raw materials, through intermediate goods, to shop goods in the retailers' hands. At each stage the productive system relies on the activities of the factors of production: land, labor and capital which are assumed to operate in a stable manner fixed by the prevailing technology. Logically, this now implies a fixed relationship between final demand and the quantity of the factors employed, a particular quantitative relation between production and consumption as well as between savings and consumption. By "savings" Mummery and Hobson mean, in good classical fashion, also "investment." In other words, they work with the assumption that all savings tend to be automatically invested, or "accumulated."

Now it is savings, elegantly defined as production minus consumption, that must go to augment capital somewhere in the production process. It is this feature that now renders parsimony problematic. Specifically, "if increased thrift or caution induces people to save more in the present, they must also consent to consume more in the [immediate] future."[4] In other words, the additional investment in productive capacity will have to be absorbed by a properly expanded consumer demand. And this creates a dangerous tension since "if saving is being effected, not merely during one day or one week but regularly and habitually, the constantly increasing total of capital thus brought about will require a regular and habitual increase in the rate of consumption to prevent oversupply in the earlier stages of production."[5] Therefore, it is consumer demand, and not aggregate supply, that is the real engine driving the economy. Too much savings and investment will merely clog the industrial channels and produce glutted markets.

In the next chapter, "The Physiology of Production," they show that the quantitative relation between production and consumption deduced earlier is in fact maintained "through the medium of price and profit."[6] With changes in consumption, capital will of necessity change simultaneously. For instance, as a result of savings consumption decreases, which will first depress retail sales and profits, and then decrease planned inventories. From the retail level the recessionary force will work itself backward to manufacturing. In the process, consumer retail demand ultimately determines the level of employment and the amount of capital needed and thereby determines their respective incomes. In other words, aggregate consumption determines aggregate production, which in turn determines aggregate income. As a corollary, wages and other factor incomes are ultimately paid by the consumer, and *not* by resources set aside in a "wages fund" by the employer. Back to the main argument: a fall in the aggregate incomes would indicate that the use of capital and labor has declined relative to their supply, thereby causing prices and incomes to fall until production no longer exceeds the level of consumption. According to Hobson and Mummery, this demonstrates that the *only* cause of depression is underconsumption, evoked by an "undue exercise of the habit of thrift." Similarly, "the East-end problem (of poverty), with its concomitants of vice and misery," can be traced to its true economic cause: "the most respectable and highly extolled virtue of thrift."[7]

Turning now to the cause of oversaving, Hobson, the social economist, shines through by accusing the economists of the fundamental fallacy of assuming that the interests of the community must always be identical to the interests of its several members. According to Hobson and Mummery:

> The statement of Adam Smith, "What is prudence in the conduct of a private family can scarce be folly in that of a great nation," has been taken too generally for a gospel of truth. This view, that a community means nothing more than the addition of a number of individual units, and that the interests of Society can be obtained by adding together the interests of individual members, has led to as grave errors in Economics as in other branches of Sociology. The confident assumption, that if individuals look carefully after their own private interests, the welfare of the whole community will incidentally be secured, is the true explanation of the indifference with which students of the mechanism of commerce have regarded all such criticism of the construction of that machine as is contained in theories of Over-production.

The authors then apply this reasoning in explaining overproduction.

The disclosure of the falsehood on which this assumption rests will also disclose the existence and nature of that force which gives to Over-Supply an actual existence in the world of commerce. If the interests of each individual in a community were identical with the interests of the community there could be no such thing as Over-Supply. It is impossible to suppose that a company of men, producing in common for the common good, would at any time produce more than was required for consumption in the present or near future. It is, in fact, the clash of interests between the community as a whole and the individual members in respect to Saving, that is the cause of Over-Supply.[8]

What is true for the individual, in this case the unlimited power to save, is not true for the community. Mummery and Hobson offer the following example: an individual can work harder than necessary for twenty years in order to then retire and consume the fruits of the past labor. What he or she does not consume right away, others will consume in exchange for money, in fact giving the saver a lien on future production. In society as a whole, this can't be done. If society produces more than it consumes for the purpose of consuming later, it will be faced with the perishability of food and many other goods: "Rust and moths, the dangers of destruction by fire or other accident, changes of fashion, etc. . . . will see to it that the value of saved goods will erode."[9] In addition, another reason why commodities cannot be stored is that some are non-material, such as services of actors, singers and repairmen. Ergo, what is possible for each, is not possible for all together.

The reason why individuals save and invest in excess of what demand can readily absorb, Hobson and Mummery explain, is the competitive spirit, which induces everyone, in rivaling others, to accumulate more or better machinery. Such competition is unlimited, even if all the necessary machinery to produce the desired output was already in existence, because a manufacturer can also produce more cheaply "by beating down wages of [his] workpeople, and thus force some of the previously existing machinery to stand idle."[10] But this process of competitive innovation and cost reduction does not affect the aggregate amount of socially usable saving in the community, it merely determines what portion of the thrift will be exercised by an individual saver-investor.

In a chapter titled "Over-Production and Economic Checks," they examine and reject two automatic market adjustments, which in the eyes of economists will effectively prevent oversupply: (1) a fall in the general price level, and (2) a fall in the rate of interest. The first is ruled out because "every . . . fall in retail prices . . . will mean a corresponding fall of the money income in the community."[11] Thus, no reason exists for consumption being increased. The second check won't help either, since people will not save less with lower interest rates. Why would the knowledge that they can get a smaller return on their investment induce the rich to buy an extra carriage and increase household expenditures?, especially under the condition or prospect of declining incomes. Neither can we expect the impoverished working class to increase their consumption significantly. The restoration of the balance of consumption and production only works by cutting output, and this is indeed what happens with declining returns on investment. But lower production and lower profits, far from being a preventive check, constitute the very malady that they are supposed to prevent: the "most pernicious form of the disease called Depression in Trade."[12]

The publication of *The Physiology of Industry* was not without consequences. It was reviewed in a demeaning fashion by a leading economist, Francis Edgeworth. Even worse, to add injury to insult, Hobson, the young heretic, only 32 years old, was suddenly barred from continuing as University Extension Lecturer teaching courses on political economy. "This was due," Hobson later explained, "to the intervention of an economics Professor who had read my book and considered it as equivalent in rationality to an attempt to prove the flatness of the earth."[13] That professor, it turned out, was H. S. Foxwell, who in a letter to the Extension Board considered Hobson as "a man only notorious for a very fallacious attempt to prove that thrift is morally and socially a vice."[14]

Hobson's exclusion from academia was sudden and thorough: invitations for speaking engagements were canceled, and his application to join the prestigious Political Economy Club rejected. Though he later mused that his exile might have very well prevented him from developing his humanist theory in a more orderly way, it also helped him avoid the stifling specialization of the ivory tower and kept him in better touch with the pulse of ordinary and concrete life. In the next few years he wrote a couple of books on poverty and the evolution of capitalism which were generally well received and helped restore some of his respectability. Meanwhile, his "partner in crime," Mummery, was killed in an attempt to climb the Nanga Parbat in the Himalayas.

Underconsumption and inequality

After an intensive but brief study of Ruskin's economics, he turned his attention once again to underconsumptionist macroeconomics, publishing *The Problem of the Unemployed* (1896). Like in the previous heresy, he again asked why the free play of individual self-interest appears to fail the common good, but this time, potentially inspired by Ruskin's assault on the "systems of inequity," he came up with a different answer of a distinctly Sismondian flavor: the failure of aggregate demand must be blamed on a maldistribution of income. In particular, the culprit was the unearned surplus income of rich capitalists and landowners. Even though the working man saves in painful abstinence, carefully postponing present consumption for future use, the logic for the rich is otherwise. Having already met all their basic needs, they go on to pile up new savings for no other reason than to see their wealth accumulate. "It would, I think, be pretty safe to conclude that a very large percentage of incomes received as rents and interest are not used for current expenditure, but are left to grow by compound interest," Hobson claimed.[15] He realized, of course, that as long as the high incomes from interest, rent and monopoly profits were spent on luxury goods, there would be no problem of aggregate demand keeping pace with production. This possibility, however, was voided by a matter of human psychology:

> Where incomes flow in, yielding a power of consumption wholly dis-proportionate to the output of personal effort, a natural tendency to "save" is manifested, which is sharply distinguishable from the reasonable "saving" made out of legitimate earnings. It is this auto-matic "saving" which upsets the balance between consumption and producing power, and which from the social standpoint may be classed as "oversaving". No class of men whose "savings" are made of their hard-won earnings is likely to oversave, for each unit of "capital" will represent a real want, a piece of legitimate consump-tion deferred. But where "savings" represent the top portion of large incomes, drawn from economic rents of land, profits of specula-tion, high interest of capital derived from monopolies, no natural limit is set upon the amount which is saved.[16]

In short, the rich cannot enjoy spending their accumulated incomes just like a man cannot enjoy a good meal unless he has earned it by some prior physical effort. To Hobson, this was simply a matter of "natural law."[17]

Moreover, a large part of so-called "unearned income" really needs to be seen as earned *by the community*, such as the growing value of town lands, taking advantage of nearby markets, the dependence of much profit on legal monopolies (protective tariffs and licenses to produce alcoholic beverages, and so on) and the prior existence of a public infrastructure. Hobson felt that these "unearned incomes," not needed to induce individual effort and merely constituting a gratuitous surplus, ought to be taxed and so legitimately passed into public possession for supplying the common wants and enrich-ment of the common life. Through this process the state would consume in lieu of the capitalists, thereby redressing the fatal imbalance caused by his "psychological law." Alternatively, the workers' movement could also be pro-moted, securing higher wages through effective trade unions. Thereby, Hobson observed, higher wages will operate as proxy to a tax on the unearned elements of income.

This last point concerning redistribution through wages to help absorb excessive savings was further developed in his next book, *The Economics of Distribution* (1900), in which he introduced the notion of "forced gain," when in the process of bargaining the stronger party appropriates all the gains from the mutual cooperation. Labor typically did not get what it deserved, since capitalists could afford to outlast their opponent, appropriating the entire surplus produced by both parties. With this notion, Hobson's under-consumption theory now resembles in all major aspects the theory articulated by Sismondi more than half a century earlier: a theory of the trade cycle, in which savings are the result of bargaining power. It's an exercise in economic dynamics, an explanation originating in the maldistribution of income caused by asymmetry in negotiating power between labor and capital. The owners of capital, awash with savings, tend to reinvest most of it, thereby changing the mix of aggregate demand from consumption by the poor to investment by the rich. It is true that overall purchasing power is initially maintained. Yet this static interpretation of Say's Law does not imply that there are no difficulties. In Hobson's own words:

> [The] saving class is therefore not necessarily causing an increase in "employment" by paying workers to put up more factories instead of using their moneys to demand consumer goods. So long as the "saving" is actually in progress – i.e., so long as the factory and machinery are being made – the net employment of the community is just as large as if the money were spent to demand commodities; more labor is engaged in making factories, less in working them. But after the new factories are made, they can only be worked on condition that there is an increase of producing power – i.e., on condition that a sufficient number of persons are actuated by motives different from those which animated the "saving" class, and will consent to give validity to the saving of the former by "spending" on commodities in increased proportion of their incomes. Where no such expectation is realized, an attempt to "operate" the new factories does not give any net increase of employment, it only gluts the market, drives down prices, closes the weaker factories, imparts irregularity to work, and generally disorganizes trade.[18]

As a result, and as a manifestation of the problem, *not* the Keynesian cause, loanable capital will not find its way into investment. Incomes will decrease and with them new savings, until the balance between investment and consumption is restored. At that stage, the economy is poised for a recovery and the cycle can start all over again.

Explaining imperialism

Hobson's *The Problem of the Unemployed* was published at an inopportune time. The British economy, and capitalism in general, was about to enter what is referred to as the *Belle Époque*, a prolonged period of relative stability and steady growth, lasting till World War I. Was Hobson's theory thereby refuted? Not in his eyes. Something new had been occurring to strengthen the system, in spite of its propensity to overinvestment and underconsumption. Gold had been discovered in South Africa and soon trouble was brewing between the British and the Dutch, eventually to escalate into the Boer War in 1899. Hobson was sent there by a newspaper to report back to the British. The information he collected during his stay provided the material for his *Imperialism: A Study* (1902), soon a classic and remaining to this day Hobson's best known work.

What had taken place in the late nineteenth century was a mad scramble by the major west European countries, except Spain and the Netherlands, to acquire tropical territory in Africa and parts of Asia. Egypt, Sudan, Kenya, Uganda, South Africa, "Niger Coast," as well as Burma, Hong Kong, Pakistan and Malaysia in Asia, all came under British rule, adding some 80 million people to the empire. Meanwhile, Germany grabbed Tanzania, Cameroon and Namibia; France incorporated Senegal, the Sahara and Indochina (Vietnam, Cambodia, Thailand); Portugal annexed Angola and Mozambique, while Belgium seized the Congo. In contrast to the earlier wave of colonization of America, India, Australia and South America, these acquisitions were not intended to provide new land for settlers from the overpopulated mother country, and very few did indeed emigrate.[19] Neither did trade between the mother land and its new tropical and subtropical areas amount to much. So, why did it happen? Hobson's answer was as novel as it was intriguing: the industrial countries, suffering from overproduction and underconsumption, needed new markets to dump surplus goods and to seek profitable outlets for their bulging savings by investing in railroads, mines and manufactures in sheltered new markets abroad. In other words, the imperialist phenomenon was to be understood as a "great safety overflow channel which has been continuously more and more widened and deepened to carry off the ever-increasing flood of new capital" fed by the excessive savings of the rich.[20] The "economic taproot" of imperialism consisted of rents, monopoly profits and, more generally, of unearned elements of income. According to Hobson, "where the distribution of incomes is such as to enable all classes of the nation to convert their felt wants into an effective demand for commodities, there can be no overproduction, no underemployment of capital and labour, and no necessity to fight for foreign markets."[21] Imperialism, therefore, must be seen as the fruit of false economy, and social reform – meaning redistribution through taxation and trade unionism – as the natural remedy. "It is idle to attack Imperialism or Militarism as political expedients or policies," Hobson emphatically concludes, "unless the ax is laid at the economic root of the tree, and the classes for whose interest Imperialism works are shorn of the surplus revenues which seek this outlet."[22]

The skeptical reader may now ask, if it really is the very force of underconsumption that induces capitalists to invest surplus savings abroad, why did the imperialist "safety valve" not operate *before* the end of the nineteenth century? In other words, Hobson's theory must also explain why underconsumption during the 1870s and most of the 1880s led to recessions and depressions rather than investment in Africa. The answer he gives is simple: the growth of cartels, pools, trusts and holding companies during the late decades of the nineteenth century, turned the earlier competitive capitalism into a more mature and monopolistic version. Under free competition overproduction induces factories to cut prices down to a level at which the weaker competitors can no longer cover costs and are forced into bankruptcy. But the "first result of successful formation of a trust or combine is to close down the worst equipped or worst placed mills, and supply the entire market from the better equipped and better placed mills."[23] Profits are increased by either reducing costs or by raising prices. In either case, trusts will limit the quantity of capital which can be effectively employed in domestic industry, and send a large part of the burgeoning profits for investment abroad. In short, imperialism was simply a new way underconsumption manifested itself. Hobson's proposed economic reforms – the nationalization of certain monopolies, the encouragement of trade unionism, a national minimum wage and a system of progressive income taxation – were the simple tools to restore competition.

The economics of the unemployed

After the tragic culmination of the imperialist struggle for markets (World War I), and with the British economy headed for two decades of stagnation and mass unemployment, Hobson again drew attention to underconsumption, producing *The Economics of Unemployment* (1922), perhaps his most sophisticated statement on the subject. Now at the age of 64, he took care to spell out his theory with utmost clarity and to avoid any unnecessary excursions by which some readers might take offense, such as attacks upon the virtue of personal thrift. He also wrote with the concerns of the orthodox economist in mind. So, for example, he observed after putting forth his theory, "controversial experience has . . . taught me that it is not enough to establish propositions by constructive argument, so long as certain deep seated implications of an opposing theory remain unanswered."[24] Being well aware that, for the economist, "oversaving," "overproduction," and "limited markets" are all mere illusions because they assume that two automatic market adjustments – a fall in the interest rate and/or a fall in the price level – render them impossible, he took extra care once again in addressing these two checks.

As to the interest rate, he grants that an undue increase in capital will cause it to decline, but much too slowly to prevent a general glut. This is so for several reasons. First, it only affects the new capital supplied by current savings, a portion constituting less than 5 percent of the total. Second, he reminds us that much of the new savings are automatically generated by unearned portions of income. And third, to the extent that much of conscious thrift aims to make definite provisions for old age or other contingencies, a lower interest rate will tend to stimulate, rather than discourage, savings. Turning to the alleged prevention of overproduction by falling prices, he points to the prevalent combinations and cartels in business, which are designed to adjust to falling demand by restricting output and "holding up" prices. Moreover, to the extent that prices fall, so do the money incomes of workers and owners fall as well, thereby tending to neutralize any potential stimulus to aggregate demand.

Hobson also devoted an entire chapter to discussing in timely fashion an idea voiced by many business leaders who, "with considerable support from economists," had been calling for wage cuts by maintaining that lower wages would curb the depression and reduce unemployment by lowering production costs and prices, thereby enabling businesses to increase their sales. Against this sop, Hobson emphasized that such policy is at best a temporary alleviation "sowing the seeds of future trouble." The acceptance of real wage reductions in bad times as inevitable and desirable, he explained, "means acceptance of the prevailing conditions of the distribution of wealth as between capital and labour, which we regard as the root cause of fluctuations and depressions." Moreover, in an economic order in which trusts and other business associations prevail, "there is no security that wage reductions will not simply be absorbed in higher profits without leading to increased production and employment."[25]

It gets especially interesting when Hobson addresses the argument that domestic wage reductions are necessary to prevent being undersold by low-wage countries, such as Germany at that time. Here Hobson, generally known as a proponent of free international trade, touched upon a topic of great relevance in today's globalized economy. He at first explained that according to the well-known theory of international trade, such wage reductions would be unnecessary. "If the economic world went round as smoothly as theorists imagined, and consumption was ready and able to take everything that could be produced, there would be no plausibility in the demand that we must cut our wages . . ."[26] According to this doctrine, England would be specializing in certain lines of production, and even though Germany could produce them more cheaply, "she would not compete because her capital and labour would be more profitably absorbed in the lines where her advantages were [even] greater."[27] But Hobson warned that the reality does not correspond to theory. The world market, too, is limited and had shrunk so much that a powerful nation such as Germany could absorb virtually all of it so as to leave little for high-wage producers. Therefore, it would indeed be in the interest of British workers to lower their standard of wages toward that of German wages, thereby gaining a greater market share. It is worth noting that Hobson here, just like Sismondi a century before him, was willing to entertain departures from reasoning sanctioned by international trade theory. Hobson also claimed that they were based on overly unrealistic and abstract assumptions such as the acceptance of Say's Law in a world of full employment. Actually, he and Mummery had already reminded their readers in the closing pages of their book that "Free Trade requires for its advantages a perfectly healthy condition of commerce, where demand always keeps pace with the possibility of Supply," but that in a "diseased state of commerce" under conditions of underconsumption, a system of protection may even increase an economy's level of employment.[28] In other words, Hobson had long been aware that his questioning of Say's Law on dynamic grounds would also preclude an unqualified acceptance of the optimistic conclusions of international trade theory.

In the present work he warned that the "supreme temptation" to meet the competition of low-wage countries by lowering labor standards is nevertheless "the greatest single peril to the progress of the working classes in the higher-waged industrial country."[29] The *only* meaningful way to defend its standards of work and life is "economic internationalism of a constructive order" supported by an intergovernmental apparatus securing minimum standards of wages, hours and other conditions for labor in less developed industrial countries. And he further warned with a prophetic voice, that

> if it be found feasible to produce standard manufactures more cheaply in Russia, China or Japan, having regard to the joint economy of improved machine production and cheap labour, it seems inevitable that a good deal of our past industry will leave England and pass into these cheaper areas of production.

To forestall such a possibility he suggested strengthening the International Labour Bureau to prevent "sweated labour in foreign countries from under-selling [England] in the world market." More generally, what was needed was a new perspective regarding the global economy: "economic peace and progress can only be attained by common rules of international conduct contributory to a more equal and more equitable apportionment of work and its product over the whole area of the world market."[30] But aside from such insightful commentary, Hobson's *Economics of Unemployment* did not add anything essentially new to the work he had already done around the turn of the century.

Hobson and J. M. Keynes

In the early thirties, after having a manuscript rejected by the *Economic Journal*, he started to correspond with its editor, John Maynard Keynes.[31] There was not much give on either side. But in 1936, when Keynes published his revolutionary *General Theory of Employment, Interest, and Money*, he sent a copy to old Hobson who must have been delighted to see that in the closing pages he was finally getting some recognition from the economics establishment. Keynes wrote:

> Theories of under-consumption hibernated until the appearance in 1889 of *The Physiology of Industry*, by J. A. Hobson and A. F. Mummery, the first and most significant of any volumes in which for nearly fifty years, Mr. Hobson has flung himself with unflagging, but almost unavailing, ardour and courage against the ranks of orthodoxy. Though it is so completely forgotten to-day, the publication of this book marks, in a sense, an epoch in economic thought.[32]

After a short sketch of *Physiology*, he also criticized it for assuming that all savings are always invested, for its neglect of the interest rate and for putting too much emphasis on underconsumption leading to overinvestment, "instead of explaining that a relatively weak propensity to consume helps to cause unemployment by requiring and *not* receiving the accompaniment of a compensating volume of new investment."[33] Nevertheless, Keynes allotted him a prominent place in the "brave army of heretics," ranking him among those who, by "following their intuitions, have preferred to see the truth obscurely and imperfectly rather than to maintain error, reached indeed with clearness and consistency by easy logic but on hypothesis inappropriate to the facts."[34] It's a flattering statement, but nevertheless somewhat double-edged praise: the picturing of Hobson' s initial work as the apex of his contribution ends up depreciating most of his labors rearticulating the Sismondian approach based on maldistribution. Perhaps Keynes may have never quite learned to appreciate Hobson's work. It is true that at one stage he apologized to Hobson in a letter dated February 14, 1936: "I am ashamed how blind I was for many years to your essential contention as to the insufficiency of effective demand." (But at the same time he indicated in his private correspondence that it was primarily Mummery that he admired: when writing to Alfred Kahn he claimed, "Hobson never fully understood him [Mummery] and went off on a side-track after his death."[35])

The 77-year-old Hobson responded with a letter sent to Keynes in February 1936, in which he suggested a way by which his theory could be made more compatible with Keynes' emphasis on hoarding and underinvestment. It's a mechanism that starts with underconsumption and, because of developing excess capacity and diminished profitability, prepares the ground for Keynesian underinvestment. As he put it in a long footnote in his autobiography, published two years later:

> It is only when the failure of current savings cannot find a profitable investment, owing to the failure of consumer markets (home and external) to keep pace with the increase in producing power, that

depression and unemployment set in. Part of the recent savings lies idle in banks waiting for an opportunity for investment, and the decline of profits which underproduction brings about, causes a reduction in the rate of savings and in the proportion of aggregate income which is saved.[36]

In the same vein, the American social economist, John M. Clark, noted in Hobson's obituary, that his approach stressing excessive investment can be seen "as a step in the process leading to [a] falling-off [of] investment [and] may deserve a place in a balanced synthesis."[37]

But one needs to keep in mind that Hobson's (and Sismondi's) theory was not the same kettle of fish as the one cooked up by Keynes. Theirs deals with instability and concomitant social fallout within an intertemporal framework of economic *growth* where new investment not only constitutes additional demand but also leads to a greater capacity to produce in the future. In this manner Hobson must be seen as a predecessor of economic growth models which were in fashion during the 1940s and 1950s. In the words of one of the founders of this discipline, E. D. Domar:

> Keynes analyzed what happens when savings (of the previous period) are not invested. The answer was – unemployment, but the statement of the problem in this form might easily give the erroneous impression that if savings were invested, full employment would be assured. Hobson, on the other hand, went a step further and stated the problem in this form: suppose savings are invested. Will the new plants be able to dispose of all their products? Such a statement of the problem was not at all, as Keynes thought, a mistake. It was a statement of a different, and possibly also deeper problem. Hobson was fully armed with the [capacity creating] effect of investment, and he saw that it could be answered only by growth.[38]

Joan Robinson, another eminent economist in the field, felt that Roy Harrod's analysis of the growth process constituted the "missing link" between Keynes and Hobson.[39] More recently, and because of this resemblance of Hobson's theory with the Harrod and Domar growth models, the economist Michael Schneider has succeeded in squeezing Hobson's theory into a mathematical form, thereby shedding new light on the relative importance of boosting investment or consumption in trying to overcome an economic slump.[40]

In conclusion, it is worthwhile to point out the irony that Hobson's early thinking about aggregate demand failure had to first lead to his excommunication as an economist, before he was recognized, even celebrated, as an important forerunner of the Keynesian revolution in macroeconomics. As with Sismondi, Hobson's emphasis on *consumption* – a humanistic disposition more interested in consumption than accumulation of wealth – led quite naturally to add a new macroeconomic dimension to social economics. Although contemporary individualistic economics has chosen to distance itself from Keynes in order to rebuild macroeconomics on a micro foundation, a social and genuine macroeconomics continues to be practiced and further developed within a relatively new school called *post-Keynesian economics*.[41] Witness the similarity of its component views with that of social economics, as brought out in a recent description of post-Keynesianism: "The economy is to be viewed as a dynamic historical process; uncertainty is a significant feature of economic life; questions of distribution are fundamental; human choice is acknowledged as real; economic and political institutions (money and structures of power) shape economic events; human emancipation is to be included amongst the goals of policy."[42] Even though there is now a primary emphasis on *monetary* macroeconomics, this school can be seen as the contemporary *macro*economic branch of social economics with a rich life of its own.[43] Therefore, the focus from here on will be on the other half: social economics in its microeconomic dress.

2. The economics of social reform

"Mr. Ruskin's first claim as social reformer is that he reformed Political Economy," Hobson said about his mentor in 1898, and immediately proceeded along the same path, eager to begin with a constructive critique of orthodox microeconomics in its marginalist dress. In Hobson's own recollection, "the need for the humanization of economic science and art was intensified by the study [he] gave to Ruskin in the mid-nineties."[44] In the same year he published his *John Ruskin: Social Reformer*, with the avowed purpose of rendering "some assistance to those who are disposed to admit the validity of the claim which Mr. Ruskin has made to be first and above all else a Political Economist."[45] The result is a marvelous and orderly presentation of Ruskin's valuable but scattered insights together with an uncompromising critique of his shortcomings, including his "fanatical abhorrence" of the doctrine of natural equality. In the years after its publication, Hobson pursued the topic of social reform with a series of public lectures to the London branch of the Christian Union. These lectures were soon published under the title *The Social Problem* (1901). Since it could serve still today as a textbook in humanistic social economics, it deserves some attention.

Hobson understood the meaning of the "social problem" as the challenge of achieving that social and economic order that would best enable "complete satisfaction" of all members of society. Such an idealistic program would hardly strike anybody as controversial, were it not for the particular spin Hobson was to put on the term "satisfaction" and how he proposed to measure different degrees of "completeness." In its negative formulation the social problem can be stated more concretely: how to minimize social problems or the social waste of unemployment, meaningless work, chronic poverty, congested cities, foul air, decay of the family, landlordism and so forth. Now, in order to grapple with all the essential facts of the "social problem," said Hobson, an economics is needed that can also incorporate "non-economic" aspects of economic activity, such as "moral wealth, culture, friendship and love." In short, he proposed a new social economics quite different from the prevailing science, which "takes money as its standard of value, and regards men as means of making money," and thereby is by its very nature incapable of facing "the deep and complex human problems which compose the Social Question."[46]

Hobson's critique of microeconomics

In proposing an alternative to the established economics, Hobson puts his finger on a number of basic issues: a standard of valuation that imports ethics into economics, the question of where to draw the boundaries of social inquiry and, last but not least, the issue of the quantitative method. His treatment of all three still provides almost a century later the core elements of a social economics centered on *human* welfare, rather than *material* wealth or income.

In order to reconstruct the prevailing science of wealth into a true science of *human* wealth or welfare, several major steps would be necessary. First, one must substitute for the prevailing commercial standard of money, a human standard reflecting various satisfactions and efforts. Next, these feelings, many of which manifest in temporary and fleeting desires, must be made congruent "with the real good or worth of the individual life as a whole." And finally, these "cleansed" individual valuations must be in harmony with the good of society as a whole. Hobson believed that since "the real and total worth of the individual life is determined by, and forms part of, the worth of the larger social life" this harmonization usually occurs naturally.[47] Therefore, a new standard of value is needed that reflects "true or absolute value" from the social standpoint. He preferred to call this new ultimate standard "social utility," but did not mind the use of other terminology, such as the satisfaction of essential human needs, or self-realization.[48] Later he preferred "organic welfare." What matters is that it is an ethical standard reflecting the common good.

Among other issues that should be discussed is a critique of the standard of money serving as an indicator of social well-being due, to the standard's blindness to values and output that are not commercially produced, such as baking bread at home. Formerly homemade goods for private use that are made increasingly for sale, are registered by economists as an increase in wealth, which in fact is "wholly fictitious." Similarly, the so-called "free goods" of nature such as sunshine, clean air and scenery do not count, unless they are privatized, so that "the squire who filches a piece of common land, the Scotch-American millionaire who encloses a mountain and charges for a right of way," will appear to have increased the wealth of the community.[49] More generally, one would think that the more of these "free goods" a nation has, the wealthier it is. But, according to the measuring rod of economics, it is poorer. Worse yet, the commercial value standard of money does very little to measure changes in the quality of life. So, for example, if national income is said to be thirteen times higher than it was a century earlier, it could imply "that we are simply making greater drudges of ourselves, toiling harder than before after commercial goods under conditions of work which disabled us from making a more pleasant or more profitable use of our increased possessions than our forefathers made of their smaller stock."[50] In other words, what one really needs to know is the comparative sum of pains and pleasures that the production and consumption of national income entails. This involves converting economic "costs" and "utilities" expressed in terms of cash into terms of human life. And for that, it would be necessary to ascertain on the cost side of the ledger the character and conditions of work, how it is distributed among the workers, and finally, the capacity of different segments of the working class to bear these costs. As to the benefits of consumption, one would have to gauge satisfaction by asking what the goods and services are, who will get to use them and to what extent consumers are capable of getting the best use of them. So, for example, the more sophisticated forms of wealth are directly related to the number and character of the "consumers" as the following quotation illustrates:

> Take a picture which ranks as an asset of £1000 in the national wealth. If it is bought up by a vulgar plutocrat for his private gallery, it may be no "wealth" but "illth" serving to feed certain evil propensities of greed and ostentation. If it hangs in the public gallery of a money ridden people, uneducated in the enjoyment of forms of beauty, their finer feelings blunted by coarse lives, its utility may still be very small. But if such a people can be educated, refined, and endowed with the sense of beauty, a value or utility is imparted to the picture which is incalculably great, as it becomes a formative influence of national character.[51]

Economics and ethics

The switch from a measuring rod of money to one of human benefits is the prelude to a more controversial step. It is one thing to reduce costs and utilities from money terms to subjective feelings, Hobson says, but "quite another thing to introduce an [ethical] standard of valuation from outside — to refer every 'is' to an 'ought'."[52] Clearly, the use of an external touchstone of "true or absolute utility" for the worth of feeling implies the subordination of the economic sphere to something wider and more encompassing. The problem requires one to discount "fleeting" and "often mistaken" individual desires, and to establish the "desirable or ideal" by an objective standard of reference, "social utility." Hobson defends this move to subordinate economics to ethics in two ways. First, he argues that there is no such thing as a value-free science based solely on facts, saying, "no collection and ordering of crude facts is possible without importing from the outside some principles of collection and order which embody the objects or ends of the process of investigation in a hypothetical way." Because of this, he concludes, "You cannot investigate phenomena effectively without possessing some clear motive for investigation, and this motive will be related to a wider motive, which will eventually relate to some speculative idea." For the social scientist, not familiar with the philosophy of science, Hobson offers a detailed illustration to clarify his point:

> A student sets himself to collect facts of the rates of mortality in a given town; if these facts are to be of scientific service they must be collected and grouped in a method which is imposed *a priori*; for example, various districts are taken, and mortality rates are arranged as they vary according to density of population, or again, the figures will be set in relation to other facts than locality – e.g. to rents or to family incomes – or a comparison may be effected between the rate of city born or country born. Whatever the direct object and the result of this investigation of crude fact may be, this prime object and result have no scientific finality. If the object of investigation is to ascertain the proportionate mortality at different ages in different social strata between town and country born, this object is itself suggested and dictated by some larger object relating to the respective advantages and disadvantages of different pressures of population. Driven far back, the whole series of investigations and reasonings at different foci will be found to relate to and depend on some hypothesis of political and social good, which is the "end," hidden doubtless, as a conscious motive for the detailed student buried in his tiny group of facts, but none the less permeating the whole process with "teleology."[53]

In short, you cannot gather data to do science unless you already have a certain idea or ideal in mind. This is no different for Hobson's social economics in which "we must have a social ideal constructed to accord with human facts and human possibilities," but at the same time "transcending existing facts, and furnishing a test for conduct."[54]

Hobson's second point in defending objective norms flatly denies the principle that fact and value can be clearly separated. In doing so, he throws himself against the authority of the father of J. M. Keynes who had just published a book on this very issue.[55] There Keynes said that "the attempt to fuse together the inquiries into what is and what ought to be is likely to stand in the way of our giving a clear and unbiased answer to either question."[56] So, for example, it is one thing to study the competitive forces determining wages, quite another to evaluate the degree of fairness of the wages so determined. But Hobson disagrees; to him "the 'ought' is not something separable and distinct from the 'is'; on the contrary, an 'ought' is everywhere the highest aspect or relation of an 'is.'"[57] In the social sciences, unlike the sister sciences dealing with nature, every fact has moral significance; it naturally is inherent in the fact, and therefore full knowledge of a fact implies also knowing the ethical dimension of the fact. Moreover, an inquiry carried out in strictly positivistic terms, ignoring as it does the "ought" in suppressing questions about the social or moral consequences of the observed facts, was likened by Hobson to "the protean fallacy of individualism which feigns the existence of separate individuals by abstracting and neglecting the social relations which belong to them and make them what they are."[58] There is certainly a basic similarity here to Sismondi's "carrying economics forward to new ground," in the sense of an impartial observer having to recognize unjust suffering that comes from man rather than coldly passing over it.[59] For example, the question of fairness cannot be ignored in an inquiry of how wages are determined in the bargaining process in which the stronger party gains at the expense of the weaker one. Here, to shut one's eyes to the moral issues, to confine one's study to the operations of supply and demand, would be to completely ignore the testimony afforded by economic conditions of the sale of labor services and to the injustice and the human waste of competitive wage determination.[60] More generally, the need for ethics arises because human beings, unlike other animal life, have ideals and the capability to shape their environment in that direction. To the extent that these ideals come to be shared within a group, they can then be seen as "ethical facts." In Hobson's view, "ethics do not 'intrude' into economic facts; the same facts are ethical and economic."[61]

Much of Hobson's case for a new ethical economics revolves around an interpretation of the essential needs or the ultimate demands of (human) nature, but he does not stop there. As if the case for a normative economics were not controversial enough, he also assails the narrow definition of economics prevailing at that time, depicted by his famous contemporary Alfred Marshall as the science preoccupied with the human activities of "getting and spending," a definition which may be agreeable if strictly confined to commerce. But as soon as one asks how a certain kind of work affects the health and character of the worker and his family, and how this kind of consumption affects the moral life of the consumer, then "the larger unity of the human organism, both in its physiological and its psychological aspects, everywhere intrudes."[62] Similarly, in many human activities, such as with genuine artists or scholars in whom greed and idleness cease to be important motives, the ongoing activities of money getting and spending are "organically interwoven" with quite different feelings and intellectual purposes. The problem is that not *all* activities of earning and spending money are homogenous in quality; even in the case of the laborer, the mercenary motive is combined and modified by others, such as "fealty to comrades, some sense of duty, some malice against an employer" and so on.[63] Different motives imply different qualities of action, and even though they often involve in one way or another the use of money, the activities cannot therefore be regarded as homogenous enough to warrant the singling out of a uniform category of conduct.

More generally, economic and social life must be treated as organically inter-related. A man "is not a mechanical but an organic composition of forces," Hobson insisted, "not a business man and a father and a student and a politician and a moralist [but] all these together in one."[64] To pretend that commerce is a department by itself may be a way to simplify science but it also falsifies it. Hobson reiterated Ruskin's basic criticism of scientists who would break a social problem into parts because of their perception that such a problem can be reduced to a mechanical composition of forces. Hobson said this method might work with a machine but not with an organism, because "the very first process of breaking it into its several parts destroys the very object of your investigation."[65] Therefore, a true social economics needs to be enriched by ethics and its scope broadened by borrowing from neighboring disciplines.

The qualitative dimension

Adding to the heresy of turning positive economics into an artful science or a scientific art aiming at social reform, Hobson devoted an interesting chapter to a question that carries extra significance today when the bulk of economics, in the name of science, is increasingly relegated to mathematics, and rapidly developing into some type of "mathematical politics."[66] He starts out with the question: "If we are to have a science of human costs and utilities, of true effort and satisfactions, will the method be mathematical?"[67] As one would expect, his answer is "absolutely not," because any mathematical treatment assumes that all desires and preferences are a question of mere quantity, and that differences of quality can always be reduced to the quantitative dimension. This is so whether the choice is between more or less, better or worse or even higher or lower. Yet there is a *qualitative* dimension to making choices and to the types of satisfaction that result. To illustrate the problem of these irreducible qualities, Hobson quotes Alfred Marshall, who argued thus:

> It may be objected that the higher motives are so different in quality from the lower that the one cannot be weighted against the other. There is some validity to this objection; for the pain which it would afford an earnest and good man to do deliberately a wrong

action is *so great* that no pleasure can compensate for it; it cannot be weighted or measured. But even here, what hindered the pain from being measured is not its quality, but its amount; the pain is practically *infinite*.[68]

To Hobson, this very defense proves his point: after granting that mathematicians are in fact treating "infinity" as if it were some kind of positive quantity, he claims that logically speaking it is "not a quantity at all, but just the negation of quantity" and explains that "if I say this pleasure is infinitely greater than that, I mean that the difference is incapable of quantitative expression that, in other words, it is of kind or quality."[69] Moreover, when observing the individual in society, one observes a historical evolution of wants and satisfactions. It's a movement from mere survival to a quest for more "complimentary food appealing to taste, ornamental elements in clothing, commodiousness and dignity of dwelling etc.," in other words, a continued ascent of a whole hierarchy of basic human needs or values with aesthetic, intellectual and moral needs at its apex. From this, Hobson infers that one must admit "that each class [of needs], in its necessary order of development, has *infinite* real utility as compared with subsequent orders which are conditioned in their development by its priority."[70] In other words, each category of basic need is infinitely more important than the one which follows, each being an indispensable condition of all further life.

More than a dozen years later, Hobson further elaborated on this serious limitation of quantitative economics. The last chapter of *Work and Wealth* (1914) launches a broadside attack against *marginalism* (a term Hobson coined) as another example of reducing quality to differences in quantity. Being sharply critical of "the recent extensions of quantitative analysis into economics by the method of marginal preferences," Hobson voiced his misgivings: marginalism cannot *explain*, nor can it *predict*, consumer behavior. To make his case he considered the problem of allocating money between qualitatively different wants, such as spending it on some mix of theater tickets and charity. In life, although such choices are made, this is no proof that people maximize utility according to some equimarginal principle. The following example illustrates the principle behind budgeting our consumption, by a cooking analogy:

> The composition of a dish is here expressed in proportions of its various ingredients, so much flour, so many ounces of raisins, so many eggs and so much sugar, etc. The marginalists would dwell upon the crucial fact that the last penny worth of flour, raisins, eggs and sugar, taken severally, had an equal value for the pudding, and that these marginal or final increments were in some way causal determinants of the composition of the pudding, because in using the ingredients the cook took care to use just so much of each, and

neither more nor less. And it is quite true that the delicacy of the culinary art will in fact be displayed in deciding whether to put in another handful of raisins, another egg, or a spoonful more sugar. But from the standpoint of trying to appreciate the virtue or worth of the dish as a culinary creation, it cannot be admitted that any special importance or causal determination attaches to the last increments of the several ingredients. For it is evident that the "how much" of each ingredient is itself determined by the conception of the *tout ensemble* in the mind of the creator or inventor.[71]

What is true in the culinary arts also applies to every form of composition embodying some unity of purpose. As long as one uses several means in pursuit of an end, the marginal equivalence is logically implied. But while "the scientific analysis of any composite arrangement, mechanical, organic, conscious, *involves* this marginal assumption . . . it explains nothing." So, for example, after a shopping expedition, the utility of the last dollar of my expenditures on bread will equal that of books, "a fact that proceeds *not* from a comparison, conscious or unconscious, of these separate items at the margin, but from the parts assigned respectively to bread and books in the organic plan of my life."[72] As a result of all this, we do not have to imagine the almost impossible and certainly the intricate psychological operation of balancing different qualities; instead, the various utilities simply reflect the value of the organic whole. Or, to put it differently: the whole determines the parts, not the other way around.

Humanizing the economy

A demonstration that an individualistic science of economics is ill-suited to guide policy makers toward a better society constitutes but the first step of social reform. Beyond that, Hobson articulated a constructive attempt to sketch a more meaningful alternative in terms of social economics. This reconstruction, later called "economics of human welfare," was developed in two subsequent books, *Work and Wealth* (1914) and *Wealth and Life* (1929). The new perspective, together with his lifelong activism for legislative implementation of the ideas promulgated, has played an important role in preparing the way for the new social policies in Britain.

A natural right to property

Hobson's case for a more just social order is grounded not in prudence or altruism, but instead in natural law, which he interpreted in his own unique way. "The right of property may be described as 'natural,'" he explains, "because certain laws of the physical and moral nature of man mark out the true limits of property in any given condition of society."[73]

His basic argument goes as follows: the carrying out of productive effort uses up vital energy which every member of society has a right to replenish: "nature assigns to every producer, as his separate property, that portion of his product, or some equivalent in exchange, required to sustain his productive energy." In other words, everybody has a (natural) right to a "living wage." But since wages are fixed by market forces, there is no guarantee that an employer, under competitive pressure, will necessarily respect this law; in fact, self-interest often generates a temptation "to exhaust their [the workers'] vital capital, and throw their prematurely exhausted bodies upon public or private charity to keep."[74] Legislation of some minimum wage would be the first step to social reform. As a member of the Liberal Party, Hobson had actively tried to persuade the government to implement such wage legislation, an effort that was partly rewarded in 1909 with the setting up of Trade Boards having the power to fix wages in certain industries. Yet his party's continued reluctance to establish minimum wages as a general principle covering the entire economy, led to Hobson's resignation and his joining the Labour Party in the mid 1920s, where his contributions were more appreciated and also more fruitful.

Natural Law and rights of property, in Hobson's interpretation, not only dictated bare wages of subsistence, but also mandated an incentive component in inducing worker consent to produce more. Just how much more would be required depends primarily on the degree of intrinsic satisfaction the nature of work provides and the selfishness of the individual in question. For example, artists, said to work for "art's sake," do not require much in extra pay for their products, but coal miners would. Natural Law is violated not only by paying less than is necessary, but also by paying *more* than is necessary to evoke a particular productive effort. Hobson bases this claim on a more dubious psychological "law" according to which such excess earnings "will hang like a millstone around [one's] neck," thereby numbing one's energy and paralyzing one's efforts.[75] Whatever the merits of his Natural Law doctrine may be, it forms the foundation for all the reform efforts aiming at redistribution of the elements of "unearned income," money that originates as "forced gain" appropriated through bargaining power. These transfers were either to go to society (through progressive taxes) or to the dispossessed working class through measures aimed at increasing workers' rights and trade union power.

In connection with the issue of property, Hobson blames yet another individualistic fallacy inhibiting the reform of an unjust economic system: the widespread erroneous belief that *society* cannot produce any new property or wealth. But are not transactions between buyers and sellers facilitated by markets which are after all *social* institutions? Are not suppliers assisted by technological knowledge, a *social* product? Similarly, goods are more profitably marketed by being transported on *public* roads and protected against theft by a *public* legal system, and their value tends to be enhanced by the proximity of towns, another *social* institution. In short, society collaborates with individual labor as a "maker of values." In that role, it has a natural claim to an appropriate share of the wealth it helps to generate. Yet individual producers, asserting that the value of their output is the product of nothing more than their individual skill and effort, resentfully oppose taxation, regarding it as an encroachment upon their property rights. To the extent that they succeed, large chunks of socially produced value end up in private pockets, thereby preventing the reproduction and maintenance of social property; state services deteriorate, public education suffers, monetary aid for the aged poor gets cut, and, through all this, society "suffers in vigor and progress of life and character."[76]

Underlying this theory of natural property rights are the concepts of individual *capacity* which, in the interest of society, must be encouraged to be fully used or "realized," as well as basic human *needs* serving as the basis for rightful claims on the social product. "Wealth," Hobson insisted, "should be distributed according to the support it renders to the whole life of recipients. It should give each what each is capable of utilizing for a full human life."[77] He appeals to a social standard that aims at maximum satisfaction of basic needs in society. In other words, it is an economics with a strongly normative bent that considers it objectively wasteful, or "inefficient," if some members of society have more wealth than they can handle while others languish in extreme poverty.

Recognizing higher human needs

But whereas his social analysis *starts* with the need for survival and security, he refuses to abstract from the context of the higher dimensions of human nature, ranging from the needs for association and social affection all the way to the love of joy, freedom, personal virtue and social justice. All these different types of needs, in his eyes, are organically interlinked; more specifically, as we satisfy one category of basic need (for example, survival needs), a new kind of need, such as the need for companionship, will emerge and start to color our goals and motivations. It is because of these organically sequential interconnections that whatever happens at the lower or "body" level can either stifle or facilitate the development of the higher realms of personality and consciousness. But true social economy will have to make sure that the lower needs of food, shelter and rest are provided in a manner that does not stifle these self-realization needs. The narrow-minded policy of maximizing national wealth or income may be questionable when industrial life involves real human costs that are not accounted for in the price tag of the products. In defending this fundamental position, Hobson anticipated the economist's typical retort, suggested in economics textbooks, "that the inconvenient or dangerous element in trade is represented by a higher rate of wages," by answering that "the suggestion is not a whit borne out by facts."[78] But even if it were, certain risks of life-threatening injuries, such as necrosis in the match trade, could never be compensated by money: "No man or woman economically competent to enter a 'free' contract would work under existing conditions in white lead," said Hobson, and added that the plain fact was that "the lives of these unfortunate workers are simply not paid for; they do not rank among expenses of production."[79]

Because these hidden human costs are primarily non-economic in the sense that they tend to interfere with life and the development of personality, they provide the chief rationale for a more encompassing human welfare economics. The task of a true social economics is to burst through the straitjacket of the economic motive, otherwise "we cannot win the spiritual liberty needed for the ascent of man," Hobson warned.[80] It is for this reason that the higher moral needs are also of relevance to a social economist.

One of the distinctive features of Hobson's welfare economics is the realization that human nature is not static, mechanical and fixed, but dynamic, and that its growth hinges on the social environment. Moral development is stunted by selfish considerations and by caving in to the temptations of the immediate urges to the detriment of a fuller social personality. The *whole* person identifies him/herself with a higher moral and social self to which he/she "belongs by instinct and reason."

Catalysts for higher self-identification

Two decades later, in a significant and beautiful passage, Hobson specifies in more detail two psychological catalysts that enable personality growth, and the role social institutions play in its transformation.

> When moralists talk of altering human nature they are often mis-understood to mean that instincts and desires deeply implanted in our inherited animal outfit can be eradicated and others grafted on. Now no such miracles are possible or needed. But substantial changes in our environment or in our social institutions can apply different stimuli to human nature and evoke different physical responses. For example, by alterations in the organization and government of businesses and industries, so as to give security of employment and of livelihood to workers, and some increased "voice" to them in the conditions of work it seems reasonably possible to modify the conscious stress of personal gain-seeking and to educate a clearer sense of social solidarity and service. The insecurity of livelihood has been a growing factor in the discontent of modern workers, and it increases with an education that reveals the "social" cause of that insecurity in the absence of any reliable economic government. Security is, therefore, the first essential in any shift of the relative appeal to personal and social motives. The second essential is such alterations in the government of businesses as to give the ordinary

94

worker some real sense of participation in the conduct and efficiency of the business.[81]

It is this emphasis on security as the "gateway" to the higher dimensions of service and solidarity that anticipates in a truly remarkable manner Abraham Maslow's theory of personality, and must be seen as one of the key principles of a humanistic social economics. It points to the social costs inherent in competition, and a strong case could be made that much of the contemporary emphasis on "me first" and consumerism exhibited since the 1970s may be explained by the vanishing job security among the young and, more generally, the highly competitive climate found in modern life.

Moreover, Hobson repeatedly stressed the relationship of job insecurity and character.[82] In his own voice:

> A weekly wage of bare efficiency with regular employment is socially far superior to a higher wage accompanied by greater insecurity of work. The former admits of modes of living and ready money payments: it conduces to steadiness of character and provision for the future without anxiety. Rapid and considerable fluctuations of wages, even with full employment, are damaging the character and stability of standards: but irregularity of employment is the most destructive agency to the character, the standard of comfort, the health and sanity of wage earners. The knowledge that he is liable at any time, from commercial or natural causes that lie entirely outside his control, to lose the opportunity to work and earn his livelihood, takes out of a man that confidence in the fundamental rationality of life which is essential to soundness of character. Religion, ethics, education can have little hold upon workers exposed to such powerful illustrations of unreason and injustice of industry and society.[83]

A similar effect can be expected from repetitive and meaningless work. Without ever mentioning the sociological term "alienation," Hobson devoted a chapter to "overspecialization in industrial life," deploring the "narrowing and monotonizing" of labor and the way it degrades and distorts the personality of the laborer and the worker as consumer.[84] The individual victim may not be consciously aware of the problem and even deny it. Still, "a man who is not interested in his work and does not recognize in it either beauty or utility," is, according to Hobson, "degraded by that work, whether he knows it or not."[85] Here again, efficient or cheap production is likely to have as collateral a significant human cost. In order to counteract this "externality" he suggests some measures of worker participation and economic democracy that educate a "clearer sense of social solidarity and service." However, he was skeptical about the prospects of such radical reforms as "seeking to oust the owners of capital from the government of industry and putting labor in its place," because he worried about problems in the securing of finance and the maintenance of discipline. Profit sharing and co-partnership, therefore, appeared to him to be the more practical goals.[86]

Besides the catalysts of job security and meaningful work, Hobson also pointed to the need to minimize perceptions of social injustice, emphasizing again the problem of unearned income. As "long as property appears to come miraculously or capriciously, irrespective of efforts or requirements, and as long as it is withheld irrationally, it is idle to preach 'the dignity of labour' or to inculcate sentiments of individual self-help," he explains.[87] Only a well-ordered and just economic system promotes the kind of trust and faith in the future that is necessary for the growth of personality and the common good.

That perceptions of fairness in society do influence individual character and motivation is repeatedly confirmed when people cheat on their taxes "because everybody else does." More generally, the more we see others as unwilling to cooperate, the more we rationalize self-centered tendencies. Once again, economists cannot admit such social effects, regardless of how true they may be, since they would deny the basic assumption of *exogenous* preferences serving as touchstones for *economic* welfare.

Hobson's social catalysts of human growth point to three main villains: an *excessive division of labor* stifling human creativity on the job, *competition* making for anxiety and insecurity and a *maldistribution of income and wealth* breeding a cynical and self-serving attitude. In his subsequent work, Hobson adds another culprit: the investor-owned corporation.[88] Owned by an impersonal "crowd of people" who only care about how much their investment yields, property becomes divorced from responsibility. "The modern owner of property is often unaware whether he is engaged in the liquor trade, in the rackrenting of city slums, or in the conduct of some sweated industry," hiding behind anonymity which serves as an effective screen. A company structured in this way, with absolution of social responsibility, has "neither soul to be saved nor body to be kicked."[89] Yet, given its enormous power in directing investment flows, it must be seen as a formidable stumbling block to a humanistic reconstruction of the economy.

In the final pages of his *Social Problem*, Hobson explored what light the new assignment of individual and social property throws upon the role of the state. He paints a picture of partial nationalization of industry, targeting, in particular, big business with some monopoly power, the postal service, railroads, utilities and other municipal services; but being anxious to avoid the perils of bureaucracy, he carved out a predominant role for private enterprise, which would continue to supply the comforts and luxuries of life, the reason for the latter being its greater sensitivity to the refined, erratic and individualistic demands of citizens.

In this type of mixed economic system, the state will also have to assume a *protective* function by being an employer of last resort, a provider of social insurance, enforcing a "living wage," policing conditions of labor and – another item he added later to the agenda – a guardian against pollution of the common air and water.[90] As already discussed, he also advocated a *redistributive* function involving progressive taxation and social expenditures for public goods. As a whole, Hobson's theories remain an oasis of "social liberalism" or "liberal socialism" within the arid landscape of economic orthodoxy.

Hobson's legacy

In terms of *political* developments, Hobson toward the end of his life had good reason to feel gratified: one country after another paid increasing attention to lessening the human costs of labor through legislating hours of work and the use of child labor, controlling unemployment and introducing accident insurance, factory hygiene and so on. But when it came to economic science, Hobson's new social economics of human welfare did not attract much attention in academic circles. It must have been one reason he felt it necessary to repeat his message. But at the same time, his reconstruction was never subjected to a critical scrutiny and openly attacked. This raises an interesting question: why did Hobson's social economics fall on deaf ears? Hobson himself addressed this question. For one, and more technically speaking, it may have been the introduction of the Austrian "real cost doctrine," whereby the real cost of anything is *not* the money cost, but the foregone utility of other things, something that tends to rule out any human consideration related to supply side of exchange. This type of substitution of a direct and relevant approach to costs for an indirect and irrelevant one, reminded Hobson of the definition of sugar as "the stuff which makes tea nasty when you don't put any in."[91]

Hobson suggests some other reasons. First, he blamed the new vogue of abstract, mathematical reasoning in economics operating on the assumption that all qualitative differences can be reduced to one dimension and solved by quantitative calculation. The offspring of the mathematical mind constructed an abstract economic system "operated by the movement of identical and infinitesimal units whose accurate adjustments produced an 'economic harmony.'" The acceptance of this new method, he felt, involves more than the craving of scientific men for exactitude: "Its imminent conservatism recommends it, not only to timid academic minds, but to the general body of possessing classes who, though they may be quite incapable of following its subtlety of reasoning, have sufficient intelligence to value its general conclusion as popularized by the press."[92] Quite obviously, he had not much regard for academic economists who he regarded as not only timid but also of "low vitality." Already in 1901, he devoted a chapter to the overspecialization of intellectual life, in which he described an unhealthy situation where in the universities "we have hundreds of men who thus completely lose themselves in work of research, absorbed by the smallness of the task they essay, and often hypnotized to torpor by gazing at it," with the natural result "that theories of life spun by overwrought brains of those who are not living a whole life cannot themselves be whole."[93] Even worse, the people who gravitate to university life tend to be men "terribly sensitive to the approval and disapproval of rulers and other authorities in the outside world." He saw them not so much as "the intellectual mercenaries of the vested interests as their volunteers."[94] All this is especially relevant in explaining the intellectual resistance to Hobson's work. He asks: "Why must the social nature of value be refused acceptance?" and gives the following reason:

> Because the analysis of economic distribution which would flow from its acceptance would disclose the flagrant inequity, inhumanity, and irrationality of all processes of actual distribution. *The condemnation alike of wealth and poverty, could then no longer be discussed as a sentimental attitude, but must rank as a scientific judgement of supreme importance.*[95]

Be this as it may, there is yet another plausible explanation: after Hobson's early macro heresy leading to his excommunication from academia, he was considered an unworthy economist on all matters, including his social economics. His rehabilitation by Keynes and others came too late, in the sense that few bothered to reexamine his other doctrines.

Nevertheless, Hobson, unlike Sismondi, had ultimate faith in the rationality of intellectual pursuits, trusting that "seeing facts and thinking straight are more attractive to the mind than seeing falsehoods and thinking crooked," so that in the long run truth would have to assert itself. All that was needed for this to happen was a large enough number and variety of independent and creative thinkers in free intercourse and cooperation.[96] Today, one still waits for economics to straighten itself out. And it may require quite some time given the fact that both contemporary micro- and macroeconomics seem to be further from redemption than they were at the end of Hobson's life.

At his passing, at the age of eighty-one years on April 1, 1940, Hobson left a life's work of over fifty books and hundreds of articles in journals and newspapers. Whatever the ultimate merit of his contributions to economic thought may be, he was, as G. D. H. Cole reminded readers in an *Economic Journal* obituary:

> above all else a man of inflexible principle [who] in spite of the less than positive treatment that he was subjected to by the representatives from orthodoxy left no trace of bitterness in his pen; he never

succumbed to polemics and personal attacks, and spoke his mind regardless whether anybody liked it or not, and whether what he said was attended to or simply ignored.[97]

He did nevertheless have a considerable influence. Besides being seen as the "Godfather" of the British Labour Party, his social doctrines indirectly through the American social economists J. M. Clark, Rexford Tugwell and John Ryan are an acknowledged source of inspiration behind the New Deal. Father John Ryan, a longtime practitioner of large chunks of John Hobson's social economics, also helped organize the Association for Social Economics and the *Review of Social Economy*, its journal.[98] It is in organizations and publications such as these, as well as in the vast literature of the post-Keynesian school, that John Hobson's spirit lives on and is being further developed.

Conclusion

John Hobson died almost one hundred years after Sismondi. Nowhere in any of his voluminous work did he refer to his older kin, even though there is reason to believe that he must have heard about the man.[99] Yet, the similarities between the two are too striking to be ignored.[100] Each in his own environment was confronted by serious postwar slumps that drove them to look for a new and more social path in economics. Each sought to reconstruct the prevailing doctrines in such a manner as to de-emphasize the accumulation of national wealth in favor of a better distribution of national income. First and foremost, this meant a new economics able to shed some light on the trade cycle. Only by a new focus on aggregate demand and national income could the recurring booms and busts of the economy, so detrimental to the poor, be better understood and eventually controlled. In the process, each rejected Say's Law, not in the naive sense of claiming that there would not be enough purchasing power to buy back what had been produced, but in the sense that the maldistribution of income made for too little consumption and too much investment in a dynamic sense, because new investment implies a growing capacity to produce consumer goods without adding enough to workers' income to be able to sell those goods at cost-covering prices. In other words, there are real limits to the speed at which wealth can be accumulated.

This macroeconomic critique went hand-in-hand with their protest that economics was relying much too much on unreal abstractions and the myth of self-adjusting market mechanics ensuring a benign state of equilibrium. Yet, wasn't the real world plagued by ongoing disequilibrium, especially in the labor market, with all its dire social consequences? Naturally, such a more realistic perspective led to an ethical critique of existing socioeconomic institutions and an appeal to government as a protector of the social interest.

Capitalism needed to be reformed and democratized, elements of injustice removed and some of its key institutions recast. But in the advocacy of these proposals, neither ever failed in their active commitment to class harmony, preferring social peace to the fiery tension of antagonistic class struggle. The path of social economics winds between the ideological fortresses of individualistic *laissez-faire* capitalism with its neglect of society, and a clumsy bureaucratic socialism drowning the person in the collective uniformity of the mass. It's a path that is being built as we go forward, led by a compass aiming at social justice and an uncompromising affirmation of the human dignity of all. Much has been accomplished by the tireless efforts of the pioneers, Sismondi and Hobson, and the labor of many others who came later. It all centers around an economics that does not shy away from incorporating social values grounded in a distinctly *human* perspective of a rational economy. It is here that social economics stands in stark and fundamental contrast to the ways of the prevailing mainstream discipline which seeks the impossible: to guide politics in the name of science rather than ethics. Chapter 5 will help us better understand the history and legitimacy of such a claim.

Notes

1 See A. Kadish, "The Non-Canonical Context of *The Physiology of Industry*," in J. Pheby (ed.), *J. A. Hobson after Fifty Years*, New York, St. Martin's Press, 1994.
2 J. A. Hobson, *Confessions of an Economic Heretic*, London, Allen, 1938, p. 30.
3 J. A. Hobson and A. F. Mummery, *The Physiology of Industry*, London, Murray, 1889, p. iv.
4 ibid., p. 51.
5 ibid., pp. 50–51.
6 ibid., p. 86.
7 ibid., p. 99.
8 ibid., pp. 105–106.
9 ibid., p. 109.
10 ibid., p. 113.
11 They also reject what has come to be known as the "Pigou effect," where people on fixed incomes will indeed gain by a fall in prices. Some people may be less affected by the general drop in money incomes, but only at the cost of others being hurt more. "If a mortgagee still gets his interest, the landlord suffers more severely in proportion" (ibid., p. 121). Moreover, they also reckon with the question of elasticity of demand to the extent that it is relevant to the issue.
12 ibid., p. 131.
13 Hobson, *Confessions of an Economic Heretic*, p. 30.
14 A. Kadish, "Rewriting the Confessions: Hobson and the Extension Movement," in M. Freeden (ed.), *Reappraising J. A. Hobson*, London, Unwin Hyman, 1990, p. 145.
15 J. A. Hobson, *The Problem of the Unemployed*, London, Methuen and Co., 1896, p. 90.
16 ibid., p. 91.
17 ibid., p. 88.

18 ibid., p. 79.
19 Between 1884 and 1903, only 5 percent of British emigration went to those "new territories."
20 John A. Hobson, *Imperialism: A Study* [1902], Ann Arbor, MI, University of Michigan Press, 1965, p. 84.
21 ibid., p. 87.
22 ibid., p. 93.
23 ibid., p. 75.
24 John A. Hobson, *The Economics of Unemployment*, London, George Allen and Unwin, 1922, p. 39.
25 ibid., pp. 91–96.
26 ibid., p. 97.
27 ibid., pp. 97–98.
28 Hobson and Mummery, *The Physiology of Industry*, pp. 206–207.
29 Hobson, *The Economics of Unemployment*, p. 100.
30 ibid., pp. 104, 105, 107.
31 For a summary of that correspondence see J. King, "J. A. Hobson's Macroeconomics: The Last Ten Years (1930–1940)," in Pheby, *J. A. Hobson after Fifty Years*, pp. 124–142.
32 J. M. Keynes, *The General Theory of Employment, Interest, and Money*, New York, Harcourt Brace Jovanovich, 1964, p. 365.
33 ibid., p. 370.
34 ibid., p. 371.
35 Quoted in King, "J. A. Hobson's Macroeconomics: The Last Ten Years (1930–1940)," p. 140.
36 Hobson, *Confessions of an Economic Heretic*, p. 193.
37 J. M. Clark, "J. A. Hobson, Heretic and Pioneer," *Journal of Social Philosophy*, July 1940, p. 357.
38 E. D. Domar, "Expansion and Employment," *American Economic Review*, 1947, vol. 37, p. 52.
39 See Joan Robinson's "Review of R. F. Harrod, *Towards a Dynamic Economics*," *Economic Journal*, 1949, vol. 59, pp. 68–85.
40 M. Schneider, "Modelling Hobson's Underconsumption Theory," in Pheby, *J. A. Hobson after Fifty Years*, pp. 100–123.
41 See M. Lavoie, *Foundations of Post-Keynesian Economics*, Brookfield, VT, Elgar, 1992, for constructing post-Keynesian economics on a foundation of basic human needs.
42 T. Lawson, "The Nature of Post-Keynesianism and its Link to Other Traditions: A Realist Perspective," *Journal of Post-Keynesian Economics*, Summer 1994, vol. 16:14, pp. 503–538.
43 The literature of post-Keynesian economics is vast and rapidly growing. Since it is readily available, we will not cover its essential nature and evolution here. For an introduction the interested reader is instead referred to P. J. Reynolds, *Political Economy: A Synthesis of Kaleckian and Post Keynesian Economics*, New York, St. Martin's Press, 1987.
44 Hobson, *Confessions of an Economic Heretic*, p. 38.
45 J. A. Hobson, *John Ruskin: Social Reformer*, Boston, MA, Dana Estes and Co., 1898, p. viii.
46 J. A. Hobson, *The Social Problem* [1901], reprint, Bristol, Thoemmes Press, 1996, p. 38.
47 ibid., p. 39.
48 ibid., p. 64.

49 ibid., p. 41.
50 ibid., p. 43.
51 ibid., p. 50.
52 ibid., p. 51.
53 ibid., pp. 65–66.
54 ibid., p. 66.
55 J. N. Keynes, *The Scope and Method of Political Economy*, London, Macmillan and Co., 1890.
56 ibid., p. 47.
57 Hobson, *The Social Problem*, p. 66.
58 ibid., p. 67.
59 See Sismondi quote in Chapter 2, p. 38.
60 Hobson, *The Social Problem*, p. 68. A similar reservation to Keynes' point can also be found in a "Manifesto" of the American social economics movement: "If a writer confines himself to the positive side of the science, to analysis and description, in a textbook, for example, if he describes the economic causes and the prevalence of starvation wages without pointing out their immorality, some of his readers will draw the conclusion that such rates of wages are not morally wrong, or, at least, that they arouse in the writer no moral indignation. The writer will have neglected the opportunity and the duty of contributing to human betterment and promoting the common good," J. A. Ryan, "Two Objectives for Catholic Economists," *Review of Social Economy*, December 1942, vol. 1:1, p. 4.
61 Hobson, *The Social Problem*, p. 69.
62 ibid., p. 54.
63 ibid., p. 56.
64 ibid., p. 63.
65 ibid., p. 59.
66 See A. Rosenberg, *Economics–Mathematical Politics or the Science of Diminishing Returns*, Chicago, IL, University of Chicago Press, 1992.
67 Hobson, *The Social Problem*, p. 70.
68 ibid., p. 72.
69 ibid., p. 72. He proceeds to show that even economists themselves are not wholly comfortable in applying the quantitative method. It shows in the diagram of textbooks graphing a *descending schedule of marginal utility* such as Jevons in his *Theory of Political Economy* [1871] in which the economist "is obliged to admit that the utility of the expenditure upon necessaries is 'infinite' – i.e. that the quantity of money spent on them is no index or possible measure of the good got out of them" (ibid., p. 73). This is so because the first sums of money budgeted and spent are not governed by a merely passing desire but by some rough reference to a true and wider standard of utility, in this case the value of survival. A sane man will not indulge in a quantitative comparison between the "infinitely" greater value given to necessities versus the "utility" imputed to conveniences and luxuries. A similar case can be made in distinguishing between conveniences and luxuries.
70 ibid., p. 76. For a rigorous endorsement of this type of qualitative choice, see N. Georgescu-Roegen, "Choice, Expectations and Measurability," *Quarterly Journal of Economics*, 1954, vol. 68, pp. 504–534.
71 J. A. Hobson, *Work and Wealth: A Human Valuation*, London, Allen, 1914, p. 332.
72 ibid., pp. 332, 334.
73 Hobson, *The Social Problem*, p. 98.
74 ibid., pp. 99–100.

75 ibid., p. 112.
76 ibid., p. 149.
77 J. A. Hobson, *Wealth and Life: A Study in Values*, London, Allen, 1929, p. 230.
78 Hobson, *The Social Problem*, p. 45. The author's research corroborates Hobson's answer on this point. See M. Lutz, "On the Quality of the Industrial Earnings Structure in Manufacturing," *Industrial Relations*, February 1977, vol. 16:1, pp. 61–70.
79 Hobson, *The Social Problem*, p. 45.
80 Hobson, *Work and Wealth*, pp. 289–290.
81 Hobson, *Wealth and Life*, p. 45.
82 What else could be more challenging to the economist's basic assumption of exogenous preferences?
83 Hobson, *Work and Wealth*, p. 199.
84 Hobson, *The Social Problem*, ch. 13.
85 Hobson, *Work and Wealth*, p. 88.
86 J. A. Hobson, *Incentives in the New Industrial Order* [1922], Westport, CT, Hyperion Press, 1980, p. 10.
87 Hobson, *Work and Wealth*, p. 298.
88 See Hobson, *Work and Wealth*, p. 252; *Wealth and Life*, pp. 146–147.
89 Hobson, *Wealth and Life*, pp. 147, 146.
90 Hobson, *The Social Problem*; *Wealth and Life*, p. 383.
91 J. A. Hobson, *Free Thought in the Social Sciences*, London, Allen, 1926, p. 104.
92 ibid., pp. 107, 108.
93 Hobson, *The Social Problem*, pp. 231, 235.
94 Hobson, *Free Thought in the Social Sciences*, pp. 271, 55.
95 ibid., p. 246, emphasis added.
96 ibid., p. 283.
97 G. D. H. Cole, "Obituary: J. A. Hobson 1858–1940," *Economic Journal*, June–September 1940, vol. 50, pp. 351–359.
98 The new Association was founded in 1942 and Ryan's inaugural message has been reprinted as "Two Objectives for Catholic Economists" (pp. 1–5). There he sums up his inaugural message in one concluding sentence: "While economics should be treated primarily as a positive science, it is in large part also a normative science, and its main usefulness is as a means of promoting the common good and social justice." Already in his first book, *A Living Wage: Its Ethical and Economic Aspects*, New York, Macmillan, 1910, there is heavy mention of Hobson's theory of unemployment and low wages. Furthermore, in his autobiography, *Social Doctrine in Action: A Personal History*, New York, Harper and Brothers Publishers, 1941, pp. 64–69, he describes in detail the influence Hobson had on his own work.
99 See Schneider, "Modelling Hobson's Underconsumption Theory."
100 On this point, see J. Allett, *New Liberalism: The Political Economy of J. A. Hobson*, Toronto, University of Toronto Press, 1981, p. 99; M. F. Bleany, *Underconsumption Theories: A Historical and Critical Analysis*, New York, International Publishers, 1976, pp. 151, 164; Schneider, "Modelling Hobson's Underconsumption Theory," pp. 102, 122; E. E. Nemmers, *Hobson and Underconsumption*, Clifton, NJ, Augustus M. Kelley, 1972, pp. 5–9. For the kinship between Sismondi and Ruskin, see J. C. Sherburne, *John Ruskin or the Ambiguities of Abundance*, Cambridge, MA, Harvard University Press, 1972, pp. 98–99 and ch. 6.

5

ETHICS, SCIENCE AND ECONOMIC WELFARE

The picture that has been sketched of the birth, evolution and nature of classic social economics should make one thing clear: its ultimate aim is to lay down *principles of economic policy*, to guide the policy maker in ascertaining what is conducive to social welfare and what is not. This pragmatic point of view follows the lead of Sismondi, who, in the opening paragraph of his initial essay, subordinated political economy to the "science of government" with the object of securing the physical well-being of man, and of teaching government "the true system of administering national wealth."[1] In other words, social economics sees itself as an essentially *normative* science. The emphasis on social values and the social good does not, of course, preclude the traditional scientific undertakings of description, analysis and explanation as the efforts of both Sismondi and Hobson to understand macroeconomic fluctuations and depressions testify. But social economics goes beyond such factual studies to make statements also regarding policy and the institutional order, and do so as part of economic *knowledge*. This approach is especially characteristic of Hobson, whose entire life's work was a quest to articulate the requirements of a more *rational* socioeconomic order and to suggest the means toward realizing this ideal in practice.

1. The challenge of moral skepticism[2]

Elementary economics, as it has been taught for decades, rejects the normative characteristic of social economics *in principle* as incompatible with science, the factual analysis and scientific apparatus of the so-called "positive economics." Moreover, this common indictment of a normative economic approach is voiced by virtually all other schools of economic thought, ranging from right to left of the political spectrum. This all-embracing consensus can be readily illustrated: "Economics cannot pronounce on the validity of ultimate judgments of value," says Lionel Robbins, who refers values and obligations to the exclusive business of ethics.[3] Swedish Nobel Prize winner Gunnar Myrdal, in his earlier work, recommends that the economist leave the making of evaluative premises to the politician.[4] Another Nobel Prize

104

laureate, John Hicks, declares that any evaluative attempt at prescription must always depend on the personal values of the investigator, and thereby the normative economist's policy conclusions "can possess no validity for anyone who lives outside the circle in which these values find acceptance." Worse, for Hicks, a values-based economics must be seen as a "dreadful thing to accept," highly "conducive to the euthanasia of our science."[5] Others like Joan Robinson, Friedrich V. Hayek, Oscar Lange and Paul Samuelson, to name a few, hold similar opinions. Perhaps more interesting and illuminating are the observations of economic historian Joseph Schumpeter. After granting that there "is no harm in the physician's contention that the advice he gives follows from scientific premises, because the – strictly speaking extra-scientific – value judgment involved is common to all normal men in our cultural environment. We all mean pretty much the same thing when we speak of health and find it desirable to enjoy good health," he goes on to say in no uncertain terms, "but we do not mean the same thing when we speak of the Common Good, simply because we hopelessly differ in those cultural visions with reference to which the common good has to be defined in a particular case."[6] Kenneth Arrow, too, agrees that an objective social good independent of individual desires does not exist, and he endorses the "nominalist temperament" of contemporary academia in which the existence of a social ideal is relegated to the *meaningless*.[7]

Subroto Roy clarifies and explains this united front, a formidable consensus according to which this book – in claiming legitimacy as *economics* – would be seen as a "dreadful," "meaningless" and futile endeavor.[8]

Roy traces the intellectual source of this unanimity of views to the eighteenth-century teachings of philosopher David Hume. For Hume, the wickedness of a "vicious action," such as willful murder, is not a fact and does not really exist. The murder may have happened, but the attribute of wickedness, he insisted, can never be found "till you turn your reflection into your own breast, and find a sentiment of disappropriation, which arises in you, toward this action."[9] Things like "wickedness" or evil are conjured up by feeling, or sentiment, but not an object of reason. To him there is no such thing as a moral fact and, without it, no possibility of moral reasoning or moral truths. In short, Hume denies ethics any objective status and relegates it to a matter of personal opinion, an arena where differences can never be reconciled through reasoning and argument. The modern economist's embrace of Hume's moral skepticism with its denial of a cognitive ethics will similarly spoil any project of rational policy proposals, as, for example, the alleged goodness of free international trade. Social economics, therefore, since the time of Hume, has stood condemned as an essentially illegitimate enterprise in its social discourse.

Moreover, the whole idea that the scope of economic expertise can be stretched to the point of telling people what kind of policies they ought to implement, is decried as a fallback to medieval authoritarianism, or a return to Plato's philosopher kingdom. It contradicts the cherished liberal ideal that political principles and decisions in a democracy are the sole business of the electorate. The economist, after all, is not an elected official who speaks for the people. This, of course, does not preclude academic advisors in government, but, and here is the important distinction, the economist must confine him/herself to matters of *technical* detail. Once the finance minister, or any other member of government, has posed the normative premises of "what ought to be done," the economist as technician only enters at that point to counsel the best course of action for attaining the political goal. Would it not, therefore, follow that the social economics of Sismondi and Hobson – with its proposals for legislative action to minimize poverty, redistribute income and improve working conditions – in its flagrant disregard of this restrictive rule of the economist, would also have to be censured?

The dual charge of trespassing against science and democracy is the very ground on which the damning consensus is built. As illustrated, it is held up by strong and well-known personalities in the economics discipline. But its rational support, and how much it can be justified, is an entirely different matter. Obviously, philosophy has not stood still since the days of David Hume, and today one finds increasingly an acceptance of the compatibility of morality and reason. True, ethical facts are not observable in the same way as are other facts, and it may also be readily granted that many of our personal values are subjective. But these concessions do not preclude the existence of moral facts that dwell in the realm of reason. As one philosopher puts it: "moral truths are truths of reason; that is, a moral judgment is true if it is backed by better reasons than the alternatives."[10]

The difficulty with accepting Hume's point of view is that it is inherently self-destructive. For one, take note of the following direct and simple contradiction emphasized by Roy: the economist embraces a Humean brand of moral skepticism for the sake of protecting science and democracy against dogmatism and tyranny. But aren't these learned opinions themselves nothing but opinions? Thus the economist needs to rely on what amounts to a patently moral proposition, but to do so within the framework of a theory of knowledge that was explicitly coined to *deny* making any moral propositions with cognitive significance.[11] Clearly, the demand for scientific integrity and knowledge must be construed as conferring on morality some objectivity as well. To insist that we ought to eliminate statements of "ought" makes no sense. Furthermore, applying the same dose of skepticism to other fields, such as history, natural science and psychology, sterilizes knowledge claims there as well. For example, if the skeptic insists that every premise in a deductive argument must be justified by deductive reasoning, one must question the premise behind the premise in a never-ending process of infinite regress. A similar fate awaits empirical knowledge, where Hume himself applied his debilitating skepticism in raising doubts about the *possibility of induction*. "There can be no demonstrative argument to prove that those instances of which we had no experience resemble those of which we have had experience."[12] We can never, for example, be sure that the sun will rise the next morning just because we have the experience that it has been doing so every day for as far back as people can remember. It goes without saying that such skepticism will undermine much of our faith in the currently fashionable (inductive) econometric techniques – as Keynes had already pointed out when they were first conceived of in the 1930s.[13] Obviously, an unflinching and radical skepticism of this kind destroys not only ethics, but science as well, leading Roy to conclude: "We should have to admit frankly to the scholarly community that since there is nothing which may be properly called objective knowledge the Department of Economics in every university should be closed down, or there might just as well be a Department of Astrology on campus too, teaching and researching the reading of palms, the writing of horoscopes, and so on."[14] Happily, there is a more constructive antidote to the self-contradictory moral skepticism of Hume and his modern economist followers: sheer *common sense*.[15] This approach, strongly endorsed by the famous moral philosopher G. E. Moore, was explicitly invoked by John Hobson as early as 1914 for the purpose of justifying social values.[16]

All said, it appears that the "formidable consensus" shared by celebrated economic experts and brought to bear against the idea of a social economics may itself rest on a deceptive foundation and so give rise to a premature conviction that would benefit from a great deal more reflection. One should not forget that the earlier "consensus" against Sismondi's and Hobson's macroeconomics turned out to have been precocious and ill-advised.

At the same time, the moral skepticism so deeply entrenched in the hearts and minds of today's economists makes the proposing of policy objectives a highly treacherous affair, one that calls for utmost vigilance by the social economist in order to minimize controversy. Professor Schumpeter's point about human *health* serving as a *legitimate end* to the science of medicine since "we all mean pretty much the same thing when we speak of health," may be taken as a guide on how to proceed in the making of economic prescriptions for a "healthy society," understood as the common good, a point discussed in Chapter 6. More generally, for a social economics to have solid standing in a Court of Reason, it should muster not only equal but also *greater* rational appeal than its mainstream counterpart. The remainder of the present chapter clears the ground for such a challenge by showing how vulnerable the science of orthodox economic policy really is.

2. Theory and policy in historical perspective

Everything in economics starts with Adam Smith, and it is no different with the questions relating to the place and legitimacy of policy proposals. But times were different then: natural law philosophy still dominated the intellectual scene. The prevailing belief system was that the world had been created perfectly, that whatever was "natural" was the way Providence had intended it to be, or as good as it possibly could be. In other words, the natural, or what would be apart from human interference, was the ideal. To Smith and his contemporaries, the goal of political economy was the establishment and maintenance of the "simple system of natural liberty" allowing room for individual independence and initiative. It was the task of the statesman to establish and maintain this system. Smith's advice on policy amounted to an essentially negative task of dismantling all "unnatural" restrictions preventing free exchange and free competition. All other good things, including the rapid accumulation of national wealth, would follow automatically. The role of government in terms of Smithian philosophy was echoed by Thomas Jefferson in his 1801 inaugural address, in which he proposed a state "which shall restrain men from injuring one another, which shall leave them otherwise free to regulate their own pursuits of industry and improvement, and shall not take from the mouth of labour the bread it has earned."[17] It was, of course, precisely this optimistic faith in the benefice of nature (including self-interested human *nature*) against which Sismondi felt the need to protest a few decades later, demanding, among other things, state interference to rein in the often destructive force of free competition.

After Smith, it became more and more difficult to identify the actual or natural with the desirable. For example, growing apprehensions about the natural tendency of population growth to outstrip the food supply helped, in the words of Terrence Hutchison, "to strip the adjective 'natural' from some of its optimistic penumbra of benefice and justice."[18] Thereby, the stage was set for a separation of the "is" and the "ought," a new development that led Jeremy Bentham to make a distinction between the science of political economy and its application as an *art* in which the distinguishing feature of the latter was its need to draw from other "sciences" such as ethics and politics. Both science and art implied each other, both were necessary, and both were equally scientific. Such a complementary view prevailed in the England of the 1820s, but it was soon challenged by the early (and not yet quite reformed) J. S. Mill,[19] and most famously by Nassau Senior in *An Outline of the Science of Political Economy* (1836). Senior, like Bentham before him, separated science (dealing with wealth) from art (concerned with happiness), but unlike Bentham, he had no place for the practical or art dimension within political economy. To him it was not the business of the political economist to make policy recommendations, in part because he felt that meaningful policy had to go beyond mere economic premises, but also, and perhaps more importantly, because he was concerned that as soon as we advise, dissuade, approve or censure, "we cease to be scientific."[20] Not everybody agreed with Senior's hard-nosed approach: John McCulloch, another leading figure of that period, voiced strong opposition, and the more mature J. S. Mill readily mingled economics with social philosophy and moral values, some-thing that allowed him to feel much more ambivalent about competition. For the same reason, he accorded a higher priority to the *distribution* of national wealth than to its accumulation.[21] Nevertheless, as late as 1873, Senior's interdiction of rational policy recommendations was to be repeated by the last classical economist, John E. Cairnes.[22]

After the Marginalist Revolution of the 1870s, economists radically recon-sidered the "economic problem," meaning the goal of economics. Instead of economic growth, the satisfaction of consumer wants took center stage, and, with this reconceptualization, *efficiency* now became the new buzz word. It meant the best possible satisfaction of given wants and market demand with the existing resources (land, labor and capital) and the prevailing tech-nology. The ticket to such an efficient economy was once again the free market, but the highway to economic welfare was no longer the way to speed up the growth of wealth. Instead, it was built on such idealized notions as *"perfect* competition," *"perfect* mobility" of the factors of production, *"perfect* information" on the part of economic agents, and so forth. In short, economics became more of an abstract exercise, a game to be played on an increasingly theoretical level by academics eager to exhibit their command of elegant formalism and logical rigor. Against this new background, the neo-classical economists of that period, led by Henry Sidgwick and Alfred Marshall, felt that for the sake of practical use by the policy maker, a less formal and more pragmatically realistic type of theory was required. This new theory, now known as neo-classical *welfare economics*, would complement the highly abstract economics with its assumption of the various "perfections" for an efficient resource allocation. It still accepted the general idea of free competi-tion as a desirable framework for a liberal society, but now focused on various concrete *exceptions*, on cases in which *laissez-faire* and private interests would *not* be expected to lead to the common good.

The philosopher-economist Sidgwick, even though he too stressed the fundamental difference between "is" and "ought" and the fact that there "is no generally accepted axiom for judging the rightness or goodness of different modes of division," proposed in the final part of his *Principles of Political Economy* (1883) a revival of economics as an art, which would include:

> besides the Theory of provision of governmental expenditures, (1) the Art of making the proportion of produce to population a maximum, taking generally as a measure the ordinary standard of exchange value, so far as it can be applied; and (2) the Art of rightly distri-buting produce among members of the community, whether on any principle of Equity or Justice, or on the economic principle of making the whole produce as useful as possible.[23]

He proceeded to discuss cases in which socially desirable goods and services (such as lighthouses, reforestation, promotion of scientific research and so forth) were not in the individual private interest and as a result would have to be provided by the public. Moreover, he also addressed the cases in which the social and the individual interests tend to diverge, as in the excessive exploitation of natural resources, and even the inter-temporal conflict between present and future generations.[24] In a way, he has to be seen as the first orthodox *welfare* economist.

Sidgwick's proposal was not welcomed by his contemporaries. They preferred to follow the advice of Cambridge's John Neville Keynes, who warned that it was not the function of science to pass ethical judgment and that "the attempt to fuse together enquiries as to what is and enquiries as to what ought to be, is likely to stand in the way of our giving clear and unbiased answers to any set of questions."[25] Of course, it was against this view that John Hobson sought to expand the scope to include the "ought," and went about constructing his social economics.

Alfred Marshall used his doctrine of consumer and producer surplus to suggest that an efficient satisfaction of consumer demand might require tax-financed government subsidies to some industries (as, for example, electric utilities) afflicted by losses due to economies of scale. These and many more propositions of welfare were intertwined with the more "positive" microeconomic theory. In all likelihood, elements of welfare economics would have occupied a more extensive and prominent part, had Marshall — although very much concerned with the development of human character, as expressed in his footnotes and marginalia[26] — not also been so occupied with the question of precise scientific measurement. Instead, he preferred to center his economics around *given* wants, market prices and the measuring rod of money. Not surprisingly, in his *Principles* (1890) the logic of price theory came to overshadow his more sporadic and more *ad hoc* contributions to welfare economics. The obvious task was for someone who, following the lines of Sidgwick, could present in a separate and integral way a unified theory of neo-classical welfare. This was accomplished by Marshall's successor at Cambridge, Arthur Pigou, with his celebrated book *Wealth and Welfare* (1912).

Pigou's neo-classical welfare economics

Pigou's welfare economics stands as an attempt to generalize and complete the program started by Sidgwick and Marshall. His analysis steers away from formalist abstraction, logical rigor and elegance, in favor of an orientation more suitable for practical applications, explaining that "it is the promise of fruit and not of light that chiefly merits our regard."[27] Like Marshall, Pigou restricted his analytical focus to existing (and constant) tastes and preferences and "that part of social welfare that can be brought directly or indirectly into relation with the measuring rod of money."[28] He called that component of human welfare, *economic* welfare. In doing so, he still followed the other neo-classical economists in insisting on the fact–value distinction, maintaining that economics itself "cannot be an art or directly enunciate precepts of government," that it is a positive science of "what is," not a normative science of "what ought to be." His welfare economics was an attempt to reduce value judgments to a minimum, to a few general propositions that would be acceptable to reasonable people. It was mainly microeconomic in nature, discussing welfare in relation to national income in terms of its *volume* and *distribution*. Yet, in his first edition, he was also concerned about its *variability*, meaning the macroeconomic problem of fluctuations in unemployment. Concerning the variability aspect, Pigou felt that it was reasonable to suppose that "any cause which diminishes the variability of the national dividend, provided that it neither diminishes its volume nor injures its distribution, will, in general, increase economic welfare."[29] There never was, perhaps, a time when orthodox and social economics, in spite of other fundamental differences, had so much in common. But soon thereafter, involuntary unemployment was once again ignored, and to this day welfare analysis has proceeded on the traditional neo-classical assumption of full employment.

A good part of Pigou's welfare economics is still very much alive today, in particular, the distinction between social cost and private cost: very often, he pointed out, private cost/benefit calculations lead to decisions and actions that have "spillover" effects on third parties. For example, the dumping of toxic chemicals in a river may indeed minimize *private* costs, but certainly not the costs to society. Such spillovers, being *external* to the market transactions, were also called "externalities." Similarly, the private benefits accruing from some actions, such as education and vaccinations, often involve benefits to others as well. Pigou felt that such activities would not be sufficiently undertaken in the marketplace, leaving it to the government to provide additional incentives for their production or use.

But Pigou's welfare economics became much more daring and controversial when he discussed poverty and the distribution of national income. The center of the controversy is found in a chapter titled "Economic Welfare and Changes in the Distribution of the National Dividend." There one reads that "it is evident that any transference of income from a relatively rich man to a relatively poor man of similar temperament, since it enables more intense wants to be satisfied at the expense of less intense wants, must increase the aggregate sum of satisfactions."[30] Of course, this proposition was conditional on the greater equality not interfering with the level of production. Furthermore, the words "of similar temperament" were inserted to preclude the possibility that a poor person is generally unable to get the same type of benefit or utility from spending income. On that point, he later elaborates: "it must be conceded, of course, that, if the rich and the poor were of two races with different mental constitutions . . . the possibility of increasing welfare by this type of change would be seriously doubtful." Moreover, even within the same race, the rich man, "from the nature of his upbringing and training," may be assumed to spend his income more wisely. But Pigou immediately counters that, "after a time, more especially if the time is long enough to allow a new generation to grow up – [the poor's] possession of such [higher income] will make possible the development in them, through education and otherwise, of capacities and faculties adapted for the enjoyment of the enlarged income." For this reason, "the differences in temperament and tastes between the rich and the poor are overcome by the very fact of shifting of income between them," Pigou contends.[31]

The debate on interpersonal comparisons of utility

Nevertheless, the assumption of equal capacity of happiness was directly assailed by another leading economist, Lionel Robbins, and his attack led to the first round in what is now called the debate over *interpersonal comparisons of utility*. Robbins insisted that when talking about (and comparing) two different individuals and their utilities, one is bound to proceed unscientifically, since the level of satisfaction of other people cannot be observed. Pigou's assumption of equal human capacities may be reasonable and convenient, but, said Robbins, "there is no way of proving that the assumption rests on ascertainable fact."[32]

What Robbins is claiming is another aspect of extreme moral skepticism, the philosophy of solipsism, the belief that all one can possibly experience is one's own feelings. It is a position that would question the very possibility of knowledge in psychology, understood as the science of the human mind. If we cannot know, through observation, that others indeed have a mind, how could we ever theorize about the human mind? Now it is, of course, true that a person does have privileged access to his or her *own* experience. Nobody can experience my pain or pleasure the same way I can, but – and this part is overlooked – my own way of experiencing what I experience is not the *only* way to know my state of mind. There are different ways of knowing. As Roy puts it, "just as the historian can know what happened at Waterloo . . . without having to know it in the way someone who was there knows it, so I can know how you feel something without having to know it in the way you know how to feel it."[33] Women who have themselves given birth may be able to understand the pains of childbirth in a way others cannot, and women in general may be able to understand that experience better than men can. Nevertheless, this does not rule out an objective judgment that childbirth can be very painful. We can and do take another's words to essentially mean the same thing we mean by those words. So when someone complains that he is hungry, or when someone describes the pains of childbirth, we can understand what that person means. To deny this is to deny the very basis of communication: that words, any words, have meaning.

More generally, Robbins' objection, offered in the name of science, is not only bad advice for the economist, but also is contradicted by life in the real world. Take the legal system, for example. The courts regularly attempt rational judgments arrived at by careful deliberations, as to, for instance, who should have custody of a child in a divorce case. Similarly, one can readily imagine the dire implications for our legal institutions and the penal code if we doubted an essentially similar capacity for everybody to endure punishment of one kind or another. Following Robbins, we could not really say that a $5 parking ticket to be paid by Mr. A is less punitive than a $500 ticket Mr. B got for driving under the influence. Could it not be, the scientific economist would ask, that Mr. B is a "highly efficient pleasure machine" (a phrase economists liked to use to refer to someone's capacity to derive happiness from life)?[34] If Mr. A and Mr. B have different capacities, it may under some circumstances be justified to go easy on a highly sensitive driver for his OUI (operating under the influence) and to dole out a harsher fine for a coarse individual with little capacity to experience pain for parking on the wrong side of a street. How do we know, how can we really "prove" that the assumption of treating everybody equally "rests on ascertainable fact"? To treat everybody the same before the law, the scientific economist would maintain, is as arbitrary as treating people in a discriminating manner. Therefore, one might want to conclude, we should dispense with the penal code and leave each case for the judge to decide.

Returning to the debate seven years later in his 1938 presidential address to the prestigious British Economics Association, Roy Harrod reminded his colleague, Robbins, that the whole basis of *any* economic policy recommendations depended upon assuming comparability between individuals.

> If the comparability of utility to different individuals is strictly pressed, not only are the prescriptions of the welfare school ruled out, but all prescriptions whatsoever. The economist as an advisor is completely stultified, and, unless his speculations be regarded as of paramount aesthetic value, he had better be suppressed completely. No, some sort of postulate of equality has to be assumed. But it should be carefully framed and used with great caution, always subject to the proviso "unless the contrary can be shown."[35]

Of course, Harrod is advising caution, but he concludes nevertheless – equal capacity for happiness should be assumed *in principle*, unless the contrary can be shown. And this would mean, of course, that, other things being equal, a greater equality is indeed objectively desirable.

Robbins immediately responded to Harrod in an article that appeared in the following issue of the *Economic Journal*, and his answer is revealing.[36]

He begins by admitting that originally he had found Pigou's welfare proposition appealing, and felt that the approach of counting each person as one is "less likely to lead us astray." But then he came across an incident in a story he was reading that began to stir his doubts. The story involved a British official in India who was trying to explain the egalitarian meaning of Benthamism (utilitarianism) to a high-caste Brahmin. The Brahmin replied, "but that cannot possibly be right. I am ten times as capable of happiness as that untouchable over there." Although Robbins had no sympathy for the Brahmin's position, he was disturbed that there was no scientific way to prove the Brahmin wrong. This led him to conclude that the assumption of equal capacity for happiness was strictly a moral one or a value judgment, and was separate from the other propositions of economics.

But this separation did not leave him content: "For it meant, as Mr. Harrod has rightly insisted, that economics as a science could say nothing by way of prescription." Therefore, Robbins accepted the necessity for economics to make this value judgment: "I was bound to admit that what I was doing was simply to carry one stage further a very common and almost universally accepted practice. Economists recognized that their prescriptions regarding policy were conditional upon the acceptance of norms lying outside economics." Robbins, too, admitted that for economics to be useful it had to take a stand one way or the other — it had to side either with Bentham and Saint Paul that all people are considered equal, or with the Brahmin and Hitler that they are not. Robbins is quite clear where he stands with his choice: "I think that the assumption of equality comes from outside [of economics], and that its justification is more ethical than scientific. But we all agree that it is fitting that such assumptions should be made and their implications explored with the aid of the economist's technique."[37]

In coming to terms with Harrod and Pigou, Robbins seems almost apologetic for his previous criticism: "I confess I was very surprised . . . All that I had intended . . ." And in his conclusion he winds up on a note that is nothing less than humanistic:

> In the realm of action, at any rate, the real difference of opinion is not between those who dispute concerning the exact area to be designated by the adjective scientific, but between those who hold that human beings should be treated as if they were equal and those who hold that they should not.[38]

In conclusion, then, it appears that Robbins seemed willing to live with a basic proposition that was out of bounds of a strictly scientific approach. Yet, and this is rather puzzling, Robbins has been pictured as putting closure to a long debate by scoring a rather speedy knockout. So, for example, the great historian of economic analysis, Joseph Schumpeter, could observe when writing in the 1940s that the idea that satisfactions of different people can be compared and, in particular, summed up into "General Welfare of society as a whole," is one that "few economists will care to defend nowadays," and he refers to Robbins' 1938 article as an example of this rejection. Given our rendering of the debate, in particular, Robbins' concession speech, this is a curious conclusion that raises eyebrows. True, Robbins did not concede his basic point that such comparisons are impossible on scientific grounds. On the other hand, he was moved to endorse comparability as an ethical postulate that needed to be brought into economics. Knowledge being factual, does it not go beyond the scientific to embrace moral facts as well? Even Schumpeter himself softened his stand on the whole issue by recognizing that utility comparisons are not altogether meaningless.[39]

After the dust had settled, American social economist John Maurice Clark summed up the sorry state of welfare theory as follows:

> The form and theory which now bears the name can without real unfairness be described as welfare economics with the welfare left out, in a remarkably resolute attempt to meet the real or supposed requirement of economic science. Rejecting "interpersonal comparisons" this body of theory seems to end in rather complete agnosticism, aside from policies that increase the national dividend without making anybody worse off. But the existence of a single disadvantaged person acts as a veto on scientific approval of any policy — one cannot be scientifically certain that his loss does not outweigh the gains of many.[40]

Clark's disappointment merely echoes and reflects what both Harrod and Robbins had agreed on fifteen years earlier. But there remains another mystery: economists, in spite of having decided that interpersonal comparisons were invalid and had to be avoided at all costs, have *not* remained silent on policy matters. They continue with business as usual, glorifying the efficiency of free competition at home and abroad, deploring the distorting effect of monopoly on resource allocation; and they still appear to do so in the name of economic *science*. In other words, what Harrod, Robbins and Clark claimed could *not* be done, they were and are simply still doing. The puzzle might be easily solved if one allows for the possibility of a new breakthrough, a new technique that would put the welfare back into scientific welfare economics. And this is indeed what at first appeared to be happening.

3. The rise of the "New" Welfare Economics

The skepticist impasse deplored by Harrod and Robbins was believed to have been circumvented when, in the late thirties, Nicholas Kaldor, another great name of the period, proposed the idea of a so-called "compensation test."[41] If there is a choice between two alternative social states, let us say a tariff on Chinese shoes or no tariff, there are bound to be conflicting interests; whatever we end up deciding, there will always be losers and there will always be winners. But now comes the new idea: *if* the group of people that gain from a policy change are able to fully compensate the losers, and have something left over besides, it ought to be seen as a good policy move that will enhance economic welfare. So, for example, if tariffs could be reduced and *only a part* of the consumer gains used to fully indemnify the American shoe industrialists, together with their workers and suppliers, then there would be no losers, only winners.

At first sight, the Kaldor proposal does look promising. Obviously, there is the (rather formidable) practical problem of determining just who is entitled to compensation and just how much should be granted. Still, to the extent that necessary compensation ends up actually being paid, we would have a new mechanism to make statements concerning policy without having to make interpersonal comparisons of utility. Yet, such a theoretically simple (albeit practically complex) solution is *not* what Kaldor meant to propose. He cleverly sidestepped the problem of *actual* compensation by professing that such compensation does *not* need actually to be paid. The mere possibility of indemnification, or *hypothetical* compensation, is sufficient for examining the potential social benefits of a policy change. Economists applauded, the Harrod impasse seemed to be overcome and it appeared that a value-neutral and operational welfare economics had finally been worked out.[42]

Much of mainstream normative economics still stands on this foundation even today. But there have been critical voices from the beginning, one of them belonging to William J. Baumol, a respected American economist.[43] What troubled Baumol was the implicit and hidden assumption behind the hypothetical compensation idea. Here is how he rearticulated his concern in a well-known textbook on welfare economics:

> What if the compensation suggested (but not required) by Mr. Kaldor's criterion is not in fact made? Are we justified in assuming that because the money measure of gain to one set of individuals is greater than the loss to a *different* set of individuals, that society as a whole has indeed benefited? To take a crude illustration, let us assume that all persons who gain from an innovation are very rich, whereas all the losers are in a highly impoverished state. Is it then reasonable to assume that the subjective value of money does not vary from one group to another? Certainly the fact that the richer group has gained (in money form) slightly more than the poorer group has lost, is meager evidence that there has indeed been a balancing of satisfactions and dissatisfactions. Indeed it seems very plausible that the same amount of money might well represent a much greater loss to the poorer group than the corresponding gain

to the richer. *It turns out then that Mr. Kaldor's criterion has not eliminated the problem of interpersonal comparisons of utility.*[44]

This is a most subtle and significant point. Another example may make it clearer. Imagine a contemplated policy change that benefits the upper half of society by exactly the same as it hurts the lower half. In this case, we have an ambiguity, a type of tie in which a policy change seems neither good nor bad. The rich gain, let us say, £1 million, while the poor lose an equivalent amount. The rich, therefore, could indeed compensate the poor, but without any profit to themselves. In calling this a tie, one has to assume that the extra million to the rich provides the same amount of satisfaction as the extra million lost by the poor represents dissatisfaction. In other words, that £1 million produces the *same* amount of satisfaction to the rich and the poor, and therefore the utility of money for the rich man is the *same* as it is for a poor one. If this does not make a comparative assumption about people's utilities, nothing else does.[45]

In summary, far from showing that it is possible to avoid the "unscientific" interpersonal comparisons, Kaldor simply did what Pigou had done earlier, only in a different form. Rather than following Pigou (and Robbins) in assuming equal capacity for satisfaction out of a particular level of income, Kaldor, and the mass of economists following him, end up assuming that the satisfaction generated by the spending of income level, regardless of how high or low it may happen to be, is always the same for everybody. All this makes for a rather counterintuitive and hardly "scientific" foundation of orthodox normative economics. It also affects one of its practical "arms," Cost–Benefit Analysis (CBA), a policy tool that we will again encounter in Chapter 10.[46] If *this* is the accredited intellectual counterpart of social economics, can we not come up with something better? Before presenting the social economics alternative, it will be useful to focus on one more aspect of the New Welfare Economics: the question of its own scientifically unsubstantiated propositions.

The New Welfare Economics: a pseudo science?

As we have seen, modern economics would be fairly ineffectual in dealing with the real problems of welfare, or human well-being, and the formation of social policy, if it had to practice complete abstinence from value judgments. This is what Harrod pointed out, what Robbins was essentially forced to admit, and what in the final analysis Kaldor's new technique could not alter. In order to have something at all to say about welfare, in spite of the prohibitive impasse, modern economics has constructed its own unique solution to the value judgment problem. This "solution," of which Kaldor's compensation principle is an important component, was termed the New Welfare Economics, to contrast it with the earlier version that Pigou had introduced.

The New Welfare Economics, already encountered in the introductory chapter, occupies a central position in the science, as browsing through textbooks and journal articles will readily confirm. The following pages show what kind of value judgments are involved and how their presence affects the normative conclusions the welfare economist draws from his new apparatus.[47] The following statement is a good initial illustration of the dubious teaching of the New Welfare Economics:

> *Economist X:* It should not be necessary to point out that, despite its slightly misleading name, the concept of a Pareto Optimum is completely objective and that our discussions are thus of a positive rather than a normative nature.[48]

The *Pareto Optimum* concept is the guiding principle of the New Welfare Economics, first formulated by the Italian economist and sociologist Vilfredo Pareto. The so-called Pareto Optimum can be stated as follows: a social optimum exists whenever it is not possible to make somebody better off without making somebody else worse off. Conversely, if it is possible to make somebody in society better off without making anybody else worse off, it is considered a good move, and should be undertaken in the interest of maximizing social welfare. This type Optimum is now said to be "completely objective" and part of a factual or "positive" economics. We will see that such a claim is quite far from the truth. But others are more modest in their claims:

> *Economist Y:* Notice, moreover, that the necessary condition of [a Pareto Optimum] is a condition of economic efficiency whilst the additional condition for sufficiency (namely a "just" money income distribution) involves a value judgment. This suggests that we may continue to use [the necessary conditions] without inhibitions and in the usual way in discussions of such topics as "optimum tariffs," or "ideal" tax systems, provided that we bear in mind that we are concerned with questions of economic efficiency and not with questions of justice and injustice.[49]

Here a distinction is now made between the *necessary* conditions and the *sufficient* conditions for achieving such an optimum, or, what amounts to the same thing, the necessary and sufficient conditions for the socially best allocation of economic resources. In other words, whatever is not Pareto optimal, "wastes" available resources in the satisfaction of consumer preferences. Now, Economist Y emphasizes this necessary versus sufficient distinction to make an important point: the formulation of the necessary conditions only involves the technical (or engineering) term "efficiency," which can be used "without inhibitions" (meaning without having to engage in the making of value judgments) to determine *right* and *wrong*. These necessary conditions alone, although they are not enough, are said to provide some ground in ascertaining what is scientifically or "positively" in the interest of society. But beyond that, Economist Y does grant that the formulation of a sufficient condition *will* involve opinions about justice or injustice and with them a value judgment. To summarize perspective Y, the economist *can* (and also should) make policy proposals based on the necessary conditions, but he or she cannot really go any further than that without losing the credentials of science. In particular, questions of redistribution are better left to politicians. All things considered, Economist Y makes a more guarded claim than Economist X, but both would agree that the necessary conditions of a Pareto Optimum are within science. That is what thousands of students of welfare economics learn today, all too often *without* the slightest hint that the story can be told otherwise.[50]

The value judgments supporting the criteria of Paretian efficiency

There are four basic value judgments underlying the entire edifice of Paretian welfare economics. First, the concern is with the welfare of *individuals* in society, not with groups of individuals (such as future generations) or the welfare of society as a whole. Second, it confines the contribution of individual welfare to *economic* causes only, such as income, wealth and leisure. In its purest form an individual's welfare is a function of the goods and services that he or she can exchange in the marketplace. In other words, it is *economic* welfare rather than social welfare that is being discussed. Third, the individual is deemed to be the best judge of his or her economic welfare. The individual as consumer or producer ought to be *sovereign* even if somebody else could make a more informed choice on his or her behalf. Fourth and finally, there is *the* Paretian welfare judgment: if any change in the allocation of resources increases the income or leisure of at least somebody, without hurting anybody else, then such a change must be considered to have increased social economic welfare. Equipped with this quartet of Paretian value judgments, the economist will formulate, at least *in theory*, the necessary conditions for maximum social welfare.

The usual procedure in the literature of welfare economics has been to portray these value judgments as "widely acceptable," minimal, non-controversial and "more or less objective." But are they really? The first one, the individualistic focus, is the essence of the liberal creed. As such, it may not only be contentious in a monarchy or a socialist society, but even *in liberalism* its domain is limited, too; there are many people who have concerns about (the social value of) protecting the environment or the welfare of future generations. The second value judgment, with its narrow focus on economic welfare, is only meaningful provided individual market decisions won't have significant *social* side effects. Neither Sismondi nor Hobson nor any other liberal *social* economist would be willing to make that judgment and therefore reject the idea of trying to approach the common good from a strictly economic point of view. Moreover, the second assumption also prohibits those social interdependencies which are non-marketable and therefore ruled out of bounds. They include the feelings of envy, pride, compassion, guilt and other non-economic causes of welfare. Neither can the third value judgment that insists on an individual's own judgment and discretion in the quest for his or her welfare be accepted as "widely held"; witness the legislation for compulsory education, compulsory national insurance, for controlling drug, tobacco and alcohol use, for subsidized bread, milk and concert halls, and for the wearing of seat belts and motorcycle helmets. In a democracy one has to presume that such legislation has been adopted precisely because of a widely acceptable value judgment, that an individual is not always the best judge of his own welfare. Finally, the fourth Paretian value judgment, the opinion that social welfare is to be considered a (monotonic) increasing function of individual welfare, implies, among other things, that a series of economic policies only benefiting the richest households, while leaving the rest of society no better off, would in the manner of a "widely held" consensus be said to improve the welfare of a society. This, too, is a highly questionable proposition, and, as noted earlier, Sismondi already in his (more liberal) *Richesse Commerciale* did not accept it when criticizing the right of employers to appropriate the entire profits, with workers continuing to toil at subsistence wages.[51]

Economists often tend to forget that their textbook world is not at all the same as the one the rest of humanity inhabits. In reality, all four Paretian welfare judgments are controversial, and fall considerably short on representing the existing values. For any science with global aspirations, the narrowness of Paretian individualism will provoke understandable resistance in the southern and eastern hemispheres. Even in the industrial countries of the West, there are a number of Paretian value judgments that do not adequately represent mainstream values of the culture. At best, they express the values of some atomistic, materialistic and acquisitive "utopia."

Moreover, for purposes of making the whole theory operational, the New Welfare Economics also makes a number of highly abstract and unrealistic assumptions.[52] It assumes a stationary economy in which all decisions are made at once, a timeless world where there is no uncertainty about the future, a world where there is no involuntary unemployment, where human character is fixed and the preferences of individuals can never change, where the realities outside the marketplace simply do not matter, a world with no externalities and other market failures, in short, a world that does not (yet?) exist. This is a "reality" of an economy operating under a hypothetical regime of perfectly competitive markets and perfect knowledge which recalls the late-nineteenth-century world of idealized notions with all its various "perfections."

Appraising the New Welfare Economics

Whatever the ultimate value of the new welfare economics, its main use is limited to economics textbooks. Even if it would (or could) inspire public policy, its established method of developing guiding principles, for example, the need for economic efficiency, in terms of the Paretian value judgments, cannot really be said to be sufficiently value-free to justify being part of "positive economics." In this respect, Economist X shows an unwarranted optimism. Furthermore, even the meeting of the "necessary conditions" epitomized by the value-laden term *economic efficiency* is more nominal than real. "Efficient" and "inefficient," it would appear, are terms of a normative, not positive economics. Mark Blaug, a leading methodologist of economics, is very clear about that when he says: "immense confusion has been sown by the pretense that we can pronounce 'scientifically' on matters of 'efficiency' without committing ourselves to any value judgment."[53] Therefore, the impression portraying allocative efficiency as the *sine qua non* of a sound social policy must be seen in its true colors as little more than pseudo-science. Once the world of Paretian value judgments is left behind, even the necessary conditions for social welfare lose their luster. To this extent, our Economist Y is a bit guilty of false advertising as well.

The New Welfare Economics is not just poor science, but poor philosophy. Its utilitarianism is still rooted in the early-nineteenth-century thought of Jeremy Bentham. As has long been pointed out, the utilitarian vestiges include, above all, two distinguishing elements: the conviction that a person's well-being must be expressed in terms of *utility*, and the idea that the ranking of social goodness can only be done by means of summing up all of the individual utilities. Aspirants in economics soon are given to understand that *this* is the *royal road* to figuring out what is in the interest of society. It rarely occurs to the student that there could be any other way to approach welfare economics. A better future may lie ahead, however. At least one leading scholar in the field today discards this claim of uniqueness and superiority as a mere "pretension."[54] Utilitarian welfare economics simply suffers too many drawbacks to qualify as particularly suitable in discussing the good of society; it especially neglects considerations of freedom and rights, and in its "new" version even turns its face away from distributional considerations. Similarly, the Pareto Criterion, as it has been shown, cannot serve as a requirement for a good social order. Nobel Laureate Sen offers the following illustration: "A society in which some people lead lives of great luxury while others live in acute misery can still be Pareto optimal if the agony of the deprived cannot be reduced without cutting into the ecstasy of the affluent," and adds, "a state can be Pareto optimal and still be sickeningly iniquitous."[55]

Moreover, identifying welfare as utility automatically equates interpersonal comparisons of welfare with interpersonal comparisons of utility. Since the latter must involve the comparison of "inscrutable minds" and feelings, there naturally follows a blanket prohibition on *all* interpersonal comparisons of welfare. Luckily, such inference would only follow from a utilitarian ethic and the simple solution to the problem consists in bursting out of the straitjacket of that particular philosophy. As Sen reminds us:

> Welfare economics is a major branch of "practical reason." There are no good grounds for expecting that the diverse considerations that are characteristic of practical reason, discussed, among others, by Aristotle, Kant, Smith, Hume, Marx or Mill, can, in any real sense, be avoided by taking refuge in some simple formula like the utilitarian maximization of utility sums . . . .[56]

And for all practical purposes this also means leaving current economic welfare criteria behind and turning our thinking to an alternative and more practical approach: social economics.

Notes

1   J. C. L. Simonde de Sismondi, *Political Economy* [1815], New York, Augustus M. Kelley, 1966a, pp. 1, 2.
2   This section relies heavily on the early chapters of S. Roy, *Philosophy of Economics: On the Scope of Reason in Economic Inquiry*, New York, Routledge, 1989.
3   L. Robbins, *An Essay on the Nature and Significance of Economic Science* [1932], 3rd edn, London, Macmillan Press, 1984, p. 147.
4   G. Myrdal, *The Political Element in the Development of Economic Theory*, London, Routledge and Kegan Paul, 1953, p. 2.
5   J. Hicks, quoted in Roy, *Philosophy of Economics*, p. 24.
6   J. Schumpeter, *History of Economic Analysis*, New York, Oxford University Press, 1954, p. 805.
7   K. Arrow, *Social Choice and Individual Values*, New Haven, CT, Yale University Press, 1951, p. 22.
8   Roy, *Philosophy of Economics*, chs. 4 and 5.
9   D. Hume, *An Abstract of a Treatise of Human Nature*, Hamden, CT, Archon, bk. II, 1740 (quoted in J. Rachels, *The Elements of Moral Philosophy*, New York, Random House, 1986, p. 25).
10 Rachels, *The Elements of Moral Philosophy*, p. 35.
11 Roy, *Philosophy of Economics*, p. 46.
12 Quoted in Roy, *Philosophy of Economics*, p. 64.
13 In a comment on Tinbergen's work, Keynes denied the validity of the underlying assumption that the correlation coefficients obtained from analyzing the past are meaningful, adding "there is *no reason* at all why they should not be different every year" (Keynes, quoted in E. K. Brown-Collier, "Keynes' View of an Organic Universe," *Review of Social Economy*, 1985, vol. 93:2, p. 17). And already in 1926

he had stressed the fact that the necessary assumption of intertemporal continuity may be good enough in physics but not in the social sciences dealing with an open-ended and interconnected "organic" universe where "the whole is not equal to the sum of its parts, comparisons of quantity fail us [and] small changes produce large effects" (ibid., p. 18).

14 Roy, *Philosophy of Economics*, p. 68.

15 See ibid., pp. 87–88, 91–92. For a similar solution see E. Anderson, *Value and Ethics in Economics*, Cambridge, MA, Harvard University Press, 1993, ch. 5.

16 G. E. Moore, "A Defense of Common Sense," in his *Philosophical Papers*, London, Allen and Unwin, 1959, pp. 52–59. For Hobson's discussion of common sense, see *Work and Wealth: A Human Valuation*, London, Allen, 1914, pp. 320–322.

17 T. Jefferson quoted in W. Letwin, *A Documentary History of American Economic Policy Since 1789*, New York, Doubleday, 1961, p. xv.

18 T. W. Hutchison, *'Positive' Economics and Policy Objectives*, Cambridge, MA, Harvard University Press, 1964, p. 25.

19 See J. S. Mill, *Essays on Some Unsettled Questions of Political Economy* [1874], New York, Augustus M. Kelley, 1968, pp. 120–164.

20 Quoted in Hutchison, *'Positive' Economics and Policy Objectives*, p. 31, fn. 3.

21 See also ibid., pp. 27–29.

22 J. E. Cairnes, *Essays in Political Economy*, London, Macmillan, 1873, pp. 255–256.

23 H. Sidgwick, *Principles of Political Economy*, London, Macmillan, 1883, p. 403.

24 ibid., pp. 406–413.

25 J. N. Keynes, *The Scope and Method of Political Economy*, London, Macmillan and Co., 1890.

26 Moreover, to him the development of human character was more important than the mechanical problem of satisfying given wants, and he admonished the reader that policy issues cannot be settled on the basis of economic theory alone. Instead, we must consult "our ethical instincts and common sense" for that purpose to decide the extent of wanting to be a scientist or a reformer (see H. Myint, *Theories of Welfare Economics*, New York, Augustus M. Kelley, 1965, pp. 132–141).

27 A. Pigou, *Economics of Welfare* [1920], 4th edn, London, Macmillan, 1932, p. 4.

28 ibid., p. 11.

29 ibid., p. 67.

30 ibid., p. 89.

31 ibid., pp. 91–92.

32 Robbins, *An Essay on the Nature and Significance of Economic Science*, p. 140.

33 Roy, *Philosophy of Economics*, p. 178.

34 See, for example, M. Friedman, *Essays in Positive Economics*, Chicago, IL, University of Chicago Press, 1953, p. 3.

35 R. F. Harrod, "Scope and Method of Economics," *Economic Journal*, September 1938, vol. 48, p. 397.

36 L. Robbins, "Interpersonal Comparisons of Utility: A Comment," *Economic Journal*, December 1938, vol. 48, pp. 635–641.

37 ibid., p. 641.

38 ibid.

39 Schumpeter, *History of Economic Analysis*, p. 1071.

40 J. M. Clark, "Aims of Economic Life as Seen by Economists," reprinted in his *Economic Institutions and Human Welfare*, New York, Alfred Knopf, 1957, p. 59.

41 N. Kaldor, "Welfare Propositions and Interpersonal Comparisons of Utility," *Economic Journal*, September 1939, vol. 49, pp. 549–552.

42 No need to mention certain technical complications that led to a refinement of the compensation principle by incorporating the subsequent point made by Tibor

Scitovsky. It does not alter the basic principle. T. Scitovsky, "A Note on Welfare Propositions in Economics," *Review of Economic Studies*, November 1941, vol. 9, pp. 77–88.

43 W. J. Baumol, "Community Indifference," *Review of Economic Studies*, 1946–1947, vol. 14:1, pp. 44–48.

44 W. J. Baumol, *Welfare Economics and the Theory of the State*, Cambridge, MA, Harvard University Press, 1995, pp. 163–164 (emphasis added).

45 There was not much response by other economists to Baumol's deadly point. Only Kenneth Arrow, in his 1951 celebrated essay on social choice, briefly comments on Baumol's complaint. For Arrow, Kaldor's real sin was of a lesser kind: his principle was merely *arbitrary*. He could have, for example, also compared *fractions of incomes* rather than absolute amounts in assessing gains and losses; for example, reject a policy if it boosts the income of the rich by 10 percent but reduces the income of the poor by 11 percent. It is not clear whether this is a better rule. Imagine a change where one rich family gains 10 percent but the poor masses lose merely 9 percent of their income. Would the adoption of such a policy really be in the social interest?

46 In addition to making interpersonal comparisons of the kind suggested by Baumol, CBA also operates with an implicit value judgment concerning a desirable distribution of income.

47 In what follows I rely heavily on the book by S. K. Nath, *A Reappraisal of Welfare Economics*, London, Routledge and Kegan Paul, 1969. This book is an exemplarily clear and penetrating analysis questioning the logic of some commonly accepted propositions of the New Welfare Economics. It was reprinted in the United States by Augustus M. Kelley in 1976.

48 M. J. Farrel, "The Convexity Assumptions in the Theory of Competitive Markets," *Journal of Political Economy*, 1959, vol. 67, p. 378.

49 I. F. Pearce, *A Contribution to Demand Analysis*, Oxford, Clarendon Press, 1964, p. 132.

50 For the sake of brevity and simplicity, the following discussion will focus only on the *necessary* conditions of Pareto Optimum.

51 See J. C. L. Simonde de Sismondi, *De la Richesse Commerciale*, Geneva, J. J. Paschoud, 1803, ch. 2, p. 7.

52 See Nath, *A Reappraisal of Welfare Economics*, pp. 11–12, for a list of basic assumptions, some of which are mentioned in the next sentence. For an excellent critique showing the irrelevance of welfare economics in terms of information requirements, see J. Stiglitz, *Whither Socialism?*, Cambridge, MA, MIT Press, 1994, chs. 3 and 4.

53 Quoted in D. W. Bromely, *Economic Interests and Institutions: The Conceptual Foundations of Public Policy*, New York, Basil Blackwell, 1989, p. 223.

54 A. Sen, "On the Foundations of Welfare Economics: Utility, Capability and Practical Reason," in F. Farina, F. Hahn and S. Vannucci (eds), *Ethics, Rationality and Economic Behaviour*, New York, Clarendon Press, 1996, p. 50.

55 ibid., p. 53.

56 ibid., p. 61.

6

TRACKING THE COMMON GOOD

After having painted a picture of contemporary welfare economics with all its faults and inadequacies, the reader is better prepared to enter the very heartland of social economics which, as already mentioned in Chapter 1, considers itself a separate school based on an alternative approach to *normative* economics. Rather than aiming at the most efficient satisfaction of individual preferences with a given set of basic resources, the focus now shifts directly to the common good, a concept that obviously cannot be distilled from the actual preferences of members of society. Clearly, in today's society, as already in Sismondi's time, the social order is far from harmonious; witness the conflicting interests between capital and labor. Everything seems to indicate that people have quite different tastes and preferences about the goals of society and few are ready to give up the privileges they now enjoy. It would be premature, however, to conclude from these observations that the common good either does not exist or is beyond comprehension. Instead, it will have to be tracked on a different path, one that builds on a normative view of people's interests and goals. In other words, the question to be asked is not what people happen to like, but what they would like after reflection in the light of reason. Therefore, the norm must be valid for any and all rational agents. Equipped with the resulting principles, we should be well on the trail of the common good. The whole approach resembles what MIT economist Sidney Alexander labeled, decades ago, the *Humanist Criterion*: when faced with alternatives, a reasonable and well-informed person, free of personal and cultural bias, prefers one alternative over the others, one which is thereby shown to be preferable from a social point of view.[1] This chapter will rely on logic and common sense, and the work of some scholars who have used these tools. The goal is to articulate a social economic alternative to Paretian welfare economics, but before engaging in this task, the reader should be made aware of a very recent development in the theory of modern welfare economics.

1. The crumbling of the New Welfare Economics?

During the last two decades, as mentioned in the previous chapter, the stranglehold of normative utility-based economics has been challenged. Nobel Laureate Amartya Sen, as a leading expert on some of the most knotty and mathematical aspects of modern welfare theory, has been working for more than two decades to liberate normative economics from its utilitarian past. He attached the label *welfarism* to the conventional practice to represent value in terms of individual utility. Ever since, the cutting edge of modern welfare economics has been centered on his work, attempting to express well-being in a manner that bypasses utility and focuses instead on alternative conceptualizations, including such hitherto ignored aspects as rights and freedoms. He focuses on what he calls *functionings*: "parts of the state of a person, in particular the various things that he or she manages to do or be in leading a life."[2] For instance, having enough food helps promote such elementary functionings as being adequately nourished and being in good health, as well as the more complex functionings such as achieving self-respect or enjoying self-esteem. What really matters is a person's *capability* to function well, the degree to which a person can freely choose alternative combinations of functionings. So, for example, extreme deprivation would imply a lack of centrally important functionings and the corresponding basic capabilities (freedom to be adequately sheltered, socially integrated and so on). This functionings/capabilities approach lends itself to social evaluations and comparisons of well-being. To a large extent it is possible to contrast the living standard of the rich with that of the poor, to identify poverty in terms of minimum living conditions, or even to rank the living standards of different persons and groups by criteria that are widely shared (or would be so after adequate reflection).[3] Clearly, all this establishes that interpersonal comparisons of *welfare* (as measured by some capability index) are possible, even if one were to concede that interpersonal comparisons of *utility* are not. Sen fully recognizes that, given the different weights people attach to the various functionings, such evaluations are not always easy and unambiguous. Nevertheless, in a rough and ready way, they do allow us to carry out normative analysis. Furthermore, they permit us to take into account individual or group diversity in the promotion of equality. So, for example, regarding women, Sen admonishes us to consider disadvantages that may affect the capability of being nourished (demands of pregnancy, neonatal care), achieving security (single-mother family), having fulfilling work (stereotyping of women's jobs), and establishing one's professional reputation early on in one's career (asymmetric demands of family life).[4] In following the commodity-centered approach by focusing only on inequality of incomes between the sexes, one will tend to underestimate the more real inequality expressed in terms of capability; similarly with race, the aged, the handicapped and so on.

Possibly the main significance of Sen's accomplishments so far is to demonstrate that welfare economics need not be confined to the "royal road of utility" and the collateral Pareto Principle. Only time will tell to what extent other economists will follow Sen's new direction. In any case, Sen's work helps pave the way for a more open-minded and tolerant disposition in the profession toward other approaches, including the traditional social economics standard. At the same time, the focus on functionings and capabilities also suffers from a number of shortcomings, among them the classification of relative importance of the various functionings. As one reviewer asks in the context of discussing Sen's capability egalitarianism: "must we seek equality in *all* capabilities, including, say, effective access to luxury vacation resorts and fine wines?"[5] Professor Martha Nussbaum, a leading philosopher, goes one step further when making the suggestion:

> It seems to me, then, that Sen needs to be more radical than he has been so far in his criticism of the utilitarian accounts of well-being, by introducing an objective account of human functioning and by describing a procedure of objective evaluation by which functionings can be assessed for their contribution to the good human life.[6]

It is on questions and procedures of this type that the social economist claims to be able to shed valuable light, and in the process create a more operational normative economics.

2. The social economics of basic human needs

Aristotle's *Nicomachean Ethics* starts out by defining the human good as "happiness" and proceeds to give a clearer account of it by ascertaining the proper function (*ergon*) of a human being.[7] The answers he gives are expressed in terms of all the forms of good functioning that make up a complete life. It is, of course, from this ancient Greek philosopher that Sen must have borrowed the awkward-sounding term of "functionings." But Aristotle, relying on a particular philosophical anthropology, gives more detailed content to the notion of the human good. He distinguishes between "natural" desires for "real goods" necessary for our pursuit of happiness, and "acquired" desires for what may turn out to be "apparent goods." The first class may be called human needs, the second personal wants. Now the basic human needs (food, drink, shelter, health), being based on our human capacities and tendencies, are taken to be the same for all. Their fulfillment is always good, never excessive, unlike wants. The pursuit of happiness or human flourishing is controlled by a number of virtues, including the virtue of *justice* directed to the good of others. It morally obliges us not to impede others in their pursuit of the good life. We are to treat others fairly by respecting their rights, and also the laws of the state, which are meant as vehicles for facilitating the pursuit of the good life for all members of society. It's the state's duty to assure a minimum provision of certain goods that may not be within reach or control of every citizen; they include the so-called "goods of fortune," consisting of access to adequate medical care, a healthy natural environment and an adequate amount of wealth to function in a way that allows for self-realization.[8]

This short sketch of Aristotelian ethics contains in a nutshell the materials of a normative economics sensitive to the human dimension. It is an approach based on basic human need satisfaction as "the royal road" to self-realization, and it embodies the role of the state as a facilitator and executor of social justice, understood as the right of everyone to be equally able to meet their most basic needs. This view was widely held in the Middle Ages and must have inspired Sismondi and his followers. Still today the focus on basic human needs must be seen as *the* distinguishing element that unites social economists.[9]

The definition of a "need" is straightforward, as a necessary want whereby the adjective "necessary" refers to life. By embracing the standard of need satisfaction, the social economist does make a value judgment that life is good and worth sustaining. Moreover, meeting needs is necessary for the subsistence and health of the organism, otherwise the organism will *visibly* suffer. In other words, the meeting of biological needs is essentially an empirical matter quite different from the generation of pleasure or the satisfaction of mere desire. Therefore, when Sismondi held that "the first attention of society must be given to the securing of its material interests, of its subsistence," there is relatively little ambiguity as to what he meant and what society should have done.[10] Even today, the complete lack of elementary necessities of human life is generally seen as negative welfare or "illfare." The removal of the causes of extreme deprivation and destitution is seen as the prerequisite of any positive social welfare of the community.[11]

The concept of enabling basic subsistence seems clearer and more operational than some notion of an adequate "capability of functionings." Moreover, the assumption of a common humanity enables an intersubjectively valid way to compare welfares of different groups of people and so establishes a yardstick for redistribution policy. "It can hardly be denied," said the late mathematician and economist Nicholas Georgescu-Roegen, "that it makes *objective* economic sense to help starving people by taxing those who spend their summers at luxurious resorts," and adds, "there is economic sense even in taxing the latter more heavily than those who cannot afford luxuries."[12]

The foregoing clears the way for the articulation of the first of the two principles of a social economic human welfare analysis: *subsistence and physical health are essential human values, and every member of society by virtue of his or her humanity, has an equal right to these goods.* Both subsistence and physical health are the kind of concepts that mean "pretty much the same thing" to

128

everybody and would thereby have to qualify as permissible value judgments even in the eyes of the late Joseph Schumpeter. In fact, these value judgments are so much based on common sense that to the ordinary citizen their explicit mentioning must read like a rather trivial academic insight; but it should be noted that nowhere in today's orthodox welfare economics, with its grip on countless students, do we encounter this fundamental realization.

From human needs to human rights

The notion that natural needs entitle us, by nature, also to have them met, has long been one of the basic insights of natural law thinking. In spite of its intuitive plausibility, it may fall short in giving a real justification of human rights. On the other hand, a justification can be given as developed by one of the leading authorities on the philosophy of human rights: Alan Gewirth from the University of Chicago. A thumbnail sketch of his argument may be rendered as follows: first, he describes a moral right as an individual's interest for which there is a normative moral justification and which therefore ought to be respected and protected. But on what grounds would such interests ever justify the imposition of duties on others? In response, Gewirth proceeds to show that moral rights, and human rights in particular, can be justified on the basis of something that is common to all human beings and therefore can serve as a basis for a logical deduction of rights. This commonality he finds in our capability to engage in *human action*. It's a concept that entails two necessary "generic" features: voluntariness or freedom, and purposiveness. A precondition for any such action is basic well-being or the command over necessities such as water, food and shelter. If the so-called "additive goods" (education, self-esteem) that enhance one's ability to reach one's goal are included, well-being would then consist not only of physical integrity but also of "mental balance." Rights, therefore, will arise out of a concern for all persons as agents to create and protect the necessary conditions for successful action. Every human being as an agent wanting to fulfill a purpose will have to admit that freedom and basic well-being are indeed necessary goods, and that he or she has a right to these goods. The logic further implies that others, being agents too, must have identical rights. Finally, since these generic rights apply to all agents, who are after all human, these generic rights (of human action) are also human rights. Through this type of "moral geometry" Gewirth converts the basic language of human needs into a vocabulary of human rights.

Reassuringly, another philosopher, David Copp, comes to a very similar conclusion using an approach that also centers on human autonomy and agency. He argues for a moral norm enshrined in the Universal Declaration of Human Rights (article 25), a document ratified by the United States and virtually all the countries of the world – that stipulates: "Everyone has the right to a standard of living adequate for the health and well-being of himself and of his family including food, clothing, housing and medical care and necessary social services." Copp also tries to justify this right by appealing to human autonomy, and argues that a person is able to enjoy an adequate standard of living when able to meet his basic needs, and thereby empowered to live as a rational agent, "making choices that determine his own way of life on the basis of values that he has formed autonomously."[13] Both scholars show how a perspective of basic human needs also entails an obligation of society and the state to enable the satisfaction to meet those needs. A government violates human rights, says Gewirth, "when its hands-off policy lets the most vulnerable members of its society suffer harm and injuries like poverty, disease, illiteracy or unemployment," provided, of course, that it could take measures to help the situation.[14]

If Gewirth is right, it would seem to follow that the imperative of enabling everybody to meet their basic needs is far more than a noble opinion, but a requirement based on reasoning and logical argument.[15] Equipped with this type of philosophical background support, a human welfare economics can be put on a more meaningful and secure footing than the prevailing norm of social welfare maximization *à la* Pareto efficiency. It is the choice between the path of logic and common sense versus the unreal and esoteric world of economic calculus.

Dealing with the higher needs

Matters become much more challenging with the realization that there is more to life than survival and good health. It has long been recognized that "man does not live by bread alone." Such a world view makes it necessary to, following Sismondi, "consider political economy in its relation with the soul." What this implies is a broadening of the concept of need to include the higher values of personality. Hobson, for example, saw self-development as the gateway to securing "real freedom" and also stressed self-respect as a core value in the building of character. To him, all this was necessary in order to gain the "spiritual liberty needed for the ascent of man."[16] But now the question poses itself as to how to conceptualize human integrity or "wholeness" of the person. Sismondi's allusions to an "ennobling of human nature" and "perfection of Man" as the ultimate end of an economic system lack the hard edge to carve out appropriate measures of social policy.[17] Nor do the values of the American Declaration of Independence, upholding the inalienable rights to "life, liberty and the pursuit of happiness," provide much guidance. Yet, these values, intrinsic to the "higher needs," are both important and reflective of what is distinctly human. A humanistic economic system cannot afford to simply ignore them. At least we should heed the basic point already recognized by Sismondi that the *manner* in which society provides for its subsistence will also impact on the quality of life. It helps determine such things as "the feelings of sympathy or jealousy with which fellow men look upon each other as brothers eager to assist one another, or as rivals furious to destroy one another" and "the vigour of the race, or its degeneracy" and so on.[18] For example, Sismondi stressed the need for leisure that would promote the intellectual development of the worker "in order to advance in virtue."[19] Hobson, too, it will be remembered, repeatedly stressed the effect of what seem to be "purely economic" variables on human character formation. In this regard he was, above all, concerned with the social and moral impact of competition, job insecurity and the quality of the workplace.

Yet, these "higher" needs and the degree of their being satisfied are notoriously difficult to measure even for the person him/herself. As one economist put it: "The rule seems to hold that the higher and more ideal your purpose, the greater your difficulty in gaining any assurance that you have accomplished it."[20] Lack of satisfactory measurement further prevents a consensus on the relative importance of these human values which may at times even be in mutual conflict. What if a degrading workplace offers more economic security? Clearly, the situation is no better than the one faced by Amartya Sen with his array of plural values and multiple capabilities.

The plurality and ambiguity of higher values make a generally acceptable ranking of them very difficult, yet without such a priority scale it will be impossible to easily evaluate the social order. But there have been several attempts to overcome this problem. One consists in trying to impartially reflect whatever standards of value seem to be in force in a society at a given time. This has been by and large the approach of the institutionalist economists of the "social value school," many of whom have long been considered to be social economists as well, especially the influential American, John Maurice Clark. The problem with this method is, of course, that a value judgment does not become more desirable merely because it is held by a large number of people: witness the wide endorsement of slavery in the American antebellum South.

Another approach, influential among the earlier Catholic social economists, is to accept the spiritual authority and guidance of the Church and papal encyclicals in matters of sorting out the social values, and to attempt to build them into a more enlightened economics. Examples of the latter would include the principles of "subsidiarity," "the preferential option for the poor" and "the dignity of labor." The obvious drawback here, is that regardless of the truth value embodied in the results of such enterprise, it can hardly be expected to find much support among people with different religious commitments or among non-believers.

A third method, much more in tune with the humanistic approach featured in this book, is to focus on some *human standard* related to the growth of personality. A key variable here would be Hobson's human value of self-respect in the building of character as mentioned earlier. Recall that Hobson's "humanizing of the economy," stressing the higher dimensions of human personality, stipulated that the vertical dimension is organically interlinked with its base, consisting of the lower material needs. Satisfaction of one kind of prepotent category of needs (as, for example, the need for security) will promote the emergence and growth of the (higher) social and moral needs. And if, as mentioned earlier, essential job security should conflict with the provision of quality jobs, it is the lower, or more basic, need that will be given priority.

One could also turn to some particular psychology as, for example, Abraham Maslow's theory of personality with its emphasis on the higher needs, such as self-esteem and self-actualization.[21] Here, too, socioeconomic structures and policies are evaluated as to whether they promote or discourage the growth of personality, and in the process the emphasis must be on the quality of work in the workplace. The main difficulty with Maslow's psychological approach is that, in spite of its intuitive appeal, this theory no longer reigns supreme.[22] Today, there are many personality theories to choose from, with none able to command special allegiance. Under these circumstances it would be somewhat risky to want to base a human welfare economics on any one of them.

The apparent weakness of all these alternative approaches counsels caution and a retreat to safer ground in order to try a very different route – *reculer pour mieux sauter*, as the French say. The real challenge is to find a minimalist and yet widely held and rationally justifiable social value that manages to capture the essence of the distinctly human, and so can stand as a proxy for the meeting of some of the "higher" human needs. On this road we soon encounter the Kantian *principle of humanity*: "always treat humanity, whether in your own person or in the person of another, never simply as a means, but always, at the same time as an end," together with its corollary, the value of *human dignity*.[23] Much of the remainder of this chapter will be devoted to discussing the latter concept in some detail, an account made necessary by the lack of acquaintance of social science with the idea of *intrinsic* human worth, as well as in recognition of the key role that it can play in normative economic thought.

3. The value of human dignity

What is meant by human dignity? Ironically, we cannot learn much from various dictionaries, which recognize an entry for "dignity" but not for "*human* dignity." The former is a term of many meanings, all carrying various connotations that relate to relative social rank or elevation. There dignity is a matter of degree, some people or "dignitaries" enjoying it more than others. Human dignity, on the other hand, belongs to every human being *qua* human being. As part of a common humanity, it belongs to all in equal amounts and is inalienable, meaning that it cannot be gained or lost. True, we often do say that some people are at times treated in a way that "deprives them of their dignity" or that someone seems to be "losing his human dignity" by doing unworthy things, but such counter-examples are more apparent than real. They are readily avoided by distinguishing human dignity (which is unassailable) from the *claim* issuing from such dignity (which alone can be violated or disrespected).

The concept of human dignity is central to the liberal credo in politics: a commitment to the equal worth and dignity of each and every person.[24] Specifically, the concept implies that basic human rights are not just a matter of social or political attribution, but instead are intrinsic to human nature and therefore also to be respected by the state. In this same sense, personal dignity has also been enshrined as the absolute foundation of the United Nations' Universal Declaration of Human Rights and of many nations' constitutions, particularly of the German Federal Republic. Even for the United States, Justice Brennan held that the Constitution must be seen as "a sublime oration on the dignity of Man."[25] Clearly, all this goes to show the central importance of the concept of human dignity in Western thought and civilization.[26]

Human dignity in modern science and philosophy

While scientific developments such as the Copernican Revolution in cosmology had early on set in motion the long process of "decentering Man," the mainstream of authoritative wisdom, whether religious or secular, as late as the nineteenth century, still accepted the premise that human dignity was in some sense real. By and large scholars approved the notion that the human being was endowed with an autonomous intellect, a distinctly human faculty that sets the person apart from nature. And it was this particular view that came under attack from the new scientific doctrines proclaimed by Darwin, Marx and Freud. It marked a turn to a new naturalism where humankind was nothing but a product of nature and whose intellect was no longer seen as free but determined instead by nature.

With Charles Darwin the biblical account of Genesis lost much of its credibility. God as creator was replaced by a competitive struggle for existence and the principle of natural selection. The doctrine of an evolutionary continuum no longer permitted the cherished notion of an elevated and sublime status for humanity. In Karl Marx's "materialist" conception of thought, the human mind emerged as an irrational, involuntary reflection of economic class interests producing ideology. And with Sigmund Freud, deliberate thought was, in the words of one scholar, little more than "an involuntary expression of personal history and temperament, perhaps toilet training."[27] In short, the intellectual contribution of these three "doctors of modernity" aimed quite successfully to strip the person of all illusions of dignity. As a result, human dignity as a concept was soon denied any scientific or rational foundation. It is only today, after many decades of scientific progress and additional historical evidence, that the views of Darwin, Marx and Freud are held with much less certainty and with significant qualifications.[28]

As part of the revival of the concept, the German philosopher Hans Wagner in his book on human dignity points out that science by its very method can only apprehend the human being as an *object* among other objects of investigation.[29] In so learning about human nature one tends to forget that man is also the *subject* or maker of science without which we would not be able to say anything of cognitive significance. Yet, it is precisely this human capacity to recognize and freely respect epistemological norms or truths that sets us apart from nature. "Man owes his dignity to [this] circumstance," insists Wagner.[30] Moreover, it is only through philosophy, not science, that we can arrive at such understanding. Science, for inherent reasons, must be seen as incapable of coming to grips with the ontological existence of human dignity. And it is a good lesson not to equate human knowledge with scientific knowledge only.

The problem may go even deeper than that. A number of philosophers also question the materialism of science in its treatment of the human mind, an approach that would rule out genuine free will.[31] This is so because (immaterial) "intellect" and "will," by being reduced to a mere function of the brain, become submerged in the sea of physical causality. Furthermore, is the superiority of the human mind really just a matter involving *degrees* of neurological complexity of brain function? An affirmative answer to the question (and the way scientists would answer it) would imply that the higher status of human beings would also have to be only a matter of degree – *not* of kind. But if so, if we as a species have dignity only because we are a little smarter than animals, should not the smarter segments within the human race also be entitled to more dignity? It would seem then that the egalitarian essence of human dignity and equal human rights cannot be easily aligned with the materialist accounts of a human mind rooted in brain and nature.

Justifying human dignity

One should be aware of an insightful contribution by contemporary scholarship on the notion of equal and intrinsic human worth. Rather than arguing for human dignity by simply demonstrating its ontological grounds of reason and free will in an assertive manner, Alan Gewirth prefers what he calls a "dialectically necessary argument," allowing us to logically infer human worth directly from human action or agency. The basic argument is very simple: when a person chooses something, when engaging in purposive action, an agent is thereby attributing value or worth to the purpose that drives the action. That end must have, from the agent's point of view, enough value so as to merit the effort of trying to attain it. Logically, the ascribed worth of the agent's ends must also entail attribution of worth to the agent him/herself. In other words, if a person's purposes are valuable, so must be the source of that value: the person him/herself. The mere circumstance of purposive action (actual, contemplated or potential) indicates that the actor must have *as agent* human dignity. Finally, it is this worth or dignity the agent must equally extend to everybody else because they too, as agents, have the same relation to their respective purposes and the worth they embody.[32] In this way, Gewirth concludes, "the necessary attribution of inherent dignity to all human beings is dialectically established, for all humans are actual, prospective or potential agents."[33]

Gewirth's dialectical argument, deriving human dignity from agency, should be particularly meaningful to anyone immersed in economics, increasingly represented as the "science of choice." But, it must be understood that when Gewirth talks about human "action" or "agency," he does so in a strictly philosophical sense: it implies the ability to *control* one's behavior to choose what appears as really desirable and not just to follow one's inclinations or strongest desire.[34] In other words, Gewirth makes allowance for the distinctly human capacity of the freedom of the will or real autonomy when justifying human dignity.[35] Only human beings enjoy this kind of capacity, and they share it all equally.

A *universal norm*

Gewirth's penetrating logic substantiates the notion that every person has by nature intrinsic worth or dignity, a claim that is far more than a self-congratulatory, anthropocentric opinion, but must be seen as a fact established by reason. Some additional conclusions can also be derived from this general viewpoint. They include the claim that human dignity is to be attributed to all persons *equally* regardless of sex, race or class. Because personal dignity is grounded in human nature rather than conferred by society or culture, it is also a universal or transcultural value with a domain of global dimensions.

For proponents of the doctrine of cultural relativism, the last point may not be at all acceptable and, given an opportunity, they will readily point to the plurality of ethical value systems prevailing in different cultures. True, these plural moralities have long been documented by ethnologists. Nevertheless, the norm of equal human dignity is rationally, not empirically, grounded; it pertains to a *normative* morality which lends itself as a touchstone in evaluating existing patterns of social relations by a standard of how persons and groups in society ought to be treated. Once again, this universal property justifies the making of transcultural welfare propositions.

Equipped with a universal standard and recognizing that human dignity relates intimately to human rights – a connection made explicit in the text which prefaces the United Nations' Universal Declaration of Human Rights – the social economist can now wield a second principle of normative economics: *every member of society has an equal and rightful claim to human dignity and to be treated in accordance with this claim.* It upholds a right for everybody to be respected and treated as a person having intrinsic value rather than merely as "a thing" with only instrumental value and a price. Among other implications, the rights of human dignity involve injunctions against being manipulated, exploited, degraded, taken advantage of, discriminated against, being sold or rented, or being forced to act without one's consent. On the affirmative side, the right also translates into a right to be treated with respect for one's life with its vital needs for self-determination and personal freedom, as well as the right to basic equality.

4. Toward a political economy of the common good

Up to this point, two basic norms of *material sufficiency* and *respect for human dignity* and the moral rights that they imply have been established. It has also been shown that these norms or principles are not just equivalent to personal opinions, but that they rest on a rational foundation, and therefore claim to be part of economic knowledge. This answers one of the indictments against social economics voiced at the beginning of Chapter 5. What about the second charge, alleging that the laying down of such normative principles of economic policy is a challenge to citizen sovereignty, that it is undemocratic? Is not the economist *qua* economist only supposed to advise the government on how best to implement the goals of the people and their representatives?

Quite obviously, the liberal concern here is well intentioned: it is, to prevent another of Plato's "philosopher kingdoms," a system in which a selected "elite" is put in charge of the state's affairs. But at the same time it confuses the economist as commentator and maker of recommendations with the political system itself. If the system is democratic, then no recommendations, no matter what they are, can be imposed by force. Similarly, if the system is not democratic, then all recommendations that are enacted, no matter what they are, are imposed by force. The values of sufficiency and dignity are only meant to critically evaluate the status quo. By this view, the authority of the social economist rests solely on the power of reason in support of the normative claims that are being made, that is the extent to which they can withstand rational criticism. Furthermore, the insistence that the economists restrict themselves to the role of playing mercenaries to majority rule seems irresponsible and demeaning. Neither is it what ordinary economists do when they routinely expound to Congressional committees the importance of deregulation or the value of unregulated international trade. Ultimately, what is at stake is not a conflict between democracy and benevolent dictatorship purporting to be the common good, but a contest of the strength of reasons supporting different principles of public policy.

Translating these moral rights into economic rights and the social policies and institutions they call for, will cast an "economics of the common good" in more concrete form. Before proceeding, one more question needs to be addressed.

The tension between individual rights and the social good

More often than not one encounters the belief that rights are meant to protect *individual* interests while the notion of community stresses *common* interests. Underlying these different perspectives are alternative modes of seeing the person: one looks at the individual as a freewheeling atom in the social place, the other views the person as submerged in and constituted by social relations. Therefore, it is neo-liberal individualism that stresses rights. On the other hand, communitarianism as well as some feminisms emphasize solidarity, social bonds, mutualism and social responsibility.[36]

Having said this, it seems peculiar to ground the community-oriented common good in the individualistic language of rights. But the problem really lies elsewhere in a too-narrow understanding of rights and community. This is the underlying confusion in the adversarial relationship of individual rights to community. Specifically, rights are seen as negative rights only, concerned with warding off interference from other persons or the state. Valuable as the conception of "negative" rights may be, standing by itself it promotes a view of society consisting of atomistic individuals oblivious to the needs of others. What is lacking is the realization that the concept of human rights entails a mutualist and egalitarian universality: "each human must respect the rights of all others while having his rights respected by all the others, so that there must be a mutual sharing of the benefits of rights and the burdens of duties."[37] In other words, rights must also be conceived of in their "positive" aspects, for example, the right to social assistance in having one's needs met in order to live a life of purpose. Rights and community are not antagonistic but, when properly understood, are vital complements to an organic whole. This recognized mutuality intrinsic to human rights is central to the correct notion of community: a community with rights or, to use Gewirth's term, a *community of rights*.[38]

Economic rights

The logical relationship between human rights and the common good now becomes much clearer. The good that is "common" must be understood as a good that is equally shared or equally belonging to each and every member of society. What notion could better express the conception of the "common good" than the human rights to freedom, basic well-being and respect of dignity that – by virtue of a shared humanity – are common to, and equally vested in, all the members of society?[39] This concern with equal rights prompted social economists like Sismondi and Hobson to denounce a social order that by its very constitution degraded and victimized the suffering masses in order to grease the machinery of ceaseless capital accumulation.

Gewirth in his *Community of Rights* (1996) works out in painstaking scholarly manner a list of economic rights derived from basic human rights. They include, starting in order of decreasing importance, the *right to welfare* (governmental provision of adequate food, shelter, clothing, medical care and other necessities of life, including the right to education); a *(limited) right to private property*; the *right to employment*; and the *right to economic democracy*. He devotes a chapter to each and in the process entertains a discourse on various objections raised.[40]

Gewirth's extensive list appears more vulnerable to criticism than the single right proposed by his counterpart, David Copp: the *right to an adequate standard of living*. Copp's adjective "adequate" is interpreted to mean enabling "integrity" of body and mind, but there's a problem here, too: one looks in vain for an explication of what is implied by "psychological integrity." The challenge is to come up with a short but meaningful list that also promises to be operationally significant.[41]

By borrowing two items from Gewirth's list and adding a third, one can articulate principles of social economic welfare that are more immune to the attack that they are mere opinion and express a particular cultural vision. The following three normative propositions may guide public policy:

(1) the right to the necessities of life;
(2) the right of economic democracy;
(3) the right of future generations to sufficiency and respect for dignity.

The first of the "trinity" is grounded in the basic human needs, the second appeals to respect for human dignity and the third appeals to both material needs and dignity.

Much has been said about the right to welfare support and protection by means of a social "safety net." The normative principle of human dignity goes further, by mandating the manner in which assistance to the poor is to be provided: to encourage self-respect and self-reliance. Already in the 1830s, Sismondi stressed this important point:

> An English workman employed by his parish in breaking stones on the highway, is degraded even below a machine; but a man who has been made to work intelligently at works of irrigation or clearing . . . may become useful to his country wherever there is a demand for his labor, and gain complete independence.[42]

At the very least, public assistance must be provided in a manner that is neither aiming at punitive deterrence, nor degrading or otherwise creating a dependency on the state, i.e., "passive welfarism." More generally, the right to subsistence-cum-dignity is in all likelihood best met by the provision of public or private employment remunerated at a "living wage," the rate Hobson claimed was required by (his version of) natural law. If private jobs at those wages are not forthcoming, it would put the burden on the state as employer of last resort. Similarly, free basic education and especially adult retraining seem like appropriate tools in pursuit of encouraging self-reliance.

Subsequent chapters will explicate the issues of economic democracy and the need to protect the interests of future generations. As to the needs of economic democracy, that is, firms treating workers with dignity, a better idea of what is at stake may be conveyed by the economist Frank Knight, the founder of the conservative Chicago School who at one point bemoaned the fact that "it is characteristic of the enterprise organization that labor is directed by its employer . . . in a way analogous to material equipment," and added, "Certainly there is in this respect no sharp difference between a free laborer and a horse, not to mention a slave, who would, of course, be property."[43] But it is one thing to be critical, and quite another to offer a coherent alternative that has in addition met the economic test of being a winner in the competitive marketplace. The challenge will be to show what respect for human dignity would entail in terms of retooling the system from capital hiring labor to labor hiring capital. It's a question of democratizing the contemporary absentee-owned corporation.

The third leg of the trinity of rights impacts on future generations. Why should we treat them with any less respect than we treat our contemporaries? Long-term or multi-generational issues cannot, so it would seem, simply be left to the tastes and shopping preferences of present-day consumers driving the unregulated marketplace. Moreover, continued indifference for the common good on this "ultimate challenge" may lead humanity itself down the road of self-destruction.

The twin issues of human sufficiency and human dignity will also provide essential background material to Chapter 9 featuring a sober reassessment of the impact of unregulated international competition on society. There we find a perfect example of just how relevant social criticism in the spirit of Sismondi and Hobson can still be. Even more so, because the contentious logic of global capitalism is bound to sooner or later reveal its illusory character and make way for a more open-minded approach towards the common good.

Redistribution through taxation

If the state is to assume a protective function in the manner previously outlined, it must have the necessary resources to accomplish this task. How is the potentially massive public assistance to be financed? The obvious answer is taxation. And this raises another issue. Even if one were to agree with Georgescu-Roegen that "it makes sense to help starving people by taxing those who spend their summers at luxurious resorts," and even if one accepts Hobson's point that much of the surplus that is appropriated by private enterprise was really produced by society and therefore rightfully to be reclaimed through taxes, there remains a potential problem. It arises because the justification for the right to welfare hinges ultimately on the value accorded individual autonomy, as demonstrated by Gewirth and Copp. But could the concern for autonomy not also be invoked in protecting the freedom of the rich? Libertarians have long argued that transfers of income and wealth to the needy poor is an abridgment of the rights of the well-to-do. Going further, philosopher Robert Nozick has even likened redistributive taxes to forced labor![44] How is the social economist to respond against such an indictment?

Gewirth's answer is simple: he argues that while the rich do lose some of their freedom, the destitute poor will gain far more in autonomy by the transfer.[45] Reading Sen's *Inequality Reexamined* (1995) featuring the capability-based approach to freedom suggests a similar type of response. Copp, on the other hand, makes a more basic and more obvious point: "The ordinary citizens have a duty to assist the state in discharging its duty by contributing to programs intended to enable every citizen to meet his basic needs."[46] He explains that when taxing the rich, the state is only asking them to do their duty. How would it be considered a violation of one's rights if one is merely being asked to do one's duty?[47] This defense is also implicit in Gewirth's "community of rights" based on mutuality of sharing the benefits and burdens entailed by human rights. Finally, recalling Sidney Alexander's "humanist criterion" in social choice, it is to be expected that even the rich, *free of personal bias*, would prefer to live in a society in which human deprivation is mitigated through government taxation.

A social market economy

Every economic system needs a coordinating principle. Capitalist ideology has long favored the free market while socialists have been looking more toward government planning. Social economists, on the other hand, have not been willing to endorse either principle. Even though they have long opposed the idea of *laissez-faire*, they have also expressed grave concern about the bureaucratic excesses that tend to go hand-in-hand with the planning process. Instead, their vision of a market economy is one that is undergirded with social correctives, especially in the domain of workers' rights. It is a vision sensitive to security of employment and insurance against risks as well as a more just distribution of income and wealth.

On the level of basic organizational principles, the kind of economic system necessary for the promotion of human welfare and respect for dignity entails two basic tenets. First and foremost, it implies a *humanistic enterprise system* which recognizes the sovereignty of people, not capital. It is based on the premise that human beings, not money and not material resources, are the most vital resources of the economic system. It is human and social "capital" that must be given a special emphasis in the organization of the economy, a requirement that suggests labels like human capital*ism* or social capital*ism*. So, for example, free capital markets have no intrinsic worth but are instrumental to social welfare. In case of a conflict between the interests of capital owners and the common good, the latter must prevail. Second, the *economy must be embedded in society* and not the other way around. In other words, social decisions cannot be allowed to be dictated by the impersonal force of economic competition. More specifically, the political domain has to correspond to the economic sphere, a condition that gets seriously violated in a world of *national* politics and *global* economy. Logically, a reintegration of the economic domain would entail either the trimming back of economic forces to the national level, or else some expansion of government to world levels. In conclusion, both organizational principles are sufficiently radical in nature to warrant further treatment in the chapters to come.

Conclusion

The basic argument for a human welfare economics entails a very different set of welfare criteria than the economic-efficiency-based thinking of the previous chapter. The reader is invited to judge for him- or herself which of the two makes more sense.

It is hard to suppress the feeling that one of the choices seems artificial and abstract and at times counterintuitive, featuring an analysis centered on Pareto efficiency with its own value judgments. It makes a theoretical case for a market economy based on a hypothetical regime of perfect competition, and leaves the determination of the common good to the contest of individual interests. By its very make-up, it has nothing to say about poverty and human deprivation. And in upholding more of a "commodity focus," it proposes rules that allocate people, on par with other inputs, for the purpose of producing more goods.

The other choice, a more philosophical approach, recommends the social value principle of "sufficiency and respect for human dignity for all" and takes the economy as we find it. Here the common good has some substantive meaning and a protective role of government is recommended in alleviating hardships and inequities, often caused by destructive competition. It is an economics in which human destitution and degradation take center stage, a "people-centered" approach in which goods and material resources are allocated and distributed in order to enhance the quality of lives.

Preferring the humanistic alternative of a social welfare economics is not without a serious consequence, however. It entails the same bold leap forward as it did in the case of Hobson's analysis of economic distribution some eighty years ago, to the effect that the condemnation of wealth amidst poverty can no longer be discussed as a sentimental attitude, but must be given objective status. This interpretation is bound to affect the relationship between economics as an academic discipline and the centers of privilege and power. Whatever honest assessment may lead to, the criteria of sufficiency, health and respect for dignity may meet the same academic resistance Hobson met a century ago.

Nevertheless, the pursuit of truth is a long and winding road where "seeing facts and thinking straight" does not happen overnight, and may not assert itself, short of the pressure of external events. But Sismondi in his study of the social sciences gave some advice to what he called "the friends of liberty and the dignity of man," which he summarized in the exhortation "never to be discouraged." In the past, the "vanity of rules which blind presumption has given us for principles" has not stopped the members of a community from "looking above the narrow circle of personal interest and occupying themselves with the advancement of their fellow-men."[48]

Ultimately, what is at stake is the choice between an ethics based on unlimited desires in which "more" is the objective and on an ethics of "enough" which is based on needs. One, embracing the maximization principle, sees no limits to individual acquisition; the other, recognizing a social domain (as well as an ecological context), counsels responsibility, sharing and moral restraint. As the late E. F. Schumacher concluded in his *Guide for the Perplexed* (1977), "we are quite competent enough to produce sufficient supplies of necessities so that no one need live in misery"; in other words, we do know how to provide *enough* for all, and in this sense the economic problem has already been solved. Rather it is the *moral* problem that has to be faced and dealt with.[49] A meaningful economics, therefore, must at least acknowledge the very existence of a moral dimension. Yet, it is precisely this dimension that academic economists deny. It's no secret that the art of the "economic way of thinking" that is in the name of a liberal arts education annually and globally pounded into the heads of students, refuses to go "beyond the narrow circle of personal interest." Any reform aimed at the common good must therefore also explore the peculiar institution of economic science, in particular its treatment of moral obligation and its conception of rationality. This task will be the topic of Chapter 7.

Notes

1 In his own language, the *Criterion* states: "Alternative A should be done rather than alternative B if and only if a reasonable, well-informed [person], free of personal and cultural bias, would prefer to be anyone in the state consequent on A rather than in the state consequent on B," S. Alexander, "Human Values and Economists' Values," in S. Hook, *Human Values and Economic Policy: A Symposium*, New York, New York University Press, 1967, pp. 101–116.

2 A. Sen, "On the Foundations of Welfare Economics: Utility, Capability and Practical Reason," in F. Farina, F. Hahn and S. Vannucci (eds), *Ethics, Rationality and Economic Behaviour*, New York, Clarendon Press, 1996, p. 57.

3 ibid., pp. 57–58; A. Sen, *The Standard of Living: The Tanner Lectures*, New York, Cambridge University Press, 1987, pp. 29–33.

4 A. Sen, *Inequality Reexamined*, Cambridge, MA, Harvard University Press, 1995, p. 113.

5 E. Anderson, "Review of Sen's *Inequality Reexamined*," *Economics and Philosophy*, April 1995, vol. 11:1, p. 185.

6 M. Nussbaum, "Nature, Function and Capability: Aristotle on Political Distribution," *Oxford Studies in Ancient Philosophy*, 1988, supplemental vol., p. 176.

7 Aristotle, *Nicomachean Ethics*, trans. M. Oswald, Indianapolis, IN, Bobbs-Merrill Educational Publishing, 1962, pp.16–19.

8 For a reader-friendly introduction to Aristotle, see M. Adler, *Aristotle for Everybody: Difficult Thought Made Easy*, New York, Simon and Schuster, 1978.

9 See J. B. Davis and E. O'Boyle (eds), *The Social Economics of Human Material Need*, Carbondale, IL, Southern Illinois University Press, 1994.

10 J. C. L. Simonde de Sismondi, *Political Economy and the Philosophy of Government* [1847], New York, Augustus M. Kelley, 1966b, p. 123.

11 See H. Myint, *Theories of Welfare Economics*, New York, Augustus M. Kelley, 1965, p. 225.

12 N. Georgescu-Roegen, *Energy and Economic Myths*, New York, Pergamon Press, 1976, p. 318 (emphasis added).

13 D. Copp, "The Right to an Adequate Standard of Living: Justice, Autonomy, and the Basic Needs," *Social Philosophy and Policy*, Winter 1992, vol. 9:1, pp. 213, 257.

14 A. Gewirth, *The Community of Rights*, Chicago, IL, University of Chicago Press, 1996, p. 5.

15 For the more refined versions of these arguments, as well as for rebuttal of the conventional objections, the reader is urged to consult the painstakingly philosophical reasoning of Gewirth's book (ibid.); and Copp ("The Right to an Adequate Standard of Living").

16 J. A. Hobson, "Character and Society," in P. Parker (ed.), *Character and Life*, London, Williams and Norgate, 1912, p. 66.

17 J. C. L. Simonde de Sismondi, *New Principles of Political Economy* [1827], trans. R. Hyse, New Brunswick, NJ, and London, Transaction Publishers, 1991, p. 74.

18 J. C. L. Simonde de Sismondi, *Political Economy and the Philosophy of Government* [1847], New York, Augustus M. Kelley, 1966b, pp. 123–124.

19 ibid., p. 223.

20 P. Wicksteed, quoted by T. W. Hutchison, *'Positive' Economics and Policy Objectives*, Cambridge, MA, Harvard University Press, 1964, p. 176.

21 Examples of such orientation are E. K. Hunt ("The Normative Foundations of Social Theory," *Review of Social Economy*, 1978, vol. 36:3, pp. 285–309) and M. A. Lutz and K. Lux (*The Challenge of Humanistic Economics*, Menlo Park, CA, Benjamin/Cummings, 1979).

22 For a recent evaluation of Maslow's theory, see S. Lea *et al.*, *The Individual in the Economy: A Textbook of Economic Psychology*, New York, Cambridge University Press, 1987.

23 I. Kant, *Groundwork of the Metaphysics of Morals* [1785], trans. H. J. Paton, New York, Harper Torch Books, 1964.

24 R. Howard and J. Donnelly, "Human Dignity, Human Rights and Political Regions," *American Political Science Review*, September 1986, vol. 80:3, p. 803.

25 Quoted in W. Parent, "Constitutional Values and Human Dignity," in M. Meyer and W. A. Parent (eds), *The Constitution of Rights: Human Dignity and American Values*, Ithaca, Cornell University Press, 1992, p. 47.

26 As for the probable origins of the idea, we must turn to the biblical revelation of *imago dei* or God-likeness of the person. And since neither the Greek nor the Roman slave owners must have paid much attention to the egalitarian norm of human dignity, it is said that the revival of the idea of equal personal dignity had to await the triumph of Christianity, J. Messner, "Die Idee der Menschenwürde im Rechstaat der Pluralistischen Gesellschaft," in G. Leibholz (ed.), *Menschenwürde und Freiheitliche Rechtsordnung*, Tübingen, 1974, pp. 231–234.

27 R. F. Baum, *Doctors of Modernity: Darwin, Marx and Freud*, Peru, IL, Sherwood Sudgen and Co. Press, 1988, p. 111.

28 For a brief but cogent review of the evidence, see Baum (ibid.). The reader may also take note of the new theories of the mind by W. Penfield (*The Mystery of the Mind*, Princeton, NJ, Princeton University Press, 1975) and J. Eccles and D. Robinson (*The Wonder of Being Human: Our Brain and Our Mind*, New York, The Free Press, 1984), all three being distinguished scientists in their respective fields. Some already talk about a "trial of Darwinism," P. Johnson, *Darwin on Trial*, Downers Grove, IL, InterVarsity Press, 1991. In philosophical quarters it has also been pointed out that the concomitant replacement of Reason by "instrumental reason" has led to an intellectual sanction and social entrenchment of the technical imperative, leaving an alienated "one-dimensional man" in its wake, H. Marcuse, *One-Dimensional Man*, Boston, MA, Beacon Press, 1978; J. Habermas, *The Philosophical Discourse of Modernity*, Cambridge, MA, MIT Press, 1987; M. Buber, *I and Thou*, New York, Scribner, 1970.

29 H. Wagner, *Die Würde des Menschen*, Würzburg, Koenighausen and Newman, 1992.

30 ibid., p. 538.

31 M. Adler, *The Difference of Man and the Difference It Makes*, New York, Fordham University Press, 1993, and M. Adler, *Intellect: Mind over Matter*, New York, Macmillan Publishing, 1990, p. 164.

32 The deduced value of the agent is intrinsic, not instrumental, and so not a matter of more or less. Intrinsic value is absolute value and so does not admit of different degrees. Therefore, it is also totally egalitarian.

33 A. Gewirth, "Human Dignity as the Basis of Rights," in Meyer and Parent (eds), *The Constitution of Rights*, p. 23.

34 Gewirth, ibid., pp. 25–27.

35 It may need to be noted that purposes for Gewirth cannot be amoral. His agents, having universalized his ascriptions of worth and rights not only to himself but all agents, will therefore also modify and constrain his rationally justified assessments of his purposes.

36 See, for example, C. Taylor, *Philosophical Papers*, New York, Cambridge University Press, 1985, ch. on Atomism, and C. Gilligan, *In a Different Voice*, Cambridge, MA, Harvard University Press, 1982, pp. 22, 149.

37 Gewirth, *The Community of Rights*, p. 6.

38 Hence the title of his book.
39 Gewirth, *The Community of Rights*, pp. 94–95.
40 ibid., chs. 4–7.
41 Copp, "The Right to an Adequate Standard of Living," pp. 213–261.
42 Sismondi, *Political Economy and the Philosophy of Government*, p. 222.
43 F. H. Knight, *Risk, Uncertainty and Profit*, Boston, MA, Houghton Mifflin, 1921, p. 126.
44 R. Nozick, *Anarchy, State, and Utopia*, New York, Basic Books, 1974, p. 169.
45 Gewirth, *The Community of Rights*, p. 46.
46 Copp, "The Right to an Adequate Standard of Living," p. 260.
47 ibid., p. 261.
48 Sismondi, *Political Economy and the Philosophy of Government*, p. 417.
49 E. F. Schumacher, *A Guide for the Perplexed*, London, Cape, 1977b, pp. 139–140.

7

HOW REASONABLE IS ECONOMIC RATIONALITY?

Rationality is not a topic often discussed around the kitchen table. And yet, it is one of the most basic concepts in social science and economics. It's the philosophy of human conduct: to do something in a rational manner is to do it for good and cogent reasons, the "good reasons" being not just *some* reasons but the *best* and *strongest* available.[1] Finding some reason for doing something that one wants to do is not being rational but is merely to rationalize one's action. Clearly, in spite of the concept's philosophical connotation, the ability to act rationally applies to everybody in their everyday lives. Even feelings, or "the reasons of the heart," are legitimate grounds for rational conduct. Not surprising, it occupies a central place in the quest of understanding *Homo sapiens*, or what the Greeks called "the rational animal." What matters is not that we always act rationally, but that, as humans, we have the *capacity* for reason.

What has been said so far is hardly disputable. Yet, it transforms into something controversial as soon as one looks at the way economics speaks of rationality. Just as mainstream welfare economics operates with the welfare taken out, so it can be shown that economic rationality is economics with the rationality taken out.

1. Philosophical beginnings

Count Giovanni Pico della Mirandola, having studied at Bologna and traveled through Italy and France spending time at various universities, decided to mount a serious challenge to the prevailing catechism of the Church fathers. In 1486, at the age of twenty-four, Count Mirandola offered to debate the theologians in an effort to reconcile the spiritual traditions of the ancient Greeks and Jews with Christianity. The basis of the proposed debate was a list of 900 questions, many of which hung close to the skirt of heresy. When the Pope did not allow the disputation, the young scholar published the introduction he had written to these debating points, and this became the famous *Oration on the Dignity of Man*. In it Count Mirandola seeks to transcend the prevailing human image of the Middle Ages, the fallen and sinful

146

creature living under a watchful and angry God. Instead he has the Creator say to Man:

> We have given you, Oh Adam, no visage proper to yourself, nor any endowment properly your own, in order that whatever place, whatever gifts you may, with premeditation, select, these same you may have and possess through your own judgment and decision.
>
> We made you a creature neither of heaven nor of earth, neither mortal nor immortal, in order that you may, as the free and prouder shape of your own being, fashion yourself in the form you may prefer. It will be in your power to descend to the lower brutish forms of life; [and] you will be able, through your own decision, to rise again to the superior orders whose life is divine.[2]

Count Mirandola's little book became the manifesto of Humanism and gave the Renaissance one of its basic themes: the rebirth of man in the likeness of God. More specifically, the dignity of Man, according to Count Mirandola, rests in Man's freedom and his capacity and need to direct and shape his own life. Man is unfinished. He has freedom either to raise himself above the angels or to reduce himself below the beasts. We have within us both the higher and the lower, the noble and the base, and our freedom lies in the capacity to choose between the two.

Count Mirandola's stress on human autonomy and freedom of the will was to be echoed during the Enlightenment in the philosophical anthropology of Immanuel Kant. In modern times, the basic message reverberates in the moral philosophy of Princeton scholar Harry Frankfurt. In a seminal paper, he defines the distinguishing characteristic of being human as having the capacity of a free will.[3] This freedom of the will, he stresses, is very different from the freedom to do what one wants to do. Many animals share this type of freedom. Instead, "The statement that a person enjoys freedom of the will means that he is free to want what he wants to want," or better, "to have the will he wants." Frankfurt pictures the essential feature of a *human* being as being, at least in principle, capable or *free* to control one's desires. These (higher order) desires about desires imply reflective self-evaluation made possible by self-awareness. We do care about our desires, liking some and disapproving of others. So, for example, the statement "I do not like my wanting to watch TV all the time" is not a statement of a schizophrenic mind but of a true human being. Even more, we have the freedom to resist that particular indulgence by following the (higher level) aspiration not to do so. That is in substance what Count Mirandola meant when he proclaimed that we may fashion ourselves in the form we may prefer; to descend to brutish levels or to rise to more sublime orders of being.

Members of the animal kingdom, on the other hand, lack these higher order desires and with them the freedom to change whatever particular "will" they happen to have. A dog may show an ugly disposition toward somebody without moral qualms and without being able to "help it." But it is not only animals that appear to lack the human capacity for self-evaluation. Frankfurt also, and for our purposes more importantly, identifies very young children and "some adult human beings" as belonging to a category of "non-persons" or incomplete persons. He labels them *wantons*, a designation which according to the dictionary means somebody who is unruly, lewd, licentious, lascivious, undisciplined or just a frolicsome child.[4]

The essential characteristic of a wanton is that he does not care about his will. "His desires move him to do certain things, without its being true of him that he wants to be moved by those desires or that he prefers to be moved by other desires."[5] He has no identity apart from his first-order desires and inclinations. If a wanton experiences an "inner" struggle, it's merely a conflict between two opposing desires in which the stronger of the two will end up winning. He himself has no stake as to which will have the upper hand. His will is determined by the strength of his desires, something akin to an external force he does not care to control or, in the case of the unwilling addict, cannot control.

We all have the potential to act in a wanton manner. In addition, Frankfurt's theory is relevant because his wanton/person distinction within human nature provides a backdrop that helps shed light on the true idea of rationality. After what has been said, it may come as a surprise that the economist would not see in the wanton anything that contradicts rational conduct. How is this so? Because the wanton pursues any end he/she happens to have, and if he/she is a "good" wanton, he/she does this efficiently and logically. In contrast, Frankfurt's person is rational when she/he tries to determine the ends she/he believes she/he ought to have. Thus the rationality of the wanton and the rationality of the person are two very different things. This stark difference becomes obscured when the "rationality" label is used in both cases.

The meaning of rationality

To repeat, philosophy teaches that rational conduct is doing something for good reasons. It involves not only finding the best possible means to do what one wants to do, but also aligning the doer with the person one wants to be. In Nicholas Rescher's words, it's about "what I would want if I managed to make certain changes in myself (that is, made myself over more fully in the direction of my own ideals)."[6] It involves commitment to deeply held values, some more personal and others more social in nature, which prescribe conduct.

These considerations are part and parcel of what is called *evaluative rationality*, which counsels against preferences that harm our better nature and are illegitimate. In fact, evaluation is said to be at the very heart and core of rationality.[7] What really matters is the pursuit of "appropriate" ends, meaning those ends that serve the agent's best (or real) interest. To some extent, it is "a matter of meeting the needs that people universally have in common – health, normal functioning of the body and mind, adequate resources, human companionship and affection, and so on."[8] Whatever interest we pursue, in order to be deemed "appropriate," must be in *anyone's* interest acting under the same constraints and circumstances. This is so because rational ends express a *common* interest.[9] In other words, genuine rationality is intimately related to common humanity and the common good. Reject one and you have to reject them all.

Rationality and morality go together. The starting point and core of every meaningful theory insists that moral judgments must be backed by good reasons, as well as giving equal weight to the interests of each person. There are no "privileged" persons: every life has the same value, and we are not to treat persons unequally unless there is good reason to do so.[10] As discussed in Chapter 6, equal respect for human life and dignity is required by reason, and therefore it is also a requirement of rational conduct. There can be no such thing as a rational manipulator or a rational exploiter or a rational cheater. And yet economists, if true to the teachings of their discipline, will strongly object to this last statement and much of what has been said leading up to it. This puzzle needs some explanation.

2. The road to Rational Economic Man

In his *Treatise of Human Nature* (1739–40), David Hume pictures reason as only concerned with means, not ends. Its role was essentially informational, to assist in the deliberations about an action's consequences. Ends of action, on the other hand, were the result of "passion," the seat of purely subjective desires or "appetites" driving behavior. From his perspective reason was operating as a pure *instrument* informing how to best reach one's goals – reason being "the slave of the passions." Reason so narrowly construed allowed Hume to seriously claim that "it is not contrary to reason to prefer the destruction of the whole world to the scratching of my finger."[11] It's not easy to think of anything more absurd, and this proposition reveals the absurdity of the British Enlightenment project of reducing reason to mere instrumental rationality.[12]

The legacy of Humean reason permeates economic science to this day; witness the statement of one of the foremost contemporary economic experts on rationality (Nobel Laureate Herbert Simon):[13] "Reason is wholly instrumental. It cannot tell us where to go; at best it can tell us how to get there. It is a gun for hire that can be employed in the service of any goal we have, good or bad."

Classic economic man

In retrospect, the classical economists can be forgiven for seeing no harm in basing their science on such "thin" rationality. In those days, political economy was concerned with production, business and commerce. Naturally, this led to building the science around the profit motive. Under the harsh reality of competitive pressure, altruistic and moral motives could reasonably be neglected, and reasoning was naturally related to business success. Rationality was a matter of calculation.

Toward the latter part of the nineteenth century, when economics started to emphasize the theory of consumption to explain market demand, it simply adopted "utility" or "pleasure" maximization as an analog to profit maximization of the producer. However, even the British pioneer of that "new economics," Stanley Jevons, felt it appropriate to discuss briefly the relationship between economics and ethics. By proposing the object of economics to be the maximization of happiness by purchasing pleasure at the lowest cost of pain, he also realized that the new language could be misunderstood: "It may seem as if pleasures and pains of a gross kind were treated as the all-sufficient motives to guide the mind of man."[14] Not so, Jevons declared, "the feelings of which a man is capable of are of various grades . . . . He is capable also of mental and moral feelings of several degrees of elevation," and "a higher motive might rightly overbalance all considerations even to the next lower range of feelings."[15] But, he added, economics can only deal with the lowest rank of feelings in the hierarchy of values. Instead, a different type of reasoning, a "higher calculus of moral right and wrong," would be needed for rational conduct. But in the cases when "that higher calculus gives no prohibition, we need the lower calculus to gain us the utmost good."[16] In this view, economics has its own special domain, while ethics or morality dwell on a higher level. This makes economic rational choice only legitimate in choices that are morally indifferent. Hence, the problem of "freedom of the will" cannot exist within *economic* choice as such. At the same time, matters of *human* (not economic) choice and *human* rationality were accepted as a different kettle of fish. In short, "economic man" was just an abstraction with significance in the restricted economic domain.

This explicit relegation of economics to the lower sphere of human action provoked Ruskin's passionate outcries, calling it a pig science and much more. And when it became the official doctrine in the writings of Alfred Marshall, it moved Hobson to a lifelong struggle for a social economics that would reintegrate in some fashion the higher motives, and, with them, the ethical dimension.

Meanwhile, the history of economic man takes a decisive turn for the worse with the work of a Unitarian minister who was appointed in 1874 to the little Portland Street chapel in London. Philip Wicksteed held that position until 1897; meanwhile, he supplemented his income as a university extension lecturer and by writing. His concern for poverty drove him in the early 1880s to study economics. He read Marx's *Das Kapital* only to find its logic flawed.[17] Strongly influenced by S. Jevons' new theory of value in economics, he chose to devote his energies to writing book-length monographs: *The Alphabet of Economic Science* (1888) and his magnum opus, *The Common Sense of Political Economy* (1910).

Wicksteed's main message was that Jevons and the economists after him had not gone far enough in realizing the true domain of economic science. The marginal principle and utility maximization were *not*, as Jevons and Marshall believed, *only* applicable to industrial or commercial affairs, "but run as a universal and vital force through the administration of *all* our resources."[18] In short, *all* deliberate or conscious human action is part and parcel of economics. So, for example, the question of whether to study or go out with a friend is a question that needs to defer to economic science. It's a problem of how to manage our time, and we can do only so much in a twenty-four-hour day. Hence, what started as the science of commerce was turned into the science of choice.

The ramifications of this radical idea are far-reaching. It extends an often impersonal, cold and calculating approach to everyday life. The non-economic category either vanishes or is subordinated to the economic, and the new *way of economic thinking* is born. At first sight it looks like an improvement: self-interest, says Wicksteed, need not be assumed. Even though economic man may be constantly calculating to achieve his own ends, these same ends could be philanthropic. According to this view, there is nothing that would preclude the driving of a hard bargain to maximize one's profit in order to be more capable of making large donations to charity. The only thing that matters from the standpoint of economics is what he labeled the condition of "*non-tuism*": that genuine altruism or benevolence is *not* applied to the person one is dealing with and exchanging with. "All that this means," Lionel Robbins later explained, "is that my relation to the dealers does not enter into my hierarchy of ends. For me (who may be acting for myself or my friends or some civic or charitable authority) *they are regarded merely as means*."[19] It's an interesting revelation of the uneasy relationship between economic (or instrumental) rationality and human dignity.

Wicksteed's new interpretation of economic science did not get much notice until his admirer, Robbins, gave it a renewed push in his celebrated essay on *The Nature and Significance of Economic Science* (1932). He was unusually successful in injecting Wicksteed's thoughts into the main currents of economic thinking. Seeing in Wicksteed a promising avenue for deflecting once and for all the perennial charge of self-interest, Robbins declared that selfish economic man was a fiction. In the introduction to the 1933 edition of Wicksteed's *Common Sense*, Robbins makes this point crystal clear:

Before Wicksteed wrote, it was still possible for intelligent men to give countenance to the belief that the whole structure of economics depends on the assumption of the world of economic men, each accentuated by egocentric or hedonistic motives. For anyone who has read *Common Sense*, the expression of such a view is no longer consistent with intellectual honesty. Wicksteed shattered this misconception once and for all.[20]

Equally important was Wicksteed's shattering of the old idea that the economic domain, and with it instrumental rationality, is limited, even subordinated, to a moral sphere. Soon thereafter, economics, in a few short convulsions coinciding with the mathematical formalization of utility theory, altered quite dramatically in a direction consistent with Wicksteed and Robbins' perspective. The nineteenth-century clod, Economic Man, with his behavioral traits of insatiable greed and cold-hearted egomania was out, and a "new" Rational Man was in.

The new Rational Man and self-interest

If selfishness is fiction, who is this being and what does he do? J. M. Clark, in his *Preface to Social Economics* (1936), also wryly offered his apprehension:

> Our old friend, the "economic man," is becoming very self-conscious and bafflingly non-committal. Instead of introducing himself to his readers with his old-time freedom, he says: "I may behave one way and I may behave another, but what is that to you? You must take my choices as you find them: I choose as I choose and that is all you really need to know." The poor thing has been told that his psychology is all wrong, and he is gamely trying to get on without any and still perform as many as possible of his accustomed tasks.[21]

But humorous language aside, some of the key aspects of economic rationality have already been encountered in Chapter 1. There we pictured an abstract individual with a preference ordering who acts in a manner as to best satisfy those preferences. According to this picture everybody has a preference structure endowed with certain properties such as transitivity, completeness and so on. Rational action then consists in maximizing the satisfaction of those preferences in an optimal manner, within the confines of certain (external) constraints relating to income, wealth or time. It's a problem of "constrained maximization," in which reason is employed only instrumentally, to reach one's objectives determined by one's preferences. Recall that rationality is understood as a *formal* concept that does not specify the nature of the preferences; they might as well be selfish, prudent, altruistic, moral or some combination of these. Standard economics does not second-guess a rational agent's preferences; they are simply taken as given. The idea is to apply reason (or reasoning) as an instrument only. Reason no longer means "the activity of assimilating eternal ideas, or ideals, which were to function as goals for men."[22]

More generally, if a theory postulates that one is *always* motivated by one's *own* purposes, preferences, satisfactions, pleasures, however constituted, then rationality by definition is bound to be self-interested. It cannot be otherwise; there is no more contrast class, no *non*-self-interest. But, at the same time, if *everything* is self-interest, the word loses its meaning, and one could just as well say that *nothing* is self-interest. It's like everybody being in the same political party being equivalent to nobody being in any party. If self-interested means merely purposeful, or rational, then its opposite is not altruistic, but mindless, self-contradictory and impulsive behavior. Such is the nature of humankind according to pure modern theory: not really selfish but, in fact, only rational. In this theoretical and formal sense, Wicksteed and Robbins are certainly not incorrect, just making a meaningless tautological assertion.

On the other hand, in order to apply the concept in a useful manner to economic decision making, to the building of market supply and demand curves, rationality has to be given some *content* or a more substantive meaning, and here economists still choose self-interest as *the* basic behavioral assumption. Nothing reveals that more than the going practice of equating "free-riding" – generally, trying to enjoy the benefits of a group effort without contributing oneself – with rational conduct.[23] Modern economics – contra Wicksteed and Robbins – is still clinging to the old behavioral assumption of self-interest, and does so by neglecting the other more human and social motives. "Le plus que ça change, plus que c'est la même chose."

One-dimensional rationality

At a deeper level of analysis, the essential problem with instrumental or economic rationality is that it is one-dimensional: it assumes an individual driven by a *single* purpose. This is a problematic abstraction with considerable consequences: first, individuals may routinely transcend, and in the process violate, the postulates of rationality, if by individuals we mean live people. Second, by giving the entire floor to self-interest, it rules out other dimensions, in particular the social or moral dimension in the making of choices.

The first of these problems is that the "rational animal" is a much more intricate being than economists realize. And it is this complexity that throws a monkey wrench into things. People as agents, when acting to satisfy their preferences, can do so rationally when it is assumed that their preference orderings are *complete*. In simple language this means that all alternative actions are both comparable and commensurable, that they can be compared and measured on a *common* scale, and assessed in the light of a *common* criterion. If so, we can always determine whether one course of action, and the consequences to preference satisfaction that it would entail, scores higher or lower than another. In other words, we can always rank alternative actions, saying "I prefer this to that," or in the case of some tie, "I am indifferent" or "I don't care which one to pursue." Choosing the best action is reduced to picking the one with the highest value expressed in *number* form. Technically, this is known as *algorithmic* choice, a term derived from an "algometer," which in the old days was a device for measuring the intensity of pain caused by pressure. An example of such algorithmic choice would be the "choosing" of the square root of nine over the square root of four, executing such choice as a calculus of *maximization*. All that is required is a mechanical computational ability. This method of choice can be illustrated when a college admissions committee decides to rank applicants based on test scores, and to choose for admission only those candidates who score higher than a certain agreed-upon cutoff point. In this case, the procedure would work because there would be only *one* criterion for screening the applicants. It breaks down, however, as soon as the committee uses more than one criterion, let us say test scores, high-school grades, civic leadership potential, regional mix, gender and ethnic characteristics and so on. Here, admittance would no longer be a matter of comparing numbers, but of making *judgments* based on specified weights given to the various goals.

In general, the essential condition for rational choice, completeness, can no longer be assumed in the case of two or more interests motivating choices; unless, of course, some candidates score higher on *all* criteria. Normally, under non-algorithmic choice the result would be indeterminacy.[24] Thus, with plural ends, the Rational Man of modern economics can no longer function reasonably in the presumed manner. Isn't choosing between *ends* what *real* choice is all about? It explains the agony and hesitation we often experience when we have to make a choice. It's an agony, an inner tension that cannot be captured by the notion of "opportunity cost" as an economist might argue. Take the "choice" between a nickel and a dime. If I (rationally) maximize and choose (algorithmically) the dime, I have to forego the nickel, or the opportunity cost of 5 cents. But the cost or loss entailed by this decision is more than compensated for by the gain. There is no real loss, no agony of choice here. Similarly with "utility," as long as an agent successfully maximizes the available utility gains, there is really nothing to agonize about. In contrast, there is often inner conflict when the choice involves different dimensions or ends: let us say, between doing our duty or seeking personal gain. In law such a tension is, of course, recognized as a "conflict of interests." It's a choice between two qualitatively different ends. Mathematics cannot resolve this conflict, and no matter what we do, there will be some uncompensated loss along some dimension. In short, as important as making personal *judgments* may be in daily life, economics cannot account for them.

In a sense, it is rather ironic that economics, after picturing itself as the "science of choice," is not even able to grasp this phenomenon. It has led the highly respected scholar G. L. S. Shackle to remark:

> Conventional economics is not about choice, but about acting according to necessity. . . . To call [economic man's] conduct choice is surely a misuse of words, when we suppose that to him the ends amongst which he can select, and the criteria of selection, are given, and the means to each end are known . . . choice in such a theory is empty, and conventional economics should abandon the word.[25]

So much for Wicksteed's science of choice. After transvaluing "welfare" and "rationality," one is compelled to add: economic choice takes real choice out of economics.

The second problem of one-dimensional economic rationality is the exclusion of the moral dimension, or the denial of moral conduct *by assumption*. Recall, that economic choice, assuming self-interest, by its very nature must reduce all other dimensions to self-interest. For this reason, true altruism or morality does not really exist; it must be regarded as being so in appearance only, mere pretensions with ulterior motives. No wonder so many economists tend to be cynics. But, as one scholar has observed, why would faking altruism really work, if there was not indeed something like genuine altruism in the first place?[26] Could we really fake or imitate, let us say cheesecake, if there was no such thing in the first place?

Of criminals, mice and men

Stanton Samenow, in his book *Inside the Criminal Mind* (1984), makes a disturbing observation when he writes that "a detailed and lengthy examination of the mind of a criminal will reveal that he is anything but sick, [he is instead] rational, calculating and deliberate in his actions."[27] People become criminals not in response to forces beyond their control, but by choice. The direct cause of criminal behavior, Samenow demonstrates, is criminal thinking. And he goes on to picture something that looks strikingly similar to Rational Economic Man:

> They all regard the world as a chessboard over which they have total control, and they perceive people as pawns to be pushed around at will. Trust, love, loyalty, and teamwork are incompatible with their way of life. They scorn and exploit most people who are kind, trusting, hardworking, and honest. Toward a few people they are sentimental but rarely considerate. Some of their most altruistic acts have sinister motives.[27]

For decriminalization and rehabilitation, Dr. Samenow prescribes "a process [that] calls for criminals to acquire [the] moral values that have enabled civilization to survive."[28] The missing social dimension seems to be the pathology shared by both the criminal and economic man.

The existence of social motives like altruism and morality poses grave problems for an anthropology of one-dimensional man. It gets us back to the human capacity of self-awareness and reflective self-evaluation. Do we ever worry about our (economically rational) pursuits? Or do we just go ahead and maximize skillfully our preferences and inclinations, whatever they may be? Didn't Abraham Maslow stress the point that "the human being is simultaneously that which he is and that which he yearns to be"? And is not this aspiration to instantiate better preferences what it means to be human?[29] Answering these questions in the affirmative will imply that human nature is intrinsically dual, that we have a momentary set of preferences and a set of preferences we aspire to; call them *aspirational preferences*. What do we do if the two conflict? It does entail (in Frankfurt's terminology) choosing the will we want to have, or the distinctive capacity of human free will and the moral struggle to fight temptation that often goes with it. It involves the rich tapestry of guilt, shame, self-respect and pride. In short, it means that we are dealing with a person, not a wanton. Laboratory experiments have shown that the theory of rational choice can be applied quite successfully in studying rats, pigeons, snails, even rotifers.[30] But it must fall considerably short as a picture of *human* rational conduct.

Reducing morality to self-interest

What about trying to squeeze morality (or altruism) onto the same dimension as self-interest? Economists sometimes operate as if this were possible. In this vein, there are two alternative strategies to attempt to get rid of the problem. One of these was recently explored by economist Sean Hargreaves Heap.[31] It consists of treating the desire for self-worth as one of the motives which underlies a particular person's preferences. To many economists this may sound like the obvious solution. But it won't work: a sense of self-worth makes choice *context dependent*, something that Hargreaves Heap illustrates with a clever example:

> Suppose a person chooses an apple when offered a choice between an apple and a banana. Now suppose they are offered the same choice again in the presence of a third option, a smaller apple, the person may well now choose the banana so as to avoid the imputation of greediness which might come from choosing what is seen to be a "large" apple.[32]

Here, the concern not to appear greedy has induced a preference change, something incompatible with rational choice theory based on "given" or unchanging preferences.

Potential attempts to nuance this type of problem by modeling the choice in a manner that declares the apple of the first choice as being in some sense different from the (physically same) apple in the second choice due to its different context does not pass muster either. The reason here is a technical one: it violates the requirements of basic (axiomatic) decision theories: that the objects of choice are to be defined independently of the field of choice, or the context of choice.[33] Furthermore, when preferences do not just apply to "apples," but "apples *in their context*," empirical testing of the theory gets prohibitively complex and ambiguous. It seems, therefore, that a concern with self-worth emanating from upholding social norms must be a *separate* type of motivational influence on behavior, other than individual preference satisfaction. Or, to look at it from a different angle, all these attempts at reducing non-self-interest to the dimension of self-interest by incorporating an additional objective aiming at self-worth into the utility function are bound to fail. The objectives are not of the same quality, or of the same order, with the result that the adding of a social or moral dimension will tend to *reorder* choices.

The second basic strategy consists in trying to capture moral considerations by means of some "overarching utility function." Here the agent first would choose between one preference ranking based on self-interest and another that is based on morality. Depending on the outcome of that initial calculation, the agent would then proceed to operate according to the utility of self-interest or morality.[34] This scheme too runs into logical difficulties, as the following thought experiment demonstrates. Suppose that *all* choices can be characterized as being either self-interested or non-self-interested. How do I choose one criterion or the other? Since the two standards by definition exhaust the possible categories, one would have to proceed either according to the reasons of self-interest or the dictates of morality. Either course of action would be inappropriate and beg the question. We simply lack some over-arching *third* criterion necessary to solve this problem.[35]

In conclusion, as has been shown, the economist's instrumental rationality, being one-dimensional and algorithmic, fails to acknowledge the human dimension in the making of reasonable choices. It denies freedom of judgment and personal discretion. "To assume that all values can be graded on a scale, so that it is a mere matter of inspection to determine the highest," says philosopher Isaiah Berlin, "seems to me to falsify our knowledge that men are free agents, to represent moral decisions as an operation which a slide rule could, in principle, perform."[36] How much longer can a meaningful social science afford to ignore this basic point? A hopeful sound is voiced by Amartya Sen who, in unmasking Rational Economic Man, likens him to a "social moron." Sen, too, bemoans the fact that "economic theory has been much preoccupied with this *rational fool* decked in the glory of his *one* all-purpose preference ordering."[37]

3. The dual self

A realistic picture of the person is one that fully acknowledges the human capacity for free will, and a good conception of rationality in economics or any other social science needs to incorporate and reflect this basic fact.

The duality of the self consists in what can be called a higher and a lower human nature, or a higher or lower self. The "higher self" need not be some elusive metaphysical entity; for the present purpose it is sufficient to describe it as the *aspirational self*, the self that is aspired to and concerns our innermost values and personal principles. It reflects what we consider to be true, fair, honest, lovable, virtuous and so on. It also points the way toward a more authentic life and the higher human needs that this implies. The "lower self," on the other hand, is much closer to the self of standard economics: the self involving urges, inclinations, a taste for pleasure, power, vanity and other expressions of self-interest. Or in terms of Frankfurt's philosophical anthropology, it is the self that one happens to have and which lets itself be moved by the strongest desires, in short: the wanton self.

Marred by linguistic ambiguity, the word "self" refers to what from the dual perspective is one of three possibilities: the lower self (such as "self-less" or "self-renunciation"), the higher self (as in "self-fulfillment" or "self-realization"), or the place of interaction between the two (such as "self-determination"). It is this last meaning that is at the heart of the dual-self conception of the active self or the ego. This interpretation fully reflects Pico della Mirandola's basic point that human nature is neither divine nor animal like, but that we are able, through our own choices, to rise to the "superior orders" or descend to the "brutish form of life." Our freedom (and dignity) lies in the capacity to choose between the two levels of our self.

In terms of authentic rationality, the dual self perspective recognizes two basic ends of action: action for the good of one-self (self-interest) and action for the good of others (altruism and morality). Obviously, in many if not most of our actions, the desires of the lower self are not in conflict with the demands of the higher self. Yet there are, even in economics and the marketplace, many occasions in which considerations of personal integrity and social values would go against purely self-regarding conduct. Should we be truthful even if honesty doesn't pay? What is more important, respect for the bottom line, or respect for the needs and dignity of one's co-workers? Other instances concern the issues of loyalty, fairness, public accountability, the common good and so on. In situations like these, there is a choice to be made: either to all-out maximize the gratification of the desires reflected in our preferences, or to choose under a self-imposed constraint invoked by the aspirational self. In simple terms, it's a choice between maximization and moral

158

restraint, and the outcome often depends on strength of character or moral backbone.

Analytically, and somewhat abstractly, the choosing agent is now modeled as having an irreducibly *dual* preference structure: first the preferences expressing the lower self. Second, perched above, are the higher order preferences of the aspirational self, reflecting the preferences about one's preferences, a *meta-preference* ordering. Any choice with moral aspects will involve a struggle between following without self-restraint the algorithmic ordering of the lower self, or instead, the morally constrained preference ranking sanctioned by the higher self. Clearly, what we have here is a choice between two incommensurable selves. Logically, as was previously demonstrated, it cannot be executed according to the formula of single-dimension utility maximization. The fact that we can and do make such choices simply indicates that there are *limits* to economic rationality. Instead of mere calculation, genuine rationality implies an intuitive balancing between two basic simultaneously held but incommensurable ends. In ordinary language, we do make judgments.

Instrumental rationality must now give way to a non-algorithmic rationality of ends as well, a new view resembling what Alan Hamlin calls "extended rationality." Essentially, it implies "that own utility is not the sole motivator of individual action, and that there exists an internal tension between self-interest and other rational goals."[38] Extended rationality also provides a potential escape from the prisoners' dilemma[39] and provides a more satisfactory model of choice under uncertainty.[40] Moreover, it also yields a greatly enriched perspective of work, intrinsic- or self-motivation, and the qualitative dimensions of the workplace. But, above all, it is a view of the self that claims to be intuitively highly plausible, even self-evident, and it seeks merely to describe people as they really are: persons with a moral capacity that is also the very root of human dignity. The next section illustrates the potency of the dual self view of rationality to capture a number of important everyday phenomena that are otherwise incomprehensible within the vocabulary of theoretical economics.

Dual self in action: trust, rights and respect for the law

In an abstract world where self-interest exhausts all possible kinds of human motivations, there is simply no room for anything like trust, "the belief in the honesty and reliability of another."[41] We do not "trust" somebody to behave opportunistically. Quite the contrary, we have trust in another to the extent that we believe that he or she will identify with the higher self, and not with the self of self-interest. Neither is this merely a sophistic theoretical point. Trust is undoubtedly an important interpersonal economic resource that tends to lubricate economic exchange by minimizing so-called transaction costs necessitated by the writing and legal enforcement of detailed contracts. At the same time, it is also a vital good in and of itself, affecting the quality of life in general, by affirming our common humanity and self-respect. Would it therefore not also follow that an economics unable to accommodate its meaning and significance would tend to embrace institutions and policies that might inadvertently also breed social distrust and cynicism?

The irrational limiting of Rational Economic Man to self-interested pursuits would also make him incapable of approaching others as ends with intrinsic value. His instrumental mentality prohibits respect for anything other than himself, which explains why economic theory cannot grasp the phenomenon of human dignity or any other kind of intrinsic value or principle. Respect for the rights of future generations, or for a person's basic rights on non-instrumental grounds, are two more social values that elude the economist's language. A revealing example in this respect pertains to voting rights when economist James Tobin mused: "Any good second-year graduate student in economics could write a short examination paper proving that voluntary transactions in votes [i.e., purchasing votes] increases the welfare of the sellers as well as the buyers."[42] Once again, intimations of a strange world.

Instrumental reasoning also affects respect for the law. The passing of a law as such will have no effect on personal conduct but only the probability of punishment making illegal behavior more costly. As Hamlin demurs, "the neo-classical rational individual reacts to the threat of punishment rather than the law itself, so that we may model the law in terms of changing the relative prices of alternative actions rather than placing any new constraints on acceptable behavior."[43] In other words, obedience to the law is wholly contingent upon calculations of self-interest. Albert Hirschman agrees: "a principal purpose of publicly proclaimed laws is to stigmatize antisocial behavior and thereby influence citizens' values and behavioral codes."[44] As a result, economists, in discussing pubic policy options, cannot see beyond the manipulating of *incentives* in channeling individual behavior. In their view, ends are "given," and if they happen to be antisocial, all we can do is to raise the stakes of such behavior. Only after one accepts, that, in principle at least, persons are free to question their conduct and invoke meta-preferences to change it, will it be possible to consider the value-molding influence of new legislation.

Human need and economics imperialism

Basic human needs are not recognized in conventional economics. They are reduced to wants or the more neutral-sounding (but one-dimensional) concept of "preferences." As a vestige of the old emphasis on pleasure or satisfaction, the selfish Rational Economic Man is moved by momentary desires. He lives not *in* the moment but *for* the moment, going through life according to the wanton creed: "eat, drink and be merry, for tomorrow we die." In contrast, it is the aspirational self that pursues a meaningful *life* by ordering the wants, assigning to them importance with regard to purposes deemed vital. These necessary wants are therefore understood as needs ranging from survival to self-realization.

When a wanted good that is not really needed is acquired, one could say that the good is misallocated or wasted. Avoidance of such waste, cutting back on some consumption, is the essence of an ethics of moderation or conservation. The notion that restricting one's wants to needs is in this sense "efficient" and also "rational" is bound to be alien to an all-is-self-interest economics. It's a world of a "need" here or a "need" there, but these "needs" refer simply to personal gain or advantage and can be traded off against each other. When Rational Economic Man says, "I do not need this commodity," he is expressing that there is something else that better suits his self-regarding purposes, a perfectly cogent statement in the one-dimensional world of self-interest. But where other-regarding purposes compete with self-interest, the word "need" takes on a different meaning. I do not really need a commodity or a service because *others* need it more, because it may have a socially more beneficial use elsewhere or in time. "Avoiding waste" here refers to the waste of unnecessary resource consumption, to respecting others and the ethic of conservation.

The notion of a structured self and plural ends does not render standard economic theory patently false, but simply relegates instrumental behavior to a special case, to a particular domain where explanation and prediction may be attempted in terms of social conduct. Commerce has long and correctly been seen as a separate sphere where for many purposes we can afford to neglect the higher human propensities. But even in a world of selfish economic traders, opportunistically dodging any kind of social values that would counsel moderation and restraint, a world devoid of moral character and conduct and respect for others, a world in accord with the postulate of economic rationality, it is questionable that commerce would prosper. The real problem arises when that limited view of the person is used to engineer social institutions to accommodate such traits. It is at that point that humanity can no longer afford to operate without a more complete picture of the rational person.

One of the founders of the Chicago School of Economics, Frank Knight, warned that "there is no more important prerequisite to clear thinking in regard to economics itself than is recognition of its limited place among human interests at large."[45] That caution has only been honored in the breach, ironically in the efforts of that same faculty including Gary Becker, Robert Fogel and Richard Posner who launched the *economics imperialism* movement. This movement applies the economic way of thinking about rationality to education, economic history, sociology, anthropology, political science, crime and even the law. According to Posner, building on such cherished notions as utility maximization, opportunity cost, scarcity, the law of demand and other such concepts, reduce all human sciences to economics.[46]

One of the most hideous manifestations of this new imperialism is its application to jurisprudence, proposing that judges, too, make decisions on the basis of economic rationality, or at least that they *should* do so. In Posner's own words: "economics turns out to be a powerful tool of normative analysis of law and legal institutions – a source of criticism and reform."[47] Good judges, the ones to be applauded and promoted, are not the ones who are (still) guided by considerations of justice but who strive for economic efficiency, defined instead as wealth maximization (the market value of output of all tangible and intangible commodities).[48]

The new economics of law is a foremost challenge to the last remaining bastion of true or reasonable rationality. The invasion seeks to oust *Reasonable Person* – defined in the philosophy of law as a person who is not only protective of his own rights, but also has a fair regard for the welfare of others – who still underlies legal reasoning. In the making of legal judgments, Werner Hirsch explains: "the law holds that a person whose acts deviate from the standard of 'reasonable' can be found negligent and held liable," while economics, in contrast, "is built around the concept of 'rational [economic] man' who in the extreme is totally self-serving, seeking to maximize his self-interest."[49] Here, too, instrumentally *rational* is a far cry from *reasonable*.

To fight against the reduction of reason to instrumental rationality, to make room for a Reasonable Person besides Rational Man, is one of the key tasks facing social economics today. The law must be regarded as the primary antibody to the frequent destructive greed of the marketplace. Obviously, the aim of economics imperialists and their conservative supporters knowingly or unknowingly also infects the very immune system of the social organism. Perhaps it could also be said that in a very real sense, economic incursions into law are the academic equivalent of AIDS. If such illicit intercourse is not stopped, the future may very well be characterized by an accelerated social deterioration with unprecedented consequences.

Conclusion

In this chapter, two alternative theories of rationality have been juxtaposed, each of which claims to be true. But the economics version logically defeats itself: if someone makes the statement that *all* motives are merely instrumental, then *that* will imply that such a claim must be instrumental too. Hence there would be no such thing as intrinsic truth and honesty in communication – that is, propositions unencumbered by ulterior motives – that would lend any credibility to the claim. On its own terms, this inherently self-contradictory element compels one to conclude that there is little that is rational about economic rationality.

Notes

1 N. Rescher, *Rationality*, Oxford, Clarendon Press, 1988, p. 4.
2 G. Pico della Mirandola, *Oration on the Dignity of Man* [1486], trans. A. R. Caponigri, Chicago, IL, Henry Regnery Company, 1956, pp. 7–8.
3 H. G. Frankfurt, "Freedom of the Will and the Concept of a Person," *Journal of Philosophy*, January 1971, vol. 68:1, pp. 5–20.
4 *Webster's Collegiate Dictionary*, 5th edn, Springfield, MA, G. and C. Merriam and Co., 1948, p. 1133.
5 Frankfurt, "Freedom of the Will and the Concept of a Person," p. 10.
6 Rescher, *Rationality*, p. 113.
7 ibid., pp. 95, 100.
8 ibid., p. 100.
9 ibid., p. 101.
10 See J. Rachels, *The Elements of Moral Philosophy*, New York, Random House, 1986, ch. 1.
11 D. Hume, *A Treatise of Human Nature* [1739], Oxford, Clarendon Press, 1978, bk. II, pt. iii, sect. 3.
12 Subsequently Hume was to make a distinction between worthy and unworthy passions, but he did so by appealing to sentiment; more specifically to what he called "natural sympathy." His longtime friend, Adam Smith, continued the building of moral philosophy on the grounds of sympathy with his celebrated *The Theory of Moral Sentiment* (1759), Boston, MA, Wells and Lilly, 1817.
13 H. A. Simon, *Reason in Human Affairs*, Stanford, CA, Stanford University Press, 1983, pp. 7–8.
14 S. Jevons, *The Theory of Political Economy* [1871], reprinted, New York, Augustus M. Kelley, 1965, p. 23.
15 ibid., p. 25.
16 ibid., pp. 25, 27.
17 Wicksteed deserves the honor of having been one of the first to speak out against Marx's Labor Theory of Value. See his *"Das Kapital*: A Criticism," in *Today*, October 1884, reprinted in his *The Common Sense of Political Economy*, vol. II, London, George Routledge and Sons, 1933, pp. 705–733.
18 ibid., vol. 1, p. 3.
19 L. Robbins, *An Essay on the Nature and Significance of Economic Science* [1932], 3rd edn, London, Macmillan, 1984, p. 97 (emphasis added).
20 See L. Robbins in his "Introduction" to Wicksteed, *The Common Sense of Political Economy*, p. xxi.
21 J. M. Clark, *Preface to Social Economics* [1936], reprint, New York, Augustus M. Kelley, 1967, pp. 9–10.
22 M. Horkheimer, *Critique of Instrumental Reason*, New York, Seabury Press, 1974, p. vii.
23 For evidence on this point, the interested reader may want to look up intermediate textbooks. For example, E. Browning and J. Browning, *Microeconomic Theory and Application*, New York, Harper and Collins, 1992, p. 659; W. Nicholson, *Microeconomic Theory*, New York, Dryden Press, 1992, p. 765; E. Phelps, *Political Economy: An Introductory Text*, New York, W. W. Norton, 1985, p. 141; R. H. Frank, *Microeconomics and Behavior*, New York, McGraw-Hill, 1991, p. 651.
24 See, for example, the article by T. K. Seung and D. Bonevac, "Plural Values and Indeterminate Rankings," *Ethics*, July 1992, vol. 102, pp. 799–813.
25 G. L. S. Shackle, *Decision Order and Time in Human Affairs*, Cambridge, Cambridge University Press, 1961, p. 272.

26 A. P. Hamlin, *Ethics, Economics and the State*, New York, St. Martin's Press, 1986, p. 36.

27 S. E. Samenow, *Inside the Criminal Mind*, New York, Times Books, 1984, p. 10.

28 ibid., p. 252.

29 A. Maslow, *Toward a Psychology of Being*, New York, Van Nostrand Reinhold, 1968, p. 160.

30 G. Tullock and R. McKenzie, *The New World of Economics*, 4th edn, Homewood, IL, R. D. Irwin, Inc., 1985.

31 S. Hargreaves Heap, "Norms and Reasons," unpublished paper presented at the International Conference for Socio-Economics, Geneva, July 13, 1996.

32 ibid., p. 3.

33 Such accepted axiomatic theories are by Savage and von Neumann-Morgenstern. See R. Sudgen, "Rational Choice: A Survey of the Contributions from Economics and Philosophy," *Economic Journal*, July 1991, pp. 751–785.

34 An example of such strategy can be found in J. Buchanan, "Markets, States and the Extent of Morals," *American Economic Review*, May 1978, vol. 62:2, p. 366.

35 Another rather graphic way to illustrate the ultimate limit of economic choice analysis works as follows. Imagine two interests, self-interest and "non-self-interest," plotted on the two axes of a conventional indifference curve type graph, suggesting that they are on the same dimension and can be traded off against one another. The budget curve will reflect the respective costs of identifying with either of the two basic interests. Question: What is the interest behind the "utility mountain" with its contour lines? If it is neither self-interest nor non-self-interest, what could it be?

36 I. Berlin, *Four Essays on Liberty*, Oxford, Oxford University Press, 1969, p. 171.

37 A. Sen, "The Rational Fools: A Critique of the Behavioral Foundations of Economic Theory," *Philosophy and Public Affairs*, 1977, vol. 6, p. 335.

38 Hamlin, *Ethics, Economics and the State*, p. 22.

39 A. Sen, "Choice, Orderings and Rationality," in S. Koerner (ed.), *Practical Reason*, New Haven, CT, Yale University Press, 1974, pp. 54–67.

40 Hamlin, *Ethics, Economics and the State*, pp. 35–52.

41 *Webster's Collegiate Dictionary*.

42 J. Tobin, "On Limiting the Domain of Inequality," *Journal of Law and Economics*, 1970, p. 13.

43 Hamlin, *Ethics, Economics and the State*, p. 53.

44 A. O. Hirschman, "Against Parsimony," *Economics and Philosophy*, 1985, vol. 1:1, p. 10.

45 F. Knight, quoted in A. M. Polinsky, "Economic Analysis as a Potentially Defective Product: A Buyer's Guide to Posner's Economic Analysis of Law," *Harvard Law Review*, vol. 87, p. 1658.

46 R. A. Posner, *The Economics of Justice*, Cambridge, MA, Harvard University Press, 1981, p. 2.

47 R. A. Posner, *The Economic Analysis of Law*, 2nd edn, Boston, MA, Little, Brown, 1977, p. 5.

48 For a detailed discussion of wealth maximization and legal justice, see M. Lutz and K. Lux, *Humanistic Economics: The New Challenge*, New York, Bootstrap Press, 1988, ch. 9.

49 W. Hirsch, *Law and Economics*, New York, Academic Press, 1979, p. xii.

8

RETHINKING THE CORPORATION

Much of modern economic theory is a brilliantly executed piece of applied mathematics served up with a thick sauce of myths and metaphors. But when this "sauce" is brushed away, much older and long forgotten concepts reemerge, such as people's claim to the fruits of their labor, naturally invalid contracts, and inalienable rights.[1]

This provocative remark, made by one of the great living social economists, introduces a chapter that gives a brief rendition of his work. The task before us is to examine the "sauce" by sorting out its ingredient allegories and metaphors about property rights and firms; only then can the "long forgotten concepts" be laid bare and analyzed. Thereafter, David Ellerman's critical analysis will be applied to one of today's most prevalent economic institutions: the investor-owned corporation. In the spirit of constructive criticism, an alternative corporation, more in tune with the principles of social economics, is proposed.[2]

The issue of property has long been central to social economists of all colors, and is something one would expect with a concept so suffused with moral overtones. Moreover, property arrangements are *social* relations; they endow one person with an object, denying it to others. It's the natural playing field of an economics centered on the social dimension. For example, Hobson had already repeatedly stressed the key role that property has played in social economics. "Until we get a clear conception of the part which property should play in human personality and society," he admonished his readers, "we can hardly hope to bear upon the economic activities from which property emerges and in which property functions."[3]

Leon Walras, as noted in Chapter 1, singled out the problem of property and its appropriation as one of the central preoccupations of a social economics: the issue was to ascertain what mode of appropriation reason recommends as compatible with the requirements of moral personality. He is quoted here at greater length:

While appropriation by itself is an objective fact, pure and simple, property, on the other hand, is a phenomenon involving the concept of justice; it is a right. Between the objective fact and the right, there is a place for moral theory. This is an essential idea, which must not be misconstrued. It is entirely besides the point to find fault with the natural conditions of appropriation or to list the different ways in which men have distributed social wealth in different places and at different times throughout history. It is, however, very much to the point to scrutinize these various systems of distribution from the standpoint of justice, originating in the moral personality of man, or from the standpoint of equality or inequality, to inquire in what respects past systems were, and all present systems still are defective, and to describe the only good system.[4]

Perhaps it is because of Walras' well-known division of economics, into "pure," "applied" and "social" parts, that economic matters concerned with rights and justice rather than mere efficiency only, are no longer accorded a place in mainstream thinking. Be this as it may, today's aspiring economics student will find next to nothing on the subject of property in her/his densely packed textbook. In contrast, in the decades before Walras, particularly when John Stuart Mill and Karl Marx were active, the property question held a central place in political economy. An explanation for the current mainstream neglect of the ownership question follows, as well as a critical examination of the currently prevailing system of appropriation from the standpoint of justice. Finally, an outline of organizational principles of "the only good system" will be developed. Much of this intellectual edifice is the brainchild of Ellerman, and this chapter honors him by restating some of his key insights and arguments.

1. Tales of property

Deeply ingrained in modern economic thought, both capitalist and socialist, is the erroneous conception that the output producing firm is naturally part and parcel of the corporation and therefore also a piece of property. There is no real distinction made between the corporation (as a shell or assemblage of capital goods and other assets) and a firm (turning inputs into outputs). Corporations and firms are falsely assumed to go together, just as the process of digesting food belongs to the person. This habit of treating the firm as being "locked" within the corporation has been the source of confusion. Because of this "myth," the opportunity to operate that firm, to make a profit, will appear as automatically entailing a *property right* to "the means of production," a right that now looks as if it naturally belongs to the stockholders. In technical jargon, operating the corporation also entails ownership of the firm in its role as "residual claimant," pocketing the profits or making up for losses, as the case may be. But, and here is the crucial distinction, whereas corporations can be owned, "firms", like entrepreneurs, cannot.[5]

The supposition of an ironclad link between the ownership of productive assets and residual claimancy (net profits or losses) is, Ellerman shows, far from factual. It is easy to show cases in which the legal party with the role of residual claimant is *not* the same as the legal party owning the factory building and the machines, that is, the means of production. All that is needed is to imagine the renting of these facilities: "If the means of production, such as plant and equipment, are leased out to another legal party," Ellerman explains, "then the lessor retains the ownership of the means of production . . . but the lessee renting the assets would then have the residual claimant's role for the production process using those capital assets."[6] Thus, a corporation owning the capital assets does not have to be the party undertaking the production, or "the firm": for example, automaker Nissan has in the past leased some of the production facilities of the troubled Subaru company to build Nissan cars. Those automobiles coming off the assembly lines owned by Subaru were in fact "Nissan cars," and owned by the Nissan company.

Quite clearly, the question of who is to be the firm is the outcome of a *contractual* effect rather than an in-built byproduct of the right of capital ownership. The firm is the party that hires the inputs, bears all the costs, produces the output and sells it for profit. That party owning the production facility *could* be the corporation, but it need not be. In this case, capital hires labor. But in principle, at least, labor could hire (rent) the facility (capital) and so be the firm. This raises the question of *why* the investor-owned corporation typically ends up being the firm.

The explanation is twofold. First, if a corporation has customarily done the hiring, it would be quite costly for a new party to take over. Most existing contracts with suppliers would have to be rewritten, creating a potentially high transaction-cost-induced barrier. An interested party normally finds it easier to simply buy the investor-owned company, thereby acquiring the existing patterns of the hiring contracts. Although these transaction costs make it look as if there is a property right in the production process, transaction costs are not property rights. The second reason why investor-owned corporations usually do the hiring is the result of asymmetrical (or lopsided) market power. Capital owners have more power to hire labor than owners of labor services have the power to rent capital. Furthermore, the bargaining power of the capital-owning class also "includes the social power of having successfully indoctrinated workers and the workers' trade union representatives that 'their role' is to hire out labor, not to hire in capital and go into business [for themselves]."[7]

In summary, it is these barriers which give the commonly observed hiring patterns the appearance that they are in fact a manifestation of a property right owned by the stockholders. Understandably, economists, more familiar with intricate mathematics than with the accounting of assets and liabilities or finely spun legal reasoning, typically do not see that appropriation continues to take place because it is part of the traditional production process. As a result of this impaired vision, economists must believe that property rights in some erstwhile or primitive state were carved out of common ownership. Contrary to this myth, new property rights are constantly being created (production) and existing property rights are being used up (consumption). The legal party that buys or already owns all the necessary inputs, advances the costs and thereby would also be entitled to the outputs produced, in other words, be the "firm." This appropriation of the input liabilities and the produced wares can be summarized in technical fashion by saying that the residual claimant appropriates the "whole product." Expressed in value terms, it is the residual between sales and costs, that is, profits or loss. Under the present arrangements, the corporation and its owners legally appropriate what the staff (managers and workers) using equipment and material have produced, the whole product. In the market economy the party that *legally* seeks to appropriate the whole product is the hiring party.

In short, misunderstanding the legal subtleties explains why economists think that the corporation has no need to appropriate the products it makes, since it is believed that the corporation already owns the results of its production activity. Accordingly, the entire process of appropriation is ignored. The question of who is to be the firm is not being asked, but is erroneously thought to be attributed to the initial endowment of property rights.[8] The next section explores this very question.

The property question in normative economic thought

The whole circle of economic life rests on law. It is formed by the existing system of legal relations, or the body of positive law supporting the social organism. Most economists have always had a tendency to take for granted, without much thought or discussion, the existing laws and institutions. They tend to forget that underlying the existing positive legal doctrines are social conceptions of *ideal* right, or normative law. Positive law is an imperfect but very much elaborated embodiment of normative law. The two concepts of law are readily distinguished in Latin as "jus" versus "lex," in French as "droit" versus "lois," and in German as "Recht" versus "Gesetz." It is only in English that the single term "right" carries both meanings, hence the differentiation between *ideal* (or "natural") and *positive* right. The early economists, too, distinguished between actual human institutions and, to use Adam Smith's expression, "the natural order of things." And even around the turn of the last century there was much confidence that society would evolve in the direction of more ideal institutions. As one economist put it: "If positive law is the basis of order, ideal right is the active factor in progress."[9]

Chapter 3 alluded to the increasing labor unrest of the 1820s and 1830s. In 1824 the (anti-trade union) so-called Combination Laws were repealed, only to be partially resurrected a year later. In the context of the political debates, Thomas Hodgskin, an economic journalist with strong philosophical interests, wrote several passionate works based on his belief that the fruits of labor should belong to the worker, including *Labour Defended against the Claims of Capital* (1825), *Popular Political Economy* (1827) and *The Natural and Artificial Right of Property Contrasted* (1832). As also indicated by the last title, Hodgskin's case was based on a normative perspective of property rights, arguing that according to natural law it was labor, not capital, that was entitled to the whole product of the firm. In so doing he thought to be relying heavily on John Locke, the classic philosopher on property rights.[10] However, this belief turned out to be unwarranted.

Locke, in his *Two Treatises of Government* (1690), is often believed to have established labor as the moral basis of private property rights. He wrote that, because every man has a property in his own person, "the Labour of his body, and the Work of his Hands, we may say are properly his." As a result, "Whatsoever then [the worker] removes out of the State that Nature hath provided, and left it in, he hath mixed his Labour and joined to it something that is his own, and thereby makes it his property."[11] The straightforward principle that each man has a right to the product of his labor becomes highly ambiguous once we realize that there are two very different interpretations of "*his* labor": it could be the labor one *does* oneself, but it could also be the labor that one *owns*. Yet, Locke in another passage goes on to say that "the Turf my servant has cut . . . become[s] my property without the assignation or consent of any body," suggesting that he meant the latter. To him, labor bought in the labor market becomes the property of the buyer, who is then entitled to appropriate the fruits of that labor.[12] A critical point overlooked by Hodgskin.

Instead, Locke merely described how the market mechanism appropriates: the master had paid for the input of the servant's labor and is *ipso facto* also legally entitled to claim the output – as with the turf cut from the commons. *And*, if the master provides a spade for use by the servant, then the employer is entitled to the fruits of "his" labor and "his" capital. This basic point was also recognized by James Mill, Sismondi's contemporary, when he explained in the context of discussing the use of wage labor: "the capitalist is the owner of both instruments of production" and therefore "the whole of the produce is his."[13]

Subsequently, when addressing the role of wages in the distribution of income, Mill returns to the case in which the laborer works with the capitalist's tools and raw materials in making a product. Here he holds that the *value* of this commodity is to be *shared* between them, "and the reward of both makes up the whole of the commodity." And under the guise of the freshly conceived wage fund theory (in which the laborer receives his share in advance), he further adds that "when that share of the commodity, which belongs to the laborer, has been all received in the shape of wages, the commodity itself belongs to the capitalist, he having, in reality, bought the share of the laborer and paid for it in advance."[14] With these comments on wages and an analysis in value terms, Mill himself helped initiate the demise of property theory in economics.

This now leads to what Ellerman calls the *Distributive Shares Metaphor* made prominent in the latter part of the nineteenth century and still featured in today's textbooks. It represents the firm as some sort of partnership in which each factor of production or supplier of inputs is pictured as having a direct claim to its share of the product. This metaphor blurs the real picture; it now makes it possible to "jump over" the firm and picture the right of the basic input suppliers "as if" that right were a direct entitlement to a share of the revenue.[15] Labor "owns" its share (as measured by the income it got), capital "owns" another, with the residual claimant taking what is left. But in the real world, outside the "as-if" pattern, neither factor owns any share in output; it is the firm that owns it all.[16] The upshot is that, by looking at the economy through the lens of the distributive shares metaphor, one no longer sees the firm, and with it vanishes the question of who should be the firm. Property theory gives way to income distribution theory.

The socialist followers of Marx also became embroiled in the unhappy talk of "the ownership of the means of production." Moreover, they also felt that when practicing science it was not their business to condemn the capitalist ownership on moral grounds. Instead, it would be more productive to fan the fires of class struggle, thereby speeding up the day when the capitalist expropriators would themselves be expropriated. As a result, in both the Marxist and orthodox camps, economic thought was now caught between warring factions in which one banked on the creative destruction of history, the other on the rhetorical power of metaphor, leaving no room for moralizing about property.

The Labor Theory of Property

Within the existing vacuum of normative theories of appropriation, Ellerman seeks to revitalize the early nineteenth-century contention that *only labor* should be the firm and so reap the profits or the losses of economic production. Conventional economists, trained to think in terms of the symmetrical (proportional) treatment of the *rights* of all basic inputs to a share in the output, have trouble following Ellerman's point. This difficulty gets compounded with yet another overlay of allegorical thinking: a basic symmetry of the *activities* of labor and capital in the production process. In this view there is nothing special or unique about human labor; it is just another factor of production on par with raw materials and equipment. All inputs appear to be *co-responsible* for the output produced.

Even though it is, of course, true, contra Marx, that capital is indeed productive (that is, causally efficacious), this new way of thinking does slur over the basic human fact that *only* human beings act with intention and are in this sense held responsible for what they do, unlike a piece of equipment. In order to make this intuitively clear, Ellerman puts forth what he calls the "parable of the hired criminal." Suppose that someone rents a van and then hires an employee to do some delivery services. Suppose, further, that the employer decides that his new employee should use this rented van to rob a bank – a surefire thing, he persuades the employee. Furthermore, for the duration of the robbery, the employee will remain under contract as a hired worker (but now with higher wages). Unfortunately for both of them, they are caught and charged with the crime.

In court the employee advances the argument that he was not guilty, just like the U-Haul dealer who hired out the van. As with the dealer, he had merely rented the services of his "factor of production" to the employer, in other words – just as the U-Haul dealer sold the use of his van, so he sold the use of his labor. Fairness, he claims, would dictate equal or symmetrical treatment for both of them. The defendant might even quote from economics texts: "labor service is a commodity like any other," and argue that what the employer does with these commodities is the employer's business, not his.

Ellerman then properly notes that the judge, no doubt, would be unmoved by these arguments. She/He would point out that although all of the factors involved in the crime were productive or "useful," only the employee and his boss were legally *responsible* for having done it. Vans, as other things, cannot be responsible for anything; only human beings by their intentional action can be held accountable for what they do and so incur legal responsibility. Because the U-Haul dealer was not personally involved, he is out of the picture. The responsibility for using the van flows to the employer and his employee, not the owner of the van. The unique characteristic of labor is precisely this responsible agency, and it cannot be contracted away to another party, as the van driver would like to maintain.

With the logic of this parable in mind, Ellerman then goes on to consider the case of regular (non-criminal) production. Is there any more reason in the production process why wage earners should suddenly give up their actual responsibility and become mere "instruments of production" like the van? The obvious answer is no. Regardless of the employment contract, they remain, in principle, fully responsible agents intentionally collaborating with the other members of the firm. Labor is responsible for what it does, and should therefore, by the generally prevailing legal doctrine of imputation, also pay for or receive the consequences of their action. This, in short, is the argument for the *labor theory of property* holding that labor alone is entitled to the whole product. It is labor which ought to be the firm, which ought to hire capital and be the residual claimant. Walras would smile: the "only good system" has been found.

Few economists have studied law and most are relatively ignorant of principles of jurisprudence. One notable exception was the Austrian Friedrich von Wieser who graduated at the University of Vienna in 1872 with a degree in law. When he later became an economist, he demonstrated full awareness of the legal rule of imputation in its relationship to production, as the following illustrates:

> If it is the moral imputation that is in question, then certainly no one but the laborer could be named. Land and capital have no merit that they bring forth fruit; they are dead tools in the hand of man; and the man is responsible for the use he makes of them.[17]

This is a clear statement of the moral implication of the legal imputation principle underlying the Labor Theory of Property. But this rare and profound insight did not lead him to question the status of the capitalist process of appropriation on normative grounds. To Wieser, one must understand imputation and responsibility from the *economic* point of view; therefore, what counts is not a judicial doctrine of imputation but its metaphorical reformulation as an economic theory of imputation. It is almost like saying that although "right" means right in law, this does not preclude that "right" should mean "might" in economics. In any case, in relying on the distributional share metaphor, Wieser could then establish that, under certain idealized conditions, each factor of production gets that share of the product that it is "responsible for."

Wieser's metaphorical leaps can probably be blamed on the ideological threat posed by Karl Marx's Labor Theory of Value. This becomes clear in a later work by Wieser. There, when discussing the role of labor and capital in a "simple economy," he again stresses the fact of labor being "by no means coordinate" with the other factors of production, that tools to him are "dead instruments" and that labor alone is conscious of its ends. He readily grants that "in this sense one may say that labor *alone* is the producer" and that "every product is fundamentally a labor-product." But his next sentence indicates where and why he goes from there: "It would be a serious blunder, however, to assume that in the practical economy the entire productive yield should be ascribed to labor alone." Why? Because he objected to the view that because material instruments are dead, this also implies that they must be unproductive.[18] Therefore, labor does not produce the whole product; the Marxist Labor Theory of Value is clearly wrong, and so in this *other* sense of productive "responsibility," labor is indeed fully "coordinate" or symmetrical with the other factors of production. In a way, it could be said that the Labor Theory of Property — in the role of innocent bystander —

became a victim of an intellectual combat animated by the ideologically charged issue of whether or not all income of capital (that is, profits, interest and rent) is the fruit of exploitation clawed from (all-productive) labor.

"Metaphors are like lies," Ellerman declares. "One requires others to round out the picture," and so there were others to follow to complete the picture that is known today as the marginal productivity theory of distribution.[19] One more "lie" required for this purpose was the idea that all factors of production can be treated as if they were all symmetric and coordinate. The traditional way to do this was to imbue life to all things. Thomas Hodgskin already drew attention to the problem encountered in common language: "We speak . . . in a vague manner of a windmill grinding corn, and of steam engines doing the work of several millions of people," and in doing so we overlook the fact that "it is not the instruments which grind corn, and spin cotton, but the labour of those who make, and the labour of those who use them."[20] In short, there is a qualitative difference between live workers and dead tools. Personification of *all* inputs is one way to accomplish the badly wanted symmetry in the treatment of inputs; another and more recent approach prefers commodification of *all* inputs. Ellerman calls the latter an "engineering view": human actions are pictured as causally effective in the same manner as land and capital. By this approach the production process reduces to the formal description: "given input K and L, the outputs Q are produced."[21]

With metaphor piled on metaphor, the road to victory was paved for marginal productivity theory, and it was not long before the principle of reward measured by one's contribution was enthroned as the principle of social justice.[22] The more essential question of whether justice requires capital to hire labor or vice versa is simply declared redundant and beyond the established limits of serious economics and is seen as something out in left field. But, at the same time, one should keep in mind that the blind spot concerning judicial imputation and human responsibility is intimately entwined with the notion of human dignity. Despite the Labor Theory of Property, persons in the market economy and in economics are treated as things and non-persons as if they bear no legal responsibility for their actions. Workers are legally treated as rented instruments of production, reduced and degraded to the same level as beasts of burden or a van (at least as long as they do not commit crimes). In short, what are offered are soulless wantons with use value only. Not much dignity here.

2. Of democracy and contracts

Democracy is the right to self-determination. This implies that the decision-making rights governing people are to be assigned to the people who are governed by those decisions. In other words, self-government is government by the governed. So much is generally accepted in political discourse. And yet, most people when asked about the meaning of democracy, will answer: government with the *consent* of the governed. This second characterization is not correct, and certainly not what the Founding Fathers of the United States had in mind. If *consent* were all there is to worry about, the following hypothetical situation would also have to pass muster: American citizens and their government representatives *consent* to surrender and transfer their political decision-making rights to a foreign power. Whatever the possible reasons and benefits behind such a scheme, we would no longer call that sort of United States a political democracy.

The tension between the true and the false definition of democracy reflects a deeper divide within political liberalism that goes back centuries. On one side, we find scholars like Hugo Grotius, Thomas Hobbes, Samuel Puffendorf and John Locke who all treat the right to liberty as a *property* right that can be voluntarily given up. On the other side of the divide, a list would include, among others, Benedict de Spinoza, Immanuel Kant, Charles L. Montesquieu, Jean Jacques Rousseau, Francis Hutcheson and Thomas Jefferson.[23] This latter group insisted on the *inalienability* of a person's thought, action and liberty; human beings are "born free," meaning that this autonomy is also innate and can never be disposed of, even with their consent. This inalienist tradition of liberalism still constitutes the foundation of the notion of human rights, civil rights and democracy. It alone is consistent with the notion of intrinsic human dignity.

All this has to do with economics too. If, as argued in the last section in the context of production, personal responsibility cannot really be alienated and transferred to another, similarly for the right to personal decision making. More specifically, a being without responsibility and without the power to make decisions is not a *human* being but a thing. Similarly, persons or workers would be reduced to the legal role of "things" if they are not a legal party to the decisions made about the services they are to perform. Consider the rental of a car. When we rent a vehicle, we not only obtain the right to take possession of the car (by being given the keys) but along with it we are granted the legal responsibility and decision-making power to use it however we see fit, although sometimes subject to certain constraints. (For good reasons, many rental companies forbid the driving their cars in certain parts of countries, such as to the southern part of Italy.) The rental contract transfers decision making about the use of the car from the owner (let us say, Avis) to the renter. In legal jargon, then, the legal decision-making power is conveyed to the renter and in the very process *alienated* from the owner. The end result of this analysis is that the categorical prohibition to alienate a person's decision-making power must rule out rental contracts for people, not to mention entire nations. What prohibits this alienation is the inalienable dignity of the person.

Before we go further, it should be understood that the impossibility of giving up one's decision-making power does not imply that each and everyone has to make all decisions him/herself. There is an important distinction between *alienating* and *delegating* decisions. For example, when we delegate decision-making power to an investment broker about how to invest our money, we legally expect those funds to be managed in *our name* and in *our best interest*. Legally, the decisions so made are ultimately still regarded as *our own* decisions. Of course, this is also what happens in political democracy, when we delegate political decision-making power to Congress and the president. It is only when we surrender our powers to another party that may pursue its own interests that we alienate our powers and become a thing. If this is so in politics, why not also in economics? Wherein does human nature differ between "politics" and "economics"?

Slavery and self-rental contracts

There were times when slavery was an economic institution legitimized by positive law. In a large part of the United States this was not that long ago. In Britain slavery was not abolished until 1833. One might ask how the early economists cohabited with *legal* slavery. Not surprisingly, they showed little interest in the issue. Many of them, like David Ricardo or Thomas Malthus, had nothing to say about it. At one point Smith characterized slavery as "unfortunate" and Say added that it degraded the industry of a free man who has no slaves at his command and that it bred indolence and inactivity among the masters. The older Mill, as will be discussed shortly, even referred to slavery as a model explaining why wage labor is not entitled to profits.[24] This apathetic, even puzzling, response of nineteenth-century economists to this ultimate degradation of humanity can be somewhat excused by the fact that their sensitivities were blunted by their way of thinking. John Stuart Mill, writing *after* the Abolition Act, devoted an entire chapter to sketching the history of slavery and demonstrating the wastefulness of "so detestable a constitution of society."[25] But by far the most timely and uncompromising condemnation will be found in Sismondi. Much of his chapter-long discussion centers on the question of justice, especially the evil of unjust positive law. He wrote in 1819:

> Power over slaves is not a right, but only robbery which in certain countries and under certain circumstances, the law does not punish. The slavemasters, the planters, speak of their rights, the guarantees the laws of their country owe to their property; but silence of the laws would not be able to change the morality of deeds; the impunity guaranteed to him who takes away the welfare of another does not abolish the distinction between right and wrong. Land ownership is a grant of the law for the advantage of all; but the ownership of one's person, and in the fruits of one's labor, is prior to law . . . The European master can have no illusions about the

criminality of his acts; they are as much against natural law as they are against the civil law of his country.[26]

Almost 200 years ago this was an unusually bold statement. Slavery was seen as a part of how the world worked, and most educated people did not seem to care that much about it, except for scattered cases of excessive abuse and cruelty. Ellerman explains the relative apathy and complacency among intellectuals in the following way:

> Societies do not promote to positions of status and influence those individuals who are likely to attack the foundations of the society. And any individuals who aspire to positions of status and influence are unlikely to harbor "unsound" opinions. Moral and intellectual leaders . . . "grew up" with a "moral sense" endowed by their ambient society as to what opinions were sound and unsound. Any line of inquiry that looked like it would lead in the wrong direction was quickly abandoned as "unfruitful."[27]

In spite of intellectual inertia, the evil of slavery was abolished, when necessary by military force. But, even in modern times, it would be premature to declare it intellectually passé. Harvard philosopher Robert Nozick believes that individuals should have the right to voluntarily sell themselves into slavery.[28] Here is a vestige of the alienist liberalism discussed earlier, the view that puts mutual consent on a higher pedestal than human dignity. But as Ellerman points out, Nozick's position may not be that much out of sync with ordinary economic thinking. He quotes a leading textbook, that "since slavery was abolished, human earnings power is forbidden by law to be capitalized. A man is not even free to sell himself; he must *rent* himself at a wage."[29]

What is the difference between consenting to sell oneself and renting oneself? Is there anything more to it than a matter of duration and extent? The Greeks already knew that a slave was a "laborer hired for life" and economist James Mill had similarly stressed that the slave owner "purchases at once the whole of the labour, which the man can ever perform [while] he who pays wages, purchases only so much of a man's labour as he can perform in a day, or any stipulated time."[30] One is forced to conclude that Nozick's self-sale contract is in essence just a lifetime employment contract. There is no real difference *in kind* between selling oneself and renting oneself. Even more disturbing is the fact that the much heralded mathematical proof that the competitive capitalist economy is Pareto efficient (that is, meets the necessary conditions for maximum social welfare) needs to assume that individuals are permitted to sell or mortgage their persons for proper compensation.[31]

176

The case against the wage system

As previously suggested, it is not easy to come up with good reasons why voluntary self-enslavement is regarded as both immoral and illegal, while the shorter-term equivalent of renting oneself is not at all seen as morally deficient. Ellerman now drives home the point, explaining why the contract that establishes and regulates the "renting of oneself for a wage" – the employment contract – is so deeply problematic. It is at this juncture that the theory takes on quite a radical flavor. Before re-presenting the basic argument in a more direct fashion, several points need to be made.

First, it should be noted that the employment contract and the employer–employee system is a relatively new socioeconomic institution. In the United States, for example, as late as 1850, almost three-quarters of the non-slave work force was still self-employed.[32] Today that figure is less than 10 percent.

Second, since World War I, the employment contract has been equally pervasive in both capitalist and socialist countries and now seems an almost universal permanent-looking fixture. In terms of socialist complicity, it should be remembered that Marxists objected primarily to the *capitalist* employer, believing that under state ownership exploitation would cease. Not all socialists agreed: in fact there was a whole school of thought, associated with the German Marburg University, which professed a type of neo-Kantian socialism that was quite influential in the two decades before World War I. Led by philosopher Hermann Cohen, it argued that the main fault of the capitalist system was its violation of the Kantian imperative enjoining us to treat people as ends rather than merely as means. In other words, the moral law should also be applied to the nature of economic relations. This line of criticism is perhaps best expressed by Karl Vorlaender, another member of the School, who held that "all rational beings, including the most miserable wage earner, the poorest proletarian, exist as ends-in-themselves, they are no machines, no mere means for capricious use for this or that will, in one word, no thing but a person, a personality whose humanity ought to be sacred."[33] For an alternative, the Marburg School proposed worker cooperatives, something that the Marxist mainstream likened to "bourgeois revisionism" and "worker capitalism."[34] The whole matter is an interesting illustration of the different policy implications derived from either the Labor Theory of Value (public employees) or the lesser known Labor Theory of Property (worker cooperatives).

Finally, it should be noted that when Ellerman questions the employment contract, he also questions the investor-owned corporation. Based on the earlier discussion relating to the misconceived myth of an "ownership of the means of production," it is easy to see that the essence of the corporation as a productive firm is its ability to function as the hiring party, the capital that hires labor. Do away with the employment contract and the corporation is reduced to an asset-holding shell, a mere supplier of capital.

Treating workers as things with no responsibility

The first indictment of the employment contract is that it goes against the general principle of jurisprudence of matching legal responsibility with *de facto* responsibility; the legal principle is to hold those legally responsible who have actually "done it." Within the scope of the contract, the employee is given the role of a non-responsible instrument. He/She is not legally responsible for the losses of his/her actions, neither for the profits. But as a person, an intentional agent actively participating in the production process with co-workers and with management, he/she is *in fact* responsible for the new assets produced as well as for the used up (input-related) liabilities. Here the employment contract is really fictitious, describing something that cannot take place. It treats persons as non-persons, and, as with slaves, it imputes responsibility for human work back to the master or employer.

To remedy the situation, all that is needed is to reverse the hiring and make labor the firm. Under these new circumstances, the staff would hire the capital equipment and the raw materials and pay for all the inputs, thereby also giving them the right to appropriate the net output. In other words, a worker-managed firm.

Treating workers as things with no decision-making power

The second indictment of the employment contract refers to the inalienable human capacity and right to make decisions, to be self-determining agents. Yet the employment contract makes the employee alienate that power to the employer for the duration of the agreement. Within its confines workers consent to be bossed around, to spend their time and efforts the way the employer sees fit. And, as mentioned earlier, it's an alienation (not delegation) of decision-making authority: the employee surrenders her/his will and interests to that of the employer and his/her interests. Here, too, the employment contract demands the impossible, the alienation of something that is inalienable.

In order to correct this contradiction, workers would have to run the firm. In their capacity as non-managerial staff, they would still be suspending their power of decision making, but doing so by *delegating* (not alienating) it to superiors who would be deciding on their behalf and for their own good. The capitalist corporation would thereby be turned into a democratic enterprise.

One further point: the democratic firm, in treating workers as persons rather than as instruments, conveys to its members the morally inalienable right to run the company. Such rights are *personal* rights rather than *property* rights. They are assigned to individual members who meet the qualifying function of membership just as voting rights in a township are assigned to the functional role of residing within the political boundaries of the town.

As a result they cannot be transferred to outsiders either by mutual consent or otherwise. There is a simple but decisive test to establish whether a right is a personal or a property right: the former are automatically extinguished with the death of the bearer, the latter can be inherited.

The factual basis for indicting the corporation

On both counts, the employment contract, and the wage system that it implies, are from the point of view of legal doctrine illogical and wrong. "If and when this contract for the renting of human beings is recognized as being invalid," Ellerman muses, "then the legal foundation and modus operandi of the conventional corporation will be removed." Only then will "the capitalist corporation based on the employment relation . . . be replaced by the democratic corporation where all the people working in the firm are jointly working for themselves."[35]

Clearly, the view represented here is very much at odds with orthodox economic thinking. It is as radical as it is novel. But, unlike many other dissenting claims, it is based on cold facts, facts pertaining to institutions and human nature. In a recent presentation to the Brookings Institution, Ellerman lists the following five factual points:

(1) The identity of the residual claimant ("firm") in a production opportunity is determined in a market economy by the *contractual* fact-pattern of being the last legal owner of the inputs (and not some mythical "ownership" of the production set)

(2) The ownership of the whole product of a production opportunity is legally *appropriated* (as opposed to being an already owned part of the "mythical ownership of the firm")

(3) The whole product is appropriated by *one* legal party, the residual claimant (as opposed to the "distributive shares" or "nexus of contracts" metaphors, which picture each factor as owning part of the product)

(4) Human actions (as opposed to the services of things) are the only *de facto* responsible and decision-making factor in production (in contrast to the engineering picture that all inputs are passive or the poetic picture that all inputs are active)

(5) The *de facto* responsibility and decision-making capacity of persons is in fact *non-transferable* from one person to another (in contrast to, say, the responsibility for the use of a tool like a truck or a van).

Ellerman concludes by challenging his audience: "If the above theses be admitted, the heretical conclusions will follow closely behind, so to resist these heresies, it is incumbent on the objective scientist to show wherein the theses are false."[36] As a social scientist trying to be objective, the author of this text has not found any of these facts to be otherwise, and feels therefore moved to help disseminate their uncanny implications until any one of them has been shown to be false.

The Labor Theory of Property and small business

The purpose of this chapter has been to "rethink the corporation," especially the investor-owned company that now dominates the economic international landscape. When John Hobson wrote about the need for reconstructing industry, it was *this* type of company he had in mind, criticizing the *depersonalized* structure of the "Compagnie Anonyme" (the French name for the Jointstock Company) with "capital belonging to a crowd of persons, who are strangers to one another." There the owners have no effective responsibility for the influences exercised on others by their property, thereby making this very structure less effectively human than the small workshop which it displaced.[37]

Within the impersonal world of the corporation, the Labor Theory of Property has strong intuitive appeal, and its application is straightforward. But when it comes to the small business operator and the family farm, the implication of the theory is less transparent.

Take the family farm: when a farmer harvests the crops – grown on land that had been worked by his great-grandfather – and needs some helping hands, can he *hire* anybody? The answer is clearly yes if the employment is temporary in nature, as for bringing in the harvest. In democratic worker cooperatives, for example, the bylaws usually specify that a new person has to work in the company for some minimum period continuously in order to qualify for membership. Similarly, immigrants are usually required to live in a democratic country for a few years before being able to ask for citizenship and the vote.

In the case of long-term employment, however, one is faced with a conflict. The owner of a farm (or firm) supplying both capital and labor is an example of democratic self-employment. The owner's control rights are the right to the whole product and would flow directly from the labor theory of property, but so also would the rights of the co-workers. Here the conflicting rights have the same root, and it is unclear as to which of the two parties ought to be more privileged. A similar conflict occurs when an inventor–entrepreneur sets up a small firm with several employees. It is not clear if the co-workers ought to be promoted to co-owners.

Another complicating twist comes from the same Kantian philosophy that underlies the Labor Theory of Property. A careful analysis of the categorical imperative never to treat others as mere means suggests that it is not necessarily against the moral law to treat people as means, provided they are so treated for an end that can be *shared*. In Kantian terms, "shared ends" must be understood to mean the same thing as morally acceptable ends.[38] In other words, an employee for a moral cause would be something more than just a tool. Therefore, to the extent that a proprietor is willing to sacrifice profits in order to help his neighborhood (for example, by offering work to unemployed co-citizens), we may have another possible exemption to the moral prohibition of hiring employees. A non-profit operation of a local soup kitchen may be similarly exempt.

Nevertheless, the contention that the labor theory may in certain cases permit wage contracts does not in any way exempt the (absentee-owned) corporation from the moral imperative. And it is for this reason that it must be rethought and restructured.

3. The investor-owned corporation in social perspective

If Ellerman's analysis is factually and logically correct, then there are over-powering reasons to believe that the modern investor-owned corporation *ought not to exist*. Economics, meanwhile, as it does with all existing social institutions, takes the corporation as an unquestionable "given." Permissible questions can, at the most, pertain to peripheral modifications, such as how to make the corporation more democratic or more socially responsible. The following discussions consider these two queries.

Democratic corporations?

The question of whether or not conventional corporations are democratic institutions can be answered decisively in the negative. True, they utilize the trappings of a democratic political structure: the shareholders are the elec-torate; the board of directors, the legislature; and management, the executive branch. And in this superficial sense the typical corporation appears like a "shareholders' democracy" in which there is government with the *consent* of the governed. Yet, as already mentioned, consent is not enough. In the economic sphere, as in the political domain, genuine democracy is self-government, that is, *government by the governed*. Clearly the stockholders are the governing party, but the "governed," the party that takes orders, is the staff of the firm. The *only* way to have a democratic firm would be to make the staff also the governing party, in other words, implementing worker self-management.

As with shareholder democracy, so also with the well-intentioned proposal of "stake-holder" democracy. The latter seeks to empower *all* the various interest groups affected by corporate decision making: the employees, the consumers, the community, the suppliers together with the shareholders. The problem with the proposal is that it fails to make the crucial distinction between groups that are merely *affected* by corporate decisions and those that are also *governed* by them. The merely affected parties (consumers, suppliers and local residents) do have a legitimate interest to constrain, even veto, certain decisions that negatively affect them. As citizens in the political arena they may legislate constraints in form of taxes and regulations. As suppliers or consumers, they have the right not to trade with a corporation deemed harmful to their interests, exercising control "by exit" rather than "by voice."[39] But management and workers, being under the authority of the owners, are the only governed party and, therefore, the only party that should have a voice, or better, *the* voice. Thus, by ignoring the essential asymmetry among the various stake-holders, the entire corporate governance debate misses the point.

Socially responsible corporations?

Everywhere corporations are considered legal "persons" with certain rights. Yet, legal persons and natural persons are far from resembling each other. One is reminded of John Hobson's comment that the corporation "has neither a soul to be saved, nor body to be kicked." For him, stock-based companies entailed a divorce of ownership and responsibility, which was made even worse with the rise of trusts and holding companies. The latter he saw as "the final step in dispose[ing] of any scruples which the investor might entertain in selecting the channel of employment for his money, as regards the utility or human services rendered by the business into which his money flows."[40] Implicitly, at least, Hobson suggests that, in earlier times, before business was "rationalized by being depersonalized," there was no such separation between ownership and responsibility. Similarly, a good case can be made that a non-public or family-held corporation can indeed act in a socially responsible way not much different from a small proprietorship. Such business organizations, just as the self-employed, can *in principle* put social values high on their agenda, even if to the detriment of profits, both short and long run.

What about the absentee investor-owned, "public" corporation? It is here that a fundamentally different situation arises. Its executives are employees who, as shown earlier, have alienated their responsibility and decision-making rights to the employer. In that capacity they are managing on behalf of shareholders who are first and foremost investors keenly interested in getting a good return on their money. Under such an institutional structure, it matters little if both employees and most investors share a strong belief in social values of one kind or another or not. Whatever may be their humanity or their generosity, both parties are tied together through the stock markets, which ultimately and impersonally determine corporate goals, actions and the permissible degree of corporate "responsibility." Unfortunately, it's one of those games in which the "good guys finish last" syndrome tends to prevail. For example, suppose a corporation puts environmental or community concerns above profit considerations, because not only management but also a majority of its investors subscribe to the same goal.

Under ordinary circumstances, these social concerns will raise the costs of the enterprise, thereby narrowing profit margins and dividends. In a competitive capital market, the price of the stock will suffer as short-term investors sell and invest their funds elsewhere. Such a scenario paves the way for a takeover bid and a situation in which a new and more scrupulous party assumes control. In other words, the best defense against losing one's job or control over the firm is to be *fiscally*, not socially, responsible. Alternatively, a company may enjoy such a monopoly for its product that it can afford to be socially responsible without being punished by the equity markets. But in a world replete with competitive pressures, such an outcome is unattainable for most.

A common response to this pessimistic analysis is to suggest that being a "good corporate citizen" *pays*, that social responsibility on the contrary may even help profits. But is there that much room for socially responsible investment in a competitive market economy? To verify a claim like this, one must reduce the argument to an empirical question, one that is far from settled and one that cannot be pursued here. What is more relevant is to ask the right question, not whether prudent or "enlightened self-interest" ultimately "pays," but rather whether absentee-owned corporations in a competitive economy can afford to put social commitments *above* the profit motive. To the extent that social values are taken into account only in an instrumental fashion ("because it pays"), to that extent the bottom-line mentality still reigns and socially responsible behavior is just another investment akin to spending money on public relations or advertising.

From the preceding considerations it would follow that socially responsible investment can only flourish in the absence of equity markets and takeover threats. It is not really clear that a sound economic system needs to have a well-functioning stock market trading corporate shares. The value of equity markets for the efficient allocation of capital can be greatly overestimated, something that is readily conceded by a leading World Bank economist: "To a large extent equity markets are an interesting and fun sideshow . . . in the allocation of capital," says Joseph Stiglitz.[41] Be this as it may, a system based on corporate cross-ownership, such as Japan, in which group holdings provide an effective shield against outside interests, appears as more compatible with the demands for socially responsible business than the ones dependent on equity markets.

4. An alternative to the investor-owned corporation

Any serious critique of the conventional corporation in terms of violating human dignity and the principles of jurisprudence, needs to suggest a better alternative, one that is feasible and one that also works. Again, Ellerman has worked out in considerable detail new legal structures necessary for the task. At the same time, and independently, there is now a remarkable real world case study or experiment that is testing these organizational principles.

The democratic corporation

How to build a "people-based" corporation? Recall that it will have to be a firm in which labor is in charge, pocketing the profits, and a firm in which capital is relegated to the role of supplier. It will also have to be a democratic firm, a "company owned and controlled by all the people working in it – just as a democratic government . . . is controlled by all its citizens."[42] The staff elects on a one-person, one-vote basis the management that will govern in their name. There is no employment contract, nor are there employees, and there is no employer in this model, just co-workers or members of a firm.

What may sound rather easy on the level of principles, is much more difficult to carry out in practice. Historically, it has been challenging to set up an operational democratic worker-owned firm. Jaroslav Vanek offered the following telling metaphor:

> The new firms (cooperatives), akin to the biological evolution of species, need their own environment, as mammals need air – and not water – to live in. If the production cooperative and other democratic forms did not flourish, it was because they were, unwittingly, forcing mammal babies into water in which they were bound to drown.[43]

Traditionally, the "waters" into which democratic firms have been birthed have been the legal instruments of common stock. The use of this elementary building block has created formidable problems. What we think of as conventional property, is really a bundle of three basic rights. They are (a) the *voting rights* (to elect the board of directors); (b) the *residual claimant rights* (to a share in profits or loss); and (c) the *right to a share of the net worth* (assets minus liabilities). These ABCs of capitalism work well for capitalist firms, but not for democratic enterprises. There is a conflict between it being all bundled up in the form of a single *property* right, which can be sold to anyone, and the requirement of democratic self-government obliging a one-member, one-vote principle. Votes cannot be for sale. Another problem arises from the fact that ownership of shares also entails the right to share in capital gains. Yet, years of accumulation of net worth and rising share prices make it often prohibitively expensive for a new prospective member to join a democratic firm. Simultaneously, there will be a temptation for a profitable labor-based firm to hire non-members or otherwise sell out to another company. Either way, worker cooperatives tend to degenerate into conventional capitalist firms, something that has happened only too often in the unhappy history of worker cooperatives.

184

In order to avoid these problems, the various rights embodied in common stock will have to be unbundled, separated out and reassembled in a different manner. First, the (a) voting rights and the (b) net-income rights must be made into *personal* rights attached to the worker's functional role of being a member of the firm. Both rights are represented by a *membership certificate* that cannot be sold. Such arrangements assure that voting will be on a one-member, one-vote basis, and that only working members of the firm will enjoy the fruits of their labor. Also, the (c) remaining right for net-worth remains a property right which ultimately accrues to the worker-members; it represents the reinvested fruit of the past labor.[44] Traditionally, this capital has been held collectively, creating in the process common property that can generate economic problems.[45] A better way is to have net worth recorded through some system of individualized internal capital accounts, which keep track of each member's contribution over the years. The working member, in a sense, loans her own accumulating capital to the enterprise where it can grow in value and then recoups it (with interest) upon leaving the firm.

The democratic firm is a social community, a community of work. Who then owns the democratic firms? Who owns labor unions, clubs, city governments and other organizations? Nobody does; they are simply not for sale. It is through this kind of legal restructuring that "the corporation itself is transformed from a piece of property into a democratic social institution."[46]

The case of the Mondragon Cooperative Corporation

Mondragon is a small town in the Basque region of Spain. Over the last few decades, it has developed into a major industrial center with dozens of co-operative factories, some quite large. After World War II, Don Jose Maria Arizmendiarretta, a young priest known as Father Arizmendi, organized with some of his students the first cooperative producing cooking stoves. Soon there were 170 worker-owners. In 1960, the Caja Laboral Popular (CLP), a credit union type bank, was set up, which provided financing for a whole set of new cooperatives. Today the CLP is a large bank with hundreds of branches and assets of almost $10 billion. Similarly, the associated worker cooperatives have grown into large companies with group sales of nearly $10 billion and a combined staff of some 26,000 persons. Among its products are household appliances under the brand name of Fagor. Only recently, the entire complex has been reorganized into one large Mondragon Cooperative Corporation (MCC), one of the largest and most successful Spanish firms competing in the European Union. What has been the formula for such unprecedented commercial success of the cooperative idea?

The answer, reassuringly, is that it is a democratic firm with a legal structure very similar to that expounded by Ellerman. The members ultimately have control over the firm. They meet in an annual general assembly and elect their officers who then hire a team of managers. Each member has a membership certificate that entitles him or her to a vote in the general assembly and a share of the annual profits (or losses). There are no shares in this corporation, instead, each member worker has an *individualized capital account* into which every year retained earnings are credited by a formula based on pay that tries to reflect the relative productive contribution of each worker. Through this formula most of the profits are reinvested; however, they do not belong to the corporation but are equivalent to long-term loans by the workers themselves. The overall moneys in these accounts trace the net asset value of the MCC. When the worker retires, he or she is cashed out of what amounts to the reinvested fruit of their labors as long as the worker had been active. The departing worker is replaced by a new member, at least under normal conditions, who then opens a new account in his or her name.

As mentioned earlier, the traditional problems of cooperatives related to collective ownership are now avoided. So, for example, there is no longer a "horizon problem" of the kind that bedeviled a Yugoslav labor-managed system where the older workers with a relatively short horizon of job tenure were naturally reluctant to vote for reinvesting profits in long-run projects, the benefits of which they would probably not work long enough to enjoy. What followed was a strong preference for short-run investments or large pay-outs in the form of dividends while leaving the firm's investment needs to bank finance. Moreover, like the Yugoslav firm, but in contrast to the traditional worker cooperative, the Mondragon cooperatives, no matter how successful or unsuccessful, are not for sale. Outsiders cannot buy ownership or control, which shields management's ability to be socially responsible and to function with the long-run interest of the community in mind, as for example, to pursue a policy of job growth.[47]

The last chapter of the Mondragon success story still needs to be written. So, for example, it is not clear how well the cooperative will be able to compete with products made in low-wage, offshore plants and sold by its rival transnational corporations. It could also be argued that due to the internal accounts, workers incur a greater risk; they are putting all their eggs into one basket. But, consider that because the Mondragon cooperatives are associated in a number of regional groups, they are highly diversified. "Instead of a worker diversifying his or her capital in six companies," Ellerman explains, "six companies partially pool their profits in a group or federation and accomplish the same risk-reduction purpose without transferable equity capital."[48] Possibly, the greatest drawback is the lack of labor mobility, something that could be alleviated if more companies adopted this system and allowed the transfer of capital accounts between firms. Still, it is a vivid example of how even large firms *can* function successfully without employees and in a democratic manner, thereby fully meeting the humanistic norms previously outlined. Reassuringly, there is an alternative to the investor-owned corporation, and it works well.

Finally, the new organizational form is not confined to worker cooperatives. In both the United States and the United Kingdom, there has been a strong growth of Employee Stock Ownership Plans (ESOPs) in which employees become co-owners of a firm's equity. The law in the United States now allows several important additional features, which come close to a Mondragon-type equivalent. First, employees can, with a bank loan (secured by the asset value of the firm), buy the company and so obtain majority ownership and control. Such leveraged worker "buyouts" are a giant stride, but they still fall short of allowing workers to effectively exercise their control rights. Until the loan is paid off, the shares are voted by appointed trustees according to management's recommendations. To circumvent this problem, American law now also permits a two-tier voting scheme, through which the employees (through one person, one vote) can instruct the trustees how to vote their shares. By such modifications, the staff emerges as the only residual claimant and is also empowered to make all the decisions. Similarly, the annual stock contributions to individual employees are, like the Mondragon model, based on relative salary. In other words, workers' individual contributions to their companies' net worth will be reflected in their stock ownership, very much similar to Mondragon's individualized internal capital accounts. Upon retirement, the accumulated stock is sold back to the company.

In practice, however, leveraged ESOPs with worker control have had very little success, although there are some exceptions to the rule – witness the case of United Airways. Unfortunately, virtually all such buyouts occur in corporations that are no longer commercially viable, such as old textile plants or shoe factories. These leveraged ESOPs are seen as a last resort to protect jobs in a community, often company towns. In addition, employees are understandably reluctant to risk their pension plans and invest all their savings in just one struggling company. All things considered, the Mondragon version of democratic firms holds much more promise.

Conclusion

The law of property is one of the most basic social institutions. Even minor changes can produce major social consequences. At one stage in American history, such change was so strongly resisted by the vested interests in power, that it took a bloody Civil War to break down the barriers. In the twentieth century, the decades-long cold war, too, was waged with the issue of property at the very core of the conflict. Even in academic circles, talk about property is likely to arouse tempers. Economists, on the other hand, will be more disinclined to open any kind of dialogue on this question since they take the basic legal structure of property rights as simply given and only worth questioning in terms of their economic efficiency. Yet they should be reminded that economic efficiency is a poor substitute for human dignity.

Nevertheless, economists are not alone in resisting the kind of right-based arguments offered here. There is little popular demand to end the wage system, just as there was a surprising lack of popular support for the abolitionist movement, despite pockets of antislavery sentiment, even as late as the first half of the nineteenth century.[49] Another, and perhaps more palatable, illustration of the uncritical acceptance of ambient social institutions pertains to the legal status of women. There, too, the law long upheld the view, enshrined in the coverture marriage contract, that husband and wife are legally one person and that this person is the husband. A wife could not own property or make contracts except in the name of her spouse. How long did it take for a popular movement to arise to challenge this legal fiction? It will probably take as long or longer for a similar movement to question the rental of human beings and promote equal human dignity and partnership both in the home and the work place.

The issue of ownership is *one* important aspect entailed in fixing the economy; the other is competition. Ever since Sismondi, social economists have been voicing opposition to the idea of entrusting the fate of the national economy to *laissez-faire* market competition. During the last century and a half, the general trend of reining in the market has by and large validated their concern. But today we experience a revival of market ideology, a movement that marches under the banner of "free trade" and that appears to want to set back the clock. Chapter 9 explains this revival and asks some hard questions.

Notes

1 D. Ellerman, *Intellectual Trespassing as a Way of Life: Essays in Philosophy, Economics, and Mathematics*, London, Rowman and Littlefield Publishers, 1995, p. 8.
2 This summary rendering of the relevant work by Ellerman relies primarily on two of his books: D. Ellerman, *The Democratic Worker-Owned Firm*, Boston, MA, Unwin Hyman, 1990a, and D. Ellerman, *Property and Contract in Economics*, Cambridge, MA, Blackwell, 1992. Moreover, I also had the benefit of having David Ellerman comment on an early draft of this chapter, thereby limiting the problem of distortion in presenting his views.
3 J. A. Hobson, *Wealth and Life: A Study in Values*, London, Allen, 1929, p. 141.
4 L. Walras, *Elements of Pure Economics* [1926], New York, Augustus Kelley, 1977, p. 77.
5 In technical language, if we have a production function $Q = f(L, K)$, one could own Q, L and K, but not f.
6 Ellerman, *Intellectual Trespassing as a Way of Life*, p. 56.
7 ibid., p. 15.
8 This fallacy has a significant theoretical fallout that affects the very core of theoretical economics. Modern economists work with an idealized and highly abstract model of the free market economy. It's a mathematical picture of an economy being in "general equilibrium." This general equilibrium economics is often

derided for its lack of realism and relevance, but Ellerman takes a different tack in launching a potentially more deadly broadside. In the famous Arrow–Debreu model proving that there can be a competitive equilibrium with economic profits he recognizes the erroneous assumption that the corporation (and its stockholders) own the production function or the "production set." But once we correct this error, the entire proof falls apart. The reason is this: if a corporation is making profits – and without the aforementioned transaction costs in this frictionless world – other parties will have an incentive to bid for all the inputs by offering slightly better deals to the suppliers. This production arbitrage will work as long as there are above normal profits; the process terminates only when there are *no* more economic profits. Hence, "the Arrow–Debreu 'proof' of the existence of competitive equilibrium with positive profits is based on assuming a non-existing property right which rules out of court a certain form of arbitrage – [one] that is perfectly possible in the idealized frictionless capitalist economy," Ellerman maintains, and concludes in wry fashion: "Models that live by the sword of arbitrage must also be prepared to die by it" (ibid., p. 196). The argument against Arrow–Debreu sketched here is worked out in greater detail in chapter 11 of his 1992 book as well as in an unpublished paper presented at the American Economic Association Meetings in San Francisco, January 5–8, 1996. Its title: "Property Rights Fallacies in the Arrow-Debreu General Equilibrium Model." In both sources one can also find some discussion of the defensive strategies postulating "hidden factor" or "owner specified outputs."

9 H. S. Foxwell, "Introduction," in A. Menger, *The Right to the Whole Product of Labor* [1899], New York, Augustus M. Kelley Publishers, 1970, p. xi.

10 See, for example, T. Hodgskin, *The Natural and Artificial Right of Property Contrasted* [1832], Clifton, NJ, Augustus M. Kelley, 1973, pp. 25–26.

11 J. Locke, *Two Treatises of Government* [1690], New York, New American Library, 1960, ch. 5, sect. 27.

12 This is the interpretation favored by C. B. MacPherson, *The Political Economy of Possessive Individualism: Hobbes to Locke*, Oxford, Oxford University Press, 1962, p. 215. See also Ellerman, *Property and Contract in Economics*, pp. 51–54, on this theme.

13 James Mill, *Elements of Political Economy* [1826], New York, George Olms Verlag, 1971, p. 22.

14 ibid., p. 41.

15 Ellerman, *Intellectual Trespassing as a Way of Life*, p. 35.

16 Another metaphor was introduced more recently to explain away the fact of the uncontracted residual. By this view the firm is now a nice symmetry of contractual claimants, as nothing more than a nexus of contracts where even "The *nexus of contracts* picture mops up that untidy detail by presenting the residual claim as just another contractual claim" (ibid., p. 54).

17 F. von Wieser, *Natural Value* [1889], New York, G. E. Stechert and Co., 1930, pp. 76–79.

18 F. von Wieser, *Social Economics* [1914], New York, Augustus Kelley, 1967, p. 112 (emphasis added).

19 Ellerman, *Property and Contract in Economics*, p. 206.

20 T. Hodgskin, *Popular Political Economy* [1827], New York, Augustus M. Kelley, 1966, p. 251.

21 Ellerman, *The Democratic Worker-Owned Firm*, p. 19.

22 See, for example, J. Rawls, *The Theory of Justice*, Cambridge, MA, Harvard University Press, 1971, p. 308.

23 For a detailed discussion of these two traditions, see D. Ellerman, "The Employment Contract and Liberal Thought," *Review of Social Economy*, April 1986, vol. 44:1, pp. 13–39. For the influence of F. Hutcheson on Jefferson, see G. Wills, *Inventing America: Jefferson's Declaration of Independence*, New York, Vintage Books, 1979.

24 Mill, *Elements of Political Economy*, pp. 21–22.

25 See also A. Smith, *An Inquiry into the Nature and Causes of the Wealth of Nations* [1776], vol. II, Chicago, IL, University of Chicago Press, 1976, p. 100; J. B. Say, *A Treatise on Political Economy* [1803], 4th edn, Philadelphia, PA, Lippincott, Grambo and Co., 1850, pp. 207–208; J. S. Mill, *Principles of Political Economy with Some of Their Applications to Social Philosophy*, vol. II, New York, D. Appleton and Co., 1891, ch. 5.

26 J. C. L. Simonde de Sismondi, *New Principles of Political Economy* [1827], trans. R. Hyse, New Brunswick, NJ, and London, Transaction Publishers, 1991, pp. 153–154.

27 Ellerman, *Intellectual Trespassing as a Way of Life*, p. 30.

28 R. Nozick, *Anarchy, State and Utopia*, New York, Basic Books, 1974, p. 331.

29 P. Samuelson, *Economics*, New York, McGraw-Hill, 1976, p. 52.

30 G. H. Sabine, *A History of Political Theory*, New York, Henry Holt and Co., 1958, p. 150; Mill, *Elements of Political Economy*, pp. 21–22.

31 See Ellerman, *Property and Contract in Economics*, pp. 101–102.

32 S. Lebergott, *Manpower in Economic Growth: The American Record since 1800*, New York, McGraw-Hill, 1964, p. 139.

33 K. Vorlaender, *Marx and Kant*, Vienna, Deutschen Worte, 1904, p. 16. For a general description of the Marburg School, see H. van der Linden, *Kantian Ethics and Socialism*, Indianapolis, IN, Hackett Publishing Co., 1988.

34 Historically, the decisive moment was the defeat of the idealist wing at the Party Congress at Dresden in 1903.

35 D. Ellerman, "The Corporation as a Democratic Social Institution," in M. A. Lutz (ed.), *Social Economics: Retrospect and Prospect*, Boston, MA, Kluwer Academic Publishers, 1990b, p. 381.

36 D. Ellerman, "The Human-Capital-ist Firm: An Approach from Property Theory and Democratic Theory," unpublished paper presented at the Corporations and Human Capital Project at the Brookings Institution, May 23, 1997, pp. 35–36.

37 J. A. Hobson, *Work and Wealth: A Human Valuation*, London, Allen, 1914, p. 252; Hobson, *Wealth and Life*, pp. 146–147.

38 Several chapters in H. E. Jones' *Kant's Principle of Personality*, Madison, WI, University of Wisconsin Press, 1971, chs. 2 and 3, are devoted to clarifying this particular point. It all centers on the significance of the word "merely" in the categorical imperative: "act in such a way that you always treat humanity, whether in your own person or in the person of any other, never *merely* as a means, but always at the same time as an end." It turns out that self-interested ends cannot be shared, and therefore, using (or employing) somebody for one's own or shareholders' profits must *always* be in violation of respect for human dignity.

39 A. O. Hirschman, "Against Parsimony," *Economics and Philosophy*, 1985, vol. 1:1, pp. 7–21.

40 Hobson, *Wealth and Life*, pp. 146–147.

41 J. Stiglitz, *Whither Socialism?*, Cambridge, MA, MIT Press, 1994, p. 228. Compare this, however, with a different perspective favored by Wall Street. "Financial markets don't just oil the wheels of economic growth, they *are* the wheels," Lawrence Summers of the Treasury Department is quoted as saying, *Wall Street Journal*, vol. CCXXX: 112, December 8, 1997, p. A1.

42 Ellerman, *The Democratic Worker-Owned Firm*, p. 1.

43 J. Vanek, "Some Fundamental Considerations on Financing and the Form of Ownership under Labor Management," in H. C. Bos (ed.), *Economic Structure and Development*, Amsterdam, North-Holland, Elsevier Science, 1973, p. 139.

44 The "net asset value" of the cooperative is not the same as the "value of the investor-owned corporation," because the latter includes the net value of the fruits of all future workers, something that in the cooperative will have to go to the future workers.

45 There is a vast literature on the so-called "common ownership" firms in England and the self-managed companies in the former Yugoslavia focusing on property rights failures, the "horizon problem" and other such topics. See E. Furubota and S. Pejovich, *The Economics of Property Rights*, Cambridge, MA, Ballinger Publishing Co., 1974; M. Jensen and W. Meckling, "The Theory of the Firm: Managerial Behavior, Agency Costs, and Ownership Structures," *Journal of Financial Economics*, 1976, vol. 3:4, pp. 305–360.

46 Ellerman, "The Corporation as a Democratic Social Institution," p. 385.

47 There is a large body of literature on Mondragon. Probably the best guide is W. Whyte and K. Whyte, *Making of Mondragon*, Ithaca, NY, Cornell University Press, 2nd edn, 1991. Unfortunately, after the events of the late 1980s and the internal reorganization that followed, all of these studies are to a large extent out of date. For a newer account, see M. A. Lutz, "The Mondragon Cooperative Complex: An Application of Kantian Ethics to Social Economics," *International Journal of Social Economics*, 1997, vol. 24:12, pp. 1404–1421, or M. A. Lutz, "The Mondragon Cooperative Enterprise System in Today's Global World," in R. C. Dyck and M. Mulej (eds), *Self-Transformation of the Forgotten Four-Fifths*, Dubuque, IA, Kendall/Hunt Publishing Co., 1998, pp. 39–54.

48 Ellerman, "The Corporation as a Democratic Social Institution," p. 104.

49 See, for example, W. H. Harris and J. Levey (eds), *The New Columbia Encyclopedia*, New York, Columbia University Press, 1976, p. 2535.

9

WHITHER THE MARKET
AND GLOBALIZATION?

Five decades ago, the Viennese social economist Karl Polanyi wrote a celebrated essay, "Our Obsolete Market Mentality," arguing that market-driven thinking was a vestige of the industrial revolution. Polanyi claims that this approach transforms "a human economy into a self-adjusting system of markets, [thereby casting] our thoughts and values in the mold of this unique innovation."[1] Now was the time, he suggested, to transcend the age of the market and to re-embed the economic system into society; little did Polanyi suspect what history had in store for contemporary Man. Today, half a century later, the market mentality is anything but obsolete. In fact, we are witnessing a market revival of an intensity and scope rarely encountered since the Middle Ages. Virtually everywhere the role of government is being trimmed; venerable social programs questioned, weakened or abolished; social controls of the market being deregulated; and public enterprise privatized. In short, we are falling back head-over-heels to an age of economic *laissez-faire*, a frightening age similar to the inhumane times that provoked Sismondi to speak out. This surprisingly rapid resurgence of the market, threatening to reverse 150 years of gradual progress in social policy, strikes at the very heart of social economics and cries out for some explanation.

1. Competition and the market system

The reason why the market has been on a winning streak can hardly be explained in terms of moral considerations or a revival of traditional values of liberty understood as the freedom to choose and the just rewards for talent and hard work. These moral underpinnings of free exchange and the market have always exerted a steady influence. Similarly, the popular idea that unencumbered markets tend to promote economic efficiency is hardly new. Instead, the real reason for the sudden resurgence appears to be not so much any change in the market's appeal *per se,* but rather a strong deterioration of the public confidence in the market's archetypal rival: the government. In the public consciousness the latter increasingly appears inept, indifferent, bureaucratic, unfair and, if nothing else, certainly "too big." Furthermore, because "big government" is a relatively new chimera since the Vietnam War, it is a likely target for the recent malaise in industrialized society. More-over, scandals both numerous and widespread involving government officials have raised the specter of moral corruption on an international scale. Not surprisingly, market ideology has capitalized on these developments.

Although understandable, this new thinking is not justified. The charge of government corruption does lose much significance when one remembers that government, at least in a democracy, literally represents the people in the sense that to a very large extent the government itself is composed of ordinary people. Why are so many of our officials more prone to corruption? Perhaps the answer is money, money stemming from the commercial domain that taints the political sphere; witness, for example, the scandals associated with campaign financing in which political favors are granted in exchange for financial contributions. Today, more than ever, politicians are increasingly seen to be beholden to various powerful interest groups to the detriment of the common good. It appears that corruption, broadly defined as putting private interests ahead of public values, is more of a *social* problem pervasive in all of society. We might sensibly ask about this general rise in corruption. Why does money speak with a louder voice today?

Markets and morality

In an eloquently written paper, Albert Hirschman examined the changing cultural attitudes toward the market during the last two centuries in the West.[2] Before the French Revolution, it was commonly believed that commerce was a civilizing and moralizing agent; by polishing and softening human interaction, people became more gentle and cordial. Hirschman quotes one Frenchman explaining that "commerce attaches [men] one to another through mutual utility," that it "affects the feelings of men so strongly that it makes him who was proud and haughty suddenly turn supple, bending and serviceable," and that "through commerce [he] learns to deliberate, to be honest, to acquire manners, to be prudent and reserved in both talk and action," and so on.[3]

This "Doux-commerce" thesis was not to survive the industrial revolution with all its havoc, human suffering and violence. Instead, the market now appeared to be a relentlessly blind and brutalizing force, a viewpoint shared by Sismondi, Carlyle and Ruskin. Hobson, too, was quite outspoken on this point, condemning the stress put on competition as a "dehumanizing and de-nationalizing influence" and he added "no graver injury has been inflicted on the mind of man . . . than the preponderance which the early science of Political Economics assigned to competition and combative aspects of industrial life."[4] Such dehumanizing views led to what Hirschman calls the "self-destruction thesis" according to which market competition needs

193

a moral foundation, deriving from pre-industrial times, in order to function.[5] This creates a serious problem addressed by Fred Hirsch, who astutely observed, "as the [moral] foundation weakens, the structure rises ever higher . . . threatening in a self-destructive game the functioning of a liberal economic system."[6] To save the system Hirsch proposed a "moral reentry" in which participants in the economy feel obliged to cooperate, to respect unwritten laws grounded in traditional social ties, religious beliefs and civic duty. Twenty-five years earlier, in Max Horkheimer's *Eclipse of Reason* (1947), a similar point was made. The German philosopher blamed the deterioration of the West on the enthronement of self-interest and instrumental reason, which he believed are the underpinnings of capitalist practice. He argued that the progress of instrumental reason "destroyed the theoretical basis of mythological, religious, and rationalistic ideas [and yet] civilized society has up until now been living on the residue of these ideas."[7] In short, market competition, far from "doux," was now pictured as deeply corrosive of social values, an agent of demoralization and even corruption.

There is an uncomfortable tension between human values and market values. Its damaging influence is illustrated by the following story.[8] An artist painted pictures and sold them for what he felt they were worth, a value that he determined according to how much work and effort he put in. Soon his paintings sold so well that he entrusted their merchandising to an agent. After some time, the agent complained that he was unable to accommodate all the would-be buyers and suggested a greatly increased price for the works. The artist refused, explaining that by his standards the pictures were not worth that much. But when it was brought to his attention that some of the buyers were reselling his paintings at the higher market price, he relented. The market makes a *fool* of an idealist.

Another example will help to emphasize the problem. Suppose there is a (professional) book publisher who needs to make money, like any other firm, but would like to produce and sell some *quality* books as well. In other words, profits is one goal, quality another, and at times the two do not go hand-in-hand. Suppose further, that the quality books in the publisher's list can only be marketed at a price that is *below* the costs of production. Thus the publisher will have to cross-subsidize, taking some of the profits from the sale of the popular books in order to cover the loss of the quality books. Now enters competition. This cross-subsidizing provides an opportunity for a rival, with no moral qualms and heedless of a public service mission, to sell popular books at a big discount. The "rational" consumers are soon attracted to the new company, while at the same time counting on the continued availability of quality books from the other seller. Is this a realistic expectation on the consumer's part? Probably not. The established bookseller will no longer be competitive in the popular book domain, and therefore will also no longer be able to afford to offer the (money-losing) quality books in his list. Hence the choice offered by competition will amount to: stop publishing altogether, or stop subsidizing (and producing) the quality books. The market makes a *loser* of an idealist.

The two examples are not isolated ones. Rather, they point to a fundamental problem intrinsic to any kind of competition.

Competition: constructive and destructive

The preceding title comes from an unusual book published by a remarkable social economist: John Culbertson. It was written in the mid-1980s when the deregulation movement had begun to sweep politics in the United States. Culbertson does not doubt the efficiency of competition in acting as a goad, or incentive for action, but he does question the idea of using competition as a guide. As to the common good, what matters far more than the effectiveness of the goad is the *goal* of competition. After all, competition is nothing but a rivalrous relation among people or organizations engaged in the same activity. How beneficial or harmful these actions are does not depend on the strength of competition but on the type of activity and its effects. Culbertson explains: "Raising cattle is constructive. Stealing cattle is destructive. Therefore competition at raising cattle is constructive. Competition at stealing cattle is destructive. If competition at stealing cattle is not curbed, competition at raising cattle will be destroyed."[9] Standard economic science after Wicksteed and Robbins, due to its *de facto* elimination of a social or moral dimension, is poorly equipped to make the necessary qualitative distinctions, and therefore tends to look at competition only as a beneficial force: the more we have of it, the better.[10]

Clearly, two or more firms can compete with one another in many different ways: effective production management, deceptive advertising, sub-standard wages or working conditions, effective lobbying and much more. How can we make sure, then, that competition, whether in industry, fisheries, sports or anywhere, is of the constructive kind? When, for example, the ancient Greeks organized the first Olympics, they had to deal with these same issues by making rules and setting standards that determined what was allowed and what wasn't, as well as establishing an enforcement procedure. Activities that did not fit into the larger picture were discouraged.

The next question, addressed by Culbertson, is who should make these rules? In American football, for instance, should the players make their own rules, quarterbacks propose the rules for quarterbacks, centers the rules for centers and so on? Due to various player interests, it is unlikely that such a set of rules would create the desired kind of game. Instead, what is required is some coordinating organ, fitting the many parts into a larger whole. By analogy, we cannot rely on firms and individuals to judge what kind of competitive behavior is in the social interest, and what is not. Society as an organization has to accomplish that.

At this point, we are reminded of the relevance of the fallacy of composition: what is true for each part is not always true for all parts. Contra *laissez-faire*, the solution to social economic problems is not built into the private and self-seeking viewpoints and actions of firms or individuals. After all, if individual interests always harmonized with social interests, there would be no need for rules in the first place. Moreover, individuals lack the information and knowledge to think in such large terms. Their lives, and with them also the time horizon of their concerns, are shorter than that of society, not to mention humanity. Therefore, problems such as "how shall the rules and social framework of the nation be defined in order to perform successfully and provide a good life for this generation and future generations of people?" are better not left to be solved by individuals.[11]

Once rules are in place, in any organized activity, there can only be two kinds of winners: a superior performance within the rules, or a skillful bending, manipulation or evasion of the rules. Examples of the latter type of competition are the devious ways of saving costs by disregarding safety standards, misrepresenting securities, falsifying inspections, bribing government officials and doctoring balance sheets. In addition, skillful bending includes the more-innocent-sounding *standard-lowering* competition by local governments that aims to offer a better "business climate" (tax concessions, lax regulations and so on) in order to attract industry. Internationally, such destructive standard-lowering competition translates into a beggar-thy-neighbor type of lowering of labor and environmental standards.

Destructive international competition, like Culbertson's example of the raising and stealing of cattle, reveals a dysfunctionality that tends to undermine the enforcement of existing labor and environmental standards at home. The market does not respect, and will not permit, pockets of decent behavior in a world of unfair competition. Rather, good guys are condemned to finish last.

The social economics of laissez-faire

As the previous discussions of Sismondi, Ruskin and Hobson have shown, what unifies their work into a school of thought is, above all else, their outspoken opposition to *laissez-faire*. Two centuries ago, Adam Smith initiated the doctrine that in the pursuit of self-interest, an individual is "led by an *invisible hand* to promote an end which was no part of his intention" and that "by pursuing his own interests he frequently promotes that of society more effectually than when he really intends to promote it."[12] Characteristically, the social economists were unwilling to trust this "invisible hand" and its alchemy of transmuting private acquisitiveness into the common good. Why trust the invisible hand? What makes it really trustworthy?

The concept of an "invisible hand" is a vestige of Deistic Natural Theology, according to which a benevolent God created the Universe and left its operation to a set of impersonal natural laws. By assigning economic matters to the natural self-interest implanted in our breasts by Providence, it seemed sensible to expect a socially beneficial outcome. Smith, therefore, came out strongly against government meddling in the workings of the free market, a stance that has been echoed by many of his followers to this day.[13] But even Smith was not for *total laissez-faire*. Besides advocating such matters as public education and usury laws, he was willing to embrace some regulation in the banking field to protect the people. He maintained that "the natural liberty of a few individuals which might endanger the security of the whole society" ought to be restrained by the laws of government, just as "the obligation of building [fire] walls, in order to prevent the communication of fire is a violation of natural liberty."[14]

In any case, the number of believers in the intellectual creed of Natural Theology's "Deism" has been shrinking to virtually zero, a process sped up by the Darwinian revolution, which stripped the invisible hand doctrine of its heavenly justification, thereby depriving it of much of its intellectual appeal. Today, we know that the *laissez-faire* philosophy is based on a myth and is not likely to be a reliable guide for the conduct of public affairs. Social economists were simply far ahead of their time, and their long track record for speaking out remains one of their distinguishing accomplishments. If poverty was a problem, if the poor had to be protected, it was not the market to which they turned, but the visible hand of government. Appalling social problems were too urgent to be entrusted to an impersonal mechanism, said to be self-regulating. Rather, it was to the government, not the market (or some abstract notion of perfect competition in a world of perfect information), that social economists have traditionally addressed their concerns for social justice and a better social order.

Society, through its agent the state, is to control the market, rather than vice versa; or to put it differently, the economy needs to be "embedded" in society. One necessary condition for achieving this is the alignment of market economic forces so that their domain does not overreach the socioeconomic and political jurisdiction of government. Otherwise, society is immediately confronted with the problem of *standards competition*, rendering competition a socially destructive force. As will be discussed, free international trade has the unfortunate byproduct of expanding the economic domain to the global level, while the social control of a country's economy cannot reach beyond its own borders. By 1922, this was of great concern to John Hobson. He proposed to counteract this imbalance by his "economic internationalism," a policy that would create an international governmental apparatus establishing a floor for labor standards.[15] Meanwhile, the tension between national policy and the global economy has been growing exponentially. The former Mexican president, Lopez Portillo, for example, spoke from experience when he lamented in 1982:

We have been a living example of what occurs when that enormous, volatile, and speculative mass of capital goes all over the world in search of high interest rates, tax havens and supposed political exchange stability. It decapitalizes entire nations and leaves destruction in its wake.[16]

In conclusion, the battle over *laissez-faire* is not yet over. Even those modern economists who have long questioned the unalloyed goodness of unrestricted competition within the national economy, appear often unwilling to question the doctrine of *laissez-faire* in the trade between countries. Nevertheless, opposition to *laissez-faire* on *all* levels must remain a distinguishing feature of an economics that operates from the social point of view.

Why the market resurgence?

There is no easy answer to this question because of the many casual suggestions currently competing for recognition. But one hypothesis, at least, attributing the fall of communism to the pro-market teachings of welfare economics, can be ruled out. In fact, the market revival movement started around 1980, long before the events of 1989. One of the main themes in Joseph Stiglitz, *Whither Socialism?* (1994), is that the collapse of the Soviets was not the result of the power of economic ideas.[17] Others, still, believe there is a continuing dynamic of a "double movement" between market and society that creates wide pendulum swings back and forth. Currently the revival of the market mentality is understood "to meet an increasing need to decentralize decisions as a response to the increased complexity of social and economic systems," a structural trend reinforced by a flood of technological innovations enhancing the growth of global interdependence. Thus, it is suggested – more optimistically than persuasively – that the revival "can only be of a partial or transient nature" and that "free trade thought should be relegated to where it belongs: to the museum of ideologies."[18]

From a social economic perspective, the current swing can be explained as the natural outcome of the humanistic catalysts stressed by Hobson put into reverse. Just as security and perceptions of fairness promote, all else remaining the same, personality growth away from selfish concerns toward a more social and moral character, so will an increase in basic insecurity and unfairness make people less civic-minded. The voting population becomes more cynical and finds in government a convenient scapegoat for their frustrations. As the state retreats, *laissez-faire* fills the vacuum by default.

What accounts for the loss of security during the last quarter century? The most plausible answer is suggested by the increasing importance of *international* economic developments. Industrialized nations of the West, including Japan, find themselves in fierce competition with economies having recourse to a large pool of both unskilled and skilled labor that can produce at a fraction of their costs. Competitiveness dictates a shift of production facilities abroad, causing "downsizing," part-time work, wage stagnation and/or mounting unemployment at home. Not surprisingly, workers fear for their jobs. A recent poll, cited by Alan Greenspan, showed that, in the United States, 46 percent of employees at major companies were frequently fearful of being laid off in 1996, almost twice the level of insecurity as during the 1990 recession.[19] One obvious casualty of this internalization of economic activity has been the welfare state, one of the main pillars of economic security. Countries with a generous support system for the poor, the sick, the unlucky and the elderly simply cannot compete with others who cavalierly dispense with safety nets and social regulations. Even for those who seem more secure in their jobs, there is the new and hot issue of how to finance retirement. As a staff reporter for the *Wall Street Journal* writes in analyzing a recent opinion poll: "Working adults of all ages have retirement on their minds, and for many, the thought makes them shiver."[20]

Besides insecurity, perceptions of unfairness have become paramount. In Anglo-Saxon countries, income inequality, one of the main determinants of unfairness, has been rapidly increasing in the last twenty years.[21] At least in the United States, growing levels of production, combined with the stagnation of real wages, suggest to many that productivity gains have not been sufficiently shared. Add to this the open wound of constant displacement of workers, and it becomes readily apparent that the postwar social contract between capital and labor is no longer in force. Industrial life is becoming more of a jungle in which each individual does well to concentrate his or her efforts toward self-protection and self-advancement. Concern for others and for the poor, together with the tax burden that this implies, have become dispensable luxuries. The result is the almost libertarian type of individualism one can so often witness among the young today.

If the real background force for the individualization of the culture comes from the globalization of the market economy, it is time to take a closer look at this new source of social insecurity.

2. The social economics of globalization

Humanity is once again experiencing an economic transformation that at times resembles in its scope and manifestations the social convulsions of the early nineteenth century, the decades of the industrial revolution. The surprisingly sudden collapse of communism in the late twentieth century opened the entire world to the play of market forces under the label of *globalization*: the integration into a new global market and culture of trade, finance and information flows. The current reality is a worldwide economic system driven by the imperatives of a global industrial revolution. Old ways are being destroyed and a new world created with all the uncertainties and apprehensions that go with it. William Greider renders a vivid portrait of the times:

> The logic of commerce and capital has overpowered the inertia of politics and launched an epoch of great social transformations. Settled facts of material life are being revised for rich and poor nations alike. Social understandings that were formed by the hard political struggles of the twentieth century are put in doubt. Old verities about rank ordering of nations are revised and a new map of the world is gradually being drawn. These great changes sweep over the affairs of mere governments and destabilize the established political orders in both advanced and primitive societies. Everything seems new and strange. Nothing seems certain.[22]

Although nothing may seem certain, the experience of the last ten years has not been reassuring: growing inequality of income and wealth, falling real wages, heavy unemployment in Europe, mounting insecurity due to corporate "downsizing" and mega mergers, the development of a contingent work force, the emergence of a new "Lumpen Proletariat" manifest in homelessness, and the undermining and disintegration of social cohesion and family by economic forces. Yet, just like in Sismondi's day, the current transformation is to a large extent supported, even encouraged, by the (now global) teachings of economists who never tire of reminding the public about the great merits of free enterprise, free international trade and free capital movements.

For social economics the recent tremors provide a welcome opportunity to approach the globalization issue in a free spirit, unhampered by ideology, vested interests and an unsuitably narrow theoretical apparatus developed long ago in order to understand the logic and the economic effects of trade in the nineteenth century. Like Sismondi, one does well to distrust an economic interpretation that tends to suppress institutional content, and is therefore at times liable to mistake abstract theory for reality.

In the early 1980s, John Culbertson started to predict a steady decline in the living standards of the West; and he had no qualms about fingering unregulated international trade as the culprit.[23] He soon inspired others, notably Herman Daly, who was about to take a position at the World Bank.[24] Ever since, Daly has been a leading opponent of free trade and its intellectual foundation: modern trade theory.[25] The following analysis of the new international economy emphasizes the role of the growing inadequacy of conventional wisdom, especially the notion of "comparative advantage" as the conceptual centerpiece of international trade theory. Much of the substance of this part of the chapter synthesizes the major insights of Culbertson, Daly and the more recent work of some "renegade" trade economists.

The theoretical merit of "free" international trade

The notion of comparative advantage as driving trade between nations dates back to David Ricardo, who first articulated the idea that international trade always benefits both trading partners. He demonstrated this with an abstract example: imagine two countries, Portugal and England, each producing two commodities, wine and cloth. Both commodities are produced by labor only. Now suppose that one week of labor produces more wine in Portugal than in England, while English workers are better at producing cloth. Naturally, it would follow that to the extent that Portugal specializes in wine and England in cloth, trading the surpluses would allow for more production and consumption of both goods in both countries. This is an example of one country having an *absolute* advantage in one good, the other in another. In Ricardo's example, common sense dictates specialization and trade.

But now suppose, and here is Ricardo's brilliant analytical insight, that Portugal has an absolute advantage in *both* goods. It can produce both wine and cloth with less labor time, that is, at a lower cost. More specifically, assume that it can produce cloth 20 percent cheaper and wine 50 percent cheaper. Ricardo showed that both countries would still gain if Portugal specialized in wine making and England employed all its resources in the manufacture of cloth. The reason is that Portugal has a *comparative* advantage in wine production while England has a *comparative* advantage in cloth.

To understand this counterintuitive "law," Milton Friedman offers the following illustration: "Should a lawyer who can type as fast as his secretary fire the secretary and do his own typing? If the lawyer is twice as good as a typist, but five times as good a lawyer as his secretary, both he and the secretary are better off if he practices law and the secretary types letters."[26] Therefore, just like secretaries, so too the British workers need not fear losing their jobs to more efficient partners in a world of free exchange. Every country, regardless of whether it does or does not enjoy an absolute advantage, will by logical necessity always have a comparative advantage in the production and export of those commodities in which it excels, and a disadvantage requiring them to import those commodities which they cannot produce economically.

The gospel of comparative advantage has been repeated in economics textbooks ever since and helps to soften any apprehensions about a country, such as the United States, encouraging trade with low-wage countries abroad. What the student is usually never told, however, is that the mainstay behind comparative advantage in the past was that capitalists in England would *not* invest their capital in a foreign country. Ricardo explained that experience shows that "the fancied or real insecurity of capital, when not under the immediate control of its owner, together with the natural disinclination which every man has to quit the country of his birth and connections, and entrust himself with all his habits fixed, to a strange government and new laws, *check the emigration of capital.*" He added: "These feelings, which I should be sorry to see weakened, induce most men of property to be satisfied with a low profit in their own country, rather than seek a more advantageous employment of their wealth in foreign nations."[27] It is capital's lack of mobility across borders that makes foreign trade special. Because of it, we are supposed to approach trade from the viewpoint of comparative, rather than from the usual considerations of lowest (absolute), cost. Ricardo's crucial qualification was echoed more than a century later by one of the co-founders of a newer version of the trade theory, Bertil Ohlin, who emphasized that the theory "is based on a far-reaching abstraction, namely that trade will not affect [a country's relative] supply of productive factors" (as would happen if capital crossed national borders).[28]

In order to look at trade through the lenses of comparative advantage, economists soon made it a habit to stick with the far-reaching assumption of zero factor mobility between nations. The principle behind Friedman's lawyer and secretary analogy fits this approach because one's labor power, or talent, cannot be invested in somebody else. This assumption guarantees factor immobility, and, probably for this very reason, the theory makes some intuitive sense. But does it really explain trade between nations in a world of enormous capital mobility? Doesn't the shift from nations to an analogy based on individuals obscure reality? Deliberately or inadvertently, the popular lawyer/secretary parable misleads many. Despite record-high levels of international capital mobility, economics students have blindly accepted assertions like the following:

> International trade is mutually profitable even when one of the countries can produce *every commodity* more cheaply than the other country. . . . Whether or not one of two regions is absolutely more efficient in the production of every good than the other, if each specializes in the product in which it has a comparative advantage (greatest relative efficiency), trade will be mutually profitable to both regions. Real incomes of productive factors rise in both places.[29]

Theoretically, a country, let us say China, could be blessed with the ability to produce *everything* cheaper than any other country and yet will always want to import as much as it exports to the rest of the world. Hence America, or any other high-wage country, need not worry – logically, it too *must* have its share of industries with a *comparative* advantage relative to China. Trade in such a textbook world is bound to be a mutually beneficial game allowing international cooperation rather than competition.[30]

There remains, however, even in this artificial view, one area of potential concern. Imports from low-wage countries are now generally conceded to be capable of hurting the wages of unskilled workers in the high-wage countries. This tendency of *factor price* (or wage) *equalization* in a theoretical world *without* capital mobility works in an indirect fashion through prices of goods. Because trade in merchandise is ultimately trade in the factors that it embodies, theory predicts a fall in the relative prices of those goods embodying a lot of unskilled labor. Through such price effects trade depresses the wages of unskilled labor and so creates more inequality in the high-wage countries. Despite the fact that the growth of inequality during the last few decades has been a striking characteristic among many industrialized countries, economists have been slow to blame trade, preferring instead to make technology the culprit. However, since the mid-1990s factor price equalization is increasingly accepted as a primary cause of growing economic inequality.[31]

The failure of comparative advantage theory

Consider now where and why the claims of mutually beneficial trade are likely to be mistaken. The strong assumption – perhaps true in Ricardo's time – of no international capital mobility is by no means the only weak spot.

Suppose, for instance, a Ricardian world of England and Portugal and no capital mobility, and that the more productive Portuguese workers can produce both cloth and wine cheaper than English workers. Would it not be reasonable to expect that this wage (and cost) advantage would cause the British workers to be undersold and their home market to be taken over by Portugal? It would all happen with Portuguese capital, a stock that would be continuously augmented by hefty profits. At the same time, the losses of English firms would soon diminish their capital stock. Even though capital did not move across borders, England would not benefit from the trade. Something very much like this happened, of course, between Japan and the United States between the 1960s and 1980s.

This kind of lopsided benefit, however, within the context of international trade, is ruled out by a couple of theoretical *assumptions*. One is *full employment*, the other *balanced trade*. As to the first, Portuguese full employment prevents that country from supplying both markets, a vestige of Say's Law of which Ricardo had been an early proponent. The second, more implicit, assumption pictures trade as mutually balanced in terms of value akin to intercountry barter. The governments arrange to barter an equivalent amount of wine for cloth, making sure that such trade deals are indeed to their mutual advantage; otherwise they would not trade in the first place.

In the real world, however, both of these assumptions (full employment and balanced trade) seem overly optimistic and unwarranted. The first need not be commented on. Everyday experience reveals the contrary to be true. The second assumption is based on an equally counterfeit representation of international commerce as negotiated between nations rather than between international firms. This institutional fiction of two nations exchanging in a barter-like manner takes us back to the part–whole distinction brushed aside by individualistic classic liberalism.

People establish *organizations* to ensure that independent actions by the parts will be in harmony with the interests of the whole. John Culbertson illustrates this basic point as follows:

> [The] organizations within the national economy act on their own behalf. To do this, the organization must designate a person or group as its agent, to act on behalf of the organization. It is understood that, say, a purchasing agent for Xerox Corporation is acting on behalf of the Corporation, not acting to make money for his own pocket. For the purchasing agent to seek his own profit, by taking a bribe to give Xerox's business to Firm Z, would be violating the trust imposed on him, violating the rules of the Xerox Corporation, and likely breaking a state law as well. It would seem nonsensical to propose that any employee of Xerox – or even that anyone whatever – should be permitted to take action affecting the interests of the Corporation, for example, to make a decision as to what one should buy, and from whom, at what price. The organization can be effective, and survive, only if it has control over actions that affect its interests.[32]

Extending the same logic to cross-border trade would imply that the nation as an organization must be overseeing the actions of its constituent parts to assure that they are in the public interest. This means that international trade should not be "free," but regulated or managed. Such rules are necessary because what is "efficient" for the trading firm as to the minimization of its costs might otherwise be accomplished by production arrangements in which labor is only paid subsistence wages.

Trading in a world of mobile capital

Firms capable of taking advantage of international wage differentials are appropriately designated as *multinational corporations*. Their quest for border-crossing trade or international finance is driven by private profit, not the national interest. Why would one expect that what is good for one company (e.g., General Motors) is always good for the country? This tension between the part and the whole is what interests social economists. When production is shifted to nations that offer the lowest labor standards, even socially responsible competitors are pressured to emulate the practice. Ultimately, corporations will tend to ignore moral considerations and human rights with impunity; the upshot is a trade regime that functions according to the canons of absolute advantage in a vacuum without socially protective rules. Unfortunately, there is no foothold in such an environment for raising

204

questions of social morality and socially responsible management; rather the mechanism of the global marketplace gently nudges even managers of moral integrity toward capricious and exploitative behavior.

Most likely, the drive to take advantage of low-wage offshore production sites acts as a far stronger lever to equalize wages than the force exerted by the factor price equalization transmitted through changes in relative prices of output. Currently, industrialized countries are experiencing direct competition in a global labor market with a virtually unlimited supply of unskilled labor. Today, for practical purposes, this increasingly implies that the market principle of *one price* prevails, that there is one "world market wage" to be determined, in China or elsewhere. Just how much of this equalization will be achieved by pulling China up or by drawing the industrialized nations down, is an empirical question related to the world's growth in productivity and population. But, in principle, internationally fluid capital has the same ultimate effects as does free migration across national borders. Imagine how Europe would be affected if, overnight, it were filled up with 500 million Asians looking for work and subsistence. It's unlikely that such an over-crowded Europe would benefit anybody.

Meanwhile, the process of gradual equalization continues. In this context it is also important to realize that actual foreign investment is not necessary for the dynamic force to work. All that is needed is a credible threat by a domestic employer to relocate unless unions consent to wage restraint, even pay reductions. Workers, both unskilled and skilled, have been under mounting pressure to negotiate their pay with utmost moderation, which helps explain the American phenomenon of stagnation in the growth of labor compensation. A classic example is the Xerox case in which employees accepted pay cuts averaging 30 percent in exchange for job security.[33]

Moreover, under absolute advantage, "a country can theoretically be 'undersold all around' and end up with zero employment and output," as one of the more enlightened trade economists concluded, noting that "technical progress or wage reductions elsewhere can cause the emigration of industries *with no mechanism to ensure their replacement*."[34] True, if most things end up being produced in China at much cheaper costs, the consumers of the importing countries will potentially benefit from lower prices across the board. However, will a nation of longshoremen, teamsters, sales clerks, cooks and funeral directors, together with the under- and unemployed, command sufficient purchasing power to take advantage of those bargains?

Orthodox economics is not at all alarmed by all these allegations. According to them, lower wages abroad are not that meaningful. Low pay does not necessarily translate into lower labor costs because labor productivity is believed to be equally low due to meager educational standards, lack of technology and a deficient infrastructure making communication and transportation tedious and expensive. But is this still a reasonable argument today? True, a quick look at national statistics will readily confirm that *average* labor productivity of a country like Indonesia or India is indeed extremely low.[35] Yet, that is hardly relevant for direct investment. What counts, is the expected productivity of a brand new plant in a particular sector of a low-wage economy. Here the latest technology will be imported and built into a new plant that can be located so as to minimize transportation costs and make use of available skilled labor pools. Finally, modern communication technology is such that the traditional disadvantages of operating at a remote site can now be largely overcome. Hence, while non-labor costs are fairly homogenous throughout the world, labor costs remain a fraction of domestic levels. All this explains why competitive wage pressures are indeed a strong force in the global spread of industry.

Even so, trade theorists remain optimistic. By clinging to the comparative advantage doctrine and the assumption of balanced trade, they are convinced that the loss of industries to the Pacific Rim must imply corresponding gains in domestic export industries. Since the latter are usually more capital and skill intensive, more productive and better paying than the industries lost, society is said to gain. So, once again, high-wage nations have little to lose by competing with their low-wage trade partners.

The problem with this argument is, of course, that trade is *not* necessarily balanced. The decades-long American trade deficits attest to this fact. Neither is there a reliable self-regulating mechanism to restore the equilibrium, witness the exceedingly slow and sluggish adjustments in currency markets. Moreover, the fact that a country with a depreciating currency would only regain the prospect of balanced trade by impoverishing itself in direct proportion to the devaluation is often forgotten. Even if it were smoothly functioning as a self-regulating mechanism, there is no reason to expect this system to be mutually beneficial.

Another orthodox sedative, that the pockets of highly skilled service sector workers are immune to low-wage competition from abroad, is losing its potency. Skills, understood as embodied knowledge, are no longer internationally immobile. With the aid of recent information technology, not only unskilled but also many highly skilled jobs are being moved between nations.[36] This new situation is the result of two developments, the first being the new technologies, allowing knowledge to be "disembodied," codified and "re-embodied" somewhere else. All that is needed is software, a modem and a phone connection. The second development is that there is an increasingly large reservoir of well-educated professionals, often English-speaking as in India, capable of doing good work but at a substantially lower price. Highly skilled Americans are increasingly witnessing their skills being moved around the globe by US corporations. Every year these corporations import more than 100,000 qualified foreigners as trainees to work alongside Americans. Subsequently these newly trained workers are assigned to overseas plants to practice what they have learned.[37] The only skilled occupations that may successfully resist being shifted to where labor is the cheapest are those in which physical contact with clients is an essential element. As with capital mobility, it is once again the transnational corporation that lubricates the wheels by serving as "global knowledge brokers." Without multinational firms, one might still live in a world resembling that of comparative advantage based on a country's relative endowment of skills, but this is no longer the world one lives in.

Gains and losses from international trade

Introductory courses in economic science teach that free trade maximizes aggregate, or social, welfare and that, conversely, ordinary tariff protection hurts society. The argument is usually carried on in terms of theory, typically utilizing graphical or mathematical analysis. Sometimes, the results are bolstered by quantitative estimates, showing the annual costs of protectionism to American consumers to be $10–15 billion.[38] What usually is not made clear to the novice is that these demonstrations and estimates rest on many artificial assumptions beyond balanced trade, no capital outflows, and no unemployment.

More assumptions

Associated with the no-unemployment supposition is the presumption that labor displaced by imports can transfer without costs to another industry. So, for instance, to use the Ricardian example, the gains from specialization would imply that the English wine growers will become weavers, and the Portuguese weavers start tending new vineyards. All this happens in an instant, without pain or the cost of dislocation. In other words, there is *perfect* mobility in labor markets. Perhaps economists do not consider it important to reckon with such costs because of yet another subsidiary assumption: there can only be one single equilibrium wage level in all sectors of the economy, and whatever wage differentials are observed are explained away as merely reflecting different skill levels. Obviously, in such a "reality," imports cannot hurt displaced workers who instantaneously find new jobs without any loss in pay. At the same time, the cheaper imports will benefit consumers, hence the social gain.

Leaving the textbook world behind, there are plenty of frictions in labor mobility causing considerable hardship among laid-off members of the labor force. Similarly, it has long been established that there are real and persistent wage differentials even among manufacturing industries.[39] These differences may become even more pronounced when comparing the service sector with manufacturing. To the extent that an industrialized country "de-industrializes" by adding jobs in such areas as tourism, higher education, movies and TV shows, the loss of wages also has to be figured in.[40] Making allowances for these service/manufacturing wage gaps changes the picture radically. The rebel trade economist Ravi Batra, for example, demonstrates with a back-of-the-envelope calculation that in 1990 free trade cost the United States hundreds of billions of dollars.[41] But, by the same token, countries that trade in order to build up their manufacturing sector, such as China, India, Thailand, Korea, and, earlier, Japan, will gain even more from such trade than economists realize.

This leads to yet another orthodox assumption, that no sector of the economy carries any special significance, that offhand there is no reason to prefer manufacturing over agriculture or the service sector. Nothing expresses this better than the statement attributed to Michael Boskin, former chairperson of the Council of Economic Advisors: "It doesn't make any difference whether a country makes potato chips or computer chips."[42] What is at stake here is an empirical question that depends not just on relative wage levels but, more importantly, on the strategic position of an industry. There are a host of good reasons to believe that from an intertemporal (dynamic) point of view, computer chips are a much better investment; consider the state of embodied technology in the products and the way jobs in more technically sophisticated areas create knowledge, experience and skills that will benefit other industries in the future.[43]

A final point must be added to the restrictive assumptions issue. It's not just an academic problem that ends up misleading students as to the nature and impact of trade. Beyond that, an economics resting on such counterfactual premises spills directly into public policy by misleading, perhaps inadvertently, public opinion. Every time economists are asked to assess the likely impact of a new trade agreement, such as NAFTA, they usually program all these assumptions into their CGE computer models.[44] This creates a rather embarrassing situation: the citizen is given reassuring estimates as to the effects of trade liberalization on real wages, unemployment, lay-offs, and so on, without having been told that the friendly looking numbers were obtained by *assuming* no trade deficits, no unemployment, no capital mobility and the like, in the first place!

Winners, losers and compensation

When Paul Samuelson, together with Wolfgang Stolper, conceded in an important article that the removal of tariffs from low-wage imports of labor-intensive products may hurt workers, he still insisted that the welfare of society as a whole would increase.[45] That claim was made on the basis of the new welfare economics (discussed in Chapter 5). As long as the prospective gains of the rich are more than sufficient to compensate the poor for their losses, one infers that society is better off. And this regardless of whether any attempt is made to actually compensate the losers. In other words, low-wage competition, in spite of the fact that it hurts the least skilled and most vulnerable members of society, all things considered, remains in the social interest of high-wage countries. Little did Samuelson know at that time that the US economy during the latter decades of the century would approximate such a trading situation. Real wages have stagnated despite continued productivity gains and rising national income, implying that trade has boosted profits at the expense of the less privileged.[46]

One has to object to this type of welfare interpretation. Recall that the "potential compensation" theorem works on the questionable assumption that a dollar for the winning rich has the same value or utility for the losing poor. On what scientific basis can such an interpersonal assumption of comparison of utilities be justified? Moreover, on moral grounds alone, this type of trade liberalization is questionable. Any change in public policy that is recommended because it will help the rich at the expense of the poor shows little respect for basic rights and for human dignity. How can it be justified that a large number of the most deprived and vulnerable citizens are deliberately used as pawns for the welfare of the better off? Not surprisingly, for a social economist, the doctrine of free trade holds very little fascination and credibility in the pursuit of the common good.

Trouble brewing on the macroeconomic front?

Ever since Sismondi and Hobson, a deep concern with macroeconomic equilibrium has been central to a more humane social economics. It is therefore tempting to briefly sketch the new economic forces unleashed by globalization in the spirit of these two pioneers by stressing the hazards of overproduction and underconsumption threatening the industrialized nations. The picture to be painted is based on two related primary forces: the competitive pressure to reduce costs to which a corporation is increasingly exposed, and a collateral tendency for income distribution to tilt in favor of capital and against labor.

Competitive cost reductions and production capacity

During the European industrial revolution, Sismondi had decried the relentless pressures exerted on an entrepreneur to undersell his rival producers, in part by introducing more machinery, sometimes even by cutting the wages of the workmen. These individual actions, when considered collectively, had unwelcome macroeconomic effects. The competitive cost and wage reductions tended to replace high-income consumers with low-income consumers, resulting in a propensity to create excess capacity, or glutted markets, together with deprivation and social suffering.

Today, industrial society is again in the midst of a similar revolution, but now it is taking place around the globe. The opening up of markets, together with new low-wage competitors in Asia, has plunged the firms of industrialized nations back into the whirlpools of almost unprecedented and seemingly endless competition. An affected enterprise, in order to defend its profitability, has little choice other than to invest in factories equipped with the latest technology. The race in the automobile industry to cut the man-hours necessary to produce a car by employing more and more robots, all preferably in a low-wage country, is one illustration.[47]

One result of such ceaseless investment is a cumulative industry-wide build up of industrial capacity, which, by itself, puts a downward pressure on prices and profits, thereby further aggravating the pressure to cut costs. But this is only half of the story.

Economic inequality and consumption

In his pioneering work on macroeconomics, Sismondi was the first to stress the crucial role of the *"diffusion* of wealth" in the reproduction of national income.[48] Like Hobson two generations later, he blamed growing inequality for creating underconsumption and crisis. Since there are now signs that the same kind of affliction may be haunting present-day economies, it is tempting to analyze the present crisis-prone situation according to that type of macro-economics. A simplified argument would run something like the following: Responding to ever more intense competition, firms rein in their costs by "downsizing" (or, making for better PR, "right-sizing" or "econo-sizing"), lay-offs and the hiring of a contingent workforce. Displaced workers join the unemployed or seek a new, often poorer paying job, in the expanding service sector. Whatever the particular road chosen, the consequence of such corporate endeavor to lower their costs of production is to reduce labor incomes and with it consumer spending. Moreover, the income of capital in the form of profits grows and is pumped into the stock market to be reinvested in the economy. Together this creates a tendency for the productive capacity of industry to rise faster than consumption power. Markets are glutted with unsold goods, prices tend downwards, profit margins decline, thereby preparing the ground for another round of competitive cost reductions.

A crisis in the making?

To the extent that firms, awash with finance, choose to locate their new investments in low-wage countries, competition will correspondingly heat up, thereby adding additional fuel to the vicious circle illustrated in Figure 9.1.

Figure 9.1 represents the dynamic process, with its mounting pressures, of both overproduction and underconsumption. Witness how so many arrows point to the lower left, indicating redistributions from labor (wages) to capital (profits), thereby affecting consumer expenditures negatively and investment positively.

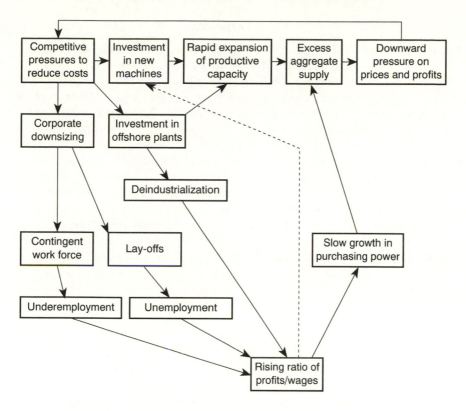

Figure 9.1 Competitive pressures in an industrialized economy

Contemporary mainstream economists, having pledged allegiance to Say's Law, will not be easily convinced. Even the increasing indications of global excess supply now observed in the automobile industry are unlikely to soften their opposition.[49] Instead, just as in the days of Hobson, when the creed of the benefice of self-adjusting markets seemed to have lost little of its seductive power, economists point to various automatic "checks" that they believe will prevent trouble; one of them being the belief that capitalists will consume more of their income the moment prospective returns on their investments fall too low. Furthermore, the tendency toward under-consumption in today's economy is checked, it could be argued, by meeting the new counteractive forces of massive advertising expenditures and rising consumer debt.

Yet, the unexpected Asian crisis of the late-1990s may have served as a reminder that excessive optimism is unwarranted; especially when one considers that it all started in Thailand after its exports dramatically declined – a collapse attributed to the intensified competition from India, Vietnam and especially China.[50]

The China card

There is a new card in the deck. The significance of China in the global equation is an economic reality of sobering proportions. Here is an emerging giant with a population of 1.2 billion and bent on becoming the world's foremost economic power. The scary combination of a massive labor pool of educated and highly motivated workers, extremely low wages controlled by an authoritarian state, together with the expressed and ambitious desire to pursue a high-tech, export-oriented development strategy, promises to serve as the ultimate testing ground of orthodox international economics. It is going to be quite an accomplishment if trade relations with such an economy can still be visualized or squeezed into a framework of comparative advantage and mutually beneficial trade. And if the Sismondi–Hobson macro perspective is essentially correct, then competition with China must be expected also greatly to exacerbate the pressures threatening the well-being of the industrialized countries. It would be difficult to imagine a better opportunity to learn by real-world events. Fortunately, truth is wedded neither to orthodoxy nor heterodoxy, but given enough time, it has a way of asserting itself.

Productivity and wages

Before suggesting some basic steps of how to align international commerce with the common good, some of the economic misconceptions that have been serving as popular anodynes in matters of trade deserve to be mentioned. One of these "pain relievers" would certainly be the often heard assertion that it was the Hawley–Smoot Tariff Act of 1930, boosting American tariff rates from 45 percent to 59 percent by 1932, that caused the Great Depression. No serious examination of that historical event justifies any such conclusion, and today even strongly pro-trade economics spokesmen will ridicule such an assertion.[51] However, other more enduring confusions, all relating to productivity, require some commentary.

According to economic theory, there is a link between labor productivity and wages: in a *competitive* market economy, a worker is paid according to the contribution he or she makes to the value of a firm's output, *ceteris paribus*. However, it is in this expression, akin to the fine print in a contract, "other things being equal," that abstraction comes in, simply because in the real world many other factors do *not* remain the same after the extra output is produced. This explains why productivity in US agriculture could increase sevenfold between 1950 and 1990, while real wages on the farm have less than doubled during the same period. Output per worker has gone up, but *farm prices* have gone down. Similarly, in US manufacturing, labor productivity has more than doubled during the same period while real wage gains have not kept up. In this case, too, the culprit has been price decreases caused by world market values driven down by imports from low-wage countries, together with the (defensive) response of installing lower-cost technologies.

The other qualifying factor in the theoretical productivity–wage link is an assumption of *competitive* wage determination in which workers, if underpaid in one firm, will readily get what they are worth in another. But what happens if there is one dominant employer, such as the Chinese state? Even in the private sector, as long as the state has a strong interest in being internationally competitive, and as long as it has the power to regulate wages directly or indirectly, it would be unrealistic to expect the employees' pay to rise with their productivity gains. Data from Mexico, for example, strongly confirm the likelihood of a de-linking between productivity and wages.[52]

As a corollary of the preceding, the well-meaning idea of rescuing a nation's beleaguered labor force through more education and training may promise more than it can deliver. Upgrading the workforce only increases pay or employment if it produces positive results *relative* to competing countries, and if the output prices can be protected from low-wage import competition. As already discussed, even some of the most highly skilled workers in the service sector are no longer working in isolation of service workers abroad.

Related to a training/education focus on productivity is also the often heard contention that American workers are still far more productive than their counterparts abroad and thus can earn far more without pricing American goods out of world markets. Although this claim is in and of itself (still) true, it neglects the other side of the coin, the equally true assertion that wages in the United States, and even more so in Germany, are much higher than in the developing countries of Asia. Obviously, what ultimately is decisive is not just productivity or wages considered in isolation, but *labor costs* which involve a ratio of both factors. Research on this question indicates that today labor costs are much higher among the industrialized nations. For example, William Greider summarizes a 1994 study for the US Labor Department as follows:

> American garment makers could make a shirt with 14 minutes of human labor, while it took 25 minutes in Bangladesh. But the average US wage was $7.53 an hour, while in Bangladesh it was 25 cents, an edge that would not be erased even if Bangladeshi wages were doubled or quadrupled. Or steel: US industry required 3.4 hours of human labor to produce a ton of steel, while Brazil took 5.8 hours. But the wage difference was 10 to 1: $13 an hour versus $1.28.[53]

Available figures from Mexico concerning the production of automobiles, television sets and computers tell a similar story. As a general rule, workers in newly built foreign plants in Asia obtain a rate of efficiency that is 50 percent to 90 percent that of workers in the West, but their wages are more like

10 percent to 30 percent of US levels. In the special case of China, the wage gap is much larger, more like 50 to 1, a difference that is almost incommensurate with whatever the productivity gap may be. All in all, it does not bode well for the advanced market economies.

Social regulation of trade

Concerns about national competitiveness usually take globalization simply as a given, non-reversible fact to which one has to adjust, usually by making wages "more flexible" or reducing the social benefits of workers. Far from it; globalization, and the competitive pressures that come with it, are a human artifact, the result of a prolonged policy initiative. Once there is sufficient evidence that it does not serve the common good, why not moderate, stop or even reverse the trend of the last thirty years? In this spirit some ameliorative measures are in order.

The need for international labor standards

The problem today is that global economic competition is becoming destructive. Developing countries, desperate to attract foreign investment, outdo each other by offering prospective investors conditions that are attractive to capital but not at all to labor. Transnational corporations can shop for the lowest possible labor standards consisting of a docile labor force with no rights to join trade unions of their choice, and willing to work at subsistence wages. The very logic of international competition produces a "race to the bottom" in which workers, more often than not young women, have to contend with degrading jobs in order to help their families make ends meet.

This tendency is *intrinsic* to competition and was one of the main motivations in setting up the International Labor Organization (ILO) in 1919. Before that there were already international agreements to eliminate slavery, and, subsequently, to prohibit the trafficking of children and young women. Contemporary international jurisprudence, as also manifested in the Charter of the United Nations, declares liberty, dignity and regard for basic human needs to be the very basis of a just social order. Moreover, worker rights – especially so-called "core" rights consisting of a prohibition of forced labor, child exploitation and discrimination, as well as the guaranteeing of freedom of association and collective bargaining – have long been seen as inseparable from human rights. Over the years, through the signing of various ILO conventions, participating nations have pledged to honor these basic labor rights. Yet enforcement is weak and less than a third of the nations have signed-on to all the relevant pacts. According to a recent OECD study, the most popular convention concerns forced labor, in which 135 out of 173 countries have chosen to participate, followed by the right to organize and collective

214

bargaining (signed by 124 nations). At the same time, China, Korea, Botswana and Zimbabwe have to date declined to ratify any of the various core conventions. Even the United States is party to only *one* of the five basic conventions: the prohibition of forced labor.[54]

Deliberate non-compliance with basic international labor standards is a competitive tool that strengthens exports and direct investment of foreign capital. Above all it manifests in the establishment of so-called "export processing zones" that either prohibit or otherwise severely restrict union activity and allow for a more lax enforcement of existing labor legislation. Not surprisingly, the OECD study found that from 1973 to 1992 the worst offenders of labor rights (including China, Egypt and Indonesia) enjoyed a huge gap between annual manufacturing productivity growth (4.8 percent) and average real wage increases (1.5 percent).[55] Unfortunately, this type of data fully confirms the earlier voiced apprehensions about trading with China, but a legitimate concern goes beyond that. How can Malaysia, Thailand, the Philippines, Taiwan and Korea afford *not* to compete with China? It does not involve sophisticated economics to know that in such standards competition, as with destructive competition in general, good guys finish last.

The need for managed trade

Once the faith in *laissez-faire* is seen as ill-founded, it won't take long to realize that the real choice is between destructive chaos and managed competition within a framework of social rules and regulations. In this respect there are a number of basic policy options that ought to be considered. Some, but not all, are enumerated as follows.

First, and foremost, every country would be well advised to follow the example of Japan and others and create a ministry of international trade whose mandate would be to assure that private gain does not come at social cost. It also implies the international negotiation of a fair set of basic labor standards that would apply to all players in the world market. Unless a country agrees to such fair competition, new direct investments there would not be permitted. Similarly, enforcement of such standards will be strengthened by other sanctions, particularly with an imposition of a *social tariff* altering the terms of trade by adding the *human* costs to the already embodied production costs.

More generally, such a national trade agency would also have the responsibility of guaranteeing balanced trade between countries. Such a goal could be accomplished by a mechanism that would, in the case of a persistent trade deficit with a commercial partner, impose a significant and uniform new tariff on such imports until equilibrium is restored. The entire revenue of such a "disequilibrium tax" might then be spent in development aid to those less-developed countries that honor basic labor standards.

Finally, the Trade Ministry would adopt measures to help consumers make their choices in a more informed and ethical manner. Significant first steps in this direction would involve a system of *social labeling* and a requirement to list labor content by the different nations involved. A good example of the former is the already successful Rugmark campaign in Europe that discourages the importation of hand-knotted rugs produced by child labor. Toy imports could be handled in a similar way. The requirement of providing information about the origin of imported products would permit citizens to exercise their own value judgments when making purchases.

It is, of course, true that the remedies suggested so far might be classified as "protectionist," but what is being protected here is not the profits or wages of a particular industry, but rather the living standards of industrialized nations as well as the health and human dignity of the workers in less developed countries.

The need for community enterprise

As in Sismondi's day, many of the problems of contemporary society are a result of the divorce of work and ownership. Profit sharing schemes can certainly be expected to moderate a threatening macro-imbalance, but they would not do much to ameliorate disequilibrium in global trade. Sismondi could not have known that it would one day be possible to have large labor-owned firms, overcoming the two-century-old split between labor and capital. The Mondragon cooperative experience (see Chapter 8) promises, at least in theory, to be an antidote to another key element of the trade problem: a truly democratic worker-owned firm, unlike an investor-owned corporation, will have little incentive to spin off a new democratic and autonomous cooperative abroad, regardless of the relative attractiveness of prospective labor costs.[56] This would effectively put an end to the leakage of capital into low-wage countries such as China and the acceleration of wage equalization that goes with it. Nevertheless, significant labor differentials would still remain, continuing to undermine balanced trade.

Imagine, however, a whole world economy without investor-owned corporations but featuring the Mondragon alternative. Democratic firms in China and elsewhere would automatically see to it that worker members alone would participate in the productivity gains. Under such an idealistic regime, North–South pay differentials would now reflect relative productivity differences, a situation that would come closer to the abstract and benign trading world depicted in textbooks. Another reason for taking economic democracy seriously.

Conclusion

Nowhere does the difference between an individualistic and a social economics become more pronounced than in the assessment of competition and the prospects of entrusting the well-being of society to impersonal market forces. The central message of the social economic perspective insists on the need to coordinate the drive for private gain with the common good. Competition, unrestrained by ethical considerations or by a social regulatory framework, will wear and tear the moral fiber of a society to breaking point. This somber view pertains to both domestic and international competition, but its effects are more visibly illustrated under a regime that relies on, and applauds, unregulated trade across international boundaries.

As with Say's Law, contemporary economic theory goes back to the abstract world of David Ricardo, embracing a so-called "law" contingent on highly implausible assumptions. Paul Samuelson is said to have hailed the doctrine of comparative advantage as one of the very few propositions that is both true and non-trivial. He may be right, but is it relevant as well? Can it really be justified as the basis for holding that every nation must benefit from liberalizing the way cross-border trade is conducted? Given common sense and the recent evidence on the horizon of approaching cargo ships weighted down by surplus merchandise, it is easy to despair. Is it possible that an excessive academic diet of abstract mathematical reasoning might promote a self-contented mind averse to criticism, even in light of contrary intimations? It reminds one of the joke about economists clinging to the maxim that the idea of blaming trade for this and that reason "may be fine in practice, but does not work in theory."[57] Meanwhile the signs of mounting social destruction and human degradation proliferate. Sadly, the dogmatic ideology of comparative advantage theory is likely to keep the globe enchained for many years. And if it ever should lose its grip on humanity, in all likelihood, it won't be as a result of academic argument. It's too tempting not to repeat one of Sismondi's choice quotes from 160 years ago:

> writing makes little impression when it attacks a dominant system. Facts are more obstinate and more rebellious. They do not manifest themselves less from its being supposed that they can be refuted without being heard, as if they were only writings; they often increase from having been neglected, and then they fall with their whole weight on the most skillfully constructed theory, crushing and overthrowing it at the very moment when its author was congratulating himself on having victoriously refuted all his adversaries.[58]

The present critique of markets, globalization and trade theory has focused on the social consequences. But there is another, perhaps even more deadly,

217

outcome in terms of potential long-run *environmental* consequences. This will be addressed in Chapter 10.

Notes

1 K. Polanyi, "Our Obsolete Market Mentality," *Commentary*, 1947, vol. 3, pp. 109–117.
2 A. O. Hirschman, "Rival Interpretations of Market Society: Civilizing, Destructive, or Feeble," *Journal of Economic Literature*, December 1982, vol. 20, pp. 1463–1484.
3 S. Ricardo, quoted in ibid., p. 1465.
4 J. A. Hobson, *Work and Wealth: A Human Valuation*, London, Allen, 1914, p. 251.
5 Hirschman, "Rival Interpretations of Market Society."
6 F. Hirsch, *Social Limits to Growth*, Cambridge, MA, Harvard University Press, 1976, p. 124.
7 M. Horkheimer, *The Eclipse of Reason*, New York, Oxford University Press, 1947, p. 34.
8 Even though the story is true (it was printed in the late seventies in the *New York Times*), its meaning is just as real when considered as a mere thought experiment.
9 J. M. Culbertson, *Competition, Constructive and Destructive*, Madison, WI, 21st Century Press, 1985, p. 5.
10 This does not preclude the fact that many classical economists before that time did recognize the moral limitations of competition. See M. A. Lutz, "Doubts about Competition," in E. O'Boyle (ed.), *Social Economics*, New York, Routledge, 1996, pp. 109–124, for a survey of some of the views expressed by Adam Smith, J. S. Mill, Alfred Marshall, J. B. Clark, F. Y. Edgeworth and others.
11 ibid., p. 10.
12 A. Smith, *An Inquiry into the Nature and Causes of the Wealth of Nations* [1776], Chicago, IL, University of Chicago Press, 1976, bk. 1, pp. 477–478 (emphasis added).
13 For a survey of the attitudes of the classical economists on this point, see R. K. Kanth, *Political Economy and Laissez-Faire: Economics and Ideology in the Ricardian Era*, Totowa, NJ, Rowman and Littlefield, 1986.
14 Smith, *An Inquiry into the Nature and Causes of the Wealth of Nations*, bk. 2, ch. 2.
15 J. A. Hobson, *The Economics of Unemployment*, London, George Allen and Unwin, 1922, p. 104. See also his *Rationalisation and Unemployment: An Economic Dilemma*, London, George Allen and Unwin, 1930, ch. 9.
16 Lopez Portillo in a speech to the United Nations, September 1, 1982.
17 "If the neo-classical model (or its precursors) had provided a correct description of the economy, then market socialism would indeed have had a running chance of success." And Stiglitz concludes: "Thus the failure of market socialism serves as much as a refutation of the standard neoclassical model as it does of the market socialist ideal." J. Stiglitz, *Whither Socialism?*, Cambridge, MA, MIT Press, 1994, pp. 2, 13.
18 L. Berti, "Society and the Market: Remote and Less Remote Sources of a Present Issue," in O. Nudler and M. A. Lutz (eds), *Economics, Culture and Society: Alternative Approaches*, New York, The Apex Press, and Tokyo, United Nations University Press, 1996, p. 64.
19 *Wall Street Journal*, February 26, 1997, p. A4. See also *The 1997 Economic Report of the President*, Washington, DC, US Government Printing Office, February 1997,

showing that in 1996 only half of the workers felt "not at all likely" to lose their jobs over the next 12 months.

20 E. Graham, "Dreams of Cushy Retirement Clash with Meager Savings," *Wall Street Journal*, December 12, 1997, p. R1.

21 The latest news on this score is the most shocking. According to *The Economist* (December 20, 1997, p. 28), between the late 1970s and mid-1990s the real family income of the richest quintile of Americans rose by 30 percent, while at the same time that of the poorest fell 21 percent. Source of data: Centre on Budget and Policy Priorities, Washington, DC.

22 W. Greider, *One World, Ready or Not: The Manic Logic of Global Capitalism*, New York, Simon and Schuster, 1997, p. 11.

23 J. M. Culbertson, *International Trade and the Future of the West*, Madison, WI, 21st Century Press, 1984.

24 In private communication, Herman Daly told me that it was his co-author John Cobb, a philosopher, who first brought Culbertson's book to his attention, and only after prolonged discussions was able to persuade him, the economist, of the irrelevance of comparative advantage theory. It certainly goes to show that interdisciplinary co-authorship can be a most fruitful approach to economic problems.

25 H. Daly and J. Cobb, *For the Common Good: Redirecting the Economy toward Community, the Environment, and a Sustainable Future*, Boston, MA, Beacon Press, 1989, ch. 11.

26 M. Friedman and R. Friedman, *Free to Choose: A Personal Statement*, New York, Harcourt Brace Jovanovich, 1990, p. 45. Ricardo himself used a similar example: "Two men can make both shoes and hats, but in making hats he can only exceed his competitor by 20 percent, and in making shoes he can exceed him by 30 percent − will it not be for the interest of both, that the superior man should employ himself exclusively in making shoes, and the inferior man in making hats?" P. Sraffa (ed.), *The Works and Correspondence of David Ricardo*, vol. I, Cambridge, Cambridge University Press, 1951, p. 136.

27 Sraffa, *The Works and Correspondence of David Ricardo*, pp. 136–137, emphasis added.

28 B. Ohlin, "The Theory of Trade" [1924], in H. Flam and M. J. Flanders (eds), *Heckscher–Ohlin Trade Theory*, Cambridge, MA, MIT Press, 1991, p. 164.

29 P. Samuelson, *Economics*, 11th edn, New York, McGraw-Hill, 1980, pp. 627, 630.

30 Because of this trade theory, protagonist Krugman rails against anybody who talks about countries competing against each other as "pop international economists," P. Krugman, *Pop Internationalism*, Cambridge, MA, MIT Press, 1996. The list of offenders also includes his colleague at MIT, Lester Thurow, and the reader may want to consult a recent feature story in *The New York Times* comparing the two economists (*The New York Times*, February 16, 1997, sect. F, 1, 10).

31 Adrian Wood has recently challenged that type finding as strongly underestimating the effect trade has had. According to his analysis, about three-quarters of the 20 percent drop in demand for unskilled workers during the last two decades can be attributed to manufacturing imports from the South. He points to the timing, magnitude and cross-country variation of the relative deterioration of unskilled earnings. A. Wood, *North–South Trade, Employment and Inequality: Changing Fortunes in a Skill-Driven World*, Oxford, Clarendon Press, 1994, p. 17. His new findings must have been unsettling for many economists; witness, for example, how the (strongly pro-free-trade) magazine, *The Economist*, quite adroitly referred to his results as "something nasty in the woodshed," October 1, 1994, p. 16.

Nevertheless, Wood's study still accepts the theoretical framework of comparative advantage; he merely modifies some of the empirical findings based on that theory. Similarly, there is the new evidence put forth by E. Leamer, *In Search of Stolper–Samuelson Effects on US Wages*, NBER Working Paper no. 5427, 1996, A. Krueger, "Labour Market Shifts and the Price Puzzle Revisited," unpublished paper, Princeton University, October 1995, and J. Sachs and H. Shatz, "International Trade and Wage Inequality in the United States: Some New Results," unpublished paper, Harvard University, December 1995.

32 Culbertson, *International Trade and the Future of the West*, p. 39.

33 T. Lee and R. Scott, "Third World Growth," *Harvard Business Review*, November–December 1994, p. 18.

34 A. Brewer, "Trade with Fixed Real Wages and Mobile Capital," *Journal of International Trade*, 1985, vol. 18, p. 180, emphasis added.

35 See, for example, the estimates by S. Golub, "Comparative Advantage and Absolute Advantage in the Asia–Pacific Region," Federal Reserve Bank of San Francisco, Working Paper no. 9, 1995.

36 There is plenty of anecdotal evidence today of this new phenomenon. The *Wall Street Journal* abounds with front page stories about skilled work being shifted to Irish and Indian engineers; Boeing has passenger jets being developed in China, the German giant Hoechst shifting the bulk of its genetic research to lower-wage USA. Swissair has been outsourcing its accounting to India. Intel and Hewlett-Packard are increasingly relying on bargain-priced Malaysians, while in Moscow we are told that "almost every programmer worth his salt works for a Western company." *The Economist* tells us that "more than 100 of America's top 500 firms buy software services from firms in India, where programmers are typically paid less than a quarter of the American rate." Moreover, outsourcing now also stretches to processing hospital records, credit reports, insurance claims, and virtually all production of television cartoons being done abroad, *The Economist*, September 28, 1996, p. 32; and February 22, 1997, p. 75.

37 *Wall Street Journal*, March 17, 1993, p. A1.

38 S. Hickok, "The Consumer Cost of US Trade Restraints," Federal Reserve Bank of New York Quarterly Review, Summer 1995, pp. 1–12; D. Tarr and M. Morkre, *Aggregate Costs to the United States of Tariffs and Quotas on Imports*, Bureau of Economics Staff Report to the Federal Trade Commission, Washington, DC, December 1984; G. Hufbauer, *Trade Protection in the US: 31 Case Studies*, Stockholm, Institute for International Economics, 1986.

39 M. A. Lutz., "On the Quality of the Industrial Earnings Structure in Manufacturing," *Industrial Relations*, February 1977, vol. 16:1, pp. 61–70.

40 E. Hagen, "An Economic Justification of Protectionism," *Quarterly Journal of Economics*, 1958, vol. 72, pp. 496–514; J. Bhagwati, "The Pure Theory of International Trade: A Survey," *Economic Journal*, 1964, vol. 74, pp. 1–78; R. Batra, *Studies in the Pure Theory of International Trade*, London, Macmillan, 1973, ch. 9. Also see R. Batra, *The Myth of Free Trade: A Plan for America's Economic Revival*, New York, Charles Scribner's Sons, 1993, p. 258.

41 Batra, *The Myth of Free Trade*, pp. 162–163.

42 Quoted in R. Batra, *The Great American Deception: What Politicians Won't Tell You about Our Economy and Your Future*, New York, John Wiley and Sons, 1996, p. 111.

43 Culbertson, *International Trade and the Future of the West*, pp. 135–137.

44 For a comprehensive analysis on this vital point, see J. Stamford, "North American Economic Integration and the International Regulation of Labor Standards,"

in B. Stein (ed.), *Contemporary Issues in Labor and Employment Law*, Boston, MA, Little, Brown and Co., 1994, pp. 3–46.

45 W. Stolper and P. Samuelson, "Protection and Real Wages," *Review of Economic Studies*, 1941, vol. 23, pp. 58–73.

46 For illuminating data on these fateful trends, see Batra, *The Myth of Free Trade*, chs. 1–3, and also OECD, *Trade Employment and Labour Standards: A Study of Core Workers' Rights and International Trade*, Paris, 1996, pp. 87–89.

47 The time it took to make a car in the US used to be roughly 40 hours just twenty years ago. Today, in response to Japanese competition, that figure is less than 30 hours, *Harbour Report*, Harbour and Associates Inc., Troy, Michigan.

48 J. C. L. Simonde de Sismondi, *Political Economy and the Philosophy of Government* [1847], New York, Augustus M. Kelley, 1966b, p. 63.

49 Witness the accumulating evidence from industry forecasts reported in Greider, *One World, Ready or Not*, ch. 6.

50 K. Richburg and S. Mufson, "Warning Signs Unheeded on Road to Asian Crisis," *International Herald Tribune*, January 5, 1998, pp. 1, 4.

51 For a brief analysis see Batra, *The Myth of Free Trade*, pp. 150–154. For an ortho-dox rebuke of the claim, see P. Krugman, *The Age of Diminished Expectations*, Cambridge, MA, MIT Press, 1994, p.125.

52 See H. Shaiken, *Mexico in the Global Economy*, San Diego, CA, University of California Press, 1990; "Advanced Manufacturing and Mexico: A New International Division of Labor?," *Latin American Research Review*, vol. 29:2, 1994; the OECD study that concluded that for the period 1973–92 developing countries enjoyed average annual productivity gains of 3–5 percent, while the corresponding growth rate of real wages was only between 1.25 and 1.75 percent, OECD, *Trade Employment and Labour Standards*, pp. 88–89. Finally, there is the telling data by A. Jackson, *Incomes and Productivity in North America*, Commission for Labor Cooperation, Dallas, TX, Bernan Press, 1997, pp. 99–110.

53 Greider, *One World, Ready or Not*, p. 75. The data are from R. Rothstein, "Workforce Globalization: A Policy Response," for the Woman's Bureau, US Labor Department, 1994.

54 OECD, *Trade Employment and Labour Standards*, pp. 34, 40.

55 ibid., p. 89. However, the study also found that Singapore, Malaysia and Thailand were among the few countries of the world where real wage growth outpaced productivity gains (ibid., p. 88).

56 Of course, this precludes setting up *non-democratic* subsidiaries abroad, something that the Mondragon Cooperative Corporation has been compelled to do during the last decade in order to be able to compete with the multinational corporations. MCC now owns conventionally managed factories in Morocco, Egypt, Mexico and even China.

57 A. Ehrenhalt in *The New York Times*, February 23, 1997.

58 Sismondi, *Political Economy and the Philosophy of Government*, p. 150.

10

THE ULTIMATE CHALLENGE

Assume for the moment that the fear of a trade-induced global depression is unwarranted, that modern macroeconomics has indeed made progress since the days of Sismondi and Hobson. Instead of bracing for a sudden and possibly violent interruption of global expansion, let us now proceed on the presumption of a successfully growing world economy. But far from celebrating this possibility, this chapter will demonstrate that the notion of unlimited economic growth is one of the most serious problems that humanity has ever faced. It threatens our physical well-being and even more so that of generations to come. Overcoming this new predicament will constitute the *ultimate* challenge to an individualistic conception of economics.

1. International trade and the environment

It has been estimated that it took thousands of years for the world economy to reach an output of $600 billion at the beginning of the twentieth century. By the end of the millennium the planetary (gross) product is expected to be $31 trillion (1995), and by 2040 the figure is likely to have tripled or quadrupled.

During the last three decades, world economic production has been growing at roughly 3 percent a year, but international trade during this period has been increasing significantly faster, at around 5 percent. The rapid expansion of world trade, despite its potentially troublesome effects on the standard of living of industrialized nations, has indeed had a strong and positive effect on world growth. But there is another consequence that is rarely considered or mentioned: an increasing reliance on imports also produces global pollution. Despite an appalling lacunae of statistical data and serious analysis, several points can be made.

Trade and transportation

Untold billions of tons of cargo and merchandise are annually trucked, shipped and flown between nations around the globe. This requires a tremendous amount of energy, a consumption that depletes fossil fuels as well as introducing carbon pollutants. Transportation (including private automobiles and travel) is much more energy-intensive than production, accounting for nearly twice the carbon dioxide emission in developed countries. In the United States, for instance, the level of energy consumed by freight transport alone accounts for as much as 60 percent of the total transportation consumption.[1] Similarly disconcerting is that more and more international trade is shipped by truck and air, the two most energy-intensive means of moving goods. A ton of goods is estimated to consume forty-seven times more energy when flown by air and five times more when trucked on roads than when transported by boat or train. Global air freight (as measured by million ton kilometers) between countries has been growing since 1991 at 11 percent a year and is expected to reach 100 million tons/km in 1999.[2] Simultaneously, fuel efficiency gains in air transport are improving by less than 1 percent annually.[3]

Moreover, the bulk of this growth in trade does not consist of raw materials shipped by tankers, but is driven by exchanging relatively similar commodities across borders. Americans drink European beverages while Europeans drink American soft drinks, beer and California wine. Much of this growing trade has little to do with necessities, but with a growing preference for fancy imports satisfying refined consumer tastes: Americans sip orange juice shipped from Brazil, eat grapes and decorate tables with flowers flown in from Chile, while the Japanese dine on Australian ostrich meat and American sea urchins and cherries flown in by the airplane load. Increasing affluence has led to imports, allowing for a wider range of products than readily available at home.

The apparent affordability of foreign goods hides or discounts their hidden costs to the environment imposed by the burning up of energy in their transportation. Affordability of such foreign goods does not include the costly transport emissions. The solution: incorporate the estimated social costs into the price by making the polluter pay through some measure of emission charges or pollution taxes. But once again, international trade and competition stand in the way of such remedial policies.

Environmental standards and international trade

Suppose there are two countries, each blessed with a bountiful fish population in large lakes that are entirely within their borders. Both countries also make a steel alloy product. One of them, let us call it Sotopia, carefully manages its stock of fish by monitoring water quality and prohibiting its steel producers from dumping any toxins into the lake. The other, call it Martopia, prefers to run its economy according to free market principles. Such a situation does not make for a level playing field: one steel producer, situated in Sotopia, has been burdened with higher disposal costs, giving its Martopian rival a significant market advantage. Clearly, in a competitive world – the kind usually assumed by economists – it is just a matter of time until the Sotopian steel producer will be forced into bankruptcy. That is *unless* they fight back in one of two ways: first, they could seek protection from the cheap Martopia imports; or second, they could relocate their business to Martopia and so evade their home country's environmental laws. In the first case, by enforcing protective measures, environmental social standards are upheld. In the second case, firms, by freely choosing the lowest environmental standards, see to it that the playing field is "degraded" to a uniformly debased level. In other words, under free trade or free capital movements, some industries are unable to compete while hampered by costly environmental standards. It's either free trade and minimal environmental protection or regulated trade with the kind of environmental protection that reflects socially responsible values. Here free trade and sound environment are simply incompatible: choose one or the other.

The problem of standards competition is that Martopia, for whatever reason, does not seem to care much about toxins in their lake. Under a world regime of free trade and mobile capital, the government of Sotopia will have good reason to be concerned about Martopia's environmental measures. Without trade it would be none of Sotopia's business, but with trade it is. A natural solution would be to push for a "social tariff" that would offset the artificially low costs (equivalent to a government subsidy) of Martopia production. Simply good social economics, and the kind of solution hinted at by Vice President Al Gore in *Earth in the Balance: Ecology and the Human Spirit* (1992), when he writes: "Just as government subsidies of a particular industry are sometimes considered unfair under the trade laws, weak and ineffectual enforcement of pollution control measures should also be included in the definition of unfair trading practices."[4]

Most economists prefer to keep silent on the social tariff issue; however, the distinguished trade economist Jagdish Bhagwati denounces the idea of implementing social tariffs, saying it is impractical to calculate and would be imposing the values of one country on another, some sort of "eco-imperialism."[5] Social economist Herman Daly counters:

> This tariff policy does not imply the imposition of one country's environmental preferences or moral judgments on another country. Each country should set the rules of cost internalization in its own market. Whoever sells in a nation's market should play by that nation's rules or pay a tariff sufficient to remove the competitive advantage of lower standards. . . . No standards are being imposed through "environmental imperialism": paying the costs of a nation's environmental standards is merely the price of admission to its market.[6]

In other words, Martopia can do whatever it wants, using the standards it deems best, only as long as it doesn't want to have access to Sotopia's markets. Anybody who chooses to play chess by the established rules implicitly accepts to play by those rules and is not thereby an unconsenting victim. Similarly, if a country wants to sell its product in a foreign market, then it has to play by the rules governing that market. Otherwise, would it not be forcing its own values or standards on the country it exports to?

The fact that Bhagwati seems unable to see this must be attributed to a numbing power that economic thinking tends to exert on the mind, specially when questions regarding free trade are broached. Furthermore, in responding to the concerns about the relocation of factories to countries with lower environmental standards, Bhagwati makes the following apparently serious suggestion:

> The governments of higher-standards countries could do so without encumbering free trade by insisting that their businesses accede to the higher standards when they go abroad. Such a policy lies entirely within the jurisdictional powers of a higher-standards country. Moreover, the governments of lower-standards countries would be most unlikely to object to such an act of good citizenship by foreign investors.[7]

Restated in terms of the previous example, the steel-maker of Sotopia could produce in Martopia by using the same costly but pollution-free technology as mandated at home. No social tariff would then be needed, according to Bhagwati. Once again, the argument is very shallow, since it ignores the fact that nothing would stop the competing steel makers of Martopia from producing more cheaply, selling their product in the market of Sotopia, and underselling the environmentally friendlier steel produced both home and abroad by Sotopia. Before too long, no foreign companies behaving as "good citizens" would be able to survive within Martopia's borders. The only way that Bhagwati's proposal could work would be for Sotopia to ban any import produced by firms that do not subscribe to its environmental standards, a restriction that would fly in the face of free trade doctrine.

The previous case for a social tariff becomes still stronger when the damage to nature spills over national borders, as in atmospheric pollution or the sullying and exploitation of the oceans. One important case in point is the Mexican method of catching tuna fish in the Pacific using purse seine nets that hurt and kill dolphins. Why should American fisherman, prohibited by US law from using the less costly method, have to compete with the quasi-subsidized catch from Mexico? The prohibition of Mexican tuna imports, a sensible way to help preserve the dolphin population, has been successfully challenged under the rules of international free trade. Under the current framework of the World Trade Organization (WTO), any attempt to defend environmental standards by discouraging trade is considered suspect, a protectionist act in disguise. Any domestic law or regulation has to meet the test of being "least trade restrictive," a requirement that often clashes with political feasibility, especially to tax-adverse citizens. Moreover, a country must *prove* to trade experts that there is a scientific merit for any standard that has the side effect of inhibiting trade; some uphill battle. Another illustration of the way economics can frustrate environmental goals is the Kyoto Agreement to Curb Global Warming, which exempts developing countries from doing their part in the reduction of the so-called greenhouse gases. It provides an open invitation for producers in the industrialized nations to evade the costly environmental rules by relocating their plants to where the rules do not apply.

For many reasons, including the export of toxic waste to less developed countries, free trade and environmental protection do not mix. One must embrace either one or the other.

2. Questioning economic growth

The concern that economic activity and growth exhausts natural resources is not a new one; in the last 300 years there have been recurrent fears concerning the adequacy of timber supplies, of population outgrowing the world's food supply, about running out of whale oil and about the depletion of coal reserves. Happily, all these resources have not disappeared, nor did the disasters occur. But the worries seem to stay.

Environmental limits to economic growth?

Anxiety about the sustainability of economic growth resurfaced in the 1970s when *The Limits to Growth* (1972), sponsored by the Club of Rome, made headlines and, perhaps aided by the ensuing energy crisis, sold 4 million copies. Using a computer model of the world economy, the authors simulated the interactions between the economy and the environmental limits of land available for agriculture, extractable non-renewable natural resources and the environment's capacity to absorb industrial and residential waste. The computer runs yielded the alarming conclusion that if the past growth trends of population, industrialization, food production and resource depletion were to continue, "the limits to growth on this planet will be reached sometime within the next hundred years."[8] At the same time, they urged the immediate redesigning of the economic system so that the basic material needs of all could be met. In other words, economics had to be weaned from its traditional preoccupation with growth and put on a diet that featured national and global redistribution.

Limits to Growth was not well received by most economists. They countered

226

that the model ignored the potential benefits of recycling, the substitution of manufactured capital for natural capital (like the building of sewage-treatment plants, insulation to diminish the use of heating oil), the expanding and environmentally more benign service sector, and, most importantly, the role of the price mechanism encouraging necessary substitutions. Moreover, they claimed that the prices of raw materials in the United States had not increased since 1870.[9] Meanwhile, the energy crisis subsided and the price of oil returned to more normal levels.

In 1987 there was another shock with the publication of the United Nations' World Commission on Environment and Development.[10] The "Brundtland Report" gave prominence to a new concept of *sustainable development*, a world development strategy that "seeks to meet the needs and aspirations of the present without compromising the ability to meet those of the future."[11] Unlike *Limits to Growth*, the report encouraged economic accumulation, advocating a "new area of growth" in which developing countries play a much larger role and reap most of the benefits. In short, sustainable *development* meant a kind of sustainable *growth*. Economic expansion could be made environmentally sustainable "if industrialized nations can continue the recent shifts in the content of their growth towards less material- and energy-intensive activities and the improvement of their efficiency in using materials and energy."[12] Rather than emphasize the depletion of *non-renewable* natural resources, as did *Limits to Growth*, Brundtland emphasized the limited absorptive capacity of nature and the perils for *renewable* resources such as fish, water and air quality. Calling for an international conference to review progress made and promote the necessary benchmarks for continued "human progress within the guidelines of human needs and natural laws,"[13] resulted in a United Nations Conference on Environment and Development. This June 1992 Rio de Janeiro meeting also produced the (non-binding) *Rio Declaration* and *Agenda 21*.

Economists were less hostile to the Brundtland Report, in part because the principle of growth was not under assault, and in part because the market mechanism does not offer ready-made solutions to such problems stressed in the report as the pollution of the common property aspects of air and water. Nevertheless, the report may have been much too cavalier in its assumption that economic growth *per se* poses no real threat to the planet.

The case for limits: the common sense case

World economic growth must have limits simply because the biosphere is fixed and the economy, being a subsystem of that sphere, is fixed as well. The diameter of the earth is not expanding. However, the logic that no part can grow to be larger than the whole is not accepted by some economists.

Herman Daly, an eminent social economist, recounts asking Lawrence Summers during a conference whether he thought that the scale of the economy relative to the environment mattered, only to get the reply that "that's not the right way to look at it."[14] What is the *right* way? Daly explains that Summers' answer is rooted in a different world view or "preanalytic vision": one in which the economy receives inputs from nowhere and exports wastes to nowhere. In other words, an economy entirely independent of the surrounding ecosphere, entirely independent of the energy flows, past and present, coming from the sun. Hardly a common sense way of looking at things. But again, this is one of the pitfalls when looking at the world through the lens of economic theory; reality has to conform to theory, in this case the conventional circular flow diagram that accounts for households, firms, governments and other countries, but certainly no ecosphere. In this case the economy parades as the overarching system, with nature as its subsystem.

Needless to say, "having limits" is not the same thing as having *reached* those limits. In other words, in the *short run*, there may be no limits. Nevertheless, one should ask: can the earth carry a world economy where all countries share in a level of prosperity similar to our own? Gandhi is said to have dealt with a similar question, whether India after independence would ever attain a British standard of living, by answering: "It took Britain half the resources of the planet to achieve its prosperity; how many planets will a country like India require?"[15]

The case for limits: the scientific case

In physics, the "science of energy" or *thermodynamics* includes the law of entropy (from energy and tropos, that is, evolution), which has special relevance for the question of limits of economic growth. This Second Law of Thermodynamics states that although the total *quantity* of energy is the same, that energy evolves irrevocably in time, changing *qualitatively* from free energy able to do work into a state in which it is degraded or "locked-up" and unable to do any more work. In a thermodynamic system, the flow of energy, therefore, is from a state of low to a state of high entropy (dissipated or unavailable energy).

The great social economist Nicholas Georgescu-Roegen devoted the last twenty-five years of his career to exploring and expounding the relevance and implications of this law of entropy for the economic process. The economic system, as an (open) subset of a larger biophysical environment, draws from the latter low entropic matter and energy and, through production and consumption, deposits high entropic energy in the environmental "sink." In the process, valuable natural resources (consisting of a terrestrial stock of past sun energy in the form of oil, coal and natural gas), together with the incoming energy of the sun, are manufactured into goods only to be eventually transformed into valueless waste, or pollution. Any form of production, even the recycling of matter, leads to a greater depletion of (available) energy. Moreover, since, according to the law of entropy, energy with its one-directional flow *cannot* be recycled, the stock of "natural resources [must] represent the limitative factor as concerns the life span of [our] species."[16] The only sustainable economy would be one that leaves the stored-up terrestrial resources unencumbered, in Georgescu-Roegen's own words: "Man could continue to live by reverting to the stage of a berry-picking species – as he once was."[17] Otherwise, the more we grow our global production by indulging in the extraction of fossil fuels, the sooner comes the time when we reach nature's inexorable limit, showing us the way back to the cave or the tree.

Rebels without a cause?

Economists are prone to ignore this limitation; after all, economic growth has long been seen as the magic carpet that will, like the tide, slowly but surely raise all hopes, including those of the poor, for a better standard of living. Without it, the question of redistribution and equity would have to take center stage. Yet, as long as the entropy law is indeed a *law* of nature, turn and twist as we may, a fact remains a fact.

Some economists, unprepared to accept the relevance of the entropy law to economics, say the Second Law applies only to *isolated* systems but not to the economy, which is open to an influx of energy.[18] This is akin to the mistaken idea that life contradicts the entropy law. Just as an organism or any life-bearing structure maintains itself in a quasi-steady state by "sucking low entropy from the environment and transforming it into higher entropy," so also the economy exists by drawing energy and matter from the environment, processing it and discharging it as waste.[19] There is no contradiction of the entropy law here. Neither should much weight be given to the related point of what J. Martinez-Alier calls "social-Prigoginism": the doctrine that human social life can "self-organize" in such a way as to overcome the threats of depletion and pollution.[20]

Similarly, some economists deny that the entropy law also pertains to matter. They say that with sufficient energy resources there could never be a physical shortage of natural resources: mineral extractions of the past are simply recovered by recycling. There is some dispute as to whether entropy does apply to matter, whether matter exists in available and unavailable states, and whether over time it degrades from the former into the latter, as, for example, through oxidation. Georgescu-Roegen insists that "matter does matter," whereas others have argued that it is *theoretically* possible to have complete recycling, but that in *practice* the necessary expenditure of energy would cause such an increase in entropy as to be unsustainable for the biosphere.[21]

At times, economists like to point out that the entropy law does not really add anything worthwhile to theory or policy. Under competitive conditions, the implications of the entropy law are already reflected in markets and the workings of the price system. Scarcity drives up prices, thereby also encouraging the utilization of substitute materials. Against this argument, Daly correctly maintains that the market equipped to deal with the micro-economic problems of efficiency in response to individual demand is unable to deal with macroeconomic issues of scale, with physical and objective limits that are not reflected in individual preferences. Rather, such limits need to be first explicitly acknowledged and socially implemented by con-straining allowable resource use before the price system is capable of reflecting the social value of sustainability.[22]

Perhaps the greatest opposition from economists comes from the notion that somehow technological progress, knowledge and information can trans-cend any growth limitation imposed by entropic degradation.[23] Witness the triumphant realization by George Gilder in his *Microcosm*:

> Gone is the view of a thermodynamic world economy, dominated by "natural resources" being turned to entropy and waste by human extraction and use. . . . The key fact of knowledge is that it is anti-entropic: it accumulates and compounds as it is used. . . . Conquering the microcosm, mind transcends every entropic trap and overthrows matter itself.[24]

The entropy law succumbs to knowledge and information. The problem stems from semantics, a confusion that dates back to 1948 when Claude Shannon, in the context of studying information flows in communication cables, coined a mathematical formula analogous to that proposed by Ludwig Boltzmann for entropy. Shannon referred to the average number of messages per signal as "the entropy of information," thereby setting the problem in motion. Georgescu-Roegen explains:

> A muddled semantic metamorphosis has then led even to the identi-fication of knowledge with low (negative) entropy. But Shannon, at least, showed his scholarly stature by denouncing in his 1956 article, "The Bandwagon" the absurdity of the trend that has "ballooned [the entropy/information link] to an importance beyond the actual accomplishments." Not surprisingly, however, the parade with the naked emperor still marches on.[25]

Because economists continue to deny the energy problem, the promise of renewable energy remains tangential to the academic debate: to assure con-tinued growth by switching from the mining of non-renewable fossil fuels to cheap and renewable *solar energy*. But the idea has fascinated many citizens concerned with the health of the environment. The Worldwatch Institute makes the following optimistic assertion: "Today's fossil-fuel-based energy economy can be replaced with a solar/hydrogen energy economy that can meet all the energy needs of a modern industrial society without causing disruptive temperature rises."[26] This message sounds too good to be true. Is it true?

Sunlight, the "lowest quality" type of all energy sources, comes to us in a highly dispersed or scattered form, like a "fine mist," to use Georgescu-Roegen's term. To make it usable, it has to be collected through photovoltaic cells. These solar collectors are energy-intensive contraptions. One must mine materials for the solar panels, produce them in factories, ship them where they are to be used and eventually dispose of them. The energy underwriting the life cycle of a solar cell does not come from (low quality) solar energy but from fossil fuels. It is for this reason that Georgescu-Roegen referred to active solar energy as a "parasite technology" riding on cheap oil and pointed out that "like all parasites, any solar technology based on the present feasible recipes would subsist only as long as its 'host' survives."[27]

Even more controversially he makes the argument, bolstered by a logical proof, that "any presently feasible recipe for the direct use of solar energy causes a deficit in the general balance of energy; that is, any such recipe indirectly consumes more of some other forms of energy than it produces directly."[28] In short, solar energy is depicted as a "non-viable technology" incapable of reproducing itself; in the final analysis, it, too, increases entropy.

Although solar energy is not likely to be the grand solution to keep a modern industrial economy going and growing, that does not, of course, impugn its usefulness in helping to prolong the life span of an industrial world. Like recycling, the Sun God ameliorates, but does not eliminate, the energy problem.

The signs of the times

How close are we to the limit of the earth's *carrying capacity*? At what level of population, at what level of affluence will it top off? This intriguing question has traditionally been stated and examined in terms of available *food* supplies and the underlying limits of global photosynthesis. But now the sufficiency of available *water* supplies has also come under scrutiny as well as the more recent and much publicized concern about *atmospheric* pollution that impinges in its own way on the capacity of global life systems.

Photosynthesis

Life is made possible by a chemical reaction (photosynthesis) transforming solar radiation into biomass (grass, leaves, trees and so forth) that in turn directly feeds herbivores and (indirectly) carnivores. Given the estimates of the magnitude of this (what biologists call) "net primary production" of the global food base, the question can be asked: how large a human population will it support? That was the question posed by Dutch biologist C. T. de Wit in an anthology edited by A. San Pietro appropriately titled *Harvesting the Sun* (1967).[29] His answer, depending on the assumptions made, indicated a maximum population range between 79 billion and 1 trillion. One of the study's limitations was assuming that available sunshine is the *only* determinant of photosynthesis. Obviously, plant growth is also dependent on climate, the availability of water and the quality of the soil. Adding these factors into the equation sharply decreases the maximum population to a range of 4 to 33 billion people.[30] In 1987, biologists estimated that the human species was already using 40 percent of the net primary product of all terrestrial photosynthesis.[31] At that time, the world population was estimated to be 5 billion. Implicit in the 1987 study, once the earth reaches a population of 13 billion, the absolute maximum potential will be attained. Population projections depend on assumed fertility levels. United Nations estimates which assume the highest levels of fertility point to a period around the middle of the twenty-first century. Under the medium fertility level forecasts, the 13 billion will never be reached, only approached with a figure of 11.5 billion in 2150. Under the low-range estimates based on a fertility rate of 1.7, the maximum population will be reached in 2050 at a level of 7.8 billion and decline after that. These figures are broadly consistent with the alarming projection of humanity, even in the absence of economic growth, approaching nature's limits within the next few generations. Not much room here for an expanding economy.

Fresh water

The human prospect darkens considerably when assessing available fresh water supplies.[32] Even though our planet has a lot of water, only about 3 percent is accessible fresh water consisting primarily of groundwater and, to a lesser extent, of lakes and rivers. It has been estimated that in 1990 the maximum daily possible renewable fresh water withdrawals per person was about 5,500 gallons. The problem is that it has been typically difficult to capture more than 20 percent of this, effectively making the daily supply more like 1,000 gallons of water.[33] This would constitute little more than twice as much as was actually withdrawn in 1987.[34]

How much water does a person really need? Not much for drinking: only about 1 gallon per person per day. For washing and cooking another 26 gallons per day is needed. The real demand for water comes from food production. For example, the growing of wheat necessary for a 1 kg loaf of bread uses 1 whole ton of water, or roughly 250 gallons. A simple vegetarian daily diet needs about 300 gallons of water, and for a more (American-like) meat-intensive diet, the figure is more like 700 gallons of water per day.[35] Add to this water for industrial use (approximately 23 percent of the total use in 1987) and one is close to the 1,000 gallons/day limit. Exact figures are hard to come by, but Joel Cohen's algebra suggests that maintaining an average diet (4,000 kilocalories per day) through methods of irrigation from rivers and aquifers – the most efficient way to water by minimizing transpiration losses – the maximum population that could be sustained is scarcely more than the present level of 6 billion. And he observes: "Unless there is an unanticipated revolution in the productivity of rain-fed agriculture, the Earth's production of human food is likely to be limited by renewable fresh water for irrigation before it's limited by photosynthesis."[36]

Of course, there are tremendous differences in the availability of freshwater supplies around the globe. Some forty-four countries, primarily in Africa and the Middle East, are considered "water stressed," with barely enough to meet the basic needs of a vegetarian diet. It is estimated that the number of people living in water-stressed countries will rise from an estimated 335 million in 1990 to something like 3 billion by 2025. Even more in jeopardy are the twenty-six countries declared "water scarce" (with less water than needed), particularly Egypt and Saudi Arabia, and millions of people elsewhere, a number that is expected to grow to 817 million people by 2025. In other words, by that time, about one-half of the globe's population (according to the low UN projection of 7.6 billion) is expected to live in countries that have either "stressed" or "scarce" water supplies. One of the reasons for this high proportion is that even small increases in population in China and India will push these large countries into the "water stressed" category. Clearly, limits to economic growth are already visible on the horizon and will likely become manifest with the coming of acute water shortages.

Atmospheric and oceanic pollution

Today there are many signs that the levels of pollution have started to overwhelm the natural absorptive capacity and are therefore seriously interfering with the maintenance of the globe's life supportive service systems.

Since 1985, there has been mounting evidence that the global atmospheric ozone layer is thinning and rupturing, thereby exposing more and more people to ultraviolet B radiation. The result is more skin cancer and cataracts, as well as the weakening of human immune systems, the lowering of crop yields and the depletion of the world's fisheries. Ozone depletion is linked to chlorofluorocarbons or CFCs. These chemicals, invented in the postwar period, serve as aerosol propellant, foam blowing agent and coolant in refrigerators and air conditioners.

There was some initial hesitation to face the problem, a delay very much encouraged by economists,[37] but with the discovery of a seasonal ozone hole over Antarctica in 1985, international pressure prevailed. It soon led to the Montreal Protocol (1987), signed by twenty-four countries, calling for a 10 year, 50 percent reduction in CFC production by each of the signatories from their 1986 levels. Ten years later, the CFC phaseout is mostly accomplished in the industrialized countries, although China has been bucking the trend. Because airbound CFCs take about 10 years to float up to the ozone layer, and once there, they do their damage for a 100 years or more, there is a time lapse that renders the extent of the damage pernicious, a malignant legacy for generations to come.

Other pollutants besides CFCs exceed the biosphere's absorptive capacity; among them, perhaps most prominently, are the *carbon emissions* from burning fossil fuels. These emissions increased dramatically in the 1960s and 1970s and at a slower pace since then, with the exception of China's coal-driven economy, which has increased its emissions by a third since 1990. When released through combustion, carbon reacts chemically with oxygen to form carbon dioxide (CO_2), a gas that can trap heat in the atmosphere and create the greenhouse effect. In the past the earth was able to absorb most of this gas through forests and oceans. However, this buffer has for some time now been overwhelmed, allowing a significant carbon dioxide buildup in the atmosphere. High levels of these concentrations are believed to cause the globe's temperature to slowly rise. According to some observations, global temperatures have indeed risen by nearly half a degree since 1950; this calculation takes into account counteracting short-term forces, such as the Mount Pinatubo volcanic eruption of 1991, the solar cycle and the effect of a Niña. Computer models employed to research climate change suggest current carbon dioxide concentrations may double by the year 2100. Global temperatures are predicted to rise about 1 to 3.5 degrees Celsius by that year, and the sea will be warming, with its levels rising by as much as a yard.[38]

No one knows exactly what the consequences of global warming may be, but there is much anxiety regarding melting ice caps, expanding oceans, flooding of low-level land areas and the effect all this may have on the potential salination of aquifers. It is for these reasons that the international community has at the close of the century been attempting to curb emissions. Meanwhile, carbon emissions, being the exhaust of the economic engine, continue to spew into the atmosphere.

Another manifestation of global stress in the environment can be seen in our oceans. International fisheries are suffering from a serious resource scarcity brought about by depletion and pollution. One-third of all fish species – freshwater and saltwater – are now threatened with extinction.[39] Other warning signs include the following observations:

> Eleven of the world's 15 major fishing areas and 69 percent of the world's major fish species are in decline. . . . Catches of Atlantic cod, for example, declined by 69 percent between the peak in 1968 and 1992. West Atlantic bluefin tuna stocks dropped by more than 80 percent between 1970 and 1993. . . . Looking at particular fishing grounds reveals a similar picture. Fishers in the Northwest Atlantic have seen their bounty fall by 40 percent since the early

1970s, while Southeast Atlantic fishers off the coast of Namibia and South Africa have experienced a more than 50 percent decline since then.[40]

The picture is similarly bleak in the North Pacific, the Black Sea, the Mediterranean and elsewhere. Stocks of swordfish are at their lowest level in history. Overfishing also manifests in the catching of progressively smaller and younger fish. For example, nine out of ten swordfish harvested are now too young ever to have spawned.[41]

In this general demise, pollution and climate change are much to blame. Two-thirds of the world's largest cities are coastal and growing. There will be more and more runoff of industrial and household waste. Coastal spawning grounds are encumbered. The warming of the sea is especially problematic since fish cannot change their internal temperature. Rising ocean temperatures, and possibly increased ultraviolet radiation, have reduced the microscopic zooplankton forming the basis of the marine food chain by 70 percent over the last twenty years. Not surprisingly, some experts now believe that in the next 50 to 100 years, climate change will have a greater impact on the health of world fisheries than overfishing itself.[42]

At the same time, overfishing is a problem aggravated by changing technology that includes cyanide fishing, factory trawlers, sophisticated gear enabling pulse fishing, and a constantly growing, government-subsidized, fishing fleet. Like the air and water, the oceans seem to have reached their economic limits too.

The moral limits to economic growth

Just exactly how close is the world economy today to its absolute limit, a boundary imposed by nature that can only be transgressed at the peril of a looming catastrophe? There is more than enough accumulated evidence that economic growth at the current level is straining the environment to such an extent that expanding material production cannot be sustained much longer. How can the economy of China grow – as optimistically projected by the World Bank – to more than five times its current size during the next two decades without transgressing the global limits of water and energy supplies? Time will tell just what the limits are, and, until then, nobody knows to what extent the health and well-being of future generations is at risk.

When confronted with such radical uncertainty and given the fact that some of the prospective damage may be difficult, if not impossible, to reverse, an ethical economics will have to opt for a *principle of precaution* to inform policy. So, for example, the *Rio Declaration* of 1992 reads:

In order to protect the environment, the precautionary approach shall

235

be widely applied by States according to their capabilities. Where there are threats of serious or irreversible damage, lack of full scientific certainty shall not be used as a reason for postponing cost-effective measures to prevent environmental degradation.[43]

Similar recognition of the principle can also be found in the Maastricht Treaty (1991). This international concern recognizes that there are *moral* limits to unnecessary environmental depletion and extinction. Humanity's formidable challenge is to protect the ability of future generations to satisfy their basic needs without endangering minimal life standards of third world populations. This implies cutting back on many of the unnecessary wants that inhabitants of industrialized nations expect to see gratified. It is only a matter of intra- and intergenerational social justice. One must ask: on what grounds is one generation entitled to impose irreversible costs on another? Social fairness demands that humanity do all it can to guarantee future life, to respect a criterion of "permanent livability."[44] Clearly, social justice and ecological sustainability are two sides of the same coin, and for this reason an authentic social economics must be an ecologically *sustainable* economics. Reining in market activity in the name of an overriding social value such as "the protection of future generations" is a prime manifestation of the dire necessity to overcome the methodological individualism of conventional economics.

3. Joining ecology and economics

The perception of a serious environmental threat to the future of humanity requires not just a change in lifestyle, but recommends some changes in the way one learns about the problem and the extent of options available in coping with the situation. Such improved understanding is predicated for appropriate assessment of the interconnections of economic activity and the natural environment. To the extent that economic science has been developed without a proper understanding of this interconnection, to that extent it must be reformed.

This idea has come up before. Frederick Soddy, a British chemist who won the Nobel Prize in 1921 for his studies of radioactive decay, knowing that a new nuclear age was right around the corner, worried that this improvement was likely to be abused for military purposes and mass destruction. Therefore, he felt it necessary to prepare the ground for a more peaceful world by focusing his attention on what he considered to be the main villain: the teachings of economics. Inspired by John Ruskin who "in solitary and picturesque protest against the hallucinations of his age, pleaded in vain for an economics founded upon life," and "who was able to see beneath mere appearance,"[45] Soddy strove to put the concept of wealth on a more logical foundation that would be compatible with the laws of thermodynamics. Specifically, he charged that what passes for wealth in a mercantile economy goes hand-in-hand with debt – the right of the creditor to demand wealth and the duty of the debtor to supply it. This entanglement of the two concepts, Soddy felt, was the source of real trouble: debt, growing at compound interest according to the laws of mathematics, increasingly overshadows its counterpart of physical wealth, which does not grow at all, but, subject to wear and tear and entropic rot, even shrinks with age. Readjustment of the two magnitudes necessitates periodic bouts of debt repudiation creating social discord, international conflict and the likelihood of war. As a solution, Soddy proposed the minimizing of debt by abolishing fractional reserve banking and by *flexible* exchange rates minimizing the need for international loans. A sympathetic account of Soddy's argument can be found in the twelfth chapter of Daly's *Beyond Growth* (1996). But with his insistence that the laws of thermodynamics must be reckoned with by all serious economists, Soddy anticipated Nicholas Georgescu-Roegen, the mathematician turned economist whose pioneering insight we have already encountered.

For Georgescu-Roegen the fundamental error consists in the mechanistic approach of modern economics. The economy is pictured as a self-contained system based on a circular flow model rather than as an open subsystem of the biosphere with a throughput of low entropy natural resources. Naturally, this also leads to a view that neglects to see energy as a factor of production, not to mention as the *primary* factor, without which neither labor nor capital can produce. Worse still, the economist's mistaken "world view" encourages several other errors of omission and commission that inhibit the detection of undue environmental stress and timely remedial action. Consider the following three examples.

Social accounting

What is national income? Sismondi defined it as follows: "We take this word, income or revenue, in its largest sense, as comprising all that part of a fortune which is reproduced annually, so that whoever has the disposal of it may consume the whole, and employ it entirely for what he wants, without being poorer."[46] The same basic idea was repeated by John Hicks a century later and is now seen as a perfectly adequate description of the level of income a certain capital stock can *reproduce* or *sustain* year after year. In other words, the Sismondian or Hicksian notion of income is nothing other than the *sustainable national income*. In rough conformity with this notion, prevailing national income accounting procedures follow this notion in determining income by subtracting depreciation (the costs of wear and tear for the annual use of capital) from gross national product yielding net domestic product.

However, this method of applying the Sismondi–Hicks criterion for income does not fully account for all the costs of production and produces an income that is too high relative to its sustainable level. The neglected costs comprise first of all the depreciation of *natural* capital (oil, gas, soil, fresh water reserves in the ground, forest and fishery resources and so on). For a proper accounting of income one needs to know the extent of depletion diminishing the stock of all these natural assets and subtract the value of this use, as with depreciation procedures with man-made capital.

The second omission of costs pertains to what is now called "defensive goods," such as pollution abatement costs, costs of reforestation, costs of cleaning up oil spills, and costs to maintain human health in dirty and over-populated cities. Such expenditures attempt to offset the environmental (and social) damage occurring in the process of production, and therefore do not really reflect a net increase of social well-being. Instead, they are intermediary goods necessary to produce the assortment of goods the consumer really wants; like any other intermediary goods, they constitute a cost that needs to be subtracted from the value of total output. Since standard national income accounting fails to recognize and subtract such defensive goods, national income may appear to increase while society's sustainable income remains the same. The problem here is that most consumption is in one way or another defensive in nature, making a precise calculation of the aggregate amount virtually impossible. Recently, there have been some commendable first steps made in remedying this defect, but there remains much to be done.[47]

Natural capital and man-made capital

The current appropriation of resources and services flowing from the earth's natural capital stock tends to be counted wholly as income with no allowance for depreciation. Economists who do not see this as a problem may be operating under yet another basic misconception: that natural capital can be easily substituted by man-made capital – what Daly called "the substitutability dogma."[48]

The assumption of substitutability allows for massive accumulation of man-made capital as compensation for any concomitant depletion of natural capital. In other words, the more machines and factories being built (that is, the more economic growth), the less one has to worry about how much natural resources are left intact for future generations to draw on. Convenient as this may sound, this "substitutability dogma" is fundamentally flawed. Daly demonstrates its falsity in *Beyond Growth*. A few of his excellent points can be summarized in the following manner.

Natural and man-made capital are first and foremost complements; each needs the other for the production of goods. Just as cars and roads are both necessary for transportation, they should be understood as complementary forms of capital, not substitutes. Yet, such distinctions become blurred if we focus, as economists learn so well to do, on the *marginal* element of substitution, considering, for example, how car maintenance may substitute for road maintenance.[49] Also, the abstract and quantitative thrust of mathematical economics does not go together well with *qualitative* distinctions made in the name of reality. Perhaps it is for this qualitative discordance that economics has long preferred to deal with (substitutable) wants, rather than needs.

Daly, seeing natural and human-made capital as complementary, notes that if the two were near-perfect substitutes, then "there would have been no reason to accumulate man-made capital in the first place, since we are endowed by nature with a near perfect substitute."[50] Another way to make the point goes like this: resources (oil, coal) serving as raw materials of production are substitutes. Labor and capital, both inputs into the transformation of raw materials into end products, are also substitutes. But this does not mean that raw materials can also be substituted with productive inputs (labor or capital). "What good is a sawmill without a forest, a fishing boat without populations of fish?" Daly asks.[51]

Since both natural and man-made capital have to be used together, and because the latter both embodies and uses the former, the expanding economic sphere has converted what once was a "free good of nature" into *the* limiting factor of economic activity. In other words, fishermen don't catch as many fish, not because there is a lack of fishing boats and equipment but because there are no longer as many fish. It follows that by accepting a sustainability constraint requiring that the capital stock must be kept intact, society must give priority to the upkeep of natural capital. "Investing" in natural capital means above all refraining from consuming it, in order to build up the productive stock and the sustainable yields of the future.[52] Frustratingly, as important and rational as such a strategy may seem for the future of the world, an unreformed economics, both unable and unwilling to understand the true character of natural capital, will continue to stand in the way of real progress.

Discounting the future

The theory of intertemporal decision making in economics is well known. It assumes that individuals have preferences concerning their consumption choices over time, and that they prefer to have things now rather than later. How much more one has to give somebody to make him or her just as happy as getting it all now, is known as the "time preference." Algebraically, the present value (*PV*) of any benefit (*B*) (or cost (*C*)) accruing in number of years (*t*) is given by the classic formula:

$$PV(B) = B(t)/(1 + r)^t$$

in which *r* stands for the rate which "discounts" the future benefits. So, for example, at a discount rate (r) of 10 percent, the value of a benefit 100 years from now ($t = 100$) will have a present value (PV) that is 13,777 times smaller. Competitive capital markets provide the opportunity for intertemporal exchange of present for future consumption. Given an interest rate, some people (with a high time preference) will be borrowing, others will choose to lend, and, in equilibrium, the market interest rate will tend to reflect a society's prevailing rate of time preference. Therefore, assuming an interest rate of 10 percent, for society the total value of enjoyment by 13,777 Grand Canyon visitors 100 years hence will be equal to one single person's enjoyment today. The higher the interest rate, the less future benefits will weigh in, and vice versa.

Since the interest rate, at least in a competitive model economy, also reflects the market return on capital investment, discounting can also make it economically irrational to invest in slow-growing renewable natural capital. Take a forest producing new timber on a sustainable yield basis at 4 percent annually. If the interest rate (and with it the discount rate) happens to be 5 percent, it would be (economically) rational for the owner to immediately clear-cut the entire stand in order to invest the proceeds in a bank account or elsewhere. This reasoning, known in economics as the Hotelling model of efficient resource use over time, is another product of the dogma of substitutability. Worse, still, discounting can lead to the policy of *rational extinction* of a species: "Any commercially valuable species that is not too expensive to capture and whose rate of reproduction for all population sizes remains below the interest rate will be exploited to extinction."[53] Rational? Perhaps, but only from an irrational point of view.

The norm of intertemporal economic efficiency also inhibits government proactive efforts to maintain the quality of the environment. Consider that any proposed action to preserve the environment (for example, protection of the ozone layer) tends to have most of its costs up front, whereas most of the benefits will accrue to later generations. In such a situation, the use of discounting will indicate that the benefits are not worth the costs, and so recommend that no action be taken. It follows, in project appraisals, that reliance on the intertemporal preferences of people alive today and the economic technique of discounting will always discriminate against future generations. One cannot expect sustainability to prevail under these circumstances.

In order to avoid such counter-intuitive results, economists interested in conservation have been recommending a modification of the conventional approach. Instead of using the private discount rate reflected in the prevailing market interest rate, they propose a special and considerably lower social discount rate for environmental project appraisals. Specifically, it can be argued that fairness or *impartiality* with respect to time would recommend a cost–benefit calculus employing a zero discount rate, or the abstaining from discounting future benefits and costs all together.

More generally, the goal of sustainability must be framed as one of justice, and not of adjusting economic efficiency by tampering with the discount rate. What is at stake are issues ranging from distribution of property rights to natural resources across generations, and as two foremost ecological economists remind us:

> Questions which are fundamentally matters of equity should be treated as such. If we are concerned about the distribution of welfare across generations, then we should transfer wealth. . . . Transfer mechanisms might include setting aside natural resources and protecting environments, educating the young, and developing technologies for the sustainable management of renewable resources. Some of these might be viewed as worthwhile investments on the part of this generation, but if their intent is to function as transfers, then they should not be evaluated as investments. The benefit from transfers, in short, should not be discounted.[54]

What is needed is a turning away from the domain of intertemporal consumer choice, economic efficiency and the standards of the marketplace, to the political sphere embodying the quality of common life. It is a switch from individual time preference to a community-based (or "civic") concept of time rooted in the consciousness of a common inheritance from the past.[55] Such creation and protection of common assets gives continuity to the common identity of a society and may also provide a physical scaffolding for a common life extending in time. In short, the criterion of environmental sustainability cannot be grafted on to an individualistic economics, but needs instead the more fertile soil of a social economics sensitive to the common good.

4. The need for sustainable development

Whether one likes it or not, humanity is approaching a historic juncture. Because of the increasingly stressed environment, and keeping the fortunes of the coming generations close to the heart, the world economy has been approaching the end of a long road. Face to face with an objective natural *constraint* to economic growth, one has to learn to live within the apparent limits. Economics too, if it is meant to be an intellectual discipline of importance to human welfare, will have to adjust to this circumstance. From its very beginning, economics has emphasized capital accumulation and growth as a means to deal with the other social goals, such as poverty, equality and (positive) freedom. In the same vein, the latest manifestations of this "growth creed" are the econometric studies trying to establish the existence of an "Environmental Kuznets Curve" (EKC): as pollution increases with industrialization, environmental quality eventually begins to improve as a developing country's income grows further. Based in part on the thesis that environmental protection is a luxury good that will only be demanded after more important needs are satisfied, this new doctrine emanates from the idea that economies pass through stages and technological life cycles, moving from agriculture to industry, and from smokestack technology to services and high technology.[56] The whole idea runs foul of the entropy law, and a careful examination of the empirical evidence reveals that, at least until now, there is no sign of an EKC to pin our hopes to.[57]

Once economic growth is dethroned, the ultimate goal and purpose of economic science must be to address the thorny question of redistribution. It is only though *transfers and redistribution* of resources, income and wealth, that levels of poverty, equality, freedom and human welfare can be effected, and this realization implies a renewed recognition of the significance of *social economics*. For purposes of redistribution, the focus has to be on human needs and fairness, not the individual wants of the sovereign consumer. Similarly, in a global economy the criteria of social justice must transcend national and temporal jurisdictions and reflect the aspirations of humanity as a whole, both across the globe and across generations.

From growth to development

Distinguishing between economic growth and economic development constitutes one of the first and foremost challenges ahead. Growth means expansion of size, a quantitative augmentation in the extraction of low-entropy energy and matter and the collateral dumping of more waste into the environmental sink. Development, on the other hand, seeks to enhance human well-being by extracting and using resources more efficiently, by making consumption less energy-intensive and a growing disposition toward a lifestyle marked by conservation. The term "sustainable growth" is a contradiction in terms, an oxymoron to be banned from intelligent discourse. Sustainable *development*, on the other hand, is a different kettle of fish: it is more possible and highly desirable, and yet by no means easy to implement.

Rechanneling and management of the interaction of human desires with the use of natural resources can, in good economic fashion, be depicted by means of the conventional categories of supply and demand.

Supply-side efforts

First of all, strictly speaking and recalling the entropy law, the *only* really sustainable economic system is one that relies exclusively on the direct use of solar energy, an economy based on the influx of energy from the sun. As soon as society dips into the non-renewable minerals and fossil fuels, constituting the dowry of humanity, sustainability is immediately impaired. Rejecting this alternative, as did Georgescu-Roegen when contemplating a society of "berry pickers" living in caves and trees, the relevant issue becomes how to make the natural resources last as long as possible.

Renewable natural resources should be managed in a manner that avoids depletion. Fisheries, forests and aquifers cannot be used in excess of their rate of regeneration, or their long-run sustainable yield. Non-renewable natural capital, the terrestrial dowry, should be tapped into as little as possible and compensated for whenever possible by the development of renewable substitutes. In addition, conservation will be helped by making goods more durable and more repairable, as well as embarking on greater efforts at reuse and recycling. Equally important is a ceaseless effort to reduce the energy intensiveness of goods through new and better technology, including new measures to minimize needless long-distance trade and transportation.

Demand-side efforts

Signifying to unfold more completely, to evolve the potential, to make something latent active, the term *develop* can perhaps be best understood, in the context of *human* development, as actualization of human potential, or the realization of the non-material self. It involves the questioning of materialism. As Schumacher put it: "An attitude of life which seeks fulfillment in the single-minded pursuit of wealth – in short, materialism – does not fit into this world, because it contains no limiting principle, while the environment in which it is placed is strictly limited."[58] Personality growth, the growth in gregariousness, self-respect and moral personality, is arguably the most desirable kind of "growth"; in light of the resource constraint, it is without doubt the only possible kind.

First and foremost, it demands a far greater consciousness of the environmental impact of our lifestyle, the avoidance of energy and material waste, an end to what Georgescu-Roegen calls the "morbid craving for extravagant gadgetry" (golf carts, "two-garage" cars), including getting rid of fashion, that "disease of the human mind."[59] Quite obviously, consumerism and advertising are major stumbling blocks to any attempt to attain sustainability. On a different dimension, but no less important, the desired number of children must be made more compatible with the requirements of sustainable population levels.

The road ahead

The Brundtland Commission Report, in its final Tokyo Declaration, understandably stresses that economic growth must be stimulated in developing countries in order to combat economic destitution there, but it specifies that it must be "a growth of a new kind in which sustainability, equity, social justice and security are firmly embedded as major social goals."[60] Yet, economic expansion by a factor of five to ten, as called for by the report, is unlikely to come from efficiency gains alone. That leaves massive redistribution of resources, capital and technology from the North to the South, the only strategy compatible with global sustainability. Under this novel approach the industrialized nations would have to realize productivity gains as more leisure (a shorter working week) rather than consumption, in addition to significant income transfers toward the poorer countries.

In terms of more specific policy options, a recent textbook coauthored by the leading ecological economists, after proposing a broad-based natural capital depletion tax, environmental assurance bonds and ecology tariffs, offers an intriguing new policy idea, attributed to Richard Schuler, to achieve global sustainability.[61] In essence, it would stabilize carbon emissions of the most industrialized countries to their present level and give an incentive to the developing world to keep population growth down. As a mechanism to achieve this dual goal, the proposal relies on emission rights being allocated to countries according to their present (but not future) population levels, and some other considerations, like protection of the rain forests (Mother Earth's lungs). The less-developed countries would then have a choice to use their permits for their own industrialization or else sell them to the industrial countries for a fair market value. The total number of global permits issued would be reviewed periodically and brought into harmony with the ecological requirements as determined by the scientific community.

Obviously, a proposal such as this is only the beginning of the type of global policy measures that will be necessary to save the planet. The earlier economists start to seriously discuss measures like this the better. The stumbling block to such healing endeavors, however, remains, as already encountered when dealing with international trade, the discipline's inclination to push an abstract economic theory accommodating mathematics more eagerly than reality. This inhibits the best minds from even detecting any problem warranting their attention.

Finally, there remains the question of whether we can muster the necessary altruism and generate the political will to help the poor and save the planet. Georgescu-Roegen already feared that such a drastic change of consciousness and of the general will was not about to happen and felt that business as usual might be a safer bet: "Perhaps the destiny of man is to have a short, but fiery, exciting and extravagant life rather than a long, uneventful and vegetative existence," adding with some sarcasm, "let other species – the amoebas, for example – which have no spiritual ambitions inherit an earth still bathed in plenty of sunshine."[62] Be that as it may, if there ever will be a no-growth industrial economy, the self-imposed constraint on growth-cum-redistribution would have to build on the pillars of security and fairness, rather than on the arbitrary income equalization brought about by North–South free trade. Workers will be understandably reluctant to carry the brunt of global environmental stabilization. Even more taxing for the latent forces of altruism is the idea of intergenerational transfers. This is an instance of the type of *pure altruism* whose existence economic theory has always tended to deny: there is absolutely nothing future generations can do to reciprocate. And yet, without it, humanity's future looks rather bleak.

Conclusion

As this book is going to press the world price for petroleum in real terms has reached an all-time low. It's not the kind of indicator that incites massive conversion to the ecological point of view urged in this chapter. Even worse, it will blow more wind into the sails of the cowboy economists who proceed as if the vessel of wild economic growth is unsinkable. Rationality gets trumped by acquisitiveness and wishful thinking. The great economist Joan Robinson put it so well, in the context of the Cambridge capital controversy, when she lamented: "he who is convinced against his will, is of the same opinion still." Intellectual argument, therefore, may have to be postponed until things get visibly worse without — one can only hope and pray — having gotten completely out of control and beyond repair.

Meanwhile, the case for considering economics embedded not only in society but also in nature, is the final lesson of a genuine social economics concerned with human welfare. Helping to avoid social decay as well as natural disaster is a step that is in our power to take.

Notes

1 R. Batra, *The Myth of Free Trade: A Plan for America's Economic Revival*, New York, Charles Scribner's Sons, 1993, p. 225.
2 The Royal Commission on Environmental Pollution's Report, *Transport and the Environment*, New York, Oxford University Press, 1965, p. 63 and recent data from the statistical office of the International Civil Aviation Organization, Montreal, CA, December 1997.
3 US Department of Energy, *Annual Energy Outlook 1997*, p. 43.
4 A. Gore, *Earth in the Balance: Ecology and the Human Spirit*, Boston, MA, Houghton Mifflin Co., 1992, p. 343.
5 J. Bhagwati, "The Case for Free Trade," *Scientific American*, November 1993, p. 46.
6 H. Daly, "The Perils of Free Trade," *Scientific American*, November 1993, p. 52.
7 Bhagwati, "The Case for Free Trade," p. 46.
8 D. H. Meadows, D. L. Meadows, J. Randers and W. W. Behrens, *The Limits to Growth*, New York, Universe Books, 1972, p. xiii.
9 H. Barnett and C. Morse, *Scarcity and Growth: Economics of Natural Resource Availability*, Baltimore, MD, Johns Hopkins University Press, 1993; and H. Barnett, "Scarcity and Growth Revisited," in V. K. Smith (ed.), *Scarcity and Growth Reconsidered*, Baltimore, MD, Johns Hopkins University Press, 1979.
10 World Commission on Environment and Development, *Our Common Future*, Oxford, Oxford University Press, 1987.
11 ibid., p. 40.
12 ibid., p. 51.

13 ibid., p. 343.
14 H. Daly, *Beyond Growth*, Boston, MA, Beacon Press, 1996, p. 6.
15 Quoted in R. Goodland *et al.* (eds), *Environmentally Sustainable Economic Development: Building on Brundtland*, Paris, Unesco, 1991, p. 15.
16 N. Georgescu-Roegen, *The Entropy Law and the Economic Process*, Cambridge, MA, Harvard University Press, 1971, p. 21.
17 N. Georgescu-Roegen, *Energy and Economic Myths*, New York, Pergamon Press, 1976, p. 59.
18 For an example see J. Young, "Is the Entropy Law Relevant to the Economics of Natural Scarcity?," *Journal of Environmental Economics and Management*, September 1991, vol. 21, pp. 169–179.
19 Georgescu-Roegen, *The Entropy Law and the Economic Process*, p. 10.
20 J. Martinez-Alier, "Ecological Perception, Environmental Policy and Distributional Conflicts: Some Lessons from History," in R. Costanza (ed.), *Ecological Economics: The Science and Management of Sustainability*, New York, Columbia University Press, 1991, p. 120.
21 C. Biancardi, E. Tiezzi and S. Ulgati, "Complete Recycling of Matter in the Frameworks of Physics, Biology, and Ecological Economics," *Ecological Economics*, 1993, vol. 8, pp. 1–5.
22 See the interchange between S. Burness and H. Daly in *Land Economics*, August 1986, vol. 62, pp. 319–324.
23 See, for example, H. Houthakker, "Whatever Happened to the Energy Crisis?," *The Energy Journal*, 1983, vol. 4:1; W. J. Baumol, "On the Possibility of Continuing Expansion of Finite Resources," *Kyklos*, 1986, vol. 39, p. 167; L. Bower, "Present and Future Oil Usage," *Forum for Applied Research and Public Policy*, 1987, vol. 2.
24 G. Gilder, *Microcosm: The Quantum Revolution in Economics and Technology*, New York, Simon and Schuster, 1989, p. 378.
25 N. Georgescu-Roegen, "Afterword," in J. Riffkin, *Entropy: Into the Greenhouse World*, New York, Viking–Penguin, 1989, p. 301.
26 L. Brown *et al.* (eds), *State of the World 1996: A Worldwatch Institute Report on Progress Toward a Sustainable Society*, New York, W.W. Norton, 1996, p. 19.
27 N. Georgescu-Roegen, "Technology Assessment: The Case of the Direct Use of Solar Energy," *Atlantic Economic Journal*, December 1978, vol. 6, p. 19.
28 ibid.
29 C. T. de Wit, "Photosynthesis: Its Relationship to Overpopulation," in A. San Pietro *et al.* (eds), *Harvesting the Sun: Photosynthesis in Plant Life*, New York, Academic Press, 1967, pp. 315–320.
30 See J. Cohen, *How Many People Can the Earth Support?*, New York, W. W. Norton, 1995, pp. 196–208.
31 P. M. Vitousek *et al.*, "Human Appropriation of the Products of Photosynthesis," *BioScience*, 1986, vol. 34: 6, pp. 277–283.
32 This section is based on the findings in Cohen, *How Many People Can the Earth Support?*, ch. 14.
33 ibid., p. 312.
34 ibid., p. 304.
35 These figures are very rough and based on certain assumptions made by Cohen, ibid., pp. 311–314.
36 ibid., p. 317.
37 See the study by M. Bailey, "Risks, Costs, and Benefits of Fluorocarbon Regulation," *American Economic Review*, May 1982, vol. 72:2, pp. 247–250, for a telling example of an efficiency-based argument against regulation.

38 K. Trenberth, "The Science of Global Change," *Jobs and Capital*, Fall 1997, vol. 6:4, pp. 21–25.

39 L. Brown, "The Future of Growth," in L. Brown *et al.* (eds), *The State of the World 1998: A Worldwatch Institute Report on Progress Toward a Sustainable Society*, New York, W. W. Norton, 1998, p. 11.

40 A. P. McGinn, "Promoting Sustainable Fisheries," in Brown *et al.*, ibid., pp. 60–61.

41 C. Safina, *Song for the Blue Ocean*, New York, Henry Holt and Co., 1997.

42 ibid., p. 63.

43 Quoted in M. Common, *Sustainability and Policy*, Cambridge, Cambridge University Press, 1995, p. 212.

44 For an application of criteria of Rawlsian Justice to the intergenerational problem, see T. Page, "Intergenerational Justice as Opportunity," in D. MacLean and P. Brown (eds), *Energy and the Future*, Totowa, NJ, Rowman and Littlefield, 1983, pp. 38–58.

45 F. Soddy, *Wealth, Virtual Wealth and Debt*, London, George Allen and Unwin, Ltd, 1926, pp. 94, 96.

46 J. C. L. Simonde de Sismondi, *Political Economy and the Philosophy of Government* [1847], New York, Augustus M. Kelley, 1966b, p. 224. Already in his *New Principles* [1819] one can find essentially the same definition: that part of accumulated wealth that could be consumed without becoming any poorer, J. C. L. Simonde de Sismondi, *New Principles of Political Economy* [1827], 2nd edn, trans. R. Hyse, New Brunswick, NJ, and London, Transaction Publishers, 1991, p. 81.

47 See the work in the United States started by H. Daly and J. Cobb seeking to replace GDP by a "genuine progress indicator," H. Daly and J. Cobb, *For the Common Good: Redirecting the Economy toward Community, the Environment, and a Sustainable Future*, Boston, MA, Beacon Press, 1989; also, C. Cobb and J. Cobb, *The Green National Product: A Proposed Index of Sustainable Economic Welfare*, Lanham, MD, University Press of America, 1994. For a general survey, see R. W. England and J. M. Harris, "Alternatives to Gross National Product: A Critical Survey," G-DAE Discussion Paper no. 5, Medford, MA, Global Development and Environment Institute, 1997.

48 H. Daly, "From Empty World Economics to Full World Economics," in R. Goodland *et al.* (eds), *Environmentally Sustainable Economic Development: Building on Brundtland*, Paris, Unesco, 1991, p. 32.

49 Daly, *Beyond Growth*, p. 77.

50 ibid., p. 76.

51 ibid., p. 77.

52 For operational details on how to do this, see ibid., pp. 81–87.

53 Daly and Cobb, *For the Common Good*, p. 156.

54 R. Norgaard and R. Howarth, "Sustainability and Discounting the Future," in R. Costanza (ed.), *Ecological Economics: The Science and Management of Sustainability*, New York, Columbia University Press, 1991, p. 98.

55 S. Tenenbaum, "Social Discounting: Retrieving the Civic Dimension," *Economics and Philosophy*, 1989, vol. 5, p. 45.

56 T. Selden and D. Song, "Environmental Quality and Development: Is There a Kuznet's Curve for Air Pollution Emissions?," *Journal of Environmental Economics and Management*, 1994, vol. 27, pp. 147–162; N. Shafik, "Economic Development and Environmental Quality: An Economic Analysis," *Oxford Economic Papers*, 1994, vol. 46, pp. 757–773.

57 See W. Moomaw and G. Unruh, "Are Environmental Kuznets Curves Misleading

Us?," G-DAE Discussion Paper no. 4, Cambridge, MA, Global Development and Environment Institute, 1997.
58 E. F Schumacher, *Small Is Beautiful*, New York, Harper and Row, 1973, p. 27.
59 Georgescu-Roegen, *Energy and Economic Myths*, p. 34.
60 World Commission on Environment and Development, *Our Common Future*, p. 364.
61 R. Costanza *et al.*, *An Introduction to Ecological Economics*, Boca Raton, FL, St. Lucie Press, 1998, pp. 236–239.
62 Georgescu-Roegen, *Energy and Economic Myths*, p. 35.

11

SOCIAL ECONOMICS AS AN ALTERNATIVE

Humanity is about to step into a new millennium. It's a time for taking stock, for reflection, but also for looking forward to the challenges ahead. We approach the future with mixed feelings. If the last decade is any guide, it will be a period of accelerating technological progress and relentless modernization. But will it also be a time of human progress and liberation? Will economic science be able to lead the world to greater prosperity and social justice? Perhaps more to the point, what does the future hold for social economic thinking? Will it continue in its traditional Cinderella role, or is it destined to gain a wider forum? This chapter explores some of these intriguing questions.

1. Humanistic social economics: a more complete picture

The present sketch of the type of social economics pioneered by Sismondi had, of course, other historical representatives besides the ones featured so far, among them Richard Tawney, Mohandas Gandhi, George Gunton, John Maurice Clark, Eli Ginzberg, Fred Hirsch, Nicholas Georgescu-Roegen, E. F. Schumacher and others. Before engaging in speculation about the prospects of this alternative way of approaching economics, it seems appropriate to make the portrayal a little more inclusive. Three members of this group deserve special mention: Gandhi, Tawney and Schumacher.

Mohandas Gandhi (1869–1948)

In his autobiography, Gandhi acknowledges the "magic spell" that Ruskin's *Unto This Last* exerted on him in 1904 when on a long train trip in South Africa:

> The book was impossible to lay aside, once I had begun it. It gripped me. Johannesburg to Durban was a twenty-four hours' journey. The train reached there in the evening. I could not get any sleep that

249

night. I determined to change my life in accordance with the ideals of the book.[1]

Years later, when back in India he translated into Gujarati a paraphrased version of Ruskin's book and titled it *Sarvodaya* (the common good). Following Ruskin, Gandhi saw economics as meaningful only if it pursued the right end: an economic system providing the basic necessities while incorporating the social values of human dignity, non-violence and creative labor. Above all, he applied Ruskin's core teachings to a new kind of philosophy of economic development that aimed to strengthen the rural village economy so much neglected during British colonial rule. He fought for decolonialization and for restructuring the economy in order to create greater self-reliance and more community control. Structural unemployment was to be countered by emphasizing the need for revitalizing the labor-intensive traditional sector and doing so with a less violent technology more respectful of human dignity. In many ways Gandhi's approach was a forerunner of the import substitution development policy, a strategy that was to rule India until the 1980s. Not surprisingly, key aspects of his thought and work can still serve as a model for less-developed countries.[2]

Richard Tawney (1880–1962)

Tawney, like Hobson and Gandhi before him, studied economics at Oxford where Ruskin had taught. But, discovering that the "austere heights" of theoretical economics were not his "spiritual home," he turned instead to economic history and social philosophy.

Authoring nearly a dozen books, Tawney's best known are: *The Acquisitive Society* (1920), an assault on consumerism and materialism; *Religion and the Rise of Capitalism* (1926), which explores the influence of Protestantism; and *Equality* (1931), a critical account of British socioeconomic institutions in the 1920s. Besides being a meticulous scholar, as one editor of Tawney's essays puts it, all his work is "shot through with passion, the passion for equality for all human beings, and the passion against the gross materialist values of the acquisitive society."[3] Like his friend Hobson, Tawney had much to say about property and was a critic of the large absentee-owned corporation, saying that with it property loses its function of providing security as well as generating creative energy. His remedy was to transfer control of production to those who perform constructive work, the workers themselves. The economy must be subordinated to the social purpose for which it is carried on.[4] At the same time, he reminded readers that no change in any economic system can avert those causes of social malaise that grow from the egotism, greed or quarrelsomeness of human nature.

E. F. Schumacher (1911–1977)

The works of E. F. Schumacher have been, in recent times, one of the more noted contributions to an economics that is human-centered and cognizant of social values, in his own words, an economics "as if people mattered." Having studied economics in Germany under Joseph Schumpeter, Schumacher enjoyed a long and highly successful career in England, moving freely among the biggest names in academia and the establishment. During the 1940s, while at the Oxford Institute of Statistics, he collaborated with J. M. Keynes on his famous "Proposal for an International Clearing Union" (1943). At the same time, he is said to have been a key figure behind the scenes for Sir William Beveridge's *Full Employment in a Free Society*, the blueprint for the British welfare state.[5] In 1950 he joined the National Coal Board. Thereafter, during a mission to Burma, Schumacher underwent an inner transformation and developed a new outlook that he expressed in his well-known *Small Is Beautiful* (1973). It sold well, and was translated into fifteen languages, and it has probably, more than any other book, served as a principal source of inspiration for the alternative economics movement of the 1970s.

The spirit of Gandhi is very much present in *Small Is Beautiful*, especially when Schumacher criticizes the modern secular mind and outlines his new strategy for economic development, stressing human need satisfaction, rural development and appropriate technology. The final chapters, when discussing the issue of ownership for the industrialized North, show the strong influence of Tawney. Schumacher rearticulated essential premises and principles of the long humanistic social economics tradition in a manner that caught the fancy of almost a generation of students, especially in the United States. But he also raised new issues such as environmental depletion and degradation, as well as other ideas, for example, the important problem of unit size or "scale" of enterprise, an issue that was more implicit in the works of Sismondi, Ruskin and Gandhi. Schumacher's logic on this point follows directly from the emphasis on *people*, not production of commodities: "People can be themselves only in small comprehensible groups; therefore, we must learn to think in terms of an articulate structure that can cope with a multiplicity of small scale units."[6] His explicit concern for smallness, of course, also led to a call for a more human technology and a village-centered approach to development.

Schumacher, when discussing education, had little sympathy for certain aspects of the modern intellect imbued with the relativism of Freud, Darwin and Marx, which he saw as undermining the idea of truth.[7] He insisted that education could only be a positive force if it aimed at the *whole person* with a center or a soul. A wholistic ethics, therefore, must be reintroduced into the economic discourse. For example, the farmer is not only a *factor of production*, but, above all, an end-in-itself, metaeconomic, and in a certain sense sacred.[8] So also, according to Schumacher, is the land he or she works.

The unity of the humanistic tradition

When stepping back and looking at the various ideas and contributions of social economics, there is diversity in the basic questions asked and the solutions offered. The prime problem for Sismondi, for example, was the emergence of the industrial system in France and Switzerland, which he saw as a menace threatening the independence of craftsmen and family farmers, and which he sought to slow down. In his preoccupation with the new phenomena of recurring business cycles and their effect on the industrial proletariat, he looked to government to be the protector of the poor. His economics must also be seen as a reaction to Ricardo's use of excessive abstraction of time and place.

Ruskin, on the other hand, when writing during the second half of the nineteenth century, took industrialization in England as an accomplished fact, entailing dehumanized jobs for the multitudes. He witnessed mounting industrial warfare and strikes fueled by a growing antagonism between labor and capital. Economic science looked the other way, confident that the welfare of society would best be served by the unregulated play of individual self-interest. Ruskin stood against the tide, especially against an abstract and pretentious economics insensitive to the social and higher aspects of human nature. Qualities such as meaning and human spirit counted far too much, and Ruskin channeled much of his work against the freshly conceived and heartless abstraction of "homo oekonomicus."

John Hobson witnessed the rise and consolidation of marginalism with its new stress on the rational consumer, the quantitative method and a theory of distribution that appeared to sanction the status quo. Add to this bleak picture the new economic imperialism and colonialism, all of which Hobson sought to explain in terms of underconsumption theory. During this period Sidgwick, Marshall and Pigou, equipped with a measuring rod of money, added a normative branch to the science. This *economic* welfare analysis with its strong utilitarian overtones provoked Hobson to attempt an alternative version centered on *human* welfare. As the labor movement gathered strength and exercised its ability to fend for workers' material interests, Hobson, like Tawney before him, started to explore more lofty issues such as the conversion of the new large-scale enterprises into more democratic institutions.

M. K. Gandhi, in contrast, found himself surrounded by the hopeless poverty and misery of colonial India. He blamed western secular, materialist and utilitarian thinking for much of it, and was eager to come up with an alternative development strategy that would be more geared to benefit the millions of peasants and craftsmen struggling for subsistence.

E. F. Schumacher reacted to the economic practice of multinational corporations imposing a least-cost technology on low-income countries. Under the influence of the energy crisis, in the early 1970s, he was one of the first social economists to call attention to natural resource exhaustion and the problematic nature of blind faith in economic growth.

More recently, social economic thinking in this humanistic tradition has been energized by such concerns as the revitalized emphasis on economic efficiency, the growth of corporate might, and trade with its threats to social cohesion and environmental degradation.

Much of the diversity within the branch of social economics is due to the fact that the socioeconomic universe that these men labored to describe and to improve is not a fixed reality. Unlike the natural sciences, it is evolving, and social economic facts change through time. Problems which appear vital at one time or in one country often diminish in importance over time and place. Table 11.1 conveys a summary of the changing aims of this tradition within the context of historical events and mainstream economic doctrines. Forthcoming twenty-first century events are likely to lengthen the table.

In contrast to this evolution of diverse thinking, social economists share moral criteria based on the satisfaction of basic human needs, respect for human dignity and social justice. These "ambassadors for justice" have all been moved by deep concern for the social consequences of excessive individualism, in particular the effects of competition and *laissez-faire* in both the micro- and macroeconomic realms. Because they have seen economic reality as a product of human intention, they have refused to accept socioeconomic institutions as "given." Instead, they have preferred to devote their energies to constructive criticism: how to re-engineer these institutions to better accord with human welfare. For example, property rights were to be brought into conformity with a more ideal conception. Social reform and economic thought were two sides of the same coin, and the ultimate goal for each was to create conditions conducive to human dignity and self-realization.

Similarly, their preoccupation with human welfare enabled social economists with a humanistic bent to keep before them the psychological importance of economic security and work, both serving as gateways for the satisfaction of the higher human needs. More generally, human nature, motivation and the formation of widely held social values have always been understood as being to some degree pliable and co-formed by the pressures and opportunities of the prevailing social order. This insight also explains the belief in a mutual interaction between individual preferences and social economic institutions.

The most distinguishing characteristic of social economics is the belief that the goal of human welfare is only in part dependent on individual preferences exercised in the marketplace. It is the task of a meaningful economics to help identify and promote institutions and policies that are congruent with the *common good*, if necessary with the aid of philosophical inquiry. Economics

Table 11.1 Humanistic social economics in a changing world

	Key historical events	Predominant economic doctrines	Humanistic problem
Sismondi	Industrialization of France and Switzerland.	Smith, Ricardo and followers.	Amelioration of material privation. Study of what makes for recurrent slumps. Need for government intervention. Need to slow down industrialization.
	First business cycles.	Economics becomes increasingly abstract and fixated on wealth.	
Ruskin	Increasing marketization of British society. Growing industrial conflict.	J. S. Mill, Senior, Cairnes.	Need to study increasingly alienated preferences of people. Focus on alienation centers on quality of labor and work.
Hobson and Tawney	Growing consumerism, i.e., England turns into an "acquisitive society." Increasing inequality. Growth of the corporation. British imperialism. Russian Revolution.	Marshall, Wicksteed, Pigou. Advocating "marginalism" in consumption, production and distribution. Money as the measuring rod in economics.	How to cope with the "Social Question," with poverty, insecurity and meaningless work. The question of "functionless property" in the form of corporate absentee ownership. The reasons and effects of imperialism.
Gandhi	British occupation of India.	"British utilitarians."	Increasing dependency of Indian economy. Modernization versus Indian culture. Counteract growing rural impoverishment, and urbanization with policy of import substitution.
	Soviet Revolution in Russia. Growth of Fascism in Europe.		

Schumacher	Growing materialism in the West. Independence for colonies. Beginning of energy crisis (Club of Rome Report).	Influence of Keynes, Kaldor, Harrod and Domar. Growing preoccupation with economic growth, measured in GDNP.	Dehumanization and depersonalization of European civilization. Economics blind to ecological destruction. Imposition of inappropriate technologies destroys third world economies.
Post-Schumacher	Globalization of economy. Fall of communism. Attack on the welfare state. Environmental threat.	Decline of Keynesian economics. Growing aversion to government intervention. Economics imperialism analytic revolution. Development economics as global Reaganomics.	Incompatibility of corporations with human dignity. Danger of international underconsumption. Threat of excessive liberalization and globalization. Environmentally unsustainable economic growth.

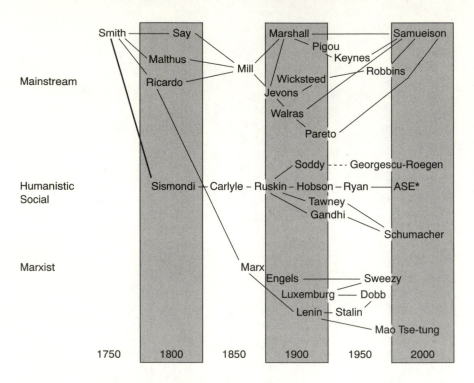

*ASE = Association for Social Economics

Figure 11.1 The family tree of humanistic social economics

does have to have a purpose, and for this reason the kind that has been offered here as an alternative has also been called *teleological economics.*[9]

The evolution of this type of social economics within the context of its two main historical rivals is illustrated by Figure 11.1. In the wake of the Marxist paradigm's recent troubles, some would say "collapse," there is now more room for the development and growth of humanistic social economics. A potential monopoly of mainstream economic thinking is sobering in view of the existing threats to the standard of living and mother nature.

The prospect of social economics

The social economics that has been described here is deeply rooted in human experience and comes from a tradition that is about as old as its main-stream counterpart. Because it grows out of a concern for social justice and an honest attempt to identify and understand social problems, its existence seems assured. Social institutions and deeply held social values, and the idea of them harmonizing with individualistic activity, are not going away.

256

Nevertheless, there have been and will continue to be challenges to this time-honored approach.

Counterfeiting social economics

Recently, economists have been playing with their dictionaries: caveat emptor. When the *New Palgrave Dictionary* published as one of its volumes, *Social Economics* (1989), the editors introduced the subject with a quote from Wicksteed claiming that economic laws have a domain that corresponds with "life in its widest extent."[10] They explain that a person's allocation of time or physical and mental effort to *any* activity (including prayers and devotions) is governed by precisely the same principle as the allocation of monetary expenditure among market commodities. Three dozen contributions are offered to demonstrate the applicability of economic thinking in Wicksteed's sense. After a short caveat that the designation "social economics" is neither much in use, nor carries any sort of commonly agreed meaning, they conclude that the label "seems appropriate as a title for a collection of articles pertaining to the use of [individualist] economics in the study of society."[11] Similarly, the fourth edition of MIT's *Dictionary of Modern Economics* defines "social economics" as:

> the application of neoclassical economic theory to social policy. The term "social" is interpreted as widely or narrowly as the individual author chooses, although it usually encompasses health, education, crime, housing and welfare services. An alternative usage of the term is that of certain radical economists who describe their work regardless of subject area as social economics.[12]

Even though the latter part of this description does grant some marginal and questionable space for inclusion of the work featured in this book, it does strongly reinforce the Palgrave transmutation of the meaning. Social economics is unjustly reduced to an application of ordinary economics to the non-market sphere of society. Nothing could be more absurd. But this perversion is merely another fruit of the noxious economics imperialism movement, which has infiltrated most social sciences and is actively working to similarly redefine and capture "political economy" and "institutional economics." As in the case of its two sister disciplines, social economics (*properly* defined) aims at limiting pure economics through implanting relevant variables and principles outside its narrow domain. The recent attempts to redefine its aims are the opposite: non-economic disciplines, to make them more fruitful and "scientific," are to be injected with a hefty dose of *economic* rationality. Contrary to the nominalist temper of modern economists, words, meanings and names cannot be arbitrarily redefined. They refer to some objective property of an underlying reality that needs to be respected. This current rage of enthroning economic man only goes to prove that this is indeed the Age of the Economist, and is even more reason to hold on to a *true* social economics as a welcome antidote.

2. Social economics, philosophy and common sense

Social economists like Sismondi and Ruskin, coming as they did from an intense interest in history or aesthetics, rooted their world view in the classic philosophy of the ancient Greeks and the republican tradition of the Romans, both of which left ample room for the recognition of an overarching social good. But this affirmation of the common good does not sit well with mainstream economists and appears meaningless to the *nominalist* temperament of the modern period. One should question if that temperament itself is appropriate and justified.

Questioning the imprint of British empirical philosophy

What is striking when looking at the history of orthodox economics (from Smith to Keynes) is that it is almost exclusively a British product. It has been formed and developed in a particular culture with a particular philosophic tradition that is not necessarily superior to its counterparts in continental Europe or elsewhere. Many of its basic tenets have found their way into economic science, and philosophers like Hobbes, Locke, Berkeley and Hume, therefore, can be seen as the "spiritual Godfathers" of economic science.

A quite powerful case has been made that in their rebellion against the dogmatic scholasticism of the sixteenth and seventeenth centuries British Enlightenment thinkers may have discarded too hastily and uncritically a tradition of almost 2,000 years of Western thought. The late philosopher, Mortimer Adler, singles out several philosophical mistakes that mar the very foundation of modern thought.[13] One such oversight, attributed to Locke, involves the treatment of perception, memory, imagination, thought and concept as "ideas" of which we are as directly conscious as we are of pleasure and pain, instead of realizing that it is only the idea's *object* of which we are aware.[14] This error prepared the ground for another fundamental mistake perpetrated by Hobbes, Berkeley and especially Hume: to ascribe to the human mind a single cognitive faculty essentially sensory in character, a faculty in which there is no room for intellect with the cognitive powers to understand, to abstract, to judge and to reason.[15]

Regarding the conception that all intelligence is entirely *sensory*, Hume anticipated by more than a century the Darwinian conclusion that the human species differs from other animals only *in degree*, not in kind. It was probably one of the earliest intellectual attacks on the notion of human dignity and human equality. But is it correct? Do animals really share with us the capacity, albeit in rudimentary form, of conceptual thinking? Can any of them generalize, say, from particular triangles to triangles as such? Laboratory experiments give us an affirmative answer to this last question. But when the objects of thought are *not* actually perceived, or not perceptible at all, as with "infinity," "mind," and with such conceptual constructs as "black hole," or "quark," the answer remains negative. The human animal is the *only* "animal" with an intellect empowered to deal with the unperceived, the imperceptible and the unimaginable.

British Enlightenment philosophy relegated reason to a mere instrument or "slave" of the passions. Chapter 7 examined instrumental reason together with Hume's absurd claim that "it is not contrary to reason to prefer the destruction of the whole world to the scratching of [one's] finger." Yet after all this time, the very heartbeat of modern economic man, instrumental rationality, is still in place.

No less important, the result of making fundamental mistakes about the nature of consciousness and the human mind leads straight to Hume's "nominalism" and its twin, "skepticism." Both doctrines make for an excessive emphasis on empiricism in the pursuit of truth, thereby also undermining the legitimacy of rationalist methods in trying to understand reality. Humean moral skepticism's stranglehold on the question of normative economic thought (see Chapter 5) recognized only two sorts of knowledge: one being mathematics involving no assertions about matters of real existence and the other empirical knowledge conveyed through the senses. He concluded his *Enquiries Concerning Human Understanding* (1748) with a famous paragraph bristling with an anti-dogmatic dogmatism:

> When we run over our libraries, persuaded of these principles, what havoc must we make? If we take in our hand any volume; of divinity or school metaphysics, for instance; let us ask, Does it contain any abstract reasoning concerning quantity or number? No. Does it contain any experimental reasoning concerning matters of fact and existence? No. Commit it then to the flames: for it can contain nothing but sophistry and illusion.[16]

Hume's primary target was the scholastic work filled with natural theology and heady metaphysics belabouring such questions as how many angels can dance on the head of a pin. At the same time, he was also belittling the legitimacy of *philosophical* knowledge in general (except, of course, his own),[17] anticipating the hard-nosed twentieth-century method of logical positivism. Since a twin reliance on both empirical evidence *and* rational philosophical discourse has long constituted the basic methodological approach of social economists, some comments on the legitimacy of philosophy in thinking about economic rationality are dealt with in the next section.

The common sense of social economics

Philip Wicksteed crowned his economic thinking with the writing of *The Common Sense of Political Economy* (1910), a book that would have probably been forgotten had it not been rediscovered and promoted by the noted scholar Lionel Robbins. As Robbins remarked, it has an unfortunate title, "not common sense in the ordinary sense of the term, and . . . not political economy"; on the contrary, the work represented one of the most exhaustive expositions of the various technical features of marginalism and pure economics as had appeared up to that time.[18]

Wicksteed, like Hobson, was destined to live in the shadow of the great Alfred Marshall. Besides being both in that sense "shadowy figures," they were about as opposite in their thinking as could be. In fact, Hobson's later critique of microeconomics was as much aimed at Wicksteed as it was at Marshall. And, historically speaking, it is also interesting to note that the economist H. S. Foxwell played a pivotal role in their teaching careers: his intervention is said to have ruined Hobson's, but he may also have encouraged and supported Wicksteed's.[19] It was probably more than a coincidence that Wicksteed started his first University Extension Lecture class in 1891, at the same time that Hobson was banned from teaching because of the economic heresies expressed in his *Physiology of Industry* (1889).[20]

Unlike Wicksteed, Hobson did embrace a philosophy of common sense in his political economy.[21] In fact, appeal to common sense experience is, and has long been, at the very heart of social economics. And this stance is not without relevance to the question of demarcating knowledge from opinion. Today, the line tends to be drawn according to the criterion of falsifiability. Statements and propositions that cannot be tested, it is maintained, do not convey useful knowledge. Perhaps so. It certainly seems to rule in empirical testing, but what about social philosophy or philosophical anthropology that also make claims about the real world?

Social economics in general, and what has been said here as a particular instantiation of this type of thought, is indeed refutable and therefore also beyond the pale of opinion. Like much of speculative philosophy, it appeals to *experience*, although not the kind of special empirical experience of laboratory research. Instead, it invokes the kind of *common* experience that all of us possess; and it is on the basis of such experience that we can have *common-sense knowledge* about matters of fact and real existence. Mortimer Adler's explanation of theoretical philosophy also pertains to social economics:

> It is an analytical and reflective refinement of what we know by common sense in the light of common experience. Our common-sense knowledge is deepened, illuminated, and elaborated by philosophical thought. There is little if any sound philosophy that

conflicts with our common-sense knowledge, for both are based on the common human experience out of which they emerge.[22]

The dual-self theory of rationality, portrayed in Chapter 7, is a case in point. As with most matters that involve the higher dimensions of human nature, measurement and quantification are rarely possible. But these higher dimensions *are* accessible to common experience, and they *can* be publicly discussed and refuted. Can we identify the higher self by observation? We must answer in the negative.[23] Yet, the construct of a higher self is not rendered meaningless by its lack of being observable. Economic man may appear observable yet be unreasonable, while the real person is equipped with a reasonableness that escapes the naked eye. In other words, part of the common experience of mankind is the avenue unique to the human sciences: our ability to look inside ourselves, to engage in introspection. The human being is both subject and object of social study, creating a fundamentally different situation than the one prevailing in the science of nature.

Besides propositions that are either falsifiable on grounds of empirical fact or common experience, statements and theories can also be refuted by rational argument. Furthermore, there are also some conclusions derived from self-evident truths. Much of the ethical foundation of social economics rests on these two pillars, and they also form the basis of a belief in moral objectivity. Moral appraisal is not something subjective that "lies in the eyes of the beholder." To quote another authority on the matter:

> Only if one subscribes to a mistakenly narrow view of "facts," one which focuses exclusively on descriptive matters and flatly excludes evaluative appraisals, can one maintain an unbridgeable divide that precludes the move from factual premises to evaluative conclusions. And this position is quite untenable. That certain items represent human needs (nourishment or companionship, for example) is a matter of empirical, determinable fact. That certain arrangements in regard to human action impede and others foster the satisfaction of people's needs is *also* a matter of empirically determinable fact. And such facts have straightforward extensive moral implications.[24]

Contrary to the confined thinking of Hume and his present-day followers, normative conclusions can indeed be logically deduced. To show that this is possible, all that is necessary is to combine a prescriptive with a descriptive premise in order to logically deduce a prescriptive conclusion. Take the following syllogism with a *self-evident* premise that yields normative truth: *We ought to desire what we really need!* Combine it with a descriptive truth concerning human needs, as for example, *All human beings need healthy and nutritious food*, and it will produce a true prescriptive conclusion, such as, *All human beings ought to desire healthy and nutritious food*. Of course, the descriptive premise is open to challenge, but in principle the normative reasoning underlying this book need not fall victim to the "naturalistic fallacy" of deriving the "ought" from the "is."

Finally, social economics, having an intimate connection with the common-sense knowledge of ordinary individuals, has from the beginning been in the province of the *generalist*, and not the specialist. Thus, some of its most striking points have been made by non-professional economists, like Sismondi, John Ruskin and Mohandas Gandhi. Worse still, intellectual overspecialization has long been seen to be counterproductive in the pursuit of knowledge. Hobson deplored the fact that "we have in modern universities hundreds of men who . . . completely lose themselves in work of research, absorbed by the smallness of the task they essay, and often hypnotized to torpor by gazing at it."[25] He felt that overspecialization affects the student in a similar manner to the industrial worker: by peering incessantly at one little group of facts, he/she blunts his intelligence and injures the focus of his/her mental eyesight.

Nevertheless, a proper conception of economics will have to make room for specialists as well as generalists. The former are better equipped to deal with questions that lend themselves to *quantitative* calculation and an analysis of the more uniform and routine aspects of human behavior. The latter have an advantage in the *qualitative* territory of inquiry into the nature and causes of social welfare; here in the domain of social economics we must rely on common sense in order to apprehend those common aspects of a human nature — self-awareness, moral integrity and freedom of the will — that are in a certain sense more uniquely human.

3. The age of the economist and the future of the world

Two hundred years ago, a New Age dawned in Europe: the Age of the Economist. The designation is attributed to the social philosopher Edmund Burke, who in 1790 bemoaned the fact that "the age of chivalry is dead, that of sophisters, economists and calculators has succeeded and that the glory of Europe is extinguished forever."[26] His comments were not so far off the mark: witness J. M. Keynes' famous statement that the ideas of economists, regardless of whether they are right or wrong, "are more powerful than is commonly understood. Indeed the world is ruled by little else. Practical men who believe themselves to be quite exempt from any intellectual influences, are usually the slaves of some defunct economist."[27] Certainly, no academic discipline has ever succeeded so much in shaping the world according to its own image. In a way, economics has been filling the vacuum left by the medieval Church, and its teachings at the introductory level all too often resemble sermons in praise of cupidity and the "economic way of thinking."[28] At the same time, civilization has become less civilized.

The age of the economist, despite all the affluence it has created in some places, is also an age echoed by W. H. Auden:

> That girls are raped, that two boys knife a third,
> Were axioms to him who's never heard
> Of any world where promises are kept,
> Or one could weep, because another wept.[29]

What does all this augur for the future of humanity? The inevitable logic of global-scale competitive capitalism points to a need for social economics.

The invisible hand as an impersonal force

For two centuries economists have been enamored by Adam Smith's powerful metaphor of the *invisible hand*: every individual acting in the pursuit of private gain is thereby led to promote "the publick interest" even though it is no part of his intention. The idea goes back to Bernhard de Mandeville's *Fable of the Bees* (1714), in which vice (licentiousness, greed, vanity and avarice) is made a virtue by which "the worst of all the multitude did something for the common good." In everyday economic discourse, the doctrine of the invisible hand has done much to legitimize self-interested profit-seeking, at least in a highly competitive economy; at the same time it has helped to de-emphasize the need for ethics in economic matters and has rendered any talk of the common good redundant.

If recent economic events foreshadow what is to come, the twenty-first century will serve as a testing ground for ascertaining the truth of the indi-vidualist creed. In the process it will either seal the fate of any social eco-nomics or generate strong pressures for the socialization of economic thought. The uncanny symbiotic relationship between competitive economic theory and the prevailing forces of modern finance capitalism sets the stage. For the first time in history, competition is free of the shackles of social control, letting loose globally a really "free" enterprise spirit. As one com-mentator put it recently:

> Globalization isn't a choice. It's the reality. There is just one global market today, and the only way [a country] can grow is by tapping the global stock and bond markets for investment and selling into the global trading system what [the] factories produce. And the most fundamental truth about globalization is this: No one is in charge, global markets are just like the Internet — every day these markets become more widespread, every day they weave us more tightly together and no one is in charge. . . . The global market today is an electronic herd of anonymous stock, bond and currency traders, sitting behind computer screens. The electronic herd cuts

no one any slack. It does not recognize anyone's unique circumstances. The herd only recognizes its own rules (what savings rate a country should have, what levels of interest rates, what deficit-to-GDP ratio and what level of current account deficit).[30]

An anonymous network of capitalist institutions is now in charge of trade, investment and production. Finance capital and other resources are increasingly allocated by means of a powerful force *with no one in charge*, creating a world of its own making, a tyranny of the bottom line. For all practical purposes, especially within the sphere of economics, this impersonal force can be identified with the old Aramaic term of *Mammon*: the false God of riches and avarice. How utterly different from the invisible hand's original attribution of "divine providence," when it was understood as being just another name given to the Deity.[31] Can one serve both God and Mammon, despite the long-noted biblical stricture? Will the unshackled impersonal force usher in a new age of human evolution or social decay?

The dynamic logic of self-interest

The impersonal force, considered from a more secular perspective, is nothing but self-interest in action, a snowball rolling down a mountain slope gathering weight and momentum. Its growing size and power enable it to overcome moral restraints, crashing through social fences. The cumulative dynamics of self-interest in action are fed by its inherent individualism, blind to the fallacy of composition and chained to the free-rider trap. Typified by entrepreneurs hustling to gain at the expense of others, these sporadic instances of opportunism can swell into a more general stream of defensive compulsion: do as the others do, otherwise you'll lose! *Underselling* one's competitors through the introduction of labor-saving technology, downward pressure on labor compensation, or both, constitutes a classic example of this phenomenon. That was, of course, the dynamics Sismondi deplored, and on which he pinned the blame for underconsumption, overproduction and the immiseration of the poor. And he also clearly recognized the impersonal character of this oppressive force, judging it to be even worse than the better known "acts of ferocity" in human history. Here is how he put it:

> In times of the greatest feudal oppression, in times of slavery, there have been, no doubt, acts of ferocity which made humanity shudder; but at least some motive excited their anger or their cruelty; there was some hope in the oppressed that they might avoid provoking the oppressor. Besides, the executioners of a ferocious act might soften the execution of it. The wife, the children, the priest may implore pardon, and sometimes obtain it. But in the cold and abstract oppression of wealth, there is no offense, no anger, no

executioner, no relation between man and man. Often the tyrant and his victim do not know one another by name, do not inhabit the same country, do not speak the same language. The oppressed knows not where to carry his prayers, or his resentment; the oppressor, far from being a hard man, is perhaps generous and feeling; he takes no account of the evil he does. He submits himself to a sort of fatality which seems at this time to govern all the manufacturing world. It is this fatality that, in spite of the promise of liberty, of equality, overwhelms with frightful oppression millions of human creatures.[32]

It is remarkable how much today's world economy resembles that of the early nineteenth century. Everywhere generous men and women with no evil intentions submit themselves to a fateful force pregnant with social destruction. This force manifests itself in the quest for maximum profit and investment return. It pressures governments to beggar their neighbors through competing "business climates" that offer lower taxes and less regulation. It encourages corporations to merge, downsize, switch to a contingent labor force, or, better yet, to seek lower wages abroad. Faced with the very real prospect of an ongoing erosion of the power to tax, governments become increasingly cost-conscious and willing to compromise human health and the provision of human services to considerations of fiscal responsibility. Many components of the welfare state and its redistributional role, including the traditional provisions for social security, are no longer affordable. A growing area of public education is now co-financed by advertising and corporate research grants. Profit and loss calculations of private insurance companies are dictating health policy, even the diagnosis and treatment of patients. The media, being more and more dependent on corporate advertising for survival, avoids friction with its donors and adjusts its news coverage accordingly. The ordinary citizen, meanwhile, adrift in a sea of powerlessness and insecurity and pelted by a constant shower of suggestive advertising, floats from day to day, from job to job, from career to career as circumstances permit, clinging to a purely materialist conception of life. One's identity is no longer fulfilled by work, but by consumption, that is, by one's shopping behavior as a consumer. On the lower end of the social scale, a growing segment of society feels more isolated, excluded and left behind, and acts from resignation, hopelessness and despair. People become deeply cynical and unable to muster any faith in the higher dimensions of human nature. It's a time when good guys finish last, and everybody knows it. It's a world where might makes right. Talk about ideals like social justice and niceties like ethical rules is met with a yawn. Meanwhile, violent redress of one's grievances becomes a natural way of life.

In short, a Rambo economy ruled by self-interest has the potential to reverse civilization as we have known it back into a barbarous state. All the evils of mounting crime, divorce, family breakdown and violence, bloody suppression of social antagonism caused by persistent unemployment, widening income disparities, tenacious poverty, social exclusion and a deteriorating environment, might be the price of nourishing the insatiable bottom line. In a way, the unchallenged reign of such an impersonal force will reveal the same brand of incompatibility between wealth and human welfare that led to the formulation of a social economics in Sismondi's day.

On the prospect of neo-liberalism and social cohesion

The revival of classical liberalism is celebrated by a number of economists as a return to the good old days of stable money, balanced government finances, technical progress, international division of labor and unhampered trade flows. To them, it's a historical tragedy that this earlier ideological commitment to *laissez-faire* and international cooperation and peace was so rudely interrupted by the mercantilist colonialism of the late nineteenth century, together with the new fashions of an activist state eager to assume the new functions of egalitarian redistribution, cranking up the welfare state and Keynesian macroeconomic management. In their eyes, these developments went hand in hand with the rise of socialism and nationalism and, ultimately, fascism. And to make things even worse, after World War II these blunders spread to the newly independent nations of the third world where the interventionist temper of their former masters was replicated and driven to new heights.

All this has changed with the fateful collapse of communism. Today, thanks to the new technological breakthroughs in communication and transportation, the world is poised to pick up where it left matters in the closing decades of the last century. Economic liberalism is pushing for a new trading regime in which the industrialized countries specialize in production of human and organizational capital while leaving manufacturing to the less developed nations. Will this trend continue?, asks UCLA economist Deepak Lal in a recent article.[33] He expresses concern about the effects on society of restructuring policies in industrial nations, which nourish doubt and feed increasingly visible protectionist undercurrents. Also, many poor nations, baffled by the events in Malaysia and Indonesia, are suddenly flirting again with currency controls and reregulation of their economies.

Nevertheless, Lal ends his speculations on an upbeat note, a theme that is revealing also in terms of what it says about the impersonal force. There are signs of hope: widespread tax aversion reinforced by the integration of global markets saps the resourcefulness of the state. Global capital markets also help to trim the traditionally confiscatory instincts of the state since governments now must worry about getting approval from these markets, and think twice about backsliding to old interventionist ways. At the push of a button, huge streams of capital can be diverted elsewhere, putting pressure on a nation's currency. Therefore, fiscal responsibility is no longer a matter of choice but of necessity. This, according to Lal, reassuringly implies that "the governments now find themselves exposed to a permanent referendum concerning their fiscal and monetary policies," and he concludes that "although the national banks and the treasuries may still have the right to *propose* policies, it is now the money markets that will *decide*."[34]

Accepting Lal's candid analysis for the sake of argument, one may wonder whether it really means the final victory of Mammon? Not really, and there are good reasons why: liberalization and markets do not operate in a vacuum but in a social and environmental context. It is likely that the implementation of the liberal creed will so encroach on social cohesion that it undermines itself. When discussing this issue at a meeting of the (currently pro-market) OECD, the conference report recognized that the success of competition and structural change is predicated on a certain degree of social cohesion: "a strong social fabric provides a secure basis for the flexibility and risk-taking, which are the life-blood of vibrant economic activity and wealth creation."[35] Far from being concerned about liberalization undermining cohesion, the report confidently asserts that the intensification of competition will provide the "motor of the economic growth and prosperity on which cohesion can thrive." This novel answer, surprising to many, is further explained:

> Robust rates of economic growth will be essential to the success of this individualist model for two reasons. First, in such a high-risk environment, almost all segments of society will need to be able to share the dream of eventually being a winner – a common, unifying belief in the chance of success that cushions the reality of extreme inequality. Second, the society will still need to be wealthy enough to attend to the minimum needs of the losers and those incapable of participating.[36]

Even though a more "flexible" economy with a deconstructed welfare system is generally believed to weaken cohesion, the OECD is banking on greater efficiency and growth following liberalization. But will it and can it? The experts hedge their bets by adding the caveat, "if for some reason the productivity gains or macroeconomic stability do not pan out, this scenario's chance of sustaining social cohesion could rapidly unravel."[37] True, the unraveling of social cohesion is one threat to the neo-liberalist dream of global hegemony; an increasingly serious environmental threat is the other. But it is revealing how, whenever economics seems to make for problems, the solution is to give it even more economics. If both social cohesion and the environment are negatively affected by economic growth, the remedy, we are assured, lies in even more economic growth. Whether this "fighting fire with fire" strategy will actually work before all is consumed by flames, only time will tell.

Wrestling with the impersonal force

The impersonal force as the cumulative product of human selfishness and greed is a formidable power. It is further helped by standard economics, which has long stamped egoism as "rational." But the force has also been misunderstood by the Marxist opponents of *laissez-faire*, who habitually saw capitalists as part of a class struggle. Marx himself left no doubt about that when criticizing other opponents of capitalism: "Where the class struggle is pushed aside as a disagreeable 'coarse' phenomenon, nothing remains of socialism but 'the true love of humanity' and the empty phraseology of justice."[38] It was, of course, exactly this "coarse" doctrine of class antagonism that drove a wedge between Marxist economists and social economists like Hobson and Gandhi.

In *Das Kapital*, Marx, having lost his earlier faith in the generic wholeness of humanity, pictures individuals as quasi-soldiers fighting a civil war for material goods, political power and social privilege. Individual wholeness and morality are unobtainable in a divided and immoral social system. Nobody has any real choice, there is no freedom to rise above oneself, preparing the grounds for a scientific socialism.

From the perspective of a humanistic social economics, what really is at the heart of history has never been class struggle, but more basically and fundamentally, an individual values struggle. The bedrock of human action is the person and the capacity of free will. Alexander Solzhenitsyn expresses this value system when he says: "The line between good and evil does not run through ideologies, philosophies, classes or nations, but through every human heart."[39]

In social theory the temptation to blame a particular malaise on some subclass of humanity leads to simplistic solutions, such as the reform or removal of the evil-doers. (One of the latest specimens is provided by certain kinds of radical feminism.) Unfortunately, the reality is that the impersonal force dwells in all of us.

The moral re-entry

This is Fred Hirsch's title of a concluding chapter of his 1976 treatise, *Social Limits to Growth*, in which he demonstrates the dynamic implications of a regime powered by individual self-interest in a world of social interaction. Seeking to recover the glue of social norms and cooperation weakened by the individualism of the market, Hirsch appeals to religion: "Modern economic analysis has kept religion firmly outside the economic sphere and has thereby obscured the role it has played in the economic system." He explains:

> Christianity sets great store by altruistic behavior. The point emphasized here is that if this is undertaken as a means to religious ends, it

also acts as a means to functionally necessary social cooperation for individualistic earthly ends. In this function, it is altruistic behavior that counts and not what motives happen to underlie it, whether Christian values, social pressures, conformist cowardice, humanitarianism, or anything else. For while such cooperation can, in some cases, be replaced by coercive rules, or stimulated through collectively imposed inducements to individuals' private interests, this will rarely be as practicable and efficient as when it is internally motivated.[40]

The appeal to an internalized system of social morality was Hirsch's natural answer to modern game theory, having expunged the old liberal fallacy clinging to the creed that morality itself could be based on self-interest. Recall Bertrand Russell's (mistaken) claim "if men were actuated by self-interest . . . the whole human race would cooperate." Morality, rehabilitated as the *sine qua non* of a kind of social cooperation, reaches further than mere exchange. As such it seems to be a necessary first step in slowing down the impersonal force, but will it also bring it to a halt?

Perhaps what is needed is nothing less than a radical reassessment of what it means to be human, a questioning of the modern mind rich in *quantitative* means but poor in *qualitative* ends. The question of quality, as E. F. Schumacher points out, implies different qualitative levels, or a vertical dimension crowned by the distinctly human quality of self-awareness and pointing to an even higher, spiritual domain. What humanity needs, according to Schumacher, is to regain a faith in meaningful existence, a purpose of life beyond self-preservation and gratification. In the process, it is important to realize that a life of universal material abundance is not a realistic ideal for this planet. Life's destiny for the human being must be something other, something more meaningful, than that. Like Adam Smith, who cautioned us that wealth and greatness are mere "baubles" and trinkets of frivolous utility, John Stuart Mill too stressed the importance of the higher "pleasures." Mill was eager to disassociate himself from "the ideal of life held out by those who think that the normal state of human beings is that of struggling to get on; that the trampling, crushing, elbowing, and treading on each other's heels, which form the existing type of social life, are the most desirable lot of human kind. . . ."[41] Abraham Maslow's psychology of personality reaffirms the wisdom of these earlier economists. If the impersonal force, being the lower self at the wheel of "progress," is the dynamo driving humanity down the dead-end road of commercialism, consumerism, self-aggrandizement and habitat destruction, there is little that can be done short of reassessing our thinking. Ultimately, modern men and women must ponder the impossibility of serving God and Mammon at the same time, whether we want to be part of an economic system that degrades and enslaves the human spirit or an alternative order that ennobles and frees it.

The step from an indulgent consumer to a socially responsible citizen is no easy matter, neither is the realignment of economic institutions with respect for human dignity and integrity of nature: but the switch from economic growth to sustainable economic development, and the massive international and intergenerational redistribution of resources that this entails, makes it even harder. At the same time, the rethinking of these matters appears to be vitally important for the survival of the human race. And if it can only be accomplished by means of some radically new spiritual awakening, so be it.

On a more secular plane, social economics in the humanistic tradition offers an alternative that also necessitates rethinking one's world view, an opening up to entertaining the possibility that the "Doctors of Modernity" (Marx, Darwin and Freud) may have made some serious mistakes.[42] The way to save humanity and the world may demand letting go of some cherished beliefs and an appreciation of the ideas that allowed humanity to progress though the ages. It may require letting go of individualism, of the idea that there is no meaning to life, that human dignity is a noble fiction, and a reassessment of the role of morality, once seen as a tool of Church oppression. And, above all, humanity must start questioning an economic way of thinking with a pre-supposition based on the realization that "rational man" of economics lacks both heart and soul.

A final word

If the world is in trouble because of excessive egoism, what it needs now more than ever is to find a way to recast the fear, hatred and anger minted from the economic realm of *laissez-faire*. This does not mean a passive submission to fate, or a turning away from the world, even less a desperate endorsement of violence to stem the tide. Fear, resignation, violence and selfishness are all part of the same coin. Rather, what is called for is to gather up all that remains to us in order to advance a renewed currency of hope. What is truly meaningful is to get involved wholeheartedly and do whatever can be done while entrusting the power of reason and truth. Being mindful of Sismondi and Hobson and their legacy of confronting mainstream economists with logic and facts, with common sense and method, today's neo-liberalist economics must be challenged in the same spirit. The work at hand has much to do with securing and improving human well-being, perhaps at the local level in one's dealings with neighbors and community, and little to do with winning a Nobel prize. The meaningfulness of this work comes from the attempt to remake the world more in tune with common-sense thinking, to help it resonate with acts of civilized behavior and human decency. To spread the intellectual legacy of social economics thinkers in pursuit of human welfare for all is to promote an ethical economics for the common good. At stake is not just a new world order, but the world itself.

Notes

1 M. Gandhi, *An Autobiography*, Ahmedabad, Navajivan Publishing House, 1927, p. 22.
2 See, for example, A. Das, *Foundations of Gandhian Economics*, New York, St. Martin's Press, 1979.
3 R. H. Tawney, *The Radical Tradition*, ed. Rita Hinden, New York, Pantheon Books, 1964, p. 7.
4 R. H. Tawney, *The Acquisitive Society* [1920], New York, Harcourt Brace Jovanovich, 1948, p. 159.
5 This information is culled from an interesting article by C. Hession, "E. F. Schumacher as Heir to Keynes' Mantle," *Review of Social Economy*, April 1986, vol. 44: 1, pp. 1–25.
6 E. F. Schumacher, *Small Is Beautiful*, New York, Harper and Row, 1973, p. 70.
7 ibid., p. 81.
8 ibid., p. 164.
9 See G. A. Smith, "The Teleological View of Wealth: A Historical Perspective," in H. Daly (ed.), *Economics, Ecology, Ethics*, San Francisco, CA, W. H. Freeman and Co., 1980, pp. 215–237.
10 J. Eatwell *et al.* (eds), *The New Palgrave Dictionary: Social Economics*, New York, W. W. Norton, 1989.
11 ibid., pp. xi–xii.
12 D. W. Pearce (ed.), *The MIT Dictionary of Modern Economics*, 4th edn, Cambridge, MA, MIT Press, 1992, p. 398.
13 M. Adler, *Ten Philosophical Mistakes*, New York, Macmillan, 1985.
14 ibid., ch. 1.
15 ibid., ch. 2.
16 D. Hume, *Enquiries Concerning Human Understanding and Concerning the Principles of Morals* [1777], 3rd edn, Oxford, Clarendon Press, 1975.
17 According to Hume there was room for "good" metaphysics in pointing out the meaninglessness of the dogmatic scholastic type.
18 L. Robbins in P. Wicksteed, *The Common Sense of Political Economy* [1910], London, George Routledge and Sons, 1933, p. xii.
19 In the preface of *The Common Sense* Wicksteed wrote: "To Professor Foxwell I am grateful for encouragement and support that have never failed since I first began the study of Political Economy" (ibid., p. xxx).
20 For the long and complicated story about those events and the roles played by Wicksteed, Foxwell and Hobson, see A. Kadish, "Rewriting the Confessions: Hobson and the Extension Movement," in M. Freeden (ed.), *Reappraising J. A. Hobson*, London, Unwin Hyman, 1990, pp. 137–166.
21 See the explicit remarks about "enlightened common sense" in the final chapter of J. A. Hobson, *Work and Wealth: A Human Valuation*, London, Allen, 1914.
22 Adler, *Ten Philosophical Mistakes*, p. 106.
23 A hard-nosed approach would have to yield the following negative answer: if, after some internal struggle, the higher order preferences lose out, if they are inoperative, we do not need to worry about them. Alternatively, in case they do succeed in effectively dictating conduct, we will observe simply a kind of action based on certain preferences, something that is fully consistent with the postulates of instrumentally rational choice theory. In both cases, the stipulation of a mystical aspirational self lurking in the background is redundant.
24 N. Rescher, *Moral Absolutes (An Essay on the Nature and Rationale of Morality)*, New York, Peter Lang Publishing, 1989, p. 74.

25 J. A. Hobson, *The Social Problem* [1901], reprint, Bristol, Thoemmes Press, 1979, p. 231.
26 Burke's phrase appears in his *Reflections on the French Revolution* [1790], as quoted in Daniel Fusfeld, *The Age of the Economist*, Glenview, IL, Scott, Foresman and Co., 1977, p. 39.
27 J. M. Keynes, *The General Theory of Employment, Interest, and Money*, New York, Harcourt Brace Jovanovich, 1964, p. 383.
28 For a classic example, see the text by H. Heyne, *The Economic Way of Thinking*, 2nd edn, Chicago, IL, SRA Inc., 1976.
29 Quoted in G. Davidson and P. Davidson, *Economics for a Civilized Society*, New York, W. W. Norton, 1988, p. 25.
30 T. Friedman in the *International Herald Tribune*, September 30, 1997, p. 10.
31 A. L. Macfie, *The Individual in Society*, London, George Allen and Unwin, 1967, p. 111. For a more general exposition of the influence of natural theology and Deism on Smith, see C. Clark, *Economic Theory and Natural Philosophy*, Brookfield, VT, Edward Elgar, 1992, ch. 3.
32 J. C. L. Simonde de Sismondi, *Political Economy and the Philosophy of Government* [1847], New York, Augustus M. Kelley, 1966b, p. 394.
33 D. K. Lal, "The Cyclical Ups and Downs of Economic Liberalism," *Neue Zuercher Zeitung*, December 27/28, 1997, p. 27.
34 ibid.
35 OECD, *Societal Cohesion and the Globalizing Economy: What Does the Future Hold?*, Paris, 1997, p. 7.
36 ibid., p. 16.
37 ibid.
38 K. Marx, "Circular Letter to Bebel, Liebknecht, Bradie, and Others" [1879], in R. C. Tucker (ed.), *The Marx–Engels Reader*, New York, W. W. Norton, 1972, p. 404.
39 Quoted in M. A. Lutz and K. Lux, *The Challenge of Humanistic Economics*, Menlo Park, CA, Benjamin/Cummings, 1979, p. 38.
40 F. Hirsch, *Social Limits to Growth*, Cambridge, MA, Harvard University Press, 1976, p. 139.
41 J. S. Mill, *Principles of Political Economy with Some of Their Applications to Social Philosophy*, vol. II, New York, D. Appleton and Co., 1891, p. 326.
42 R. F. Baum, *Doctors of Modernity: Darwin, Marx and Freud*, Peru, IL, Sherwood Sudgen and Co. Press, 1988.

BIBLIOGRAPHY

Abse, J., *John Ruskin: The Passionate Moralist*, New York, Alfred A. Knopf, 1981.

Adler, M., *The Difference of Man and the Difference It Makes*, New York, Holt, Rinehart and Winston, 1967.

—— *Aristotle for Everybody: Difficult Thought Made Easy*, New York, Simon and Schuster, 1978.

—— *Ten Philosophical Mistakes*, New York, Macmillan, 1985.

—— *Intellect: Mind over Matter*, New York, Macmillan, 1990.

Alexander, S., "Human Values and Economists' Values," in S. Hook, *Human Values and Economic Policy: A Symposium*, New York, New York University Press, 1967, pp. 101–116.

Allett, J., *New Liberalism: The Political Economy of J. A. Hobson*, Toronto, University of Toronto Press, 1981.

Amonn, A., *Simonde de Sismondi als Nationaloekonom: Darstellung seiner Lehren mit einer Einführung und Erläuterungen*, Bern, Francke, 1945–1949, vol. I.

Anderson, E., *Value and Ethics in Economics*, Cambridge, MA, Harvard University Press, 1993.

—— "Review of Sen's *Inequality Reexamined*," *Economics and Philosophy*, April 1995, vol. 11:1, pp. 182–188.

Aristotle, *Nicomachean Ethics*, trans. M. Oswald, Indianapolis, IN, Bobbs-Merrill Educational Publishing, 1962.

Arrow, K., *Social Choice and Individual Values*, New Haven, CT, Yale University Press, 1951.

Bailey, M., "Risks, Costs, and Benefits of Fluorocarbon Regulation," *American Economic Review*, May 1982, vol. 72:2, pp. 247–250.

Barnett, H., "Scarcity and Growth Revisited," in V. K. Smith (ed.), *Scarcity and Growth Reconsidered*, Baltimore, MD, Johns Hopkins University Press, 1979.

Barnett, H. and Morse, C., *Scarcity and Growth: Economics of Natural Resource Availability*, Baltimore, MD, Johns Hopkins University Press, 1993.

Barton, J., *Economic Writings*, Regina, Saskatchewan, Lynn Publishing Co., 1962.

Batra, R., *Studies in the Pure Theory of International Trade*, London, Macmillan, 1973, ch. 9.

—— *The Myth of Free Trade: A Plan for America's Economic Revival*, New York, Charles Scribner's Sons, 1993.

—— *The Great American Deception: What Politicians Won't Tell You About Our Economy and Your Future*, New York, John Wiley and Sons, 1996.

Baum, R. F., *Doctors of Modernity: Darwin, Marx and Freud*, Peru, IL, Sherwood Sudgen and Co. Press, 1988.

Baumol, W. J., "Community Indifference," *Review of Economic Studies*, 1946–1947, vol. 14:1, pp. 44–48.

—— "On the Possibility of Continuing Expansion of Finite Resources," *Kyklos*, 1986, vol. 39, pp. 167–179.

—— *Welfare Economics and the Theory of the State*, Cambridge, MA, Harvard University Press, 1995.

Bentham, J., *An Introduction to the Principles of Morals and Legislation*, London, T. Payne and Sons, 1789.

Berlin, I., *Four Essays on Liberty*, Oxford, Oxford University Press, 1969.

Berti, L., "Society and the Market: Remote and Less Remote Sources of a Present Issue," in O. Nudler and M. A. Lutz (eds), *Economics, Culture and Society: Alternative Approaches*, New York, The Apex Press, and Tokyo, United Nations University Press, 1996, pp. 17–83.

Bhagwati, J., "The Pure Theory of International Trade: A Survey," *Economic Journal*, 1964, vol. 74, pp. 1–78.

—— "The Case for Free Trade," *Scientific American*, November 1993, pp. 42–49.

Biancardi, C., Tiezzi, E. and Ulgati, S., "Complete Recycling of Matter in the Frameworks of Physics, Biology, and Ecological Economics," *Ecological Economics*, 1993, vol. 8, pp. 1–5.

Blanqui, J., *History of Political Economy in Europe* [1837/1842], translated from the 4th French edn, New York, G. P. Putnam's Sons, 1880.

Blaug, M., *Great Economists Before Keynes*, Atlantic Highlands, NJ, Humanities Press International, Inc., 1986.

Bleany, M. F., *Underconsumption Theories: A Historical and Critical Analysis*, New York, International Publishers, 1976.

Bos, H. C. (ed.), *Economic Structure and Development*, Amsterdam, North-Holland, Elsevier Science, 1973.

Bower, L., "Present and Future Oil Usage," *Forum for Applied Research and Public Policy*, 1987, vol. 2.

Brewer, A., "Trade with Fixed Real Wages and Mobile Capital," *Journal of International Trade*, 1985, vol. 18, pp. 177–186.

Bromely, D. W., *Economic Interests and Institutions: The Conceptual Foundations of Public Policy*, New York, Basil Blackwell, 1989.

Brown, L., "The Future of Growth," in L. Brown, *et al.* (eds), *State of the World 1998* (by the WorldWatch Institute), New York, W. W. Norton, 1998.

Brown, L. *et al.* (eds), *State of the World 1996: A Worldwatch Institute Report on Progress Toward a Sustainable Society*, New York, W. W. Norton, 1996.

—— *State of the World 1998: A Worldwatch Institute Report on Progress Toward a Sustainable Society*, New York, W. W. Norton, 1998.

Brown-Collier, E. K., "Keynes' View of an Organic Universe," *Review of Social Economy*, 1985, vol. 93:2, pp. 14–23.

—— "The Fundamental Difficulty in Basing Macroeconomic Policy on Microeconomic Theory," *Forum of Social Economics*, Fall 1996, vol. 26:1, pp. 47–56.

Browning, E. and Browning, J., *Microeconomic Theory and Application*, New York, Harper and Collins, 1992.

Buber, M., *I and Thou*, New York, Scribner, 1970.

Buchanan, J., "Markets, States and the Extent of Morals," *American Economic Review*, May 1978, vol. 62:2, pp. 364–368.

Buergenmeier, B., *Social Economics*, Boston, Kluwer Academic Publishers, 1992.

Buret, E., *De la Misère des Classes Laborieuses*, 2 vols, Paris, Paulin, 1840.

Cairnes, J. E., *Essays in Political Economy*, London, Macmillan, 1873.

Cate, G. A. (ed.), *The Correspondence of Thomas Carlyle and John Ruskin*, Stanford, CA, Stanford University Press, 1982.

Clark, C., *Economic Theory and Natural Philosophy*, Brookfield, VT, Edward Elgar, 1992.

Clark, J. M., "J. A. Hobson, Heretic and Pioneer," *Journal of Social Philosophy*, July 1940, pp. 350–359.

—— "Aims of Economic Life as Seen by Economists," reprinted in Clark, *Economic Institutions and Human Welfare*, New York, Alfred Knopf, 1957.

—— *Preface to Social Economics* [1936], reprint, New York, Augustus M. Kelley, 1967.

Clarke, P., *Liberals and Social Democrats*, Cambridge, Cambridge University Press, 1978.

Cobb, C., and Cobb, J., *The Green National Product: A Proposed Index of Sustainable Economic Welfare*, Lanham, MD, University Press of America, 1994.

Cohen, J., *How Many People Can the Earth Support?*, New York, W. W. Norton, 1995, pp. 196–208.

Cole, G. D. H., "Obituary: J. A. Hobson 1858–1940," *Economic Journal*, vol. 50, June–September 1940, pp. 351–359.

Common, M., *Sustainability and Policy*, New York, Cambridge University Press, 1995.

Copp, D., "The Right to an Adequate Standard of Living: Justice, Autonomy, and the Basic Needs," *Social Philosophy and Policy*, Winter 1992, vol. 9:1, pp. 213–261.

Costanza, R. (ed.), *Ecological Economics: The Science and Management of Sustainability*, New York, Columbia University Press, 1991.

Costanza, R., *et al.*, *An Introduction to Ecological Economics*, Boca Raton, FL, St. Lucie Press, 1998.

Culbertson, J. M., *International Trade and the Future of the West*, Madison, WI, 21st Century Press, 1984.

—— *Competition, Constructive and Destructive*, Madison, WI, 21st Century Press, 1985.

Daly, H. (ed.), *Economics, Ecology, Ethics*, San Francisco, CA, W. H. Freeman and Co., 1980.

—— "From Empty World Economics to Full World Economics," in R. Goodland *et al.* (eds), *Environmentally Sustainable Economic Development: Building on Brundtland*, Paris, UNESCO, 1991.

—— "The Perils of Free Trade," *Scientific American*, November 1993, pp. 50–57.

—— *Beyond Growth*, Boston, MA, Beacon Press, 1996.

Daly, H. and Cobb, J., *For the Common Good: Redirecting the Economy toward Community, the Environment, and a Sustainable Future*, Boston, MA, Beacon Press, 2nd edn, 1994.

Das, A., *Foundations of Gandhian Economics*, New York, St. Martin's Press, 1979.

Davidson, G. and Davidson, P., *Economics for a Civilized Society*, New York, W.W. Norton, 1988.

Davis, J. B., "The Science of Happiness and the Marginalization of Ethics," *Review of Social Economy*, December 1987, vol. 45:3, pp. 298–311.

Davis, J. B. and O'Boyle, E. (eds), *The Social Economics of Human Material Need*, Carbondale, IL, Southern Illinois University Press, 1994.

Denis, H., *Histoire des Systèmes Economiques et Socialistes*, Paris, V. Giard and E. Briere,1904 edn, vol. II.

Domar, E. D., "Expansion and Employment," *American Economic Review*, 1947, vol. 37, pp. 34–55.

Dyck, R. C. and Mulej, M. (eds), *Self-Transformation of the Forgotten Four-Fifths*, Dubuque, IA, Kendall/Hunt Publishing Co., 1998.

Eatwell, J. *et al.* (eds), *The New Palgrave Dictionary: Social Economics*, New York, W.W. Norton, 1989.

Eccles, J. and Robinson, D., *The Wonder of Being Human: Our Brain and Our Mind*, New York, The Free Press, 1984.

Economic Report of the President, The 1997, Washington, DC, US Government Printing Office, February 1997.

Ellerman, D., "The Employment Contract and Liberal Thought," *Review of Social Economy*, April 1986, vol. 44:1, pp. 13–39.

—— *The Democratic Worker-Owned Firm*, Boston, MA, Unwin Hyman, 1990a.

—— "The Corporation as a Democratic Social Institution," in M. A. Lutz (ed.), *Social Economics: Retrospect and Prospect*, Boston, MA, Kluwer Academic Publishers, 1990b, pp. 365–387.

—— *Property and Contract in Economics*, Cambridge, MA, Blackwell, 1992.

—— *Intellectual Trespassing as a Way of Life: Essays in Philosophy, Economics, and Mathematics*, London, Rowman and Littlefield Publishers, 1995.

, "Property Rights Fallacies in the Arrow–Debreu General Equilibrium Model," unpublished paper presented at the American Economic Association Meetings in San Francisco, January 5–8, 1996.

—— "The Human-Capital-ist Firm: An Approach from Property Theory and Democratic Theory," unpublished paper presented at the Corporations and Human Capital Project at the Brookings Institution, May 23, 1997.

England, R. W., and Harris, J. M., "Alternatives to Gross National Product: A Critical Survey," G-DAE Discussion Paper no. 5, Medford, MA, Global Development and Environment Institute, 1997.

Etzioni, A., *The Moral Dimension Toward a New Economics*, New York, The Free Press, 1988.

Farina, F., Hahn, F. and Vannucci, S. (eds), *Ethics, Rationality and Economic Behaviour*, New York, Clarendon Press, 1996.

Farrel, M. J., "The Convexity Assumptions in the Theory of Competitive Markets," *Journal of Political Economy*, 1959, vol. 67, pp. 371–391.

Flam, H. and Flanders, M. J. (eds), *Heckscher–Ohlin Trade Theory*, Cambridge, MA, MIT Press, 1991.

Foxwell, H. S., "Introduction," in A. Menger, *The Right to the Whole Product of Labor* [1899], New York, Augustus M. Kelley Publishers, 1970.

Frank, R. H., *Microeconomics and Behavior*, New York, McGraw-Hill, Inc., 1991.

Frankfurt, H. G., "Freedom of the Will and the Concept of a Person," *Journal of Philosophy*, January 1971, vol. 68: 1, pp. 5–20.

Freeden, M. (ed.), *Reappraising J. A. Hobson*, London, Unwin Hyman, 1990.

Friedman, M., *Essays in Positive Economics*, Chicago, IL, University of Chicago Press, 1953.

Friedman, M. and Friedman, R., *Free to Choose: A Personal Statement*, New York, Harcourt Brace Jovanovich, 1990, p. 45.

Friedman, T., in the *International Herald Tribune*, September 30, 1997, p. 10.

Furubota, E. and Pejovich, S., *The Economics of Property Rights*, Cambridge, MA, Ballinger Publishing Co., 1974.

Fusfeld, D., *The Age of the Economist*, Glenview, IL, Scott Foresman and Co., 1977.

Gandhi, M., *An Autobiography*, Ahmedabad, Navajivan Publishing House, 1927.

Georgescu-Roegen, N., "Choice, Expectations and Measurability," *Quarterly Journal of Economics*, 1954, vol. 68, pp. 504–534.

—— *The Entropy Law and the Economic Process*, Cambridge, MA, Harvard University Press, 1971.

—— *Energy and Economic Myths*, New York, Pergamon Press, 1976.

—— "Technology Assessment: The Case of the Direct Use of Solar Energy," *Atlantic Economic Journal*, December 1978, vol. 6, pp. 15–21.

—— "Afterword," in J. Riffkin, *Entropy: Into the Greenhouse World*, New York, Viking–Penguin, 1989.

Gewirth, A., "Human Dignity as the Basis of Rights," in M. Meyer and W. A. Parent (eds), *The Constitution of Rights: Human Dignity and American Values*, Ithaca, Cornell University Press, 1992, pp. 10–28.

—— *The Community of Rights*, Chicago, IL, University of Chicago Press, 1996.

Gide, C. and Rist, C., *A History of Economic Doctrines*, 2nd English edn, London, George G. Harrap and Co., 1948.

Gilder, G., *Microcosm: The Quantum Revolution in Economics and Technology*, New York, Simon and Schuster, 1989.

Gilligan, C., *In a Different Voice*, Cambridge, MA, Harvard University Press, 1982.

Golub, S., "Comparative Advantage and Absolute Advantage in the Asia–Pacific Region," Federal Reserve Bank of San Francisco, Working Paper no. 9, 1995.

Goodland, R. *et al.* (eds), *Environmentally Sustainable Economic Development: Building on Brundtland*, Paris, Unesco, 1991.

Gore, A., *Earth in the Balance: Ecology and the Human Spirit*, Boston, MA, Houghton Mifflin Co., 1992.

Gotesky, R. and Laszlo, E. (eds), *Human Dignity*, New York, Gordon and Breach, 1970.

Graham, E., "Dreams of Cushy Retirement Clash with Meager Savings," *Wall Street Journal*, December 12, 1997, p. R1.

Greider, W., *One World, Ready or Not: The Manic Logic of Global Capitalism*, New York, Simon and Schuster, 1997.

Habermas, J., *The Philosophical Discourse of Modernity*, Cambridge, MA, MIT Press, 1987.

Hagen, E., "An Economic Justification of Protectionism," *Quarterly Journal of Economics*, 1958, vol. 72, pp. 496–514.

Hamlin, A. P., *Ethics, Economics and the State*, New York, St. Martin's Press, 1986.

Haney, L., "The Social Point of View in Economics," *Quarterly Journal of Economics*, November 1913, vol. 27, pp. 115–139.

Hargreaves Heap, S., *Rationality in Economics*, New York, Basil Blackwell, 1989.

—— "Norms and Reasons," unpublished paper presented at the International Conference for Socio-Economics, Geneva, July 13, 1996.

Harris, W. H. and Levey, J. (eds), *The New Columbia Encyclopedia*, New York, Columbia University Press, 1976.

Harrod, R. F., "Scope and Method of Economics," *Economic Journal*, September 1938, vol. 48, pp. 390–397.

Hausman, D. M. and McPherson, M. S., *Economic Analysis and Moral Philosophy*, Cambridge, Cambridge University Press, 1996.

Hession, C., "E. F. Schumacher as Heir to Keynes' Mantle," *Review of Social Economy*, April 1986, vol. 44:1, pp. 1–25.

Heyne, H., *The Economic Way of Thinking*, 2nd edn, Chicago, IL, SRA Inc., 1976.

Hickok, S., "The Consumer Cost of US Trade Restraints," Federal Reserve Bank of New York Quarterly Review, Summer 1995.

Hirsch, F., *Social Limits to Growth*, Cambridge, MA, Harvard University Press, 1976.

Hirsch, W., *Law and Economics*, New York, Academic Press, 1979.

Hirschman, A. O., "Rival Interpretations of Market Society: Civilizing, Destructive, or Feeble," *Journal of Economic Literature*, December 1982, vol. 20, pp. 1463–1484.

—— "Against Parsimony," *Economics and Philosophy*, 1985, vol. 1:1, pp. 7–21.

Hobson, J. A., *The Problem of the Unemployed*, London, Methuen and Co., 1896.

—— *John Ruskin: Social Reformer*, Boston, MA, Dana Estes and Co., 1898.

—— "Character and Society," in P. Parker (ed.), *Character and Life*, London, Williams and Norgate, 1912, pp. 53–104.

—— *Work and Wealth: A Human Valuation*, London, Allen, 1914.

—— *The Economics of Unemployment*, London, George Allen and Unwin, 1922.

—— *Free Thought in the Social Sciences*, London, Allen, 1926.

—— *Wealth and Life: A Study in Values*, London, Allen, 1929.

—— *Rationalisation and Unemployment: An Economic Dilemma*, London, George Allen and Unwin, 1930.

—— *Confessions of an Economic Heretic*, London, Allen, 1938.

—— *Imperialism: A Study* [1902], Ann Arbor, MI, University of Michigan Press, 1965.

—— *Incentives in the New Industrial Order* [1922], Westport, CT, Hyperion Press, 1980.

—— *The Social Problem* [1901], reprint, Bristol, Thoemmes Press, 1996.

Hobson, J. A. and Mummery, A. F., *The Physiology of Industry*, London, Murray, 1889.

Hodgskin, T., *Popular Political Economy* [1827], New York, Augustus M. Kelley, 1966.

—— *The Natural and Artificial Right of Property Contrasted* [1832], Clifton, NJ, Augustus M. Kelley, 1973.

Hook, S., *Human Values and Economic Policy: A Symposium*, New York, New York University Press, 1967.

Horkheimer, M., *The Eclipse of Reason*, New York, Oxford University Press, 1947.

—— *Critique of Instrumental Reason*, New York, Seabury Press, 1974.

Houthakker, H., "Whatever Happened to the Energy Crisis?," *The Energy Journal*, 1983, vol. 4:1.

Howard, R. and Donnelly, J., "Human Dignity, Human Rights and Political Regions," *American Political Science Review*, September 1986, vol. 80:3, pp. 801–817.

Hufbauer, G., *Trade Protection in the US: 31 Case Studies*, Stockholm, Institute for International Economics, 1986.

Hume, D., *A Treatise of Human Nature*, [1739], Oxford, Clarendon Press, 1978.

Hunt, E. K., "The Normative Foundations of Social Theory," *Review of Social Economy*, 1978, vol. 36:3, pp. 285–309.

Hutchison, T. W., *'Positive' Economics and Policy Objectives*, Cambridge, MA, Harvard University Press, 1964.

Jackson, A., *Incomes and Productivity in North America*, Commission for Labor Cooperation, Dallas, TX, Bernan Press, 1997.

Jenkins, I., "Naturalism," in D. Runes, *Dictionary of Philosophy*, Totowa, NJ, Littlefield, Adams and Co., 1962.

Jensen, M. and Meckling, W., "The Theory of the Firm: Managerial Behavior, Agency Costs, and Ownership Structures," *Journal of Financial Economics*, 1976, vol. 3:4, pp. 305–360.

Jevons, S., *The Theory of Political Economy* [1871], reprint, New York, Augustus M. Kelley, 1965.

Johnson, P., *Darwin on Trial*, Downers Grove, IL, InterVarsity Press, 1991.

Jones, H. E., *Kant's Principle of Personality*, Madison, WI, University of Wisconsin Press, 1971.

Jordan, B., *The Common Good: Citizenship, Morality, and Self-Interest*, New York, Basil Blackwell, 1989.

Kadish, A., "Rewriting the Confessions: Hobson and the Extension Movement," in M. Freeden (ed.), *Reappraising J. A. Hobson*, London, Unwin Hyman, 1990, pp. 137–166.

—— "The Non-Canonical Context of *The Physiology of Industry*," in J. Pheby (ed.), *J. A. Hobson after Fifty Years*, New York, St. Martin's Press, 1994, pp. 53–77.

Kahn, A., "The Tyranny of Small Decisions: Market Failures, Imperfections, and the Limits of Economics," *Kyklos*, 1966, vol. 19:1, pp. 23–47.

Kaldor, N., "Welfare Propositions and Interpersonal Comparisons of Utility," *Economic Journal*, September 1939, vol. 49, pp. 549–552.

Kant, I., *Groundwork of the Metaphysics of Morals* [1785], trans. H. J. Paton, New York, Harper Torch Books, 1964.

Kanth, R. K., *Political Economy and Laissez-Faire: Economics and Ideology in the Ricardian Era*, Totowa, NJ, Rowman and Littlefield, 1986.

Keynes J. M., *The General Theory of Employment, Interest, and Money*, New York, Harcourt Brace Jovanovich, 1964.

Keynes, J. N., *The Scope and Method of Political Economy*, London, Macmillan and Co., 1890.

King, J., "J. A. Hobson's Macroeconomics: The Last Ten Years (1930–1940)," in J. Pheby (ed.), *J. A. Hobson after Fifty Years*, New York, St. Martin's Press, 1994, pp. 124–142.

Klamer, A. and Colander, D., *The Making of an Economist,* Boulder, CO, Westview Press, 1990.

Knight, F. H., *Risk, Uncertainty and Profit*, Boston, MA, Houghton Mifflin, 1921.

Koerner, S. (ed.), *Practical Reason*, New Haven, CT, Yale University Press, 1974.

Koford, K. and Miller, J. (eds), *Social Norms and Economic Institutions*, Ann Arbor, MI, University of Michigan Press, 1991.

Krueger, A., "Labour Market Shifts and the Price Puzzle Revisited," unpublished paper, Princeton University, October 1995.

Krugman, P., *The Age of Diminished Expectations*, Cambridge, MA, MIT Press, 1994.

—— *Pop Internationalism*, Cambridge, MA, MIT Press, 1996.

Kuthner, R., *Everything for Sale: The Virtues and Limits of Markets*, New York, Alfred A. Knopf, 1997.

Lal, D. K., "The Cyclical Ups and Downs of Economic Liberalism," *Neue Zuercher Zeitung*, December 27/28, 1997.

Landreth, H., and Colander, D. C., *History of Economic Thought*, 3rd edn, Boston, MA, Houghton Mifflin Co., 1994.

Lavoie, M., *Foundations of Post-Keynesian Economics*, Brookfield, VT, Elgar, 1992.

Lawson, T., "The Nature of Post-Keynesianism and its Link to Other Traditions: A Realist Perspective," *Journal of Post-Keynesian Economics*, Summer 1994, vol. 16:14, pp. 503–538.

Lea, S., *et al.*, *The Individual in the Economy: A Textbook of Economic Psychology*, New York, Cambridge University Press, 1987.

Leamer, E., *In Search of Stolper–Samuelson Effects on US Wages*, NBER Working Paper no. 5427, 1996.

Lebergott, S., *Manpower in Economic Growth: The American Record since 1800*, New York, McGraw-Hill, 1964.

Lee, T. and Scott, R., "Third World Growth," *Harvard Business Review*, November–December 1994.

Leibholz, G. (ed.), *Menschenwürde und Freiheitliche Rechtsordnung*, Tübingen, 1974.

Letwin, W., *A Documentary History of American Economic Policy Since 1789*, New York, Doubleday, 1961.

Locke, J., *Two Treatises of Government* [1690], New York, New American Library, 1960.

Lutz, M. A., "On the Quality of the Industrial Earnings Structure in Manufacturing," *Industrial Relations*, February 1977, vol. 16:1, pp. 61–70.

—— "Doubts about Competition," in E. O'Boyle (ed.), *Social Economics*, New York, Routledge, 1996, pp. 109–124.

—— "The Mondragon Cooperative Complex: An Application of Kantian Ethics to Social Economics," *International Journal of Social Economics*, 1997, vol. 24:12, pp. 1404–1421.

—— "The Mondragon Cooperative Enterprise System in Today's Global World," in R. C. Dyck and M. Mulej (eds), *Self-Transformation of the Forgotten Four-Fifths*, Dubuque, IA, Kendall/Hunt Publishing Co., 1998, pp. 39–54.

Lutz, M. A. (ed.), *Social Economics: Retrospect and Prospect*, Boston, MA, Kluwer Academic Publishers, 1990.

Lutz, M. A. and Lux, K., *The Challenge of Humanistic Economics*, Menlo Park, CA, Benjamin/Cummings, 1979.

—— *Humanistic Economics: The New Challenge*, New York, Bootstrap Press, 1988.

Macaulay, T. B., "Southey's Colloquies on Society" [January 1830], in *The Complete Works of Lord Macaulay*, vol. VII, London, Longmans Green and Co., 1898.

McCulloch, J., *The Principles of Political Economy*, London, Ward Lock and Co., 1825.

Macfie, A. L., *The Individual in Society*, London, George Allen and Unwin, 1967.

McGinn, A. P., "Promoting Sustainable Fisheries," in L. Brown *et al.* (eds), *State of the World 1998* (by the WorldWatch Institute), New York, W. W. Norton, 1998.

MacLean, D. and Brown, P. (eds), *Energy and the Future*, Totowa, NJ, Rowman and Littlefield, 1983, pp. 38–58.

MacPherson, C. B., *The Political Economy of Possessive Individualism: Hobbes to Locke*, Oxford, Oxford University Press, 1962.

Malthus, T., *Principles of Political Economy Considered with a View to Their Practical Application*, London, J. Murray, 1820.

Marcuse, H., *One-Dimensional Man*, Boston, MA, Beacon Press, 1978.

Martinez-Alier, J., "Ecological Perception, Environmental Policy and Distributional Conflicts: Some Lessons from History," in R. Costanza (ed.), *Ecological Economics:*

The Science and Management of Sustainability, New York, Columbia University Press, 1991.

Marx, K., "Circular Letter to Bebel, Liebknecht, Bradie, and Others" [1879], in R. C. Tucker (ed.), *The Marx–Engels Reader*, New York, W. W. Norton, 1972.

Maslow, A., *Toward a Psychology of Being*, New York, Van Nostrand Reinhold, 1968.

Meadows, D. H., Meadows, D. L., Randers, J. and Behrens, W. W., *The Limits to Growth*, New York, Universe Books, 1972.

Menger, A., *The Right to the Whole Product of Labor* [1899], New York, Augustus M. Kelley Publishers, 1970.

Messner, J., "Die Idee der Menschenwürde im Rechstaat der pluralistischen Gesellschaft," in G. Leibholz (ed.), *Menschenwürde und Freiheitliche Rechtsordnung*, Tübingen, 1974, pp. 231–234.

Meyer, M. and Parent, W. A. (eds), *The Constitution of Rights: Human Dignity and American Values*, Ithaca, Cornell University Press, 1992.

Mill, James, *Elements of Political Economy* [1826], New York, George Olms Verlag, 1971.

Mill, John S., "Thornton on Labour and Its Claims," *Fortnightly Review*, May–June 1869, pp. 505–518.

—— *Principles of Political Economy with Some of Their Applications to Social Philosophy*, vols I and II, New York, D. Appleton and Co., 1891.

—— *Essays on Some Unsettled Questions of Political Economy* [1874], New York, Augustus M. Kelley, 1968.

Mirandola, G. P. della, *Oration on the Dignity of Man* [1486], trans. A. R. Caponigri, Chicago, IL, Henry Regnery Company, 1956.

Moomaw, W. and Unruh, G., "Are Environmental Kuznets Curves Misleading Us?," G-DAE Discussion Paper no. 4, Cambridge, MA, Global Development and Environment Institute, 1997.

Moore, G. E., "A Defense of Common Sense," in Moore, *Philosophical Papers*, London, Allen and Unwin, 1959, pp. 52–59.

Myint, H., *Theories of Welfare Economics*, New York, Augustus M. Kelley, 1965.

Myrdal, G., *The Political Element in the Development of Economic Theory*, London, Routledge and Kegan Paul, 1953.

Nath, S. K., *A Reappraisal of Welfare Economics*, London, Routledge and Kegan Paul, 1969 (reprint New York, Augustus M. Kelley, 1976).

Neff, E., *Carlyle and Mill*, New York, Columbia University Press, 1926.

Nemmers, E. E., *Hobson and Underconsumption*, Clifton, NY, Augustus M. Kelley, 1972.

Nicholson, W., *Microeconomic Theory*, New York, Dryden Press, 1992.

Nitsch, T., "Social Economics: The First 200 Years," in M. Lutz (ed.), *Social Economics: Retrospect and Prospect*, Boston, MA, Kluwer Academic Publishers, 1990, pp. 5–90.

Norgaard, R. and Howarth, R., "Sustainability and Discounting the Future," in R. Costanza (ed.), *Ecological Economics: The Science and Management of Sustainability*, New York, Columbia University Press, 1991.

Nozick, R., *Anarchy, State, and Utopia*, New York, Basic Books, 1974.

Nudler, O., and Lutz, M. A. (eds), *Economics, Culture and Society: Alternative Approaches*, New York, The Apex Press, and Tokyo, United Nations University Press, 1996.

Nussbaum, M., "Nature, Function and Capability: Aristotle on Political Distribution," *Oxford Studies in Ancient Philosophy*, supplemental vol., 1988.

O'Boyle, E. (ed.), *Social Economics*, New York, Routledge, 1996.

OECD, *Trade Employment and Labour Standards: A Study of Core Workers' Rights and International Trade*, Paris, 1996.

—— *Societal Cohesion and the Globalizing Economy: What Does the Future Hold?*, Paris, 1997.

Ohlin, B., "The Theory of Trade" [1924], in H. Flam and M. J. Flanders (eds), *Heckscher–Ohlin Trade Theory*, Cambridge, MA, MIT Press, 1991, pp. 76–214.

Page, T., "Intergenerational Justice as Opportunity," in D. MacLean and P. Brown (eds), *Energy and the Future*, Totowa, NJ, Rowman and Littlefield, 1983, pp. 38–58.

Parent, W., "Constitutional Values and Human Dignity," in M. Meyer and W. A. Parent (eds), *The Constitution of Rights: Human Dignity and American Values*, Ithaca, Cornell University Press, 1992, pp. 47–72.

Parker, P. (ed.), *Character and Life*, London, Williams and Norgate, 1912.

Pearce, D. W. (ed.), *The MIT Dictionary of Modern Economics*, 4th edn, Cambridge, MA, MIT Press, 1992.

Pearce, I. F., *A Contribution to Demand Analysis*, Oxford, Clarendon Press, 1964.

Penfield, W., *The Mystery of the Mind*, Princeton, NJ, Princeton University Press, 1975.

Pheby, J. (ed.), *J. A. Hobson after Fifty Years*, New York, St. Martin's Press, 1994.

Phelps, E., *Political Economy: An Introductory Text*, New York, W. W. Norton, 1985.

Pigou, A., *Economics of Welfare* [1920], 4th edn, London, Macmillan, 1932.

Polanyi, K., "Our Obsolete Market Mentality," *Commentary*, 1947, vol. 3, pp. 109–117.

Polinsky, A. M., "Economic Analysis as a Potentially Defective Product: A Buyer's Guide to Posner's *Economic Analysis of Law*," *Harvard Law Review*, vol. 87, p. 1658.

Posner, R. A., *The Economic Analysis of Law*, 2nd edn, Boston, MA, Little, Brown, 1977.

—— *The Economics of Justice*, Cambridge, MA, Harvard University Press, 1981.

Rachels, J., *The Elements of Moral Philosophy*, New York, Random House, 1986.

Raskin, M., *The Common Good: Its Politics, Policies, and Philosophy*, New York, Routledge and Kegan Paul, 1986.

Rawls, J., *A Theory of Justice*, Cambridge, MA, Harvard University Press, 1971.

Rescher, N., *Rationality*, Oxford, Clarendon Press, 1988.

—— *Moral Absolutes (An Essay on the Nature and Rationale of Morality)*, New York, Peter Lang Publishing, 1989.

Reynolds, P. J., *Political Economy: A Synthesis of Kaleckian and Post Keynesian Economics*, New York, St. Martin's Press, 1987.

Ricardo, D., *Principles of Political Economy and Taxation*, London, J. Murray, 1817.

Richburg, K. and Mufson, S., "Warning Signs Unheeded on Road to Asian Crisis," *International Herald Tribune*, January 5, 1998, pp. 1, 4.

Richmond, W. H., "John A. Hobson: Economic Heretic," *American Journal of Economics and Sociology*, July 1978, vol. 37:3, pp. 283–294.

Riffkin, J., *Entropy: Into the Greenhouse World*, New York, Viking–Penguin, 1989.

Robbins, L., "Introduction," to P. Wicksteed, *The Common Sense of Political Economy*, London, George Routledge and Sons, 1933, pp. v–xxx.

—— "Interpersonal Comparisons of Utility: A Comment," *Economic Journal*, December 1938, vol. 48, pp. 635–641.

—— *The Theory of Economic Policy*, London, Macmillan, 1965.

—— *An Essay on the Nature and Significance of Economic Science* [1932], 3rd edn, London, Macmillan, 1984.

Robinson, J., "Review of R. F. Harrod, *Towards a Dynamic Economics*," *Economic Journal*, 1949, vol. 59, pp. 68–85.

Rosenberg, A., *Economics–Mathematical Politics or the Science of Diminishing Returns*, Chicago, IL, University of Chicago Press, 1992.

Rothstein, R., "Workforce Globalization: A Policy Response," for the Woman's Bureau, US Labor Department, 1994.

Roy, S., *Philosophy of Economics: On the Scope of Reason in Economic Inquiry*, New York, Routledge, 1989.

Royal Commission on Environmental Pollution's Report, The, *Transport and the Environment*, New York, Oxford University Press, 1965.

Runes, D., *Dictionary of Philosophy*, Totowa, NJ, Littlefield, Adams and Co., 1962.

Ruskin, J., *Fors Clavigera: Letters to the Workmen and Labourers of Great Britain* [1876], vol. III, Boston, MA, Colonial Press Co., 1880.

—— *Unto This Last* [1861], Lincoln, NE, University of Nebraska Press, 1967.

Ryan, J. A., *A Living Wage: Its Ethical and Economic Aspects*, New York, Macmillan, 1910.

—— *Social Doctrine in Action: A Personal History*, New York, Harper and Brothers Publishers, 1941.

—— "Two Objectives for Catholic Economists," *Review of Social Economy*, December 1942, vol. 1:1, pp. 1–5.

Sabine, G. H., *A History of Political Theory*, New York, Henry Holt and Co., 1958.

Sachs, J. and Shatz, H., "International Trade and Wage Inequality in the United States: Some New Results," unpublished paper, Harvard University, December 1995.

Safina, C., *Song for the Blue Ocean*, New York, Henry Holt and Co., 1997.

Samenow, S. E., *Inside the Criminal Mind*, New York, Times Books, 1984.

Samuelson, P., *The Principles of Economics*, 9th edn, New York, McGraw-Hill, 1973.

—— *Economics*, New York, McGraw-Hill, 1976.

—— *Economics*, 11th edn, New York, McGraw-Hill, 1980.

Sandel, M., "America's Search for a New Public Philosophy," *The Atlantic Monthly*, March 1996, pp. 57–74.

Sanders, Ch. and Fields, K. (eds), *Collected Letters of Thomas and Jane Welsh Carlyle*, Durham, NC, Duke University Press, 1970, vol. I.

San Pietro, A. *et al.* (eds), *Harvesting the Sun: Photosynthesis in Plant Life*, New York, Academic Press, 1967.

Say, J. B., *A Treatise on Political Economy* [1803], 4th edn, Philadelphia, PA, Lippincott, Grambo and Co., 1850.

Schneider, M., "Modelling Hobson's Underconsumption Theory," in J. Pheby (ed.), *J. A. Hobson after Fifty Years*, New York, St. Martin's Press, 1994, pp. 100–123.

—— *J. A. Hobson*, London, Macmillan, 1996.

Schumacher, E. F., *Small Is Beautiful*, New York, Harper and Row, 1973.

—— "Philosophy of Work," *The Catholic Worker*, February 1977a.

—— *A Guide for the Perplexed*, London, Cape, 1977b.

Schumpeter, J., *History of Economic Analysis*, New York, Oxford University Press, 1954.

Scitovsky, T., "A Note on Welfare Propositions in Economics," *Review of Economic Studies*, November 1941, vol. 9, pp. 77–88.

Selden, T. and Song, D., "Environmental Quality and Development: Is There a Kuznet's Curve for Air Pollution Emissions?," *Journal of Environmental Economics and Management*, 1994, vol. 27, pp. 147–162.

Sen, A., "Choice, Orderings and Rationality," in S. Koerner (ed.), *Practical Reason*, New Haven, CT, Yale University Press, 1974, pp. 54–67.

—— "The Rational Fools: A Critique of the Behavioral Foundations of Economic Theory," *Philosophy and Public Affairs*, 1977, vol. 6, pp. 317–344.

—— "The Profit Motive," *Lloyds Bank Review*, January 1983, no. 147.

—— *On Ethics and Economics*, Oxford, Basil Blackwell, 1987a.

—— *The Standard of Living: The Tanner Lectures*, New York, Cambridge University Press, 1987b.

—— *Inequality Reexamined*, Cambridge, MA, Harvard University Press, 1995.

—— "On the Foundations of Welfare Economics: Utility, Capability and Practical Reason," in F. Farina, F. Hahn and S. Vannucci (eds), *Ethics, Rationality and Economic Behaviour*, New York, Clarendon Press, 1996, pp. 50–65.

Senior, N. W., *An Outline of the Science of Political Economy* [1836], New York, Augustus M. Kelley, 1965.

Seung, T. K. and Bonevac, D., "Plural Values and Indeterminate Rankings," *Ethics*, July 1992, vol. 102, pp. 799–813.

Shackle, G. L. S., *Decision Order and Time in Human Affairs*, Cambridge, Cambridge University Press, 1961.

Shafik, N., "Economic Development and Environmental Quality: An Economic Analysis," *Oxford Economic Papers*, 1994, vol. 46, pp. 757–773.

Shaiken, H., *Mexico in the Global Economy*, San Diego, CA, University of California Press, 1990.

—— "Advanced Manufacturing and Mexico: A New International Division of Labor?," *Latin American Research Review*, vol. 29:2, 1994.

Sherburne, J. C., *John Ruskin or the Ambiguities of Abundance*, Cambridge, MA, Harvard University Press, 1972.

Sidgwick, H., *Principles of Political Economy*, London, Macmillan, 1883.

Simon, H. A., *Reason in Human Affairs*, Stanford, CA, Stanford University Press, 1983.

Sismondi, J. C. L. Simonde de, *De la Richesse Commerciale*, Geneva, J. J. Paschoud, 1803.

—— "Review of John Barton's Observations and Inquiry," *Annales de Législation et d'Economie Politique*, November 1822, pp. 82–119.

—— *Political Economy* [1815], New York, Augustus M. Kelley, 1966a.

—— *Political Economy and the Philosophy of Government* [1847], New York, Augustus M. Kelley, 1966b.

—— *New Principles of Political Economy* [1827], trans. R. Hyse, New Brunswick, NJ, and London, Transaction Publishers, 1991.

Smith, A., *The Theory of Moral Sentiments* [1759], Boston, MA, Wells and Lilly, 1817.

—— *An Inquiry into the Nature and Causes of the Wealth of Nations* [1776], Chicago, IL, University of Chicago Press, 1976.

Smith, G. A., "The Teleological View of Wealth: A Historical Perspective," in H. Daly (ed.), *Economics, Ecology, Ethics*, San Francisco, CA, W. H. Freeman and Co., 1980, pp. 215–237.

Smith, V. K. (ed.), *Scarcity and Growth Reconsidered*, Baltimore, MD, Johns Hopkins University Press, 1979.

Soddy, F., *Wealth, Virtual Wealth and Debt*, London, George Allen and Unwin, Ltd, 1926.

Sotiroff, G., *Ricardo und Sismondi: Eine aktuelle Auseinandersetzung über Nachkriegswirtschaft vor 120 Jahren*, Zurich and New York, Europa, 1945.

Sowell, T., *Say's Law: An Historical Analysis*, Princeton, NJ, Princeton University Press, 1972.

—— *Classical Economics Reconsidered*, Princeton, NJ, Princeton University Press, 1974.

—— "J. C. L. Simonde de Sismondi," in J. Eatwell *et al.* (eds), *The New Palgrave Dictionary: Social Economics*, New York, W. W. Norton, 1989.

Spiegelberg, H., "Human Dignity: A Challenge to Contemporary Philosophy," in R. Gotesky and E. Laszlo (eds), *Human Dignity*, New York, Gordon and Breach, 1970, pp. 39–64.

Sraffa, P. (ed.), *The Works and Correspondence of David Ricardo*, Cambridge, Cambridge University Press, 1951.

Stamford, J., "North American Economic Integration and the International Regulation of Labor Standards," in B. Stein (ed.), *Contemporary Issues in Labor and Employment Law*, Boston, MA, Little, Brown and Co., 1994, pp. 3–46.

Stein, B. (ed.), *Contemporary Issues in Labor and Employment Law*, Boston, MA, Little, Brown and Co., 1994.

Stevens, A., *Madame de Staël, a Study of Her Life and Times: The First Revolution and the First Empire*, vol. II, London, John Murray, 1880.

Stiglitz, J., *Whither Socialism?*, Cambridge, MA, MIT Press, 1994.

Stolper, W. and Samuelson, P., "Protection and Real Wages," *Review of Economic Studies*, 1941, vol. 23, pp. 58–73.

Sudgen, R., "Rational Choice: A Survey of the Contributions from Economics and Philosophy," *Economic Journal*, July 1991, pp. 751–785.

Tarr, D. and Morkre, M., *Aggregate Costs to the United States of Tariffs and Quotas on Imports*, Bureau of Economics Staff Report to the Federal Trade Commission, Washington, DC, December 1984.

Tawney, R. H., *The Acquisitive Society* [1920], New York, Harcourt Brace Jovanovich, 1948.

—— *The Radical Tradition*, ed. R. Hinden, New York, Pantheon Books, 1964.

Taylor, C., *Philosophical Papers*, New York, Cambridge University Press, 1985.

Tenenbaum, S., "Social Discounting: Retrieving the Civic Dimension," *Economics and Philosophy*, 1989, vol. 5, pp. 33–46.

Tobin, J., "On Limiting the Domain of Inequality," *Journal of Law and Economics*, 1970.

Trenberth, K., "The Science of Global Change," *Jobs and Capital*, Fall 1997, vol. 6:4, pp. 21–25.

Tuan, M., *Simonde de Sismondi as an Economist*, New York, Columbia University Press, 1927.

Tucker, J., *The Elements of Commerce and the Theory of Taxes*, Yorkshire, S. R. Publishers, 1755.

Tucker, R. C. (ed.), *The Marx–Engels Reader*, New York, W. W. Norton, 1972.

Tullock, G. and McKenzie, R., *The New World of Economics*, 4th edn, Homewood, IL, R. D. Irwin, Inc., 1985.

US Department of Energy, *Annual Energy Outlook 1997*.

van der Linden, H., *Kantian Ethics and Socialism*, Indianapolis, IN, Hackett Publishing Co., 1988.

Vanek, J., "Some Fundamental Considerations on Financing and the Form of Ownership under Labor Management," in H. C. Bos (ed.), *Economic Structure and Development*, Amsterdam, North-Holland, Elsevier Science, 1973, pp. 139–143.

Vitousek, O. *et al.*, "Human Appropriation of the Products of Photosynthesis," *BioScience*, 1986, vol. 346, pp. 277–283.

von Wieser, F., *Natural Value* [1889], New York, G. E. Stechert and Co., 1930.

—— *Social Economics* [1914], New York, Augustus Kelley, 1967.

Vorlaender, K., *Marx und Kant*, Vienna, Deutsche Worte, 1904.

Wagner, H., *Die Würde des Menschen*, Würzburg, Koenighausen and Newman, 1992.

Walras, L., *Elements of Pure Economics* [1926], New York, Augustus Kelley, 1977.

Whyte, W. and Whyte, K., *The Making of Mondragon*, Ithaca, NY, Cornell University Press, 2nd edn, 1991.

Wicksteed, P., *The Common Sense of Political Economy* [1910], London, George Routledge and Sons, 1933.

Wit, C. T. de, "Photosynthesis: Its Relationship to Overpopulation," in A. San Pietro *et al.* (eds), *Harvesting the Sun: Photosynthesis in Plant Life*, New York, Academic Press, 1967, pp. 315–320.

Wills, G., *Inventing America: Jefferson's Declaration of Independence*, New York, Vintage Books, 1979.

Wood, A., *North–South Trade, Employment and Inequality: Changing Fortunes in a Skill-Driven World*, Oxford, Clarendon Press, 1994.

World Commission on Environment and Development, *Our Common Future*, Oxford, Oxford University Press, 1987.

Young, J., "Is the Entropy Law Relevant to the Economics of Natural Scarcity?," *Journal of Environmental Economics and Management*, September 1991, vol. 21, pp. 169–179.

GUIDE TO FURTHER READING

The following books shed additional light on the topics covered and are strongly recommended:

Chapter 1   **[The Nature of Social Economics]**
                J. Davis & E. O'Boyle (eds): *Social Economics of Human Material Need* [1994]
                M. Lutz (ed.), *Social Economics: Retrospect and Prospect* [1990]

Chapter 2   **[J.C.L. Sismondi's Social Economics]**
                J. Sismondi, *New Principles of Political Economy* [English translation, 1991]
                M. Tuan, *Sismondi as an Economist* [1927]

Chapter 3   **[T. Carlyle, J.S. Mill and J. Ruskin]**
                E. Neff, *Carlyle and Mill* [1926]
                J. Sherburne, *John Ruskin or the Ambiguities of Abundance* [1972]

Chapter 4   **[J.A. Hobson's Social Economics]**
                J. Allett, *New Liberalism: the Political Economy of J.A. Hobson* [1981]
                M. Schneider, *J.A. Hobson* [1996]

Chapter 5   **[Ethics, Science and Economic Welfare]**
                S. Roy, *Philosophy of Economics* [1989]
                S. Nath, *A Reappraisal of Welfare Economics* [1976]

Chapter 6   **[Tracking the Common Good]**
                A. Gewirth, *The Community of Rights* [1996]
                M. Adler, *The Difference of Man and the Difference it Makes* [1993]

GUIDE TO FURTHER READING

Chapter 7 [Economic Rationality]
A. Hamlin, *Ethics, Economics and the State* [1986]
S. Hargreaves Heap, *Rationality in Economics* [1989]

Chapter 8 [Reconsidering the Investor-owned Corporation]
D. Ellerman, *Property and Contract in Economics* [1992]
D. Ellerman, *The Democratic Worker-Owned Firm* [1990]

Chapter 9 [Markets and Globalized Trade]
R. Kuthner, *Everything for Sale* [1997]
W. Greider, *One World, Ready or Not* [1997]
J. Culbertson, *International Trade and the Future of the West* [1984]

Chapter 10 [Ecological Economics]
N. Georgescu-Roegen, *Energy and Economic Myths* [1976]
R. Costanza *et al.*, *An Introduction to Ecological Economics* [1998]

Chapter 11 [The Need for a Social Economics]
F. Hirsch, *Social Limits to Growth* [1976]
H. Daly & J. Cobb, *For the Common Good* (2nd edn) [1994]

For more detailed information on these publications, see the Bibliography.

288

INDEX

and problem of induction 106–7; and
rationality 149
Hutcheson, Francis 174
Hutchison, Terrence 108

imperialism 78, 252; explained 77–9;
see also economics imperialism
Imperialism: A Study 78
impersonal force 141, 263–70; and the
freedom of the will 268–70; global
competition and the 266–8; as the
invisible hand 263–4
individualism 199, 253, 268; as a basis
for normative economics 119–21;
fallacy of 88, 92; and liberty 59; and
methodology 6–7, 236; and rights
137; vs. wholism 4
individualistic fallacy 92
Inequality Reexamined 140
insecurity; see economic (in)security
Inside the Criminal Mind 155
International Labor Office 214; Hobson
as early proponent of 81
international trade theory: and absolute
advantage 204–5; alleged theoretical
merit of 201–3; assumption of 203,
207–8; based on comparative
advantage 201–7, 217; and capital
mobility 201–7; and compensation
theorem 208–9; factor price
equalization 202–3, 205; failure of
203–7; Hobson on 80–1; and social
responsibility 205; and unskilled
wages 202–3, 205; and wage
competition 202–3
interpersonal comparisons of utility: and
cost–benefit economics 117; debate on
112–15, 126; implicit to the "New"
Welfare Economics 115, 122
invisible hand 196–7; and common
good 263–4; as an impersonal force
263–8

Jefferson, Thomas 3, 108, 174
Jevons, Stanley 256; on hierarchy of
values 150
job security; see economic (in)security
justice, positive 17; see also social justice

Kahn, Alfred 7, 82
Kaldor, Nicholas 115–17

Kant, Immanuel 5, 60, 122, 132, 147,
174, 177, 180
Kapital, Das 57, 151, 268
Keynes, John Maynard 8, 77, 107, 251,
256, 262, 266; and Hobson 81–4, 98;
and underinvestment 82–3
Keynes, John Neville 87–8, 110
Knight, Frank 139, 161
knowledge 106–7, 112, 115, 134, 259;
and entropy 230; as exportable 206–7;
and normative economics 136; perfect
120–1; social economics as 260–2;
uncertain 29
Kyoto Agreement to Curb Global
Warming 226

labor mobility 35, 186, 207; and Say's
Law 36–7
labor productivity: and education 213;
and excess capacity 210; and imports
212–13; and labor costs 205, 212–14;
linked to wage levels 212–13; and
prices 35
labor theory of value: vs labor theory of
property 170–3, 177
*Labour Defended against the Claims of
Capital* 169
Labour Party 92, 99
laissez-faire policy 1, 2, 22, 28, 41, 51,
58, 59, 60, 62, 100, 109, 188, 215;
destructiveness of 195–8; and the
fallacy of composition 196; and
international trade 204–16; and
Natural Theology 196–7; resurgence
of 192–3, 198–9; Sismondi as the first
to attack 45, 51
Lal, Deepak 266–7
Lange, Oscar 105
law 45, 154, 162, 172, 188, 197;
economic 64–5, 201, 257; of entropy
and thermodynamics 228–30, 236,
242; environmental 223–6; moral
177, 180–1; normative vs. positive
168–9, 175–6; positive 5, 17, 168–9,
175–6; of property 187; self-
enforcement of 160; *see also* natural
law
Lectures on the Rates of Wages 58
Lenin, Vladimir 57, 256
LePlay, Frederic 55
liberalism (classical) 9, 15, 119, 204;

as promoting social welfare 207;
Sismondi on 25, 40; and
underconsumption theory 209–12;
and wages of unskilled workers 203;
and welfare of the poor 208–9
trade theory: assumptions of 201, 202,
204–8, 212–13; and factor price
equalization 204–7; Hobson on 80–1;
Sismondi on 40; see also free trade,
comparative advantage doctrine
transportation and ecology 222–6, 243
Treatise of Human Nature 149
Treatise of Political Economy 26
trust 159
truth 4, 134, 142, 212, 251, 259, 270;
Hobson and 73, 82, 98; and
instrumental rationality 162; moral
105–6; self-evident 261–2; Sismondi
on 39, 50
Tucker, Joshua 5
Tugwell, Rexford 99
Two Treatises of Government 169

uncertainty 120, 159, 235; Sismondi on
29
underconsumption 28, 31–3, 35, 38, 62,
73, 209, 264; and exports 32; Hobson
on 75–9, 81, 252; and inequality
31–3, 75–7; international 209–12;
and machinery 33–5; as taproot of
Imperialism 78–9
unearned income: and consumption 76;
and natural law 92; need to tax 78–9,
92–3; and personality growth 96
unemployment 13, 21–3, 42, 111, 200,
250, 266; assumption of no 120,
207–8; Hobson on 71, 79–81, 83, 97;
as a social disease 42, 84–5; and
welfare economics 120
Unto This Last 63, 67, 249
utility 152, 154; as basis of welfare
economics 121–2, 126–7; Hobson on
90–1; interpersonal comparisons of
112–19, 121–2, 126–7; maximization
90–1, 122, 150, 151, 159, 161;
overarching 157; and qualitative
differences 89–90, 154–5, 159; and
real cost doctrine 97; social 26, 85–7;
of work 95
Utopian socialism 49, 60

value-free social science, Hobson on 87

value judgments 111, 114, 128–9, 131,
216; Paretian 117–21, 141; and
rationality 148–9, 153–5, 157–9
values 91, 130, 155, 157, 158, 160,
192–3, 224–5, 250; Christian 17–18,
268–9; common sense justification of
107; economics and 105, 108, 116,
160; hierarchy of 131–2, 150; Hobson
on 85–8, 90, 91, 98; human vs
market 194; judgment of and
efficiency 119–21; and naturalistic
fallacy 262; personal 13, 105, 106;
plural 126, 131, 135; protecting
future generations 236; Ruskin on 66;
social 1–2, 4, 11, 100, 104, 107,
131–2, 141, 160, 161, 182–3, 194,
230, 253; and social discounting
239–41; social nature of 98; of social
responsibility 182–3, 224; of
sufficiency 126–30; of human dignity
23, 132–6; universal 135–6; vs tastes
13
Villeneuve-Bargemont, Alban 56
Vorlaender, Karl 177

wage differentials 13, 207–8;
compensating for risk of injury 93–4;
international 204–5, 207–8, 216
wage reductions 38, 205, 209; to cure
unemployment 80–1; and
international trade 80–1
wage system 47; and abolitionist
movement 188; the case against
177–9; compared with slavery 45,
175–6; as historically contingent 45;
in Kantian philosophy 180–1; Knight
on the 139
Wages Fund doctrine 58–9, 62, 72, 73
Wagner, Hans 134
Walras, Leon 5, 13, 165–6, 172, 256
wantons 148, 156, 158, 160, 173
Wealth and Life 91
Wealth of Nations 40
Wealth and Welfare 110
wealth vs welfare 55, 140, 142, 241,
242, 266; Hobson on 85; Ruskin on
66–7; Sismondi on 40–3, 57
welfare economics (orthodox) 109–10,
146, 198; appraisal of 121–2;
assumptions of 120–1; based on
functionings and capabilities 126–7,
128; based on individual preferences

301